ALLEGORIES OF CINEMA

American Film in the Sixties

David E. James

PRINCETON
UNIVERSITY PRESS

This book has been composed in Linotron Sabon and Gill Sans

Princeton University Press books are printed on acid-free paper
and meet the guidelines for permanence and durability of the
Committee on Production Guidelines for Book Longevity of
the Council on Library Resources

Printed in the United States of America

James, David E., 1945–
Allegories of cinema : American film in the sixties / David E. James.
p.   cm.   Bibliography: p.   includes index.
ISBN 0-691-04755-3 (alk. paper) : ISBN 0-691-00604-0 (pbk.)
1. Motion pictures—United States—History. 2. Experimental films—
United States—History and criticism. 3. Motion pictures—Political
aspects—United States. I. Title.
PN1993.5.U6J27 1988   791.43′0973—dc19   88-9852   CIP

Designed by Laury A. Egan

10   9   8   7   6   5   4   3

For my mother and father

Contents

Preface

All who study alternative cinemas suffer in knowing that their commentary is "more immediately available to a reading public than the films upon which it concentrates" (Sitney, 1970: 3), and not the least of the anxieties of "writing about movies which you can't see anywhere" (Mekas, 1972: 84) is the realization that the number of these invisible films is unknown even to those who most vigorously pursue them. That invisibility is an institutional event whose ramifications are political. The collusion of the film critical establishment with corporate industries in resisting the propagation of the work discussed here is the mark of its threat and also of its importance. Let this recognition stand in respect to the filmmakers who are not otherwise represented.

Los Angeles, 1986

Acknowledgments

My friends have helped me in this work. Paul Arthur has been a constant inspiration; to the energy and lucidity of his conversation, his correspondence, and his scholarship, I owe more than I can calculate. Joann Edmond, Rick Berg, Stephen Eisenman, John Ganim, Beverle Houston, Bruce Kawin, Marsha Kinder, Chick Strand, and Alice Wexler all know of my obligation to them, but even they do not reckon its extent. For other assistance, it is a pleasure to remember Dominic Angerame, Stella Holmes, Cecelia Galassi, Anita Gregory, Cynthia Rogers, and Nadia Shtendera. Joanna Hitchcock and Janet Stern, my editors at Princeton University Press, have been wonderful. Janet lavished a quite disproportionate consideration upon the manuscript; there is no way I can sufficiently thank her for her generous and scrupulous care. Early stages of the research were funded by a grant from the National Endowment for the Humanities. The Louis and Hermione Brown Humanities Support fund at Occidental College assisted in the preparation of the manuscript.

thology Film Archives for stills from films by Jonas Mekas; Taylor Mead for stills from *The Queen of Sheba Meets the Atom Man*; Ken Jacobs for stills from *Blonde Cobra* and *Tom, Tom, The Piper's Son*; Museum of Modern Art/Film Stills Archive for the still from *Flaming Creatures*; Anthology Film Archives for stills from *Samadhi* and *Re-Entry*; Anthology Film Archives for the photograph of the Anthology Film Archives Cinema; Ben Van Meter for stills from *S.F. Trips Festival, An Opening* and for the photograph of Ben Van Meter; Louise Vanderbeek for stills from *Science Fiction*; George Kuchar for stills from *Hold Me While I'm Naked*; Mike Kuchar for stills from *Sins of the Fleshapoids*; Bruce Conner for stills from films by Bruce Conner; Kenneth Anger and Anthology Film Archives for stills from films by Kenneth Anger; Bruce Baillie for stills from *Quixote*; Anthony Reveaux for the still from *Peace March*; Saul Levine for the still from *New Left Note*; Émile de Antonio and the Turin Film Corporation for stills from *In the Year of the Pig*; Walker Art Center for stills from *The Cool World*; Robert M. Young for stills from *Nothing But A Man*; Mike Gray Associates for stills from *The Murder of Fred Hampton*; Agnes Varda for stills from *The Black Panthers: A Report*; Museum of Modern Art/Film Stills Archive for the poster for *Cleopatra Jones* and the still from *Coffy*; Museum of Modern Art/Film Stills Archive and Warner Brothers for the still from *Superfly*; Direct Cinema Ltd. (P.O. Box 69589, Los Angeles, CA 90069) for stills from *Sweet Sweetback's Baadasss Song*, © 1986 by Melvin Van Peebles; Museum of Modern Art/Film Stills Archive and Warner Brothers Pictures for stills from *The Green Berets*; Nick Macdonald for stills from *The Liberal War*; J. Sole and New Yorker Films for the still from *Far From Vietnam*; Robert Kramer for stills from *Ice*; Newsreel for stills from *Columbia Revolt, Summer of 68, Teach Our Children*, and *The Woman's Film*; Jon Jost for stills from *Speaking Directly*; from the Hollis Frampton film *Information* (1966, B/W), the film still by Biff Henrich, courtesy Marion Faller, © 1987, by the Hollis Frampton Estate; from the Hollis Frampton film *Zorns Lemma* (1970, color), the film still by Biff Henrich, courtesy Marion Faller © 1985 by the Hollis Frampton Estate; from the Hollis Frampton film *nostalgia* (1971, B/W), the film still by Biff Henrich, courtesy Marion Faller, © 1987 by the Hollis Frampton Estate; Anthology Film Archives for stills from other Hollis Frampton films; George Landow for stills from films by George Landow; Morgan Fisher for stills from *Production Stills*; Ernie Gehr for the still from *History*; Anthology Film Archives for stills from *The Flicker* and *Wavelength*; Paul Sharits for the still from *S:TREAM:S:S:ECTION:S:ECTION:S:S:EC-TIONED* and the installation photograph; Direct Cinema Ltd. for stills from *David Holzman's Diary*, © 1987 by DCL, All Rights Reserved; Museum of Modern Art/Film Stills Archive and Paramount Pictures for stills from *Medium Cool*; Norman Mailer for stills from *Maidstone*; Museum of Modern Art/Film Stills Archive and Universal Pictures for stills from *The Last Movie*; Anthology Film Archives for stills from *Meshes of the Afternoon* and *Notebook*; Scott Bartlett for the still from *Lovemaking*; Carolee Schneemann for stills from *Fuses*; Yvonne Rainer for stills from *Film about a women who* . . . ; Jane Weinstock for the still from *Sigmund Freud's Dora*; and Museum of Modern Art/Film Stills Archives for stills from *Deep Throat*. All Rights Reserved.

Allegories of Cinema

Considering
the Alternatives

The inert
Were rouz'd, and lively natures rapt away.
— William Wordsworth

The movies are a revolution.
— Taylor Mead

In the flowering of participatory social life we call "The Sixties" a number of previously unaccommodated and disenfranchised groups began aggressively to engage history for themselves, to make it their history. The Beat Generation, Students for a Democratic Society, Civil Rights and Black Power, hippies and the counterculture, the Vietnam War, the Weathermen, the New Morality and Women's Liberation—these were just some of the movements and issues in the United States around which a constantly fermenting and erupting chain of intertwined political and cultural activity coalesced. By any standards remarkable, these social contestations were maintained on all levels, from private consciousness to both national and international political organization.

This activity has a definite period. Internationally it can be dated from de-Stalinization and the invasion of Hungary in 1956, with Mao's change of course and Castro's return to Cuba coming to replace the hegemony of the Soviet Union through alternative models of socialism; nationally it begins with the domestic thaw in the fear and apathy of the cold war years—the end of the "passivity and acquiescence"[1] of the fifties—and is marked by the Greensboro sit-ins and the formation of the Student Nonviolent Coordinating Committee in the spring of 1960 and by the inauguration of President John Kennedy the same year. It concludes between 1973, when the withdrawal from Vietnam marked the first major political defeat for U.S. imperialism and prompted the demobilization of domestic resistance, and 1974, when the oil embargoes and OPEC's manipulation of oil prices ended the cheap energy that had fueled the generally steady expansion of the capitalist economies since their mutual integration in the postwar reconstruction.

The international economic crisis was especially punctual for the United States. It coincided with the judicial traumas of Richard Nixon's administration—Watergate and the president's resignation in August 1974—and with the domestic economic contradictions he had been unable to control. The overextension of government intervention in the economy, begun by Kennedy and continued with

1 Arthur Schlesinger's phrase (Schlesinger, 1960: 58) typifies the retrospective attitude of the self-conscious confidence that, accelerating after the election of Kennedy, marked the decade as a whole. Overviews of the sixties abound, but in addition to commentaries on specific issues mentioned below, two synoptic accounts, Jameson (1984) and Harris (1981), are especially valuable.

Lyndon Johnson's attempt to finance both the war on poverty and the war in Vietnam by deficit spending, produced in 1971 the first overall trade deficit since 1893—despite a GNP of over a trillion dollars. Stagflation thus brought to an end the longest period of secular economic growth since World War II, when, between 1961 and 1969, unemployment halved to 3.5 percent and the real GNP grew at an average rate of 4.8 percent annually. Surrounding this expanding economy that sustained the optimism of the decade were larger shifts, not the inauguration of a post-industrial society, but the full industrialization of all branches of the economy (Mandel, 1975: 191), along with the growth of private and public oligopolies and the expansion of information and service industries. Constituting a paradigmatic break—the sign or at least the premonition of the passage beyond modernity—these larger shifts split apart the social forms of modernism's stability.

The period was, then, one of great cultural innovation, one in which, as the cultural was forced into new modes of integration with the political, the autonomy of each was called into question. Reversing the inherited subservience to European models, an international passion for American arts accompanied the political and economic hegemony achieved by the United States in World War II, even if those arts were usually uncomfortable with imperialism or indeed were the product of dissent against its domestic, social, and psychological reflexes. Modernism collapsed no less decisively in the arts than in society, and as it did so American literature, painting, dance, and music all leapt from the ruins, breaking into what appeared to be entirely new concatenations of priorities, methods, aspirations, and social functions. So too with film; alongside the New American Painting and the New American Poetry, a New American Cinema stood up.[2]

Combining aesthetic and social radicalism, the formal and technical developments and the innovations in the social uses of the medium in this and several other alternative film practices of the period together constitute an epoch in the history of cinema whose significance is equaled only by its resistance to assimilation and incorporation. The present study examines the interrelation of formal procedures and social functions in these practices. It charts the interdetermination of the filmic texts and the ensemble of social and material apparatuses—the cinemas—inside which they were produced and which they simultaneously produced; and it explores the participation of these cinemas in other forms of political activity, or their self-definition against it. In this it proceeds from specific suppositions about the nature of cultural production and its proper historiography. It argues the priority of the mode of film production as the sphere in which different formal practices may be traced to the operations of the society in which they come into being. And it argues the need to jettison the essentialist binary antitheses between the aesthetic and political avant-gardes and between these avant-gardes and mass culture that film history has inherited from art history and from the ideology of modernism in general. These polari-

2 The phrase "New American Painting" was capitalized at least as early as 1953 (Rubin, 1963), though the formulation of its national specificity probably derives from Greenberg's designation of abstract expressionism as " 'American-Type' Painting" in 1955 (See Greenberg, 1961). Donald Allen's anthology *The New American Poetry* (1960) was a brilliant editorial intervention that assembled an original and authentically American writing, claiming parity for it with modern jazz and abstract expressionist painting. See Chapter 4 for discussion of the New American Cinema.

zations, and indeed the entire received concept of the aesthetic avant-garde that sustains them, must give way to an understanding of the interdetermination of all practices in the total historical field of film production, and to an analysis of how the interrelations among the different alternative cinemas that constitute that field also organize the passage of filmic codes through it. And so, following through cinema Marcuse's vacillating prognostication for the sixties as a whole—that "advanced industrial society is capable of containing qualitative change" but also that "forces and tendencies exist which may break this containment and explode the society" (Marcuse, 1964: xv)—the present essay superimposes the terms of his dilemma one atop the other to demonstrate the multiple contradictions and determinations that relate the occasions of filmic or cinematic liberation on some levels to their limitations and compromises on others.

The Mode of Film Production

Cinema is never just the occasion of an object or a text, never simply the location of a message or of an aesthetic event, but always the site of manifold relationships among people and classes. The particular pattern of optical subtractions that inflects the whole light of the projector may well be a photochemical imprint on a strip of celluloid, and the surface that returns that light to our eyes similarly a specific architecture. But neither is simply that. Each exists only as a moment in larger circulations, whose psychic and material economies are integral to social systems that produce the work of history. Like the spectacle it inhabits—the whole panoply of visual and aural media, of advertising and journalism, of the political process and the urban landscape of signs—cinema is, in the terms of Guy Debord's elaboration of Marx, "not a collection of images, but a social relation among people, mediated by images" (Debord, 1977: paragraph 4). It is as the process and the documentation of that mediation, the functions and traces of that relation, that any film is comprehensively sensible. A film's images and sounds never fail to tell the story of how and why they were produced—the story of the mode of their production.

Like the mode of material production in general, the mode of cultural production may, initially at least, be specified as a relation between the forces of production and the social relations of production. For film, the former consists of all the raw materials from which it is manufactured and the human labor that transforms those raw materials into the finished work, while the latter are the relationships among people that are entailed in and constructed by the specific ownership of the productive forces. Producing film as a commodity, the capitalist mode of film production also produces around film the social relations it produces around other commodities. While some of its activities may supply the pleasures of craft or creation and while the finished object may provide aesthetic or cognitive delight, the determining function of commodity film is the valorization of the capital invested in its production. As it is to other commodities, consumption is integral to commodity film. Surplus value is realized at the box office, and there capital returns to the money form necessary for fresh cycles of production. The historical dominance of this specific practice of film has given the medium its apparent nature and generated all the trades, machines, and institutions that are popularly supposed to be intrinsic to it—the technological, economic, and sociological phenomena that exist before the film, those that operate during its manufacture, and those that come into play after it. Following Christian Metz, we designate the ensemble of materials and social processes that produce the filmic text as *cinema* (Metz, 1974a: 12). The total form of the capitalist mode of film production, then, is the capitalist cinema, and such a cinema is a social process that inserts people into specific positions in the industries, social relationships, and discourses of film production, and thereby into society at large. As capitalist film produces the subjects of bourgeois society, so capitalist cinema produces their subjection.

The virtual containment of film within capitalist industry and its journalistic and academic extensions has concealed the historical specificity of this one mode of film. As commodity production has become naturalized as the activity of the medium's essence, as its proper and inevitable usage, it has produced the kind of fetishism, specified by Marx as peculiar to bourgeois economics, that "transforms the social, economic character that things are stamped with in the process of social production into a natural character arising from the material nature of these things" (Marx, 1977–81, II: 303). A sense of that social, economic character and of alternatives to it is not easily retrievable. Our knowledge of the shifts that have taken place over long periods of time allows us to perceive the historicity of the various modes of production of other mediums and the social relations that constitute them; but a non-commodity film practice is all but inconceivable. We can easily see how for verbal narrative the commodity novel took the place of oral recitation, distinguishing the author as an original creator supplying a textual artifact to isolated individual readers. In different societies at different times, mutations in the practice of music similarly separated an autonomous event from a communal activity integrated into play, worship, or battle, institutionalizing and eventually industrializing the difference between those who make it and those who hear it. The historian of these arts, or of painting, dance, or theater, can look back to their pre-capitalist forms or even observe their persistence in those remnants of so-called primitive societies that have lingered into the present. But such privileged perspectives are only fragmentarily available to the historian of film, which has existed only within the modern period. Apart from the few years after the Soviet Revolution and a similar period in Cuba, few noncapitalist practices of film have existed to figure functions it might have in a free society. All we have are instances, and few enough of those, in which the hegemonic regime was challenged by dissident minorities.

This coextensiveness of film with monopoly capitalism is of course partially a function of its constitutive dependence on advanced technologies. It has shared that dependence with other mediums, with modern music, for example, even before it became primarily a recording industry, and with its more recent sibling rivals, television and video. And no characterization of film via distinctions between technological and atechnological cultural practices will be of much use, for where indeed will a pure instance of the latter be found? Nevertheless, the degree of mechanization intrinsic to cinema is essential to its specificity. Its pleasures have most often followed from the pleasures of the simulacrum, and so have been those of the apparatus as such. The earliest advertisements for Edison's Kinetoscope and Vitascope in the United States and for Lumière's Cinematographe in France celebrate the projection machinery. The film is subordinate, primarily the means to the performance of the apparatus and the display of its magic—a hierarchy of priorities that continued through the inauguration of sound to the spectacular strategies of competing with television in the fifties. The projector is, however, only one component in a continuum of extensive though invisible technologies. The studios, the laboratories, and their machinery all depend on previous factories and industries, on steel and plastic, on the mining of silver and other precious metals, on electricity and power plants, whose expanding cycles of economic and social interdependence are continuous with worldwide material production as a whole. All these involve even the most casual moviegoer in the endless circuits of modern political life, as indeed they surround even the least compromising of attempts to mobilize cinematic contestation of the social order.

Though these involvements are so integral that the medium of film is inconceivable outside modernity, nevertheless its dominant historical use maximized its technological engagement and so maximized its dependence on advanced industry. Eastman Kodak made home movie equipment available as early as 1923 (Chalfen, 1975: 88), but motion picture photography did not become a means of communication like the telephone, or a means of domestic recreation like still photography. It was instead immediately organized as an entertainment industry. In this *industrial cinema*, film came into being as a commodity, as *industrial film*. Ever since, the production of film has reciprocated the conditions of modern production in general. Because the social relations of its production are those of the economy at large, as it integrates cultural production into commodity production, the capitalist cinema thus sustains the generally obtaining mode of production in two interlocking ways, ideologically and materially. It recreates in its spectators the desires and fears, the conscious and unconscious subjectivity, by which they are accommodated to capitalist society—it reproduces the relations of production, in Louis Althusser's phrasing (Althusser, 1971: 133)—

and in its own production it participates directly and integrally in the bourgeois industrial system. No less than being a social product in its languages, industrial film is then a social product in the material sense. Manufactured by people working together, it is only completed by the paying spectator, for as we have said, consumption is no less integral to production for industrial film than for any other commodity.

The industrial cinema is the mediation of the relationships among all the people it engages, the organization of the transactions among the agents of its various processes: the corporate managers and individual entrepreneurs, the financiers, the writers, directors, actors, and technicians who manufacture the film (and before these all those who manufacture the machinery by which film is made); the theater owners, the ticket sellers, and the cleaners, the publicists, journalists, and theorists who distribute it; and the audiences who consume it. Accounts, even of industrial film, typically repress most of these relations; privileging certain roles as essential and artistic rather than merely arbitrary and technical, they reduce the entire chain of labor to a single act of communication from an author (the director of an industrial film or perhaps its featured actors) to a more or less monadic spectator. But it is the totality of these concealed relations that constitutes the dominant cinema, and any industrial film is only their vehicle.

The enabling condition of the entire system is the social division that restricts access to the means of film production to the owners of film studios, concomitantly excluding the masses from production and instating them as consumers. In the industrial cinema's period of "primitive accumulation," control of the technology was the object of intense competition among the early entrepreneurs. Closely following the acceleration of the trust and merger movements of 1897 to 1902, the nine major companies pooled their patents and rights to form the Motion Picture Patents Company (MPPC) in 1909, and so assumed international control of the industry. Though it also engendered both illegal independent production and eventually trustbusting challenges to the MPPC, monopolistic production and distribution initially curtailed competition within the industry. Thomas Ince's perfection of the studio system completed the primary industrial division between producer and consumer by organizing the division of labor within production; the productive process was rationalized into more or less autonomous tasks assigned to writers, directors, cameramen, technicians, stars (already an essential means of production), and other actors, in virtual imitation of the paradigm of modern industry, the Ford production line.

Control of this labor power, especially the retention of stars as studio property under the contract system, allowed a standardized and controlled apparatus for distribution through studio-owned theaters and block-booking. This vertical integration of the industry provided the basis for a similarly standardized commodity film—a standard-gauge, post-Griffith film grammar and eventually the "classic" film text—that became the means by which the division of labor within the industry was reproduced in the division between the industry and the films' audience, society at large. The resulting correspondences between the film industry and the structure of North American society from the early twenties to the late fifties allowed the movies their hegemony in cultural life, their crucial role in mediating between private fantasy and material production. Braided to its primary function of valorizing invested capital, the cinema's other work was then the restoration and pacification of its audience—initially the urban proletariat, eventually the society as a whole—what we now understand as their production as subjects within bourgeois ideology. Since it can survive only as long as does the social status quo, industrial film is bound to legitimate it; the moral of its production is "the triumph of invested capital . . . [which] is the meaningful content of every film, whatever plot the production team may have selected" (Horkheimer and Adorno, 1972: 124).

A schematic as brutal as Horkheimer and Adorno's may be reproached with qualifications of several kinds. Though standardized in its major parameters, production in the classic period nevertheless had recourse to various forms of internal organization. Neither its Taylorized internal articulation nor even its double function within capitalist production generally precluded tensions and contradiction—spaces cracked open by uneven development that allowed resistance to be inscribed in some of the films of the twenties and after. Specific films, genres, or phases in Hollywood history have consequently been seen as breaking open the noncontradictory closure proposed by Horkheimer and Adorno: the way in which an especially devious film noir may corrode apparent ratification of the social order; the moments in a Dorothy Arzner film that may be read as disrupting patriarchal discourse; or cases in which intradiegetic dramatization of spectatorship alienates unselfconscious consumption. Such local ruptures of the system of representation may be further systematized into general taxonomies of anti-industrial functions of the kind developed during the post-1968 critical investigation of Hollywood, notably by *Cahiers du Cinéma* and then by *Screen* (e.g., Comolli and Narboni, 1971), which can restore to their own coherence specific practices previously understood only as fractured, aberrant, or ungrammatical; bad movies made good in the alembic of codic mutation.

Nor is the system itself immune to renegade uses, especially at the point of consumption where, even inside the channels of industrial exhibition, the most orthodox of works can be transformed, their messages short-circuited and turned back against themselves by various forms of misreading or recontexualization. Specific audiences may thus appropriate for their own uses what was designed to use them. These variations and even acts of resistance within the industrial mode of production as a whole, even in the period when studio productions were most formulaic, are significant enough that any investigation of alternative cinemas must take them into account.

3 For a discussion of analogous hermeneutic levels in literature from which this presentation in part derives, see Eagleton (1976: 64–102) and, informing that, Macherey (1978).

4 These are not, obviously, mutually exclusive categories: half the people who were Black were also women, revolutionaries came from all classes, and so on. Designating ideological rather than ontological identities and differences, the terms were produced and espoused in historically specific conflict with each other. Of the structural social divisions they reflect, those of race, class, and gender are primarily important, and the history of the sixties is in large part the history of these competing analytical schema. Roughly speaking, each acquired a temporary hegemony over the general field of dissent in the order listed above, and in each phase the dominance of any one tended to reduce the significance of the others. The Black movement, for example, typically dismissed the significance of gender discrimination, while the women's movement either internally reproduced the racial and class divisions of the society at large or developed new taxonomies such as Black feminism or socialist feminism to accommodate competing social analyses. The confinement of Blacks and other people of color to the working class meant that in their case racial and class groupings were virtually isomorphic, and so allowed large parts of the Black movement to pass relatively easily in the late sixties from a cultural nationalist frame of reference to an international socialist one. The women's movement, on the other hand, was less easily able to accommodate analyses predicated on race or class. The position of working-class, non-White women is the place where all three structures of inequity coincide, and filmically as well as socially they were the most disadvantaged. On these tensions, see especially Davis (1981).

Such an investigation is obliged to tread a fine line between the dialects and the language, between recognizing the variations and irregularities of the different phases of industrial film and accounting for the homogeneity that subsumes them when they are viewed from the perspective provided by radically different practices.

Despite these qualifications, the interdependence of form, content, and social function is more immediate and more immediately visible in the industrial cinema than in most other cultural practices. Unlike music, which so readily rises to a pure etheriality, or literature, in which the determining relations between a text and the social practices it sustains are so elusive, with film the contingency of the aesthetic upon the economic is always well declared. The cinema insists upon itself as material and activity, insists that it is palpably an exchange of real things. Even the classic cinema, most careful to conceal the mechanisms of its illusions, still exposed the financial transactions it involved, from the rituals of the box office ticket purchase to the glamor of the stars' salaries. Together with the extensiveness of its social presence and the plurality of its social functions, the industrial cinema's celebration of the circuits of wealth it supplies and those that supply it allows the relations among the different levels of materialist hermeneutics to be clarified especially easily. The direct and homologous relationships among industrial film's textual properties and the industrial cinema's social function all intersect at the capitalist mode of film production.[3] The mode of production mediates between cultural superstructure and economic base, between art and politics.

The alternative films considered in this volume were made by people who refused the positions the capitalist cinema assigned them. The dissidents who thought of themselves as beatniks or revolutionaries, as Blacks or working-class, as women or artists[4] all had in common the decision to take control of the means of film production, to become themselves producers rather than merely consumers. The *prise de la parole* that constituted the radical utopianism of these filmmakers enabled them to devise new modes of film production and to bring new cinemas into being. Their films' differences in content or style trace an opposition to the dominant social order that involved not merely Walter Benjamin's criteria of an attitude to the dominant relations of production of the time and a position in them (Benjamin, 1979: 222); it also involved an assault upon them. Their use of film in ideological and social self-creation allowed for and demanded new social relations around the apparatus, new relations among the people who made the films, and new relations between filmmakers and their audiences. Just as the function of the industrial cinema is to sustain bourgeois social relations by representing them as normal and others as deviant, so one of the functions of alternative film was the sympathetic representation of alternative social relations. But while dissident groups had to secure their own self-representation in order to contest their misrepresentation in the industrial media, however crucial the consequent formal and discursive innovations were, justness in representation was not always the final issue. The primacy of representation was itself called into question, and the priority of the manufactured image, particularly of the marketable image that generated the capitalist division of labor, was subordinated to other uses of the apparatus that entailed the *production* of new social relations in cinema. As these dissident groups challenged the alienation of commodity culture and the alienation of the social system it produced, they were able to propose the new forms of social interaction they constructed through film as the model and agency for equivalent changes in society at large: alternative film practices came to figure social liberation.

The present inquiry is concerned with the spectrum of these alternative practices of film that were brought into existence in a particularly tumultuous period in history; their motives variously included self-expression, phenomenological investigation, propaganda or some other component in a program of social change, or simply play. In place of my elaborating these alternatives here, the following remarks may limn the innovations of one of them, one that was so anomalous within the normative terms of cinema that it could be figured only by recourse to the analogy of an entirely different medium.

> There is a feeling in the air that cinema is only beginning; that now cinema is available not only to those who possess a high organizational and group-work talent, but also to those poets who are more sensitive, but often un-communal, who prefer privacy, whose powers of observation and imagination are most active in privacy. (Mekas, 1962: 8–9)

As we shall see, in the fifties the poet provided a model for a new film practice, not simply because poetry summarized desired formal qualities, but because the psychic and social functions of contemporary poetry allowed the process of filmmaking to be reinvented for new purposes.

As the poetic cinema, like the other alternatives, discovered the social forms of its aesthetic practice and the aesthetic forms of its social practice, it replaced the social relations of capitalist cinema with those of its own mode. No less than does the industrial cinema, an alternative mode of film production designates the social relations entered into around the production and use of film, public or otherwise, and also circumscribes the limits of formal possibilities. The mode of film production is thus also the primary concern of a materialist history of alternative cinemas; it furnishes the terms that allow any film's formal character to be traced to the social conditions of its use, and that allow these latter to be similarly located in the conditions of the dominant society in which the film is made. Here infrastructural determination may be comprehended, both the measure of autonomy the dominant cultural practice may have in respect to the social formation as a whole or to the controlling interests within it and the degree to which minority and alternative practices may create independence from the dominant ideology and the dominant mode of material and cultural production.

Though the conception of an alternative cinema may not originate at the level of the mode of production (and instances in which the desire to make a different kind of film can be absolutely distinguished from a desire to make film differently are rare, for even a minimally innovative commercial feature involves some readjustment of industrial roles), still the mode of production remains the central interpretative category. The financial and technological resources employed and the social relations of a film's manufacture and consumption mark the limits of its formal possibilities, and indeed it is only in respect to the principles and conditions of its production and consumption that a film's formal properties may be understood or evaluated. Conversely, those conditions are always encoded. In the discourse of any film is written the context of its discourses; the functions of its production are visible in that documentation of its own production that every film performs.

The description of these traces of production—whether they be a matter of gauge or length, of a formal repertoire constituting a language or idiolect and implying a specific site of projection, or of the inscription of finance or work—is the point of departure for film hermeneutics. For as every film—from the multimillion dollar epic of conspicuous investment to the fragments of a home movie—internalizes the conditions of its production, it makes itself an allegory of them. This is especially clear, though no more true, in films that transgress the dominant cinema's form or function. In cases of ideological dissent or social contestation, the filmic and cinematic alternatives are inscribed in the film itself, both as themselves and as marks of difference from the dominant discourse. In such cases— and they are the present concern—the film not only speaks of what it is, it speaks of what it is not, it speaks of its other. Even as it encodes its own mode of production, every alternative film practice encodes its position in respect to the dominant mode of production, to the mass media. And the mode of production it manifests speaks of the social relations that constitute it, the social relations of the cinema of which it is, or would be, the film-vehicle. Every film is thus an allegory of a cinema.

Allegories of Production: The Case of *Easy Rider*

Certain films articulate the limits of modes of production. Stan Brakhage's *Mothlight* (1963), for example, a film made by assembling fragments of mothwings, petals, and seeds on an adhesive strip of editing tape, and Stanley Kubrick's *2001: A Space Odyssey* (1968), costing $10.5 million and needing eighteen months of studio work for the effects alone, each stretched its respective productive system to an extreme, to the point, in fact, where their manu-

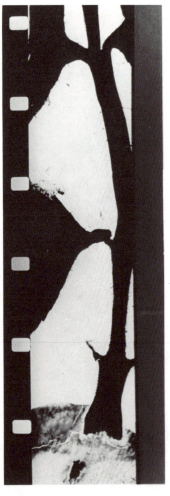

1.1 Stan Brakhage, *Mothlight*

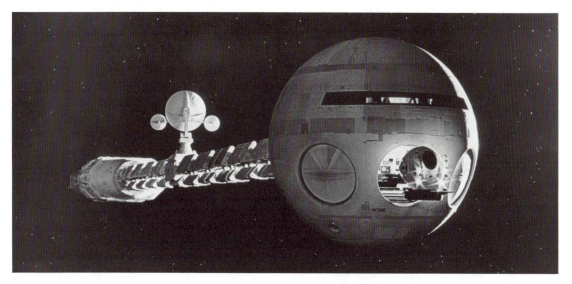

1.2 Stanley Kubrick, *2001: A Space Odyssey*

facture was so foregrounded that, in the phrase of the time, the medium did become the message. In *Mothlight* the flickering, evanescent projection of the traces of the organic material and the attempt to illuminate nature itself by circumventing a crucial and all but defining stage in filmmaking, the agency of the camera, correspond to the affirmation of the domestic, the personal, and the natural. *2001* on the other hand, so spectacular that the only comparable display of conspicuous spending, the moon landing of the following year, paled in comparison, flaunts its profligacy. Its overwhelming content not withstanding, each film also tends to a reflexive purity, in which ostensible subject matter—the moth wings or the space journey—is enfolded by the productive possibilities it sets in operation. In *Mothlight* the aesthetics of its mode of production, the laboriousness of its artisanal construction and its technological primitivism, ratify its ethic of nature redeemed. But *2001* is internally inconsistent; its conspicuous expenditure and technological excess make it a party to the militarized corporate future it predicts, and the force of its admonition is contradicted by the indulgence of its spectacle.

As this instance reminds us then, the isolation of interpretative levels—the filmic codes, the cinema in which they are produced, and the historical situation at large—is only the first step in hermeneutics, the specification of patterns of displacement and contradiction by which these levels are related. But though Brakhage and Kubrick are interesting as extremes, they are by that fact atypical; their exemplification of a relatively "pure" mode of production and its virtual containment of all other thematic, structural, or social implications is anomalous. Certain methods of production do stabilize for longer or shorter periods, but usually productive systems are in flux.

Such was the case in Hollywood in the sixties, when the declining

1.3 Stan Brakhage, *Mothlight*

audience and developments in television and popular music put the industry in crisis, both internally and in its relation to society. Films made in periods such as this frequently attempt to negotiate with surrounding social and cinematic changes, and even when they are not explicitly about the search for a satisfactory mode of production, their plots often have some metaphorical relation to their own manufacture. Consequently, as the site of conflict or arbitration between alternative productive possibilities, they invite an allegorical reading in which a given filmic trope—a camera style or an editing pattern—is understood as the trace of a social practice. In such a materialist version of the Formalist reading of texts as the mobilization of preexistent devices, formal motifs signify through the text to the material practices that produce it. Such a use of the filmic to lay bare its cinematic preconditions is especially fruitful for all kinds of sixties' film, in which the social tensions that generated them were often clearly inscribed. We may briefly consider here a historically important instance of such inscription, one that was pivotal in solving the industry's crisis. The thematic confusion and formal incoherence of Dennis Hopper's *Easy Rider* (1969), a 35mm ersatz underground film, are produced by—and so may be made retroactively to articulate—tensions among the disparate practices it incorporates in its own production.

After the nightmare climax that proves their trip to have been a bad one, Captain America remarks to Billy, "We blew it." Though *Easy Rider* immediately ratifies its hero's diagnosis with nemesis in the shape of the southern bigots, the remark itself is enigmatic. Billy's contrary claim that together they "did it," that the big money in the drug deal would allow them to retire in Florida, does bring the film's plot full circle, but the resonances of the phrase and its summary conclusion to the social alternatives witnessed by the film seem hardly satisfied here. Whether the failure derives from deficiencies in Billy and the Captain, from the counterculture's traffic with drugs, from its agricultural inexperience, or even simply from the venom of straight society is never made clear. This thematic confusion reflects conflicts in the imperatives of the film's ideological and financial work, its obligation finally to denigrate the social alternatives represented by the counterculture that gives it market value. Though its ambivalence includes a provisional and qualified approval of the counterculture (and the doubling of the picaresque hero allows both its utopian and dystopian faces to be figured), finally it must destroy Captain America and Billy.

The immediate source for such simultaneous invocation and punishment of libidinously gratifying and even utopian deviations from repressive social orders is the Western and its urban equivalent, the gangster film. Like these and their common ancestor, the rogue's tale, *Easy Rider* offers both vicarious participation in infraction and the admonitory comfort of retribution. Drugs, free love, and the excitement of the open road may be celebrated, but only as long as they are not allowed to imply such systemic change as would decriminalize them. Though it is more sympathetic to the counterculture than any previous industrial film, *Easy Rider* is finally reducible to and incorporable into the dominant ideological field. As well as ethical schemas, this field includes a specific model of film production and formal conventions which any commercial film may modify for the *frisson* of novelty but not fundamentally breach. Just as *Easy Rider* finally discredits the social alternatives it depicts, so it discredits the alternative film styles and alternative modes of film production it exhibits and exploits.

Though it relies extensively on the "biker" conventions developed by Roger Corman (with whom Hopper, Peter Fonda, and Jack Nicholson had worked), especially in *The Wild Angels* (1966) and *The Trip* (1967), the film did deviate from commercial norms, reciprocating its gestures of endorsement toward the counterculture in several key filmic codes. The most important was the rock music sound track, but several visual motifs—flash cutting between shots, an extended interlude of subjective psychedelic vision, and an overall looseness in scene construction, for instance—signal some infraction of orthodox film grammar. All these derive from previous alternative film: the basic motif of the journey from west to east and the overall ethical structure derive from Bruce Baillie's *Quixote*; flash frames which signify subjectivity or anticipation, or which diffuse transitions between scenes, derive from Stan Brakhage; the hand-held camera and the use of anamorphic lenses in the trip se-

1.4–1.7 Dennis Hopper, *Easy Rider*

quence are the staple motifs of countless underground films; the caressing attention to the technological sensuousness of the motorcycles derives from Kenneth Anger's *Kustom Kar Kommandos*, as the use of rock music structurally and as ironic counterpoint derives from his *Scorpio Rising*; the occasional "real life" confrontations, such as that with the young man in the street in New Orleans, are borrowed from cinéma vérité; and the documentation of the counterculture and its more or less scandalous rituals—drugs, nudity, communal habitation—is the defining function of underground film as a whole, originating in the various documentations of beatnik life in the late fifties. But since Hopper fails to assimilate the film practices of various dissenting and countercultural groups into a coherent style, the film remains a pastiche, an essentially orthodox industrial product, decorated with unamalgamated infractions. All are held in place in a controlled hierarchy of discourses. As interludes within a dominant and quite conventional mode of representation, they may be appropriated to secure the film's gestures of dissent, but they must finally be marked as marginal and supplementary— as deviations. The standard form is reaffirmed as normative, strengthened through its incorporations, and inoculated against their disorder. This ideological and formal recuperation expresses parallel tensions between commodity and anti-commodity functions in the film's production.

Unlike *Joe* or *The Strawberry Statement* or other studio exploitations of the youth culture, *Easy Rider* was independently produced and independently written and shot. Edited under conditions of virtual autonomy, it starred its producer and director. Despite these inflections in the industrial mode by the form of authorship associated with the avant-garde, the film was from the first undertaken as commodity production, and, distributed by Warner Brothers, it reaped a substantial return, allowing both Hopper and Fonda to proceed to new cycles of production. In this mixed mode of production, Hopper's attempt to use the industrial apparatus as the vehicle of his own authorship was countered by the financial functions of the industry. Each of the filmic alternatives he quoted manifested social alternatives, each had its own social determinations and uses, and each was constituted in specific relations to the apparatus. By incorporating them merely as style, Hopper erased those social alternatives, recuperating to the industry the traces of cinemas whose structuring conditions were their antipathy to it.

In inscribing these tensions, *Easy Rider* is in no way anomalous; indeed, the interdependence in it of diffusion and defusion of subcultural innovation is the primary syndrome in the culture of late capitalism, the process by which the industrial media neutralize oppositional practices and renew their hegemony. What is remarkable about *Easy Rider* is only the clarity by which the appropriation lit the way for a new Hollywood. The cost of that renewal was not simply filmic—*Easy Rider*'s inability to resolve filmically the formal differences among the various sources it plagiarized—but also cinematic—its failure to develop a film practice commensurate with the social implications of those sources. Its failure (and now we may read Captain America's remark "We blew it" as an allegory of the film, of the failure of Hopper and Fonda to make a film adequate to the ideals of the counterculture) is the sign of the incompatibility of the alternative film practices it invokes with the film industry and with film *as* capitalist industry—an incompatibility so fundamental that it raises the possibility that the social alternatives it considers were incompatible with film in any form. For, in the case of its central figuration of a counterculture, the hippies reject the city for a technologically primitive, communal agrarianism to which the technological dependence of the film medium is fundamentally alien. In a way that recalls purist positions in the contemporary debate about the impropriety of electronic instruments in folk music, that community culturally produces itself, not through film but through a practice that is itself communal and pre-technological, a reinvention of Elizabethan theater.

Whether the film apparatus could be wrenched free from its history and be made over in a form appropriate to this or any number of other oppositional social practices was in dispute throughout the sixties. The specter of contradictions intrinsic to cinema haunted the period, occasioning a variety of anti-films or negative films. When they did not terminate in a refusal to make films, these attempts to spring cinematic technology free from its industrial function forced the medium into the splendid new forms of the decade. But though *Easy Rider* could recognize such aspirations intradiegetically, it could not accept them filmically or cinematically. A real endorsement of the commune would have brought the film to a halt there. It would have meant abandoning the film's real destination, arresting both the death trip of Captain America and the success of *Easy Rider* in the commercial cinema.

Film and Mass Culture

Any consideration of cinema inherits a longstanding debate about the relation between mass culture and other forms of cultural production. Though since its initiation, following the mass migration to the cities in the industrial revolution, the debate has continuously been concerned with the effect of the popular press and the electronic media on working people, it became increasingly polemical after World War I, exacerbated on the one hand by popularly inaccessible high modernist art and on the other by the political use of mass communications by totalitarian governments, especially fascist Germany. The responses of artists and theorists, preeminently Brecht and Benjamin, to this latter have remained exemplary, in terms of both models of alternative art practices and attempts to rethink mass culture itself. But also in the liberal democracies—from Roosevelt on the radio to Reagan on television, and, in between, the whole articulation of the media with capitalist industry and social power—both mass culture and minority practices have been understood as political issues.

Except during a period from the late forties through the early sixties, when empirical research by academic sociologists appeared to justify the liberal belief that mass communications augmented democratic pluralism, with more primary social organizations ensuring that they circulated the information necessary to a free society without determining its reception,[5] most theories of mass culture have been adversarial. Both right and left have attacked the uniformity and superficiality of industrial media, their degradation of cultural standards to the level of the marketplace and of the lowest common denominator within it, and the susceptibility to commercial or ideological manipulation they putatively engender in the masses. Of such critiques, the most authoritative is the Frankfurt School's understanding of mass culture as a crucial nexus in the industrial organization of modern society.

As a culture industry, even as a consciousness industry—to use Enzensberger's summary extension of Frankfurt School principles (Enzensberger, 1974)—mass entertainment is continuous with industrial production as a whole and supplies the ideological conditions of its reproduction by co-opting potentially disruptive drives;

5 See Gurevitch et al. (1982: 12–13, 38–39) for a summary of these arguments.

it liquidates "two dimensional culture," "not through the denial and rejection of the 'cultural values,' but through their wholesale incorporation into the established order, through their reproduction and display on a massive scale" (Marcuse, 1964: 57). The alternative, cultural negation, retrieved another dimension through art practices so inexhorably severe that they could not be incorporated into the industrial scenarios of pleasure. At this point the Frankfurt analysis rejoins elitist critiques of mass culture, celebrating the integrity of high culture in preserving a distance between life and its mediation.

Though various lacunas in the total closure diagnosed by the Frankfurt School have been proposed—moments when one part of the system is in contradiction with another, when cracks or inconsistencies in the artwork disrupt the ideological system, or even when consumer art itself contains some utopian dimension at odds with its dominant order—the Frankfurt analysis of the structural integration of the media in monopoly capital has not been successfully challenged, and indeed other theories turn out to be partial or immature versions of it. But its model of oppositional cultural practice has proven less viable; the hypostatization and reification of high culture, the failure to address the coincidence of its defense of high modernism with the protofascist elements in modernism's self-defense, and especially the *under*estimation of the culture industry's ability to recuperate even the most recalcitrant art—all these suggest a fundamental idealism in the conception of the avant-garde practices it valorizes.

This is not to say that many such practices do not think of themselves as autonomous, but they are able to do so only by rigidly circumscribing their social function or by refusing to recognize their own social determination. Structural film is a luminous instance of such a cinema, to which we shall attend. This and cognate events in film and in other mediums must be thought of as radically contradictory attempts to secure a condition of aesthetic autonomy—as aspirations that are themselves historically determined by the same social conditions that produce the mass media. While there are occasions when Adorno recognizes the avant-garde and mass culture together as mutually sustaining manifestations of more fundamental social constrictions, his more typical supposition that the former is by definition free from all but negative determination (and that in a highly mediated form) allows him to circumvent proper attention to the conditions of the avant-garde's production and to the social relationships it entails. A similar repression in most theories of avant-garde film is equally debilitating.

A central exhibit in the debates about the mass media, film has been variously identified with both their utopian and dystopian potentials; but oppositional film practices have been so marginal that they have received little attention. While critical theories of other mediums routinely begin—or at any rate did until recently—by distinguishing an art from a commercial function, Literature from writing, for example, or Fine Art from commercial art, industrial

6 In this case, Jowett (1976).

7 The opening sentence of Lewis Jacobs's 1947 essay "Experimental Cinema in America: 1921–1947" established the foundation for subsequent orthodoxy: "Experimental cinema in America has had little in common with the main stream of the motion picture industry. Living a kind of private life of its own, its concern has been solely with motion pictures as a medium of artistic expression" (Jacobs, [1947] 1968: 543). Ironically, as if signaling the impossibility of that disaffiliation, Jacobs first published the essay in the *Hollywood Quarterly* (3, no. 2 [1947]: 111–24)!

8 Though here I take issue with Sitney's model of the avant-garde, the importance of his immensely fertile and nuanced accounts of individual films and of the careers of many important filmmakers can hardly be overemphasized; it inaugurated scholarly consideration of large areas of film history otherwise ignored. The present work does not seek to displace his crucially innovative reading of American film, so much as to frame it in a materialist analysis of the conditions of that film's production; his work everywhere informs this essay, even when it is not explicitly recognized. While in general he theorizes the avantgarde as a transhistorical category, in fact his account of it does recognize historical variations. For example, the present assertion of the specificity of the sixties' alternative cinemas may be glimpsed between his observations that "the 1950s were quiet years within the American avant-garde cinema," and that "the seventies have been a quiet period for the American avant-garde cinema" (Sitney, 1979: 137, 398). Though Heath is right to observe that "avant-garde filmmaking has suffered from being provided with a history of its own" (Heath, 1981: 175), the damage incurred is minimal compared with that which attends the repression of independent film in bourgeois histories.

film has generally been taken *tout court* for the medium as such. Adorno himself could find instances of authentic literature, drama, and especially music; but the closest he came to non-collusive film was Orson Welles—whose work he dismissed as "calculated mutations which serve all the more strongly to confirm the validity of the system" (Horkheimer and Adorno, 1972: 129).

Until television sewed mass communications entirely within consumer society, the commercial cinema was the exemplary instance of the culture industry. As the occasion either for the elaboration of general theories of the media or for distinctions within them, it was successively attacked from all points of the political spectrum; the moral-religious condemnation of its practitioners, its product, or its effect was followed by similarly wholesale condemnations of it on anti-communist and more recently left-semiological grounds. The rebuttals to these attacks have found evidence for Hollywood's probity, not just in its crusades against communism or even in its "deconstruction" of its own codes, but primarily in the fact of its centrality in mass culture. Elision of the functional distinctions between *popularity* and *populism* has allowed endless versions of *Film: The Democratic Art*,[6] proposing the commercial cinema as a model of demotic culture.

Whichever of these positions is adopted—and here it will be sufficient to note that the restriction of class, ethnic, or social leveling produced by the movies to one moment in the industrial cycle, the point of consumption, hardly accords even with liberal/pluralist models of the mass media as ensuring the free circulation of ideas—they all must recognize the dominance in cinema as a whole of the industrial mode of production and its overall cultural hegemony through the sixties. In no other medium has a single practice been able to produce itself as so entirely normative. Consequently, any non–industrial film always finds itself already politicized, already conceptualized as marginal, deviant, inconsequential—as other. For itself, alternative film has been obliged to construct an alternative history, in which it did have an existence beyond that reflected back to it as the byproduct of what it itself was not. And reflecting its marginal position, the scaffold for this history most often has been the idea of "art." Attempts to provide a history of an autonomous art practice of film in the United States, entirely separate from Hollywood, date back at least as far as 1947[7]; of sixties versions of them, formulated by the writers around *Film Culture*, and later *Art Forum*, P. Adams Sitney's is exemplary.[8]

Variously articulated (Sitney, 1969, 1970, 1975, 1978, 1979), Sitney's project contains two main components: the explication of a tradition of film-as-art in the United States since World War II and the installation of this tradition as the continuation of a similar one in Europe before the war. The genealogy parallels that of modernist painting, and indeed the U.S. branch is attributable to the flight from fascist Europe of cubists, dadaists, and surrealists (Sitney, 1970: 4), Hans Richter being the most important. The tradition is itself a formalist one, and Sitney defines it in formalist terms: "The

rejection of linear narrative . . . is nearly the defining feature of the
independent cinema" (Sitney, 1978: vi). Deriving respectively from
Dziga Vertov's investigation of the "rhetorical indeterminacy" of
the space between shots and from Peter Kubelka's concern with the
articulation of one frame with the next (ibid.: vii–viii), the two
halves of the tradition sustained film as art by clarifying its intrinsic
properties and eliminating those inessential to it. Its teleology is thus
radically reductionist: the successive stripping away of narrative,
myth, protagonist, and even the first-person "lyric" center of perception, finally to arrive at the pure interrogation of the medium
itself. Its American component especially, this avant-garde of experimental, poetic, underground, and finally structural film (the onomastic uncertainty suggests not so much the lack of appropriate nomenclature as a radical heterogeneity in the materials themselves),
is understood as virtually absolute in its independence. On occasion
Hollywood is allowed a negative influence (Sitney, 1970: 4), and in
the enterprise adjacent to Sitney's work, the establishment of Anthology Film Archives as a "nuclear collection of the monuments of
cinematic art" (Sitney, 1975: v), this history does include narrative
filmmakers such as the Soviets, Bresson, even Chaplin and Keaton;
but in general "the precise relationship of the avant-garde cinema
to American commercial film is one of radical otherness. They operate in different realms with next to no significant influence on each
other" (Sitney, 1979: viii).

In counterposing against commercial film a unified avant-garde
from Vertov to Kubelka, Sitney elides the radical social differences
among the people who produce the films he refers to and the radically different cinemas they compose. His equation of the practice
of a member of a post-revolutionary collectivity with that of an
alienated aesthete—of the art of a worker with the work of an artist—without regard to their social incomparability is an ideological
exclusion, a function of the ideology of the aesthetic avant-garde
itself, the object it purports to account for. The most comprehensive, nuanced, and lucid of the transpositions of the modernist paradigm to film, Sitney's work is able to account for certain projects
in cinema, and the importance of his accounts of specific films can
hardly be overestimated. But the elaboration of an autonomous,
self-regarding, and self-producing alternative practice that has been
continuous through the modern period and independent of industrial production distorts the historical field of cinema, and, in forcing erroneous inclusions in and exclusions from its categories, it
must falsify the practices it attends to. The most egregious distortions of such an elaboration follow not from its insensitivity to the
industry's high-art aspirations, which have been more or less continuous from the *Société Film d'Art*'s productions of bourgeois
theater to the rewriting of Hollywood in terms of the *politique des
auteurs*; rather, they follow from its inability to accommodate the
diversity of the alternative cinemas and their ongoing negotiations
with Hollywood. The former is a matter of a splintered spectrum of
formal priorities and social functions radically different from each

other and, in fact, often openly hostile. The latter, continuous since the beginnings of the avant-garde in the surrealists' and the Soviets' fascination with American culture, was aptly summarized in Germaine Dulac's observation that the "avant-garde and the commercial cinema, that is, the art and the industry of film, form an inseparable whole" (Dulac, [1932] 1978: 44).

Alternative Cinemas

The present argument that the cinemas of disenfranchised social groups are the truly populist ones disputes both the naive celebration of the democracy of Hollywood and the apotheosization of the avant-garde; neither position can account for the diversity of non-studio film practices or the political transactions they involve. The categories of the avant-garde and the industry must be dismantled, and their blank polarization opened to the play of heterogeneity and interdetermination within the field of practices the terms otherwise simply divide. In place of the single, transhistoric, self-regulating avant-garde tradition appears the spectrum of alternative practices which develop and decay with historically specific needs and possibilities. And far from being categorically defined against a monolithic, uncontradictory industry, these alternatives emerge from (and in certain circumstances merge with) a similar plurality of practices constructed in the margins of the industry or even as mutations within it.

In this total field of continuously changing practices, the binary distinction between industrial product and modernist aestheticism retains only a much reduced role, that of marking theoretical extremes rarely approached in practice. *Mothlight* and *2001* would appear to be as close as any films to occupying exemplary positions. But even here the degree to which *Mothlight* must exist in a system of commodities and the signature of the modernist author in *2001*, with its use of the underground trope of the interior trip and of avant-garde technologies (like the slit-scan processes in the Stargate Corridor sequence developed years before by John Whitney), immediately qualify the polarization. Brakhage's *Reflections on Black* against a "B" noir of the same period and *Tom, Tom, The Piper's Son* by Ken Jacobs against Billy Bitzer's film of the same name are other instances of different kinds of invocation of industry by art at the latter's most extreme reaches. But though the force of the heuristic evaporates whenever its defining limits are approached, still the great variety of ways in which all practices negotiate with industrial functions and film languages allows the polarity a second function, that of organizing gradational scales that enable local instances within the entire range of production to be differentiated.

The replacement of a categorical bifurcation by multidirectional gradational scales allows the different practices otherwise yoked together or entirely obscured by the modernist polarity to be returned to their specificity in the gestalt of mutually determining practices that forms the general field of production. Industrial cinema takes its place in this field, but, itself neither unified nor stable, it is not confronted by a single contrary but surrounded and interpenetrated by many different kinds of filmmaking. The distinctiveness of each of these appears initially as a matter of form—as the use of a nonstandard gauge and film length and the deployment of unorthodox profilmic and filmic codes. But these are only the traces of more fundamental innovations in the mode of film production that derive from the film's functions in the social unit that produces it. Constituting an alternative film practice as an alternative cinema, this register of functions determines filmic form, with alterity to the dominant mode being but one component in it.

This model of alternative film as subcultural practice organized around unorthodox modes of production makes possible the materialist investigation of the relation between aesthetics and politics. Attention to the specific practices that produce the dominant ideology and to those that enact resistance to it allows us to avoid the scholasticism of idealist generalizations about cultural autonomy (or semiautonomy) that propose transhistorical conditions applicable uniformly to all forms of art; and it allows us to clarify the social origin of art and its functions in daily life without falling into an abstract reflectionism which can designate culture only as an epiphenomenon of a historical reality existing independent of it. Attention to the socially active group as the area where general historical possibilities achieve a concrete form, on the one hand, and as the origin of cultural practice, on the other, makes visible the social transactions where determination is lived and fought, where history is made.

When analysis takes its terms of reference from the material level of production (the sphere of cinema), filmic form may be understood as the product of social necessities and aspirations, as they engage the cinematic possibilities of their historical moment. A given stylistic vocabulary is never merely itself; rather it is the trace of the social processes that constitute a practice. Films are only the form of appearance of the cinemas they organize. All models of filmic distinctions, and especially all formalist models that propose distinctions between an alternative film style and the codes of the feature industry, must then be doubled to include the social determinants of each; they must be returned to social practice. And any alternative practice, whether it be Black film, underground film, or women's film, may be understood as a response to the three other spheres of activity: the alternative social group, the dominant society, and the hegemonic cinema (see table, page 24). To take the example of underground film, which will be our most comprehensive illustration of this complex of determinations, the films of the beat generation were shaped simultaneously by the beats' own aesthetic principles and social uses for film, by their situation in respect to the commercial cinema, and by their situation as a dissident subculture in respect to the surrounding social formation. Underground film thus represents the modification of previous uses of the medium to produce a film practice formally consonant with its functions in beat society and capable of negotiating, symbolically and practically, the relations between the subculture and the social whole. Though a major procedure in underground film is the documentation of beat life, its function is not just the representation of beat society, but also the production of beat society.

Alternative film practice	Hegemonic film practice
Minority social or interest group	Dominant society

But while underground film developed from previous marginal alternative film practices and continued to interact with other contemporary alternatives (such as the European New Waves), as well as adapting the innovations of poetry, jazz, and other art forms and cultural practices, its major determinant, both positive and negative, was Hollywood. Even as the dominant mode of material production in a given social formation influences and assigns ranks to other modes of production which may coexist with it, so the dominant mode of cultural production positions and inflects minority cultural practices. In the modern period, the media industries inhabit all alternative cultural practices and so, for even the most recalcitrant avant-garde film, the film industry "is a general illumination which bathes all the other colours and modifies their particularity . . . , a particular ether which determines [their] specific gravity" (Marx, 1973: 107). The underground's codes emerged, then, as mutations and mutilations of industrial codes, and its practices were carried on either in the spaces between industrial practices or as modifications of them.

In the late fifties film was still the single most important agent of acculturation, with Hollywood the source of a national fantasy life, the vocabulary of its imagination, and the matrix of its art. As John Clellon Holmes summarized in 1965, "The movies of the 1930's constitute, for my generation, nothing less than a kind of Jungian collective unconsciousness, a decade of coming attractions out of which some of the truths of our maturity have been formed" (Holmes, 1965: 55). So while a tradition of working-class criticism of Hollywood may be traced back through such figures as Howard Lawson and James T. Farrell (e.g., Farrell, 1944) to the Workers Film and Photo League and Harry Potamkin in the thirties, still in the popular mind Hollywood was distinguished *against* high art precisely by virtue of its accessibility and general appeal. Despite their ideological and material work in monopoly capitalism, the movies had always retained some populist affiliations, standing "slightly aslant" of mainstream values (Sklar, 1975: 267), and only recently had they been freed from the stigma of specifically work-ing-class associations and even of a supposed communist orienta-tion. On the other hand, while the studios were increasingly relying on independent production, conditions were still sufficiently rigid and over-centralized that young artists had little chance of self-expression before depleting themselves in years of mechanical ap-prenticeship.[9] Surrounding this situation and the aesthetic innova-tion it forced on the beats was a social crisis, the fragmentation of the postwar hegemony and the growth of dissent and contestation, which appears in underground film as a social content, the beats' elaboration of their social alternatives and their critique of Ameri-can society. All these processes cross and recross in the text of each underground film, a total exegesis of which would clarify its deter-minations in all these areas: its function within the beat subculture; its filmic embodiment and production of beat values; its marginality in general cultural production; its critique, positive and negative, of the American consensus; and its critique, again positive and nega-tive, of Hollywood.

But even such a hermeneutic is only a beginning of a social *history* of cinema; precisely because it does make provision for other inter-determinations—for the effect of underground film *on* Hollywood and *on* the dominant society, as well as for its role in producing and disseminating the beat subculture—this model makes possible the understanding of all these diachronically and historically. The social formation and each of its various cultural practices were all continu-ally in the flux of their adjustment to developments in the others; and in the cultural totality they jointly make up, each was con-stantly negotiating and renegotiating various degrees of autonomy and control, each continuously fracturing and reforming under the stress of internal contradictions and external pressures. Each was constantly in a state of production. Though the dominant industry generally reproduces the ideology of the dominant society, which is always itself the site of competing social groups and classes, it too is the scene of conflict. And of course the various subcultures were themselves continually in process, mediating between different de-sires and social possibilities. What we think of as the sixties was a period of especially energetic activity in all these areas. The present concern is with the history of those social groups whose pursuit of their own interests or attempts to change America brought them into an engagement with film. These alternative cinemas must be contextualized, then, by a summary of the history of the film indus-try, for when it was not their ambition, it was their antagonist.[10]

The Crisis in Hollywood

The postwar crisis for Hollywood peaked in 1960. Although in both 1946 and 1948 the average weekly attendance at movie thea-ters equaled the early depression high of 90 million, by 1950 a third of this had been lost, and the figure subsequently fell to record lows

9 In France, to take the most signif-icant counter-example, the distribu-tion of production among hundreds of small companies and the system of government grants made it rela-tively easy for young filmmakers to begin work in 35mm feature pro-duction; the *loi d'aide* allowed Godard, for example, to borrow the money for *Breathless*. Stephen Dwoskin notes that in Europe, do-mestic film was accepted "as an ac-tivity open to anyone . . . like any other profession," a factor which, with the greater political freedom there, allowed the Europeans to build upon what they had, whereas "the New American Cinema started with film from scratch" (Dwoskin, 1975: 76). Similarly, Sitney notes that "without a chance to make the kind of films they wanted to make commercially, [American filmmak-ers] immediately set about doing what they could within the limita-tions of their circumstances" (Sit-ney, 1970: 4).

10 On Hollywood in the sixties, see Baxter (1972); Sklar (1975); Balio (1976); Jowett (1976); Cook (1981); and Schatz (1983).

of 40 million in 1959 and 1960, the number of movie theaters in the country declining by a third in the same period. Since the price of tickets rose, annual box office receipts declined less precipitously, from $1.7 billion in 1946 to $1.3 billion in 1956. The reasons commonly adduced for this decline are the changing social patterns that followed the end of the war, the preference for domestic entertainment explained by the sharp increase in the birthrate, and especially the commercial expansion of television. Though box office receipts had begun to fall before television made a significant impact—around 1949—after that time the number of sets rose quickly, from 1 million to 32 million 5 years later, and by the end of the fifties only 1 home in 10 was without television.

The difficulties these developments occasioned were exacerbated by the antitrust suits and by the effects of the Supreme Court decision in the *Paramount* case in 1948, which forced Paramount, Warner Brothers, MGM-Loews, RKO, and Twentieth Century–Fox, the five major studios, to divest their control over first-run theaters, thus breaking apart the vertical integration that had sustained the studios' monopoly since the twenties. And just at this point, when innovative leadership was necessary to develop new markets, the industry instead, after the citation of the "Hollywood Ten," capitulated to the Red Scare, beginning ten years of blacklisting which essentially ended whatever responsiveness to progressive causes, whatever distance from mainstream values, Hollywood had been able to sustain.

The postwar reorganization of industrial production, completed by the purchase of the major studios by corporate conglomerates in the late sixties,[11] led to the confused retrenchment of the fifties, with innovations largely restricted to attempts to capitalize on spectacular effects that television could not match. While nothing worthwhile came from the various wide screen and 3-D projects, the influence of television was not entirely negative. As television took over center stage in the mass culture, some elements in Hollywood began to redirect production toward selected minority audiences. The decentralization of production in the fifties had made the studios more and more the distribution apparatus for independently produced features, which by 1967 amounted to 51.1 percent of all features released (Jowett, 1976: 481). In the last third of the decade, this greater flexibility allowed the innovative directors of the New Hollywood—Arthur Penn, Mike Nichols, Francis Ford Coppola, George Lucas—to cement a relationship between the industry and a new audience, though even before that time there had been some responsiveness to the social changes of the period. John Ford's reversal of the Indian/white dyad in *Cheyenne Autumn* (1964), the spate of "problem" movies dealing with race relations, Roger Corman's message movies, the emergence of cynical non-heroes like Paul Newman's early sixties roles (*The Hustler* in 1961 and *Hud* in 1963), and even Sean Connery's James Bond all variously indicate some redefinition of values and adjustment to social discontent.

Stimulated by the national cinemas, the various New Waves of

11 "In 1969, MGM was taken over by Kirk Kerkorian, a hotel magnate; Warner Brothers was purchased from Seven Arts by Kinney National Service, Inc., which operated parking lots, construction companies, and a comic book empire; Embassy was controlled by the AVCO Corporation, which built aviation equipment; Paramount was in the hands of Gulf and Western, a multifaceted conglomerate; Universal Studios went from Decca Records to MCA, Inc., the monolithic talent agency, and large television production company; while United Artists was owned by TransAmerica Corporation, which also controlled banks, insurance companies and oil wells" (Jowett, 1976: 436).

the fifties, and the growing popularity of the art film circuits, such developments also drew heavily on the sixties underground. Formal innovations such as overt reflexivity that fractured invisible narration passed into the commercial vocabularies of both film and television as the industry began to represent hippies, Blacks, and eventually women and the war (though this last, until the mid-seventies, only in allegorical displacement), and to confront the violence of some of these causes. The desire and the ability of the art or the political cinemas to maintain autonomy from the industry was, with few exceptions, entirely eroded by the late seventies.

A component in the larger history of the industrial media and essentially shaped by the pressures of television and industrial music, this history of industrial cinema describes a crisis in its capacity as a means of capital valorization. The cinemas discussed in this book emerged from that crisis; but their history is the contestation of cinema as commodity production. From that of the solitary "poet" to the cooperative efforts of large groups, the various interventions they inaugurated call into question the functions that constitute capitalist cinema. Deriving from the conditions of capitalism and its alternatives, their various aspirations produced different articulations of personal production and public consumption. The expressive possibilities that became available—and in them semiology was always imbued with and surrounded by politics—may be summarized as being hinged between authenticity and irony.

The interruption between signifier and signified that is the condition of signification separates signs, not only externally from their referents, but also internally from themselves. Constituted in difference, all images are thus inhabited by an otherness that erodes the affirmation of their apparent presence. In the case of the film image, whose history is redolent with myths of its indistinguishability as such, the duplicity of the simulacrum has been seen as both the source of its particular pleasures and the stigma of its mendacity, with the antinomy between "the representation of reality" and "the reality of the representation" summarizing what has also been a history of anxiety. This semiological contradiction extends through the various realms of cinema, with the various alienations of its industrial production and consumption joining with the alienation of modern life in general.

The horizon of modern consciousness, such systemic alienation was felt peculiarly forcefully in the sixties, and indeed it forms the context for the period's characteristic political movements, the contrary articulations of dissent and counter-aspiration, whose post-Heideggerian and post-Sartrean existentialist vocabulary recurred to a gestalt of mutually ratifying terms: authenticity, the self, bad faith, free speech, self-realization, the politics of experience, the personal as political, and so on. From the Third World to the domestic rhetoric of liberation, from the Port Huron Statement to Situationist *détournements*, such concepts are primary. Their force, even their tenability, has of course been so thoroughly impugned that what once seemed axiomatic political postulates now resonate with nostalgia and naiveté. Whatever the ultimate standing of the critiques of them (and it is here necessary to remark only that the conditions of the production and circulation of the ideologies of the post-modern are no less determined by the historical moment than were the ethics of presence they have displaced), their preoccupations are not new. Rather, the ideals of the sixties were always tempered with their opposites, and, from the constructivism of perpetual revolution to the irreverant debunkings of the mass media, the cults of authenticity were always conducted through the cultures of fabrication.

In film no less. On the one hand, the drive for authenticity summarizes so many of the practices discussed here: the urgency with which film was inserted into the optical physiology or phenomenology of the individual; the social urgency of the revolutionary interventions in cinema; and the semiological crises of the image itself leading to the reduction to the essentially filmic. But all these were interpenetrated, sometimes overwhelmed, by their opposites, by the recognition of difference, by a pleasure in the inauthentic, or by despair at its inevitability. If the alternative cinemas were typically powered by obsessions with authenticity, they were as often steered by the perspectives allowed by the rear-view mirror of irony.

The most convenient point of entry into these alternative cinemas is through the concept of authorship. Pried out of the anonymous bedrock of mass culture by the *politique des auteurs*, what initially appeared as an impregnable site of authenticity was almost immediately returned by subsequent theory to the social circulations of textuality and survived only in the reduced and ethereal form of the "author-function." But between these points the concept did provide a ledge where the romantic, idealist panoply of expressive individualism was forced into confrontation with the materialist and the social, with the specific potentials and limits of film, and with the public operations of cinema. The alternative possibilities of the re-integration of an independent authorial cinema into the industrial economies of the spectacle or its total liberation from them are paradigmatically exemplified in the work of Andy Warhol and Stan Brakhage, the "slow and the quick" of the avant-garde (Mekas, 1972: 158).[12] Though these were the most infamous avatars of the underground, their programs for independent film, for the optical events it could conjure and the social events it could organize, were entirely contrary. Where Brakhage's use of the medium as the scene of obsessively personal vision demanded the innovation of practices antithetical in all respects to the industry, Warhol's project allowed him to redirect the artisanal mode and its visual splendors back toward industrial practice. Thus, they manifest two of the extremes between which other, less uncompromising practices steered. It is with Brakhage's use of the medium in a struggle to redeem the romantic self that we begin.

12 For other comparisons of Brakhage and Warhol, see Tyler (1969: 27), Sharits (1972: 34), and especially Arthur (1978).

Stan Brakhage: The Filmmaker as Poet

2

Poetry ... is the very adjective of what is consummate.
— Edward Dorn

Reduced to an eye
I forget what
                    I
was.
— Denise Levertov

Despite a continuing abstract, plastic tradition, the postwar American avant-garde film was most commonly understood in the fifties and early sixties through analogies with poetry. From the Cinema 16 symposium on "Poetry and the Film" in 1953 through the writings of Hans Richter to the early taxonomies of Jonas Mekas and P. Adams Sitney, the virtual congruency of the "experimental film" with the "film poem" bespoke their ancestry in the symbolism and mythology of French surrealism. When in 1957 Richter argued a distinction between "the entertainment film as 'novel' " and "the exploration into the realm of mood, the lyrical sensation as 'poetry' " and expressed a desire to "call all experimental films 'film poetry' " (Richter, 1957: 6), he was voicing a set of terminological equivalences that had been commonplace for a decade in the reception of films by Maya Deren, Kenneth Anger, Curtis Harrington, Ian Hugo, Willard Maas, Gregory Markopoulos, Sidney Peterson, and Stan Brakhage.

At the Cinema 16 symposium, for example, Parker Tyler noted two groups of "poetical expression": "the shorter films that concentrate on poetry as a visual medium ... a surrealist poetry of the image," such as *Blood of a Poet*, *Andalusian Dog*, and *Lot in Sodom*, and the films that develop "poetry as a visual-verbal medium," including those of Vigo, Peterson, Maas, and Hugo, but also Eisenstein's "severe formalism" ("Poetry and the Film," 1970: 172). Maya Deren, her own work already influential, attempted a more restrictive distinction, arguing that the "poetic construct arises from the fact, if you will, that it is a 'vertical' investigation of a situation, in that it probes the ramifications of the moment," as distinct from the "horizontal" construction of drama (ibid.). Forced to admit that her distinction between vertical and horizontal amounted to a distinction between lyric and narrative, she too recognized the specificity of film poetry as the elaboration of discrete incidents rather than the continuously unfolding linear action of the feature film.

Recalling formalist models of how poetic language makes itself visible against a background of automatized, standard prose by foregrounding the devices of its production, such polarizations also had evaluative capacities. Rating metaphor over metonymy and paradigm over syntagm, they justified the poetic film's density and intensity, its difficulty and its cavalier unconcern with filmic illusion, all of which were taken as a function of lyric expressivity which elevated it over narrative drama as uncommercial, a purer art. The argument is idealist, both in asserting a transhistorical essence of poetry and in phrasing that essence in formal terms, and consequently all that Deren and her successors could do was to reproduce the poetics dominant at the time, the high modernist moment of Romanticism. References to Eliot and Pound littered the symposium and subsequent theorizing, with Pound's concepts of Imagism and Vorticism facilitating comprehension of the non-narrative organization of diegetically disarticulate images.

Although his singular assertion of the primacy of vision—his commitment to letting "the *prima materia* of film, the Visual, constitute its own 'story' " (Robert Kelly, cited in Brakhage, 1963: 82)—produced one of the most rigorously coherent filmic essentialisms, Brakhage fits comfortably into this general field, and it substantially supplies the terms of his formal accomplishment. Though certainly parallels between his fragmented screen space and the visual field of abstract expressionism also locate him in the post–Len Lye painterly tradition, and though he found models of composition in music from Bach to Messaien and Cage, he has been especially responsible to contemporary poets. Gertrude Stein, Ezra Pound, Charles Olson, Louis Zukofsky, Robert Duncan, Robert Creeley, Robert Kelly, Edward Dorn, and Michael McClure all featured prominently in his attention, and all except Stein and Pound figured in his life. The formal qualities of his prolific writing and talking, by and large also those of his films, are recognizably the formal qualities of modernist poetry, with his use of repetitions, puns, and other tropes to destabilize language—even within the frame of the syllable—clearly in the post-Stein tradition. He has designated parts of his work in literary terms, and his magnum opus was to have been *The Book of the Film*. His major exegete defined the phases of his work as "lyrical" and "mythopoeic" (Sitney, 1979), terms drawn from poetics; and, initially, Brakhage understood his filmmaking as ancillary to his activity as a poet: "Like Jean Cocteau, I was a poet who also made films" (Brakhage, [1967] 1982: 113). Despite his almost complete exclusion of verbal language from his films, such proclivities refer the work of one of the most resolutely anti-literary of artists to a skein of formal and ontological priorities—a conception of the self and its negotiation in cultural practice—whose prototypical manifestation occurred at the inauguration of the modern period in the response of poets to the industrial revolution.[1]

The English Romantic poets' investigation of the individual's

1 The parallels between the avant-garde and Romantic poetry have been most fully developed by P. Adams Sitney. His decision "to trace the heritage of Romanticism" rather than to use Freudian hermeneutics (Sitney, 1979: ix) supplied the terms for his acute formal analyses and moved critical discussion to a new level. But like that of his mentors in the Yale school of literary criticism, his work is limited to stylistic and epistemological issues.

imagination as the mediator between consciousness and nature and their eventual apotheosis of it as the location of all aesthetic, spiritual, and finally social values marked a shift from the overt didacticism and ethical orientation of Neoclassic poetics. The social changes of late eighteenth-century industrialization that set the paradigms of modernism into play also created the alienation of the modern poet. Displaced from a praxis within a corroborative community environment, whether of the village, the church, or the court, he had to confront the reification of his activity, which now took the form of one more commodity in a competitive marketplace. Compounded by the difficulty of sustaining utopian republican aspirations after the failure of revolutionary movements throughout Europe, this social dislocation precipitated the poet into the scrutiny of his own consciousness and allowed the drama of that scrutiny to be elevated into an end in itself, the essential function of art. Where a general social effectiveness could be envisioned, it was supposed to follow the renovation of the individual imagination in the experience of poetry.

Variously dressed, this projection supplied the liberal tradition its critical posture against the dehumanization of capitalism and the industrialization of consciousness. By the twentieth century the presupposition of the primacy of the imagination and the individual creative act had been so thoroughly internalized that it appeared the natural condition of art; its invisibility as ideology ensured that a theology of consciousness would delegitimize concern with the material production and social uses of art. So total was the naturalization that even modernist poets like Pound and Eliot, who most vehemently attacked the Romantic tradition, still reproduced it in their conception of the artist's social role.

The chorus of idealist encomiums sustained by formalist hermeneutics has, *mutatis mutandis*, permitted the commodity function of art in all mediums in the twentieth century to go about its business unhindered; but the displacements so generated are especially complex in the case of poetry. Lacking any ready commercial viability, poetry has proven progressively more resistant to integration into the mercantile processes of capitalism or its attendant social rituals. Whereas painting has easily been recast as real estate, music and theater as class ritual, and fiction as consumer recreation, poetry has remained largely unassimilable. Despite exceptions that range from Byron's prodigious popularity to the modest cultural influence of an Eliot or a Ginsberg, for the poet economic marginality has increasingly mirrored a massive social irrelevance. The intense inwardness of most postwar American poetry, reaching its apogee in the confessional investigation of private neurosis, documents sensibility adrift without recourse to a public language or certainty of an audience, the former having seeped away in the jargons of politics and advertising and the latter almost entirely conditioned by the communications industries.

Though the propriety of the analogy between the Romantic poet and the avant-garde filmmaker first becomes visible formally, in the elaboration of "poetics in the field of the visual" (Sitney, 1978: 87) by Brakhage and others, such parallels are the form in which a more fundamental similarity in social dislocation appears. In the modern world, *poet* designates a preferred medium; but the word also implies a mode of social (un)insertion. It bespeaks a cultural practice that, in being economically insignificant, remains economically unincorporated, and so retains the possibility of cultural resistance. For poets in both words and film, the hyperbolic invocations of ultimate value—which arc from Shelley's celebration of the poet as "the happiest, the best, the wisest and the most illustrious of men" to Dorn's summary consummateness—may well be forced to compensate for an institutional neglect. But the void of functionlessness they confront, so palpably dissimilar from the context of artists in other mediums, may indeed be the space of negation. This possibility informs Brakhage's radical reaction, his attempt to bring film into the tradition of cultural practices whose supersession is summarized by the Hollywood cinema.

Apart from scattered and isolated projects like those of Robert Florey, Watson and Webber, and Mary Ellen Bute, and the very differently conceived achievements of the Workers Film and Photo League (Jacobs, 1968; W. Alexander, 1981), before the forties no tradition of filmmaking in the United States existed to provide an independent filmmaker who understood his or her work as Art—as an end sufficient to itself rather than as a means of entry into the studio industry—with a model of production methods and a theory of his or her social role. The installation of the filmmaker as a *poet* had, then, both theoretical and practical components. It involved the conceptualization of the film artist as an individual author, a Romantic creator—a conceptualization made possible by manufacturing a tradition of such out of previous film history; and it necessitated a working organization, a mode of production and distribution, alternative to the technology, labor practices, and institutional insertion of Hollywood.

In none of these respects was Brakhage entirely unique or original; his singular importance derives from the extremes to which he pushed in each area and from the integrity with which he maintained their interdetermination. Anchored ideologically and aesthetically at the center of Romantic idealism, he reproduced it in an array of film styles, in a mode of film production, and in a projection of the film artist's social function which are entirely homologous, each the others' precondition and effect. In his domestic, artisanal production, he materialized a theory of film as an entirely personal activity, erupting like Romantic poetry from a spring that is at once biological and quasi-divine. The practice he developed was so totalized that it was virtually seamless. So thoroughly overdetermined was each moment in it that primary determination seems locatable simultaneously everywhere and nowhere. Each aspect of his intervention, from the style of the films to their international ramifications, articulates the others. This, the reticulated, autotelic integrity

2.1 Stan Brakhage in *Prelude*

of his aesthetic, is the condition of Brakhage's singular achievement; it also predetermines his limitations.

*

By the time Brakhage made his first film, *Interim*, in 1952, film poetry was an established stylistic category. Three years later he had become so identified with it that his work seemed "to be the best expression of all the virtues and sins of the American film poem today" (Mekas, 1955: 17). Like the film poems of his predecessors, Deren, Anger, and Harrington, Brakhage's early films retarded narrative action by metaphoric interpolations that elaborate character and mood, though since the boiling water in *Reflections on Black*, for example, or the cat and the rose in *Cat's Cradle* were intradiegetically derived, in his case they were typically metonymy used as metaphor. Like the spatial distortions of the visual field they accompanied, such temporal aberrations were cued by the dominant structural motif, derived from the surrealists and expressionists (though also common in the contemporaneous film noir)—the use of a distressed protagonist, whose subjective experience the visual field more or less closely reproduced. The increasing congruence of the protagonist's vision with the filmmaker's in these "trance" films (Sitney, 1979), which quickly allowed Brakhage his crucial shift to an entirely first-person camera, encouraged his understanding of filmic subjectivity in general. The discovery that film could accommodate authorial psychodrama made it possible for him to reread film history for his own purposes. Prefiguring the *politique des auteurs*, but in terms derived from surrealism, he discovered an avantgarde tradition of personal films made by obsessive individual stylists uninfluenced by their historical contexts—primarily the prewar classic European directors, and then the postwar American independents.

The organization of such a lineage eventually supplied a justifying vector for Brakhage's work on two levels. First, it allowed him to understand his own use of the medium for interior investigation as properly traditional. Hence Brakhage would inevitably understand the history of cinema as the refraction of the lives of its avatars, and his *Film Biographies* would show the canonical directors using the medium to come to grips with psychic trauma. Their narratives all engage not a historical situation or a social function, but rather some kind of demon, usually of a psychosexual origin: Méliès as a magician trying to find a heroine who will restore his psyche, which was shattered by prenatal trauma; Griffith fulfilling his destiny to right all wrongs under the mental guidance of his sister Mattie; Dreyer searching out "the demon-of-himself"; and even Eisenstein fighting the animal that had ravaged his personal being in the womb. Second, it allowed him to claim the authority of a tradition of film practices, however dissimilar from those of the contemporary commercial cinema, as the matrix of his own style.

> My big problem has been, all these years, that no one has recognized that I (and all my contemporaries) are working in a lineal tradition of Méliès, Griffith, Dreyer, Eisenstein, and all the other classically accepted film makers. . . . I took my first cues for fast cuts from Eisenstein, and I took my first sense of parallel cutting from Griffith, and I took my first sense of the individual frame life of a film from Méliès, and so on. (Brakhage, 1982: 179)[2]

Brakhage's reading of this tradition completely elided methods of production, except insofar as studio mechanisms or other bureaucratic controls were seen to inhibit the creative genius of the film-

2.2 Reflections on Black

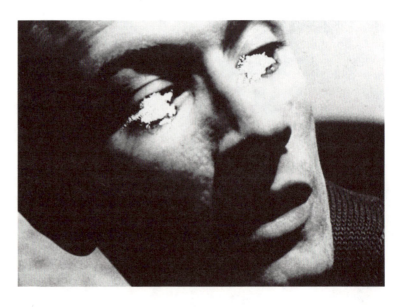

[2] Of avant-garde models for Brakhage outside the general poetic/trance cluster, Gregory Markopoulos's use of in-camera editing, as early as *Psyche* in 1947, and Marie Menken's hand-held camera in *Visual Variations on Noguchi*, in 1945, were especially important.

maker. The tradition could, then, supply a lineage for his own stylistic practice and intended use of the medium, but not a model of how a contemporary filmmaker, similarly seeking to chart the depths of his own psyche, could organize the necessary social and technical resources. None of the directors he considered worked inside the studio system proper, and not since RKO's difficulty with Orson Welles and the financial failure of *Citizen Kane* had any American studio allowed the degree of authorial power he envisaged. Though independents in the late fifties considered varying degrees of affiliation with and aspiration toward the industry, after the early sixties the underground virtually abandoned such aspirations and accepted an uneasy coexistence with Hollywood.

Brakhage adopted this position. Except insofar as the hegemonic system was taken as coextensive with the medium per se, he understood Hollywood not as a competitor or threat, but as an entirely separate enterprise.[3] A co-founder of the Film-Makers' Cooperative in 1962 and a member of the selection committee of Anthology Film Archives, he participated actively in the underground cinema, as well as in the peripheral support systems of museums, colleges, and film societies, and he depended financially on independent distribution. But his relationship with the alternative cinema was always checkered, ruptured again and again by personal quarrels and policy disagreements that, as they became especially violent with the politicization of the counterculture in the late sixties, caused him to withdraw his films from the Coop for a period and to resign from the Archives. Thus, although Brakhage was prominent and even notorious in the underground—*Desistfilm* was "the first important beatnik film with the air of a spontaneous Happening" (Tyler, 1969: 26), and by the mid-sixties his style was virtually a synecdoche for the counterculture at large—in almost as many ways as he embodied the underground, Brakhage rejected it.

Brakhage's social and aesthetic distance from the bohemian underground jelled when almost simultaneously he discovered his mature filmic mode and began a family. After the winter of 1959, when the family moved to a nineteenth-century log cabin in the Rockies behind Boulder, he was at once geographically and culturally remote from the bohemian enclaves he had passed through, and his distended and irregular engagement with the underground cinema began to resemble nothing so much as his previous sporadic employment in the commercial film world. He did, of course, maintain personal connections with other underground filmmakers and with his audience, invigorating them by his frequent presentations of new work and eventually by his teaching, and his necessary recourse to film stock and laboratories ensured his participation in the corporate state. But otherwise it was in isolation from mass society that he discovered his life's work. His importance for the modern cinema is inseparable from his removal from it. In the blankest rejection of the history of the medium, he made home movies the essential practice of film.[4]

Prefiguring a decade when such rustications would acquire in-

3 Though Brakhage characteristically inveighs against contemporary Hollywood on the grounds of its mediocrity as visual experience, just as often he admits to the pleasure of Hollywood movies, and indeed their influence on him. The echoes of film noir and fifties melodrama in trance films as late as *Wedlock House: An Intercourse* (1959) are very clear; other claims, that *Dog Star Man* (1961–64) has references to Hollywood (Brakhage, 1982: 26), for instance, are less so. He often argues the industry's debt to the avant-garde, though the interruptive flash frame is the only instance he cites.

4 The strain of the transition is summarized in the oxymoronic resonances of the title of a film of this period, *Films By Stan Brakhage: An Avant-Grade Home Movie*. In his remarks about home movies, Brakhage usually emphasizes that the personal engagement that prompts them supplies a point of liberation from the grammar of Hollywood (see, Brakhage, 1982: 47).

creasing cultural authority, Brakhage's retreat to the Colorado wilderness imitated a primary Romantic strategy—Thoreau's, of course, but more appositely Wordsworth's removal to Grasmere, 150 years before, with the social microcosm of his sister, Dorothy, and Coleridge. There, defeated by the modern world, he discovered the restorative trinity of nature, the domestic circle, and art itself. Similarly defeated, Brakhage in the mountains felt most free from the anxieties of history and urban life, free to re-create the Wordsworthian paradigm in the cycles of nature. This ideal of an antitechnological, organically human, domestic cinema, entirely separate from rather than oppositional to Hollywood, circumscribed Brakhage's life and art and the peculiarly integral relation between them. If the move and the marriage did not solve the traumas of his youth—the idiotoxic illness, the search for a community of artists, and the sexual hunger that fuels *Desistfilm, Reflections on Black,* and the other melodramas of the fifties—they did provide a relatively stable social situation and a vocabulary of human relationships in which these traumas could be investigated.

Inevitably, then, Brakhage's environment and family subsequently occupy his profilmic, and his dominant trope becomes the perception of his wife, children, or pets in their mountain home. They are the vehicle, or rather the instances, of his subject matter: "birth, sex, death, and the search for God" (Brakhage, 1963: 25). As it does in respect to the attainment of first-person vision, *Anticipation of the Night* (1958) marks this transition, even though Brakhage's expectation of his own death was almost fulfilled in the near suicide that it took to finish it. Its shooting coincided with the breakup of Brakhage's previous engagement and his meeting with Jane Collum, and he edited it during the first month of their marriage. The subsequent films of 1959–61 do represent Brakhage's attempt to engage the primary events of natural life: birth, in the films about the birth of their first and third children, *Window Water Baby Moving* and *Thigh Line Lyre Triangular*; sex, in the erotic films of the newlyweds, like *Wedlock House: An Intercourse*; and death, in *Sirius Remembered* and *The Dead*. All the concerns of these films and the stylistic innovations developed in them culminate and are synthesized in the cosmic reach of *Dog Star Man* (1961–64), in which the projection of the biological onto the metaphysical, that also includes everything in between, is most fully figured in the rhyming superimposition of the medical and astronomical imagery.

But the significance of these films and of Brakhage's subsequent exploration of the same themes is not exhausted by his use of the medium to attend to what he saw in his daily life, and to document the crises of biological cycles rather than to fabricate fictions of history—"sharing a sight" rather than "showing sights" (Brakhage, 1982: 187). In his rejection of the alienated labor of an industrial career, in which work in film could at best have financed a life outside it, Brakhage's fundamental innovation was in the sphere of production. When his project was understood simply as style or subject matter, as films separate from the cinema they implied, the films

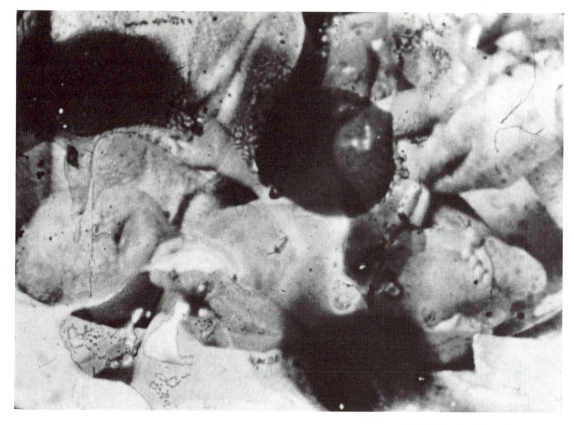

2.3 *Thigh Line Lyre Triangular*

were inevitably misread, most egregiously, of course, as pornography. By becoming an amateur—one who, according to a favorite pun, did it for love, not money—he made filmmaking the agency of his being. Bridging the aesthetic and the existential, film became identified with his life and coextensive with it, simultaneously his vocation and avocation, his work and play, his joy and terror—as integral as breathing.

Nor, similarly, is the cinematic significance of the films about birth, sex, and death exhausted by their formulation of a filmic vocabulary that made possible meditational attention to the biological processes of life. The domestication of cinema allowed an even more radical incorporation of it into life's most crucial transactions. If in telling its own story the visual tells all others, the exchange of vision between people becomes the means of social interaction; and so film—a means of seeing—becomes not just an instrument of personal documentation, or yet simply the means by which a subjectivity may be documented, but also the mode of a relationship's practice. The sign of intimacy becomes the medium of intimacy; the intercourse of sight is the site of intercourse.

As we began passing the camera back and forth, the quarrel was pitched onto a visual level. . . . Her images came out of such a quality that they could actually cut back and forth with

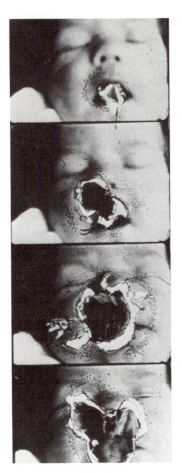

2.4 *Dog Star Man, Part II*

mine. She too grabbed the light as I had done and began taking up the same form of painting-in my image with moving light source, she automatically grasped what my style was on a feeling level, and went right on with her version of it. This was the first time we were both photographing; I photographing her, she me, but in relation to the form that was springing out of me. We got glimpses of each other, in flashes of moving light, as if emerging out of long hallways in sheer darkness. All the quarrels we were having at that time became pitched on that visual level. (Brakhage, 1963: 6)

Occasions such as this—Brakhage and his wife photographing each other at moments of heightened psychic and physical interaction, not only quarreling, as here, in what became *Wedlock House: An Intercourse*, but also lovemaking and parturition—are common in the films of the first years of their marriage; in them the mutual photography of the recording of family life is transformed into a means of negotiating family life, of articulating and understanding it.

The performative collaboration of these films tends to decline after Jane's substantial role in the photography of *Dog Star Man*, but the urgency of psychological and visual interdependence it reflects sustains Brakhage's entire oeuvre, necessitating a working process "pitched between" himself and Jane (Brakhage, 1963: 12). Eventually that source encompasses the entire family.

> "By Brakhage" should be understood to mean "by way of Stan and Jane Brakhage," as it does in all my films since marriage. It is coming to mean: "by way of Stan and Jane and all the children Brakhage" because all the discoveries which used to pass only thru the instrument of myself are coming to pass thru the sensibilities of those I love. . . . Ultimately "by Brakhage" will come to be superfluous and understood as what it now ultimately is: by way of everything. (Brakhage, 1963: 2)

There are to be sure elements of disingenuousness in such claims, and doubtless the interactive family cinema was more an aspiration than a fully achieved practice. Brakhage retained at least conscious control over the films that proceed from it, and, as in home movies in general, "the male head of household used the camera most of the time" (Chalfen, 1975: 94). But his constant deflection of authority from himself to the family unit in which he constituted himself, his constant reference to Jane's role in the films, and his insistence on his absolute psychic obligation to her represent a domestic premonition of a radical reorganization of the roles of producer and consumer in a genuinely social cinema.[5]

Beyond such heuristic value however, Brakhage's innovations remind us that in his restaging of the Romantic confrontation between the individual consciousness and what surrounds it, the affirmation of the self is always preliminary to escape from it. Inhabiting all the realms of Brakhage's cinema, this tension between individu-

5 In such a radical social cinema, distribution of authority would be maintained through all phases of production and consumption. In the case of Brakhage, his sole control of editing allowed him to appropriate the footage shot by Jane, perhaps effacing sexual difference, but certainly recuperating to an artifactual reification what at the stage of shooting was a democratic and participatory practice.

2.5–2.8 "I photographing her, she me": Stan and Jane Brakhage in *Wedlock House: An Intercourse*

ation and its transcendence, between self-consciousness and anti–self-consciousness, produces the paradoxical conjunction of an increasingly aggressive idiosyncratic style and a rejection of imaginative creation in a mode that is essentially documentary. That shift is demonstrated in Brakhage's own understanding of his endeavor, as the following remarks from 1963 and from 1972 make clear.

OF NECESSITY I BECOME INSTRUMENT FOR THE PASSAGE OF INNER VISION, THRU ALL MY SENSIBILITIES, INTO ITS EXTERNAL FORM. My most active part in this process is to increase all my sensibilities (so that all films arise out of some total area of being or full life) AND, at the given moment of possible creation to act only out of necessity. In other words, I am principally concerned with revelation. (Brakhage, 1963: 77)

I am the most thorough documentary film maker in the world because I document the act of seeing as well as everything that the light brings me. . . . I have added nothing. I've just been trying to see and make a place for my seeing in the world at large. (Brakhage, [1972] 1982: 188)

The first passage, itself a development from his previous preoccupation with his own ego as representatively human and thus potentially the access to "universal concerns" (Brakhage, 1963: 23), emphasizes existential attentiveness to biological urgency as the motor of composition, but it also contains residual notions of art as the externalization of a process other than itself, with the artist a conduit for an activity whose origin is so far behind the present that it dissolves into the divine. Brakhage continues to invoke this unknowable source, frequently designating it as "the Muses," but progressively those Muses are discovered essentially in the perceptual organs themselves, and in their physiological reaction to light. This immanentism may be understood as the post-modernist moment in Romantic poetics. Brakhage found it in "objectism," Charles Olson's critique of "the individual as ego."

Objectism, a Romantic anti-hellenism, was Olson's answer to the toxic Aristotelian dualisms, especially the polarization of consciousness and the external world, which form the prison of Western discourse. According to Olson, we are alienated from the real by a false epistemology, entrapped in an Euclidean space that informs the very structures of language; the sensuous present of our contact with the world is constantly deferred by generalized logical classification. The reintegration of man as continuous with reality rather than discrete from it requires circumvention of that historically and socially conditioned consciousness and the grammar of its language. Thus the polemical center of objectism entails "the getting rid of the lyrical interference of the individual as ego, of the 'subject' and his soul," on the grounds that it is a presumption interposed between man and the rest of nature (Olson, 1966: 24).

The identification of perception with creation in Olson's mutually dependent aesthetic and epistemology implies a situation of the self in respect to nature and a stylistic practice, both of which may be defined by distinguishing between two Romantic poetic modes. The symbolist, modernist tradition of Yeats, Eliot, and Stevens derives from Coleridge's representation of "the mind's dialectical pursuit of an ideal unity" (Altieri, 1979: 17), while the post-modernist, immanentist mode that culminates in Olson, Robert Duncan, and Gary Snyder is the essentially Wordsworthian "discovery and the disclosure of numinous relationships within nature [rather than] the creation of containing and structuring forms" (ibid.). Though as it did for both Wordsworth and Olson, this mode may have recourse to historical or philosophical paradigms, its primary imperative is the dynamic experience of what is phenomenally present, the engagement of consciousness by nature when they most illuminate each other.

Ideally foregoing "any ideas or preconceptions from outside the poem" (Olson, 1966: 20), especially large mental structures that satisfy the desolate modern ego, the immanentist mode attempts to eliminate that ego in direct contact between consciousness and nature. Rejection of the intending role of the humanist ego, and of ideas that *refer* to reality rather than *embody* it, is supposed to allow the poet to go beyond the imagination to unmediated perception, to that place where consciousness and nature are in direct contact.

Seeking not to describe but to enact, poetry becomes an articulation of that contact as well as the means to it, and so in a successful poem, "ONE PERCEPTION MUST IMMEDIATELY AND DIRECTLY LEAD TO A FURTHER PERCEPTION." Form is then organic, a function of content discovered in the experience of creation: "FORM IS NEVER MORE THAN AN EXTENSION OF CONTENT" (Olson, 1966: 16). Finally, since the ego is bypassed, the significant drama is displaced into the body, which, as both the source and agent of perception—the site of *proprioception*—produces the biological imperative of Olson's emphasis on the breath as the unit of composition.

Olson supplied Brakhage with a theoretical infrastructure and vocabulary for what he had already discovered as his essential concerns, the regeneration of the visual discourse of the West as it was articulated filmically.[6] In place of the two-dimensional representation of space by the codes of Renaissance perspective and the representation of linear causality by the codes of narrative drama—both ideologically over-determined grammars of vision to be destroyed and reconstructed in an immanentist way—Brakhage proposed attention to vision in as intense, extensive, and complete a way as possible. Since sight was the sense par excellence in which inside met outside, physical met psychological, it was the ideal site of proprioception; and since film was capable of recording the continuous present of the encounter between them, it was the ideal objectist medium.

*

but every man-<u>made-thing</u>
is nothing more <u>nor less</u>
than a direct extension
of his physiology.
— Stan Brakhage

The feasibility of the search for an untutored vision became clear when Brakhage's abandonment of the acted dramatic film allowed him to jettison both the structure of narrative and, more importantly, the normative frame of objective vision that contained the heightened perception of the trance protagonists. *Anticipation of the Night* is usually taken as marking this transition,[7] for it is in this liminary work that the extremely rapid camera movement, the use of the full range of aperture and focus, the scintillating visual arpeggios and other tropes that were to constitute Brakhage's mature style are first comprehensively articulated.

Anticipation is not however entirely first-person, and at least two protagonists supply its lyric vision. One is a baby who authorizes expanded perception of a suburban garden, rushing textures of trees and plants all infinitely refracted in the fountain of a garden hose, and extended passages of dreams of magical birds. The other is an adult male who appears to hang himself in the final sequence. A matching sequence opens the film with a similar shadow of an ambiguously swaying figure in a rectangle of light. It suggests a tentative passage over the threshold from the house to the natural vision

6 Through the sixties and beyond, Brakhage constantly reiterated the importance of Olson's thought, and echoes of Olson's ideas and phrasing are ubiquitous in Brakhage's writing. The later texts in *Metaphors on Vision* (1963) are the fullest verbal expression of his indebtedness, especially in reference to the use of the body as an epistemological instrument, and on the rejection of narrative drama; and they include an excited account of Brakhage's first meeting with Olson.

7 The pivotal role of *Anticipation of the Night* in Brakhage's formal development and his thought generally was thoroughly developed by Sitney (Sitney, 1979: 142–48). With all respect to Sitney's "It describes the doomed quest for an absolutely authentic, renewed, and untutored vision" (ibid.: 146), which is certainly justified biographically in Brakhage's suicidal impulses, I nevertheless see its structure as ironic, with the implications of the protagonist's death countermanded by the visionary achievement of the body of the film. This also precludes Sitney's proposal of a linear evolution from lyric to mythopoeic (Sitney, 1979). *Dog Star Man*, the prime exhibit in the proposed mythopoeic phase, is essentially contained inside the lyric mode rather than instancing a reversion to the modernist use of myth exemplified by Eliot, Joyce, and even Cocteau, whose works were structurally dependent on sustained references to narratives from antiquity as a means of ordering the present. Though Brakhage asserted the importance of the "mythic" image of the tree on the Cretan coin, claims for the mythic structure of the film rest finally on its "archetypal" images and its observance of seasonal cycles. The woodcutter's quest is universalized by being naturalized back into Brakhage's immediate environment and perceptions, rather than articulated against an ancient narrative. As early as *Anticipation of the Night*, Brakhage was rejecting some images as "too myth-structured" (Brakhage, 1963: 5).

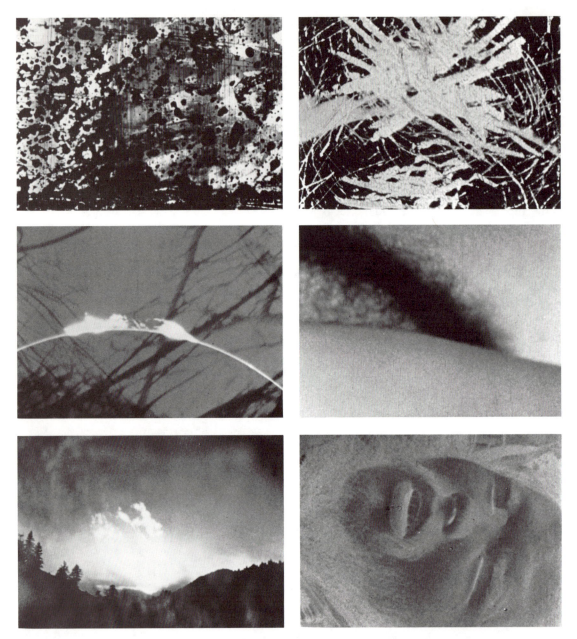

2.9–2.14 *Prelude*

of the garden outside, but the visual rhyme with the final sequence also suggests that, structurally parallel to *Incident at Owl Creek*, the entire film may be an expanded moment of redeemed vision, a Wordsworthian "spot in time" or a Blakean "open center," a death into a visionary rebirth. Whatever the status of these quasi-narrative implications, in sum they define the body of the film, not as deviant or diseased vision, but rather as a regenerated ideal.

To this extent *Anticipation of the Night* inaugurates Brakhage's attempt to regain an originary, prelapsarian vision; the Wordsworthian loss lived in the passage from infancy to adulthood is seen to recapitulate the debasement of the phylogenic acculturation of the West as a whole, a debasement that Brakhage thinks of both in terms of the fall of unmediated visual perception into the categories of verbal language and, historically, in terms of the degenerate materialism of post-Renaissance optics.

> Imagine an eye unruled by man-made laws of perspective, an eye unprejudiced by compositional logic, an eye which does not respond to the name of everything but which must know each object encountered in life through an adventure of perception. How many colors are there in a field of grass to the crawling baby unaware of "Green?" How many rainbows can create light for the untutored eye? How aware of variations in heat waves can that eye be? Imagine a world alive with incomprehensible objects and shimmering with an endless variety of movement and innumerable gradations of color. Imagine a world before "the beginning was the word." (Brakhage, 1963: 23)

This famous manifesto, itself cognate with Olson's meta-project of replacing "the Classic-representational by the *primitive abstract*" (Olson, 1966: 28), supplies the basis for Brakhage's use of the body as an epistemological instrument; and the attempt to circumvent the cultural coding of received visual languages produces the coherence of his theory and practice during the sixties.[8] The overwhelming visual presence and energy of his work, his rejection of sound as the vehicle of verbal categories as well as a detraction from the visual, and his total physical involvement in the shooting process that posits the camera as both an extension of the eye and a material-specific medium for the collection of light all manifest the insistence on the film's self-generation out of the immediate present of perception. Light is the medium of exchange in the two-way passage between the inner and outer worlds, and the site of its activity is the sight of the camera eye. Brakhage's project is thus to return to continuity what film history, in its reproduction of Western ontology, has distinguished as three separate realms: the phenomenal world; the optical apparatuses, both mechanical and biological; and the work of the brain—memory, imagination, "close-eye vision," hypnagogic and eidetic imagery, and dream. In the integration of these realms, the dualisms that sustain almost all other uses of film—the dualisms of subject and object, of physiological and psychological, of perception and creation, and of vision and its instruments—are subsumed in a single gestalt.

Once Brakhage had committed himself to first-person vision, the documentary mode was open to him. Though a career as vigorous and various as his can hardly be corralled by simple generalizations, still the bridging of the I and the eye in the interacting physiology and psychology of perception, and the mediation of subjectivity and

8 The corollary of Brakhage's insistence that "art is the expression of the internal physiology of the artist" (Brakhage, [1968] 1982: 116) may be observed in the somatic demands his films make on the spectator. The fact that they are not to be "read," but rather biologically incorporated—they must be "invisioned," "they can *only* exist *in* the eye of the viewer" (Brakhage, [1968] 1982: 23)—ensures their difficulty for people capable of experiencing visual phenomena only by recoding it into other languages.

9 As early as 1955, in *Reflections on Black*, sexual fulfillment is achieved coincidentally with unmediated subjectivity. After an introductory montage specifying the protagonist's visual idiosyncracy, he meets four women in succession. In the first instance neither sexual nor visual contact is made. In the second he stimulates the woman to her own visual subjectivity in fantasy. In the third a woman actually receives him and approaches a visual relationship by removing her glasses, though their lovemaking is interrupted by her husband. The union of the last section is successful and is shot entirely in the first person, consisting largely of close-ups on the woman's face or other isolated parts of her body. This endorsement of unqualified subjectivity resolves the previously ambiguous status of idiosyncratic vision suggested by the scratches in the emulsion over the protagonist's eyes. Figuring prominently when he is caught *in flagrante delicto*, they symbolically evoke castration anxieties, but their implications of visionary liberation also place the protagonist in the line of blind romantic seers like Tiresias and Lear. The latter alternative is finally endorsed as, immediately before the final section, the scratches pass from the protagonist's eyes to the entire screen. As we now see *through* his specific vision, the sound (which previously accompanied the imageless "sight" of the blind man and the sexual encounters which were thereby associated with his fantastic projection) ceases and the visual world is liberated into sympathetic symbolism. The coffeepot boiling on the stove achieves its climax while the visual echo of the scratches in the star-shaped spokes on the gas ring where it comes to a boil reaffirms personal vision as the site and source of ecstasy.

objectivity via light and the apparatus, form the matrix of his oeuvre. The titles of some of his most magisterial achievements— *The Art of Vision, The Riddle of Lumen, The Act of Seeing with One's Own Eyes, The Text of Light*—attest to the priority and fecundity of this major preoccupation, but also to the variety of contexts in which it was deployed.

Attention to different areas within the general matrix produce the different subgeneric divisions of Brakhage's work and the different phases of his career. The first-person perception of the major mode, the epic spectacle of his family life which begins with the lovemaking and childbirth films of the turn of the decade and continues for the next fifteen years, itself subtends various collateral forms. The autobiography of perception is variously displaced in considerations of specific topics but also in other modalities such as film letters. The pursuit of lost vision is a recurring project, though the films in which this is undertaken always involve the present perception of material objects in which traces of the past are supposed to have been preserved. Thus the reconstruction of prenatal vision and children's vision in the *Scenes From Under Childhood* series includes the present perception of children—how children look, in both senses. The more strictly autobiographical project of *Sincerity* and its cognate *Duplicity*—to rediscover his own childhood and adolescence—entails the camera's present scrutiny of old photographs, as if their appearance preserved sight itself. Other films are more critically oriented to the apparatus and to film-specific sights that can be generated by editing or other material work on the filmstrip, though these also are supposed either to simulate or stimulate optical effects otherwise available or to have some metaphoric relationship to them. In *The Horseman, The Woman and The Moth*, for example—the most elaborate of the hand-painted films—the drama of the interaction of the materials of its construction is supposed optically to recapitulate hypnagogic vision.

At other moments within this strategic oscillation between "the light *of* Nature" and "the Nature of Light" (Brakhage, 1982: 74), Brakhage is most interested in the peculiarities of his own eyesight, in respect to both phosphenes and other forms of closed-eye vision and the open-eyed perception of, for example, the streaks of light in the sky before rain or the glow with which certain objects present themselves to him. At his most extreme, he hypostatizes light itself as an ontological absolute, invoking at such times Pound's reference to Erigena's dictum, "Omnia quae sunt, Lumina sunt" (All things that are, are lights), and thus produces his "purest" films. In them, the literal or symbolic reference of the imagery is subsumed in the sensual play of light, though even in these films reflexive metaphors for the apparatus or the politics of vision appear: locks, windows, screens, and the like in the ethereal precision of *The Riddle of Lumen*, for example. Even apparently intractable works that antedate the mature mode often turn out, like *Reflections on Black*,[9] to be narrative premonitions of it, or self-negating narratives, like *Blue Moses*, that finally reauthorize the dominant mode. And an anomaly as remarkable as *Mothlight*, which circumvents the photographic process entirely, returns allegorically to the matrix; as a displacement of Brakhage's own vision into that of the moth—"what a moth might see from birth to death if black were white and white were black" (Brakhage, 1982: 246)—it conjoins two extremes in the perceptual continuum, material nature and the light of the projector, on the materiality of the filmstrip and the retina of the spectator's eye.

In addition to the purely visual relationships—continuities or contrasts of shape, color, movement, and light—discovered in those portions of the profilmic that achieve registration in the filmic and that supply the main basis of Brakhage's editing, the integration of the three spheres of subject, object, and apparatus is more or less clearly articulated by visual analogies or metaphorical relations among the profilmic, the filmic, and Brakhage's psychophysiology. Some examples of these rhymes follow. Between profilmic and filmic: the vertical green grass and the green scratches on the emulsion in *Prelude*; the sexual energy and the red edge-flares in *Cat's Cradle*; the baby's face and the "visual cramps" of the splice bars (Brakhage, 1982: 64) in *Dog Star Man, Part II*. Between filmic and subjective: the grain of the emulsion, especially of 8mm, as equivalent to closed-eye vision ("this grain field in 8 mm is like *seeing yourself seeing*" [Brakhage, 1982: 48]); the solid red frames and the soft focus shots indicating prenatal and children's vision in *Scenes From Under Childhood*. Between profilmic and subjective: the locks and doors imprisoning the child in *The Weir-Falcon Saga* as symbols of Brakhage's entrapment in adult vision.

The articulation of relations across the different realms of the filmic supplies Brakhage with his dominant shooting and editing strategies. Consequently, rhymes among body, filmic material and apparatus, and phenomenal field are so omnipresent, so insistently foregrounded, that they preoccupy the status of content to jeopardize and usually usurp priority over the literal or iconographic thrust of any represented material. The fungibility of the activity of the profilmic, the filmic, and the psychophysiological—the fungibility of style, medium, and content—centripetally reroutes potentially eccentric reference back into the field of the visual. This tendency for the specificity of the profilmic to be claimed either as evidence of the behavior of light or as a metaphor for vision produces the visual and thematic density of Brakhage's mode. But when he looks outside the family to topics that can less easily be resolved in optical terms, it precipitates a semiological tension between signification within the filmic (or sheer visual sensuality) and reference outside. Crucially, such cases involve political issues—*Western History*, *eyes*, and *23rd Psalm Branch*, for example, films about Christianity, the police, and the Vietnam War. But equivalent tensions between optical and other thematics figure even in a film situated as firmly in the biological as *The Act of Seeing with One's Own Eyes*. These occasions jeopardize Brakhage's aesthetic. As the discursiveness of this material and its threatening resistance to being reduced to the

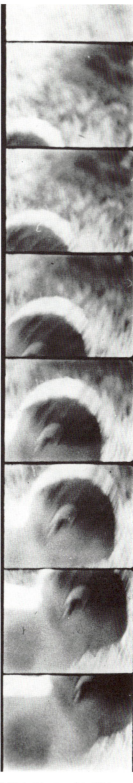

2.15 *Anticipation of the Night*

2.16 *Dog Star Man, Part III*

purely visual force him to provide a philosophical rationale for what appears as an extreme rationalization of the senses, he resorts to a theory that history is itself always configured in symbolic visual forms.

Since they efface neither the apparatus nor the artist's subjectivity but attend to both as carefully as to the diegetic field, the correspondences between the work of the apparatus and the subjects and objects of its attention not only demystify the filmic process but triple its density. The characteristic rapidity of Brakhage's cutting and the density of his superimpositions are the formal consequence of the multidimensional connections the correspondences make available; the various rhymes, allusions, and cross-references among operations in the three realms so thicken visual activity that the spectator's attention must constantly flash between the various levels. This visual energy—and could there be a better summary of a Brakhage film than Olson's "a high energy-construct and, at all points, an energy discharge" (Olson, 1966: 16)—is what asserts itself as Brakhage's style. As the authenticating presence of his body, it is the most significant feature of any film and the unifying preoccupation of his oeuvre: "There's really no problem in seeing that the same man who made *Anticipation of the Night*, then made *Dog Star Man*, then *Scenes From Under Childhood*, and is now doing the films that I'm doing. There's really no problem with that at all, because you have one absolute surety to go on, and that's *style*. I had thought to emphasize that by *signing* those works" (Brakhage, 1982: 175).

As the most crucial area of his engagement, style accounts for Brakhage's prolificacy, for once a technology for (re)producing vision has been secured, its product is as extensive as seeing itself. All Brakhage films are, finally, excerpts from the grand film that has rolled through his eyes since before birth. The primacy of style also accounts for the aridity of "new critical" interpretations of his films, listings of their shot-by-shot progression; for not simply are the dynamics of Brakhage's films so intensively visual that verbal accounts can never approximate them, but what is finally at issue is the style itself, the processes it necessitates and generates rather than anything else for which it might be the vehicle. But if a Brakhage film is the occasion for the practice of a determinate style, that style contains an erotics, an ethics, and a politics.

The demands of his style, from its frenzied, kinaesthetic, rhetorical panache to its most subtle, tentative accounts of the minutiae of the visible, forced him radically to reinvent film technology. Abandoning the codes of industrial production, Brakhage also abandoned the industrial apparatus and its processes, minimizing the technology he used, while exploiting as fully as possible the complete resources of what he retained. He understood the ideological functions of industrial optical systems fully a decade before the *Cahiers du Cinéma* theorists (though like them he ignored the economic relation between the apparatus and the corporate state);[10] he challenged these functions by introducing the physiological reflex-

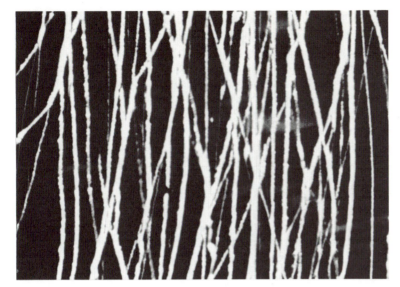

2.17 *Prelude*

iveness of proprioception into the shooting process, hand-holding
the camera to allow it the motivation of the body's pulse, and otherwise empowering it with a subtlety of apprehension matching that
of the biological eye. By using anamorphic lenses, pieces of colored
glass, and so on, from *Dog Star Man* to *The Text of Light*, he sub-
verted the optics ground so as to reproduce quattrocento perspective and the transcendental subject.[11] Paralleling John Cage's refusal
to distinguish between musical and non-musical sounds, Brakhage
employed the full range of aperture, focus, and camera speed, not
to ensure the correct reproduction of socially sanctioned perceptual
codes but rather as autonomous expressive possibilities, the source
of visual activity rather than the neutral transmitter of information
exterior to it. Like the eye, the camera was to be seen *with* rather
than *through*. A practical as well as an aesthetic imperative, minimization of technology involved his initial reliance on 16mm and
shooting in natural light (both of which he shared with the documentary movement) and his eventual use of 8mm pocket cameras.

   After the theft of the 16mm equipment used in *Dog Star Man*,
Brakhage turned to 8mm for the *Songs*, a move that summarized
the aspirations of both his films and the cinema they implied.
Whereas 16mm retained industrial if not Hollywood connotations,
8mm was affordable and symbolically identified only with home
movies. It was therefore "the fulfillment of amateur vision, that is:
of engagement leading to marriage, that is: of love to be lived with,
that is: of love within" (Brakhage, cited in Mekas, 1972: 138). Not
only was 8mm largely unfetishized, but its cheapness allowed a real
possibility of popular distribution of prints. On a small scale Brakhage did sell prints, though mostly 16mm, from his own home, but
the possibility of sidestepping commercial distribution using domestic apparatus heralded a one-to-one relation with his audience and

10 Cf. "We omit consideration of
economic implications" (Baudry,
1974: 40).

11 Of the various strategies Brakhage uses to resist the tendency
noted by Baudry (1974: 42) for the
projector to restore to monocular
centeredness the dispersal of subjectivity introduced at shooting (anamorphic lenses) or editing (machine-
gun montage), the most important is
multiple superimposition, which inserts spatial contradiction into the
spectator viewpoint. In general,
Brakhage's compositional attention
to the entire frame, especially to its
edges, produces the "all-over" de-
centeredness of abstract expressionism rather than the centered subjectivity of perspective painting.

a truly organic, noncommercial cinema, even as the possibility of domestic film libraries made feasible the multiple viewings his work demanded. The less bulky, somatically more responsive 8mm camera perfectly accommodated Brakhage's shooting, and since A and B rolling and laboratory work generally was considerably more difficult than in 16mm, it directed attention more to photography than to editing, and so accelerated a developing shift away from emphasis on the latter.

Up to the *Songs*, when Brakhage was still inclined to model himself as a modernist creative artist, his production involved shooting and editing equally. While shooting did demand attentiveness to biological urgency, it was conceived of as the collection of material preparatory to editing, where the same motivating imperatives would have to declare themselves. The form of *Dog Star Man*, to take an extreme instance, emerged only out of the edited form of its *Prelude*, the first step of which was itself determined by chance operations. Hence the elaborate activity at the site of editing: the four possible methods of inserting double-sprocketed 16mm film; the use of black leader and solid color flash frames; the use of the splice bar; the scratching, painting, dyeing, and baking of film and allowing it to mold—even the insertion of frame fragments or the incorporation of non-filmic materials (*Mothlight*), involving in *Dog Star Man*, for example, the collation of up to four synchronous rolls. Brakhage's only reservation was that the film be printable, however difficult that might be. Though the *Songs* do contain some similar work, in general the move to 8mm coincided with an increasing attention to in-camera editing and so also to shooting, such that by the late sixties Brakhage's control over the camera and especially over single-framing was so complete that editing became more and more a matter of selection from what had been secured in the now-coincidental seeing/shooting. Thus, for example, *The Text of Light* (1974) is "edited," in that the separate shots are strung together, but the film's immanentist preoccupation with the present of the perception of light rather than with any literal image dispenses with elaborate cutting within the shot or other work on the exposed film. To describe it, Brakhage preferred to use the word "arranged" or "composed" rather than "edited": "There is an energy in the amount of shooting which editing again can leak out for you. What's interesting to me is the energy of immediacy. That comes out of my involvement with Charles Olson. . . . Editing is always an afterthought" (Brakhage, 1975: n.p.).

A statement such as this, made in discussion of *The Text of Light*, or the similar claim that *eyes* was "assembled, rather than edited . . . and thus the surest track I could make of what it was given to me to see" (*Film-makers' Cooperative Catalogue*, 1975: 30) is obviously contradicted by many films, even after the *Songs*, but it does register the dominant emphasis of Brakhage's mature mode, and in fact in *The Text of Light* the relationship between the camera and the ashtray metaphorically and functionally reproduces the usual relationship between Brakhage's eye and the camera, so that the

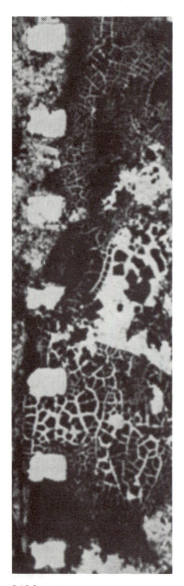

2.18 *Song xiv*

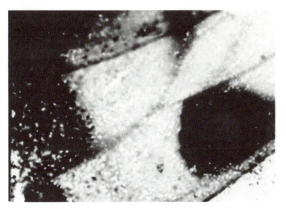 

2.19–2.20 *Mothlight*

film is entirely transacted within the hermetic impingement of the eye upon the apparatus. This extreme statement of the immanentist aesthetic returns us then to the question of the self and to the tension between Brakhage's aggressive individualism and the strategies of transcending the self that objectism speaks to.

*

That Brakhage should have so often been read by detractors and afficionados alike as an unreconstructed egotist, Romantic or otherwise, is not surprising. But his axiomatic insistence that art is personal in fact covers tensions that have both a biographical/psychological and a philosophical scope. He may claim that completion of a film ends his authority over it, and, always reluctant to speak of *his*, certainly of his *own* films, he logically prefers locutions such as "what it was given to me to see." The subordination of the imagination implied by the documentary mode, similarly prompting him to speak of his activity as discovery rather than creation, allows his work its public utility; while he can present himself as merely the vehicle of his vision, his commitment to pursuing it supplies an example for others. Remarkably, his work was for many years in the public domain, uncopyrighted. But it was signed, and with a violent inscription of himself into the very emulsion that jibes so uncomfortably with the rhetoric of disengagement. Other gestures of self-negation are similarly recouped. He claims to be merely the agent of his family's psychic energy, and there is no doubt that his debt to them and their importance to his work are real. But the concomitant of this domestication of cinema is its spectacularization of family life—its transformation of sick children, a loving or quarreling wife, and even babies aborning into hapless actors in his visual melodrama. When he simulates the vision of others—of his children in *Scenes From Under Childhood*, for example—it is as a means of reclaiming his own, and even on the rare occasions when he uses footage not shot by himself, as in *23rd Psalm Branch*, it is as a means of illustrating his memory, and so must be thoroughly internalized, fragmented, and overprinted with his signature hatchings.

Similarly for his audience, the final rewards of his work, themselves not separable from its unusual demands, are always in some sense hypothetical, their fullness deferred to that occasion when one will have at last been able to see a Brakhage film the requisite number of times.

That this last, like the virtual economic and logistical impossibility of obtaining a sense of Brakhage's oeuvre as a whole, is as much an institutional fact, a function of the political marginalization of alternative cinemas, as it is a matter under Brakhage's control, suggests that these stress marks on his achievement that appear as issues of his ego or philosophy are at the same time social events. The aporias of the immanentist aesthetic as a whole—its attempt to transcend the idealism of its Romantic heritage only compounded by its presumption of direct, alinguistic contact with the noumenal—terminate the coherence of Brakhage's aesthetic at *cinema*. While the integration of his practice into his life was so commanding in its integrity, the social disengagement of its premises was incompatible with the social relations that any use of film inevitably entails. Those moments of his manifest dependence on systems beyond his mountain home—the crises involving access to equipment that punctuate his life as crucially as they do Kenneth Anger's, the incessant struggle for funds to pay laboratory bills, the distended process of film production which halted authorial control at the laboratory door, and the difficulty of appropriate distribution—at all these points the political responsibilities of social life appear ineluctable even in the aesthetic of the wilderness. As Thoreau insisted, the first chapter of any account of life in the woods had to be "Economy."

The central political contradiction in Brakhage's endeavor is, then, a historical condition that he exemplifies so powerfully and precisely because of the uncompromising vigor and multidimensional lucidity of his attempt to practice an authentically personal cinema. This contradiction has been most acutely summarized by Annette Michelson, who advisedly contrasts Brakhage with Eisenstein as exemplary manifestations of absolutely opposite social conditions.

> Brakhage is infinitely less privileged in his lonely commitment to revelation, his guerilla stance in defiance of the culture of mid-century America. It is a tragedy of our time (that tragedy is not, by any means, exclusively, but rather, like so much else, *hyperbolically* American) that Brakhage should see his social function as defensive in the Self's last-ditch stand against the mass, against the claims of any possible class, political process, or structure, assuming its inevitable assault upon the sovereignty of the Self, positing the imaginative consciousness as inherently apolitical. (Michelson, 1973: 31)

Though we have argued that the central moment in Brakhage's aesthetic aspires more to the transcendence of the self and the dispersal of the creative imagination into the body and the family, still

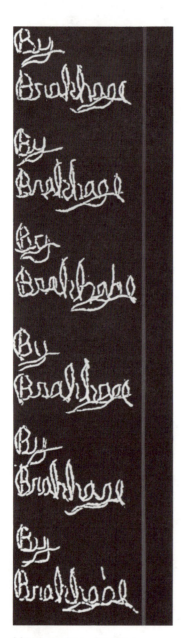

2.21 *Window Water Baby Moving*

the assertion of the individual remains intrinsic to the immanentist mode, ensuring that the family will be the largest social frame of reference properly accessible to it. And so through the individual Stan Brakhage, personal filmmaker, run the contradictory imperatives of his political context and his resistance to it. Through the introspection of his perceptual obsession run the insistent demands of the surrounding social process. We are never more thoroughly in history than when we try to step outside it. When these political tensions are strongest, when Brakhage is faced with issues that cannot be reduced into his own body or reenacted as domestic drama, they precipitate the strongest filmic tensions of his work. It is necessary, then, to note the displacements that attend Brakhage's reluctant accommodation of public matters, both when the outside world penetrated the mountain retreat or when he himself ventured into the heart of the beast. At these points, the expository limitations of his belief that "the Visual constitute[s] its own 'story'" (Brakhage, 1963: 82) mark the limit of his discourse. At worst, the idealist supposition that the visual can be the index and signature of the real produces an inarticulate empiricism; the symbolist assumption of an uninterrupted wholeness in the icon's signification completes the reification of vision to strand Brakhage in an ideologically complicit positivism.

The political ramifications of this commitment to presence and appearance are clear in what is one of Brakhage's least successful works, *eyes*, part of his *Pittsburgh Trilogy*. Made in a hospital, in a coroner's office, and from a police squad car in an industrial city, *Pittsburgh Trilogy* engages a dominant film mode of the period, the cinéma vérité documentary of public institutions, inviting specific comparison with Frederick Wiseman's virtually contemporaneous documentary on the Kansas City police, *Law and Order* (1969) and with his *Hospital* (1971). Though *The Act of Seeing with One's Own Eyes* has its own very specific *modus operandi*, most germane here is *eyes*, the police film, in which Brakhage encounters relationships informed not by nature but by the state.

Like Wiseman, Brakhage photographs the police in their encounters with the poor, the runaways, the *lumpen* dispossessed, especially Blacks. The polarization of the victims and the agents of state power recurs filmically, with the former being distinct and distinctly photographed while the police, in general lacking individuality, achieve registration only through their professional accouterments—guns, handcuffs, badges—and through the massive blue shirts that regularly fill the screen. When the police are individualized, it is always to assert their humanity, their good-humored defusion of a tense situation, or their kindliness in assisting the distressed. In place of the violence with which the police treat people of color—the brutality that Wiseman notices, for example, in the near strangling of the young prostitute—here everything is benign— and this after a decade of escalating class war between police and the poor!

The converse of this thematic effacement of social control is the

2.22 *Dog Star Man, Part IV*

2.23 Stan Brakhage filming eyes

weakness of the film's micro- and macro-articulation. The film shows an unprecedented reliance on deep-focus long takes, and the overall structure and the visual ligatures between shots are, for Brakhage, loose; structurally it hesitates between sequences of diegetically unrelated shots, erratically interrupted by extended, quasi-autonomous sequences, some of which even incorporate rudimentary field/reverse field patterns. In one of the most coherent, a body is found on the street. It is covered over, walked around, contemplated, and photographed, a form is filled out, and the body is bagged and removed—all in separate shots. In a narrative unit as strongly marked as this, a characteristic Brakhage observation such as the slight modulation of shadows over a trickle of blood from the dead man is a painful aestheticism.

These vacillations mark unresolvable tensions between Brakhage's subject and the political implications of his style. That texture of analogy and correspondence, by which he typically makes the profilmic over into a function of the filmic and vice versa, is here inhibited by the resistance the profilmic mounts against reproduction as sheer visual information or against being made over into metaphors of vision or the apparatus. Conversely, the assertion of visual presence in the imagery inhibits analytical distancing of it, while its production cerebrally as knowledge is similarly prevented by the exclusion of verbal language. Thus *eyes*'s representation of the political relationship between the people and the police is blocked by two levels of empiricism: by the supposition that the function of these specific police can be comprehended through vision alone, and by the supposition that the function of the police system as a whole may adequately be registered by observation of these instances of it.

The premise of Brakhage's scrutiny of the public world is an essentialism that takes the visual configuration of history as the index of its meaning. When not even the appearance of the acts of history is available, that premise is most strained. The diminished capacity for conceptual articulation is even more radically debilitating when the immanentist method is brought to bear on proscribed events that the filmmaker may not personally witness. Such an occlusion is at its most critical a political exclusion, and the typical response of modern artists to such events as may not be personally scrutinized is to approach them via a critique of the political uses of other, usually public, representations of them. Brakhage's own critique of institutional perception similarly attempts to overcome the impotence that separates the unaffiliated individual from the institutions of power. Thus *eyes* itself depends upon a comparison between the police as the public eyes, a notion that Brakhage derives from an Olson pun, and himself as a private eye. The comprehensive form of such a synthesis would bring the most minute register of the individual to bear upon the largest operations of history—for instance, Brakhage's eyes and the Vietnam War, and the mediation of the relationship between them by the communications industries. Inevitably, the fragility of Brakhage's social disengagement became most forcefully apparent in the period of the Vietnam War. In the film he made in response to it, *23rd Psalm Branch*, the longest of the *Songs*, his amateur aesthetic is forced into its most heroic visual confrontations and avoidances.

The war made its way into the Brakhage family via the television they used as a surrogate for going out in the evening; it precipitated domestic quarrels of unprecedented severity and bombarded him with guilt: "I couldn't deal with the television set. And it wasn't just the object itself, but that it was our only specific connection to Society with a capital 'S' or something we were expected to be responsible for" (Brakhage, 1979: 109). Rather than confront the terms of that "specific connection" or even the images themselves, Brakhage resorted to a series of strategies that do allow consideration of war in general, but only by displacing the historical specificity of Vietnam. The result is a dialogic nightmare, in which the drama of individual estrangement is played out visually in a struggle between personal vision and its nemesis.

First, in an exact recapitulation of the government and the mass media's presentation of the Vietnam War as an extension of World War II anti-fascism, Brakhage investigates it via footage from World War II, a war he had become familiar with as a child from movie newsreels. This investigation supplied the main formal strategy of attempting to incorporate that alien-ness into his own vision by montage analysis of it, and by painting and scratching that footage and overlaying it with benday dots—making it into a Brakhage movie. Similar motives inform his attempts to establish both the continuity and discontinuity between his mountain home and the atrocities of World War II by parallel montages that alternate domestic scenes with scenes of battle and concentration camps. In the most chilling of these, he establishes an extended visual rhyme between emaciated Jewish victims and the face of Louis Zukofsky, then a visitor in his home. These techniques do articulate filmically the unconscionable horror of the holocaust, especially through the violence and insight of the montage—and on this level the film is a great humanist testimony. But by the same terms the war that is produced is a function not of a specific imperialist undertaking nor even of Western culture as a whole, but of nature as such, and its traumas are those of private consciousness and memory.

This displacement was entirely consistent with Brakhage's attitude to war, which saw it as a natural disaster, an act of God-like "hurricanes and tornadoes and droughts and floods" (ibid: 116), yet with its final source in human consciousness; hence his approval, in the talks he gave in this period, of Allen Ginsberg's ostrich-like personal declaration in 1966 that the war was over. The same ahistorical essentialism informs Brakhage's analysis of the shape of crowd formations in fascist Europe and his demonstration of the parallels between the visual form of Christian architecture and fascist social space. Public behavior is the manifestation of a "war state of mind." Completing the Romantic paradigm, these terms do not explain Vietnam, but only force the film into further contradictions. As the conflict continues to be internalized within Brakhage, within his vision, the film is able neither to complete itself nor to face the implications of that failure.

First, Brakhage is reduced to words, quoting from Zukofsky, "Song, my song, raise my grief to music," to articulate the aesthetic transcendence he cannot register visually. Then he attempts to sublate this failure by incorporating it into the film, first by photographing himself writing a "Dear Jane" letter that gives a more precise interpretation of his state of mind than can be reproduced visually: "I must stop. The War *is* as thought/patterns are—as endless as . . . precise as eye's hell *is!*" and by scratching "I can't go on." But the psychological limit reached here is also a limit of his aesthetic, produced simultaneously by his inability either to confront war in an ontology of the visual or to recognize the cognitive silence that surrounds an aesthetic of the purely visual. Instead of accepting the disclosure, instead of internalizing the aposiopetic imperative in the film itself, ending it at this point and leaving its incompletion as the testimony of its inability to be completed, of the contradiction between the war and his aesthetic, he does go on and so obfuscates the formal and semantic significance his psychological impasse has brought to light. He returns to private experience, to the photography of domestic scenes with the Kubelkas in Vienna, Austrian artists, an homage to Freud, and finally to his family in Colorado and the discovery of domestic analogues to the demonic violence of the war.

While *23rd Psalm Branch* embodies the inability of Brakhage's

Romantic aestheticism to transcend privatized individual consciousness and engage history, it offers itself as a cautery for the horror of contemporary political life by presenting itself as the site of aesthetic values, public espousal of which would lead to the regeneration of the public realm. Nowhere is Brakhage's visual articulation more exact and exacting. In the Western tradition, the comprehensive term for these values is beauty, and it is appropriate finally to consider one of Brakhage's most beautiful films and an event in his life which dramatically illustrates the crippling conditions under which that beauty could be secured and the price he would pay to secure it. The whole event has the tension of an allegory.

Early in 1973, Brakhage renewed the acquaintance of an old school friend who had become a millionaire, and he decided to make a portrait of him. He went to his friend's office in Denver with a new macro lens. When the lens failed to work according to expectation, Brakhage in despair gave up shooting; the camera, with its bellows in the middle, sagged. But before he picked it up, he looked through the lens.

> And I saw a whole forest-like scene! And I said, how incredible! and I looked to see what it was pointing to, and it was pointing to his ashtray. Then I brought him around the desk and I said, look, see what I find, and he looked and said, how wonderful! and so on.
>
> And I looked again . . . and it had changed. And a little stream was wandering through it! And this is how the film began. (Brakhage, n.d.: 36)

And so *The Text of Light* was discovered, a visual odyssey, a Thousand and One Nights of optical delight, a beautiful image of liberation that can only be seen as beautiful—that can only be seen at all—when the expectations and functions of the industrial cinema are entirely abandoned. Almost entirely abstract and laboriously shot frame by frame over a period of months, it resulted in a back injury so severe it caused Brakhage to walk with a stick. The confrontation with capital, even in its most personal form, was avoided. But ecstasy was snatched from a millionaire's ashtray.

*

Between the melancholy irony of Jean-Luc Godard's belated realization that "the real 'political' film" would be a "home-movie" in which he could show himself to his wife and daughter (cited in MacCabe, 1980: 23)[12] and the entirely opposite filmmaking career it caps ring the echoes of two similarly contrary definitions of *political*. The aporias we have sketched in Brakhage's enactment in cinema of the proposition that the personal is the political are matched by the contradictions in Godard's diametrically contrary practice and contestation of the industrial media. It is worth recalling that the same year that, with *Breathless*, Godard began an engagement with the commodity cinema that would take him to the most com-

12 The entire comment reads, "As for me, I've become aware, after fifteen years of cinema, that the real 'political' film that I'd like to end up with would be a film about me which would show to my wife and daughter what I am, in other words a home-movie—home-movies represent the popular base of the cinema." Compare Brakhage's: "I believe any art of the cinema must inevitably arise from the amateur, 'home-movie' making medium" (Brakhage, [1967] 1982: 168).

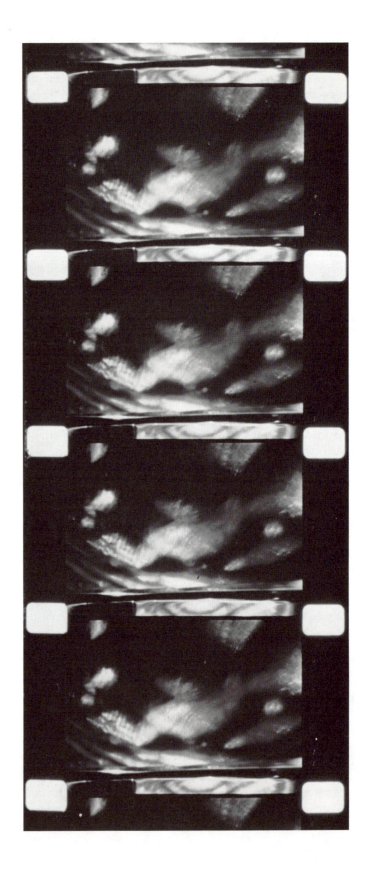

2.24 *The Text of Light*

prehensive critique of it but then back to the aegis of a Hollywood studio, Brakhage began *Dog Star Man*, the very prototype of epic domesticity, the pattern for a life's work that is the commercial cinema's most comprehensive antithesis. Brakhage's project proposes its opposition to the corporate state not by direct contestation in the public institutional sphere or yet in the sphere of industrial cultural production, but by the organization of a life that attempts to be simultaneously outside both. His films are themselves challenged, then, by two other responses to the degraded industrial cinema, which intersect precisely at Godard: radical cinema, the use of film to attack the corporate state and its programs, and the art film, the individual attempt to intervene in the culture industries. We shall attend to the American versions of both. But the most illuminating comparison to Brakhage is Andy Warhol. Like Brakhage, Warhol was essentially a home-movie maker—and probably nothing figures the difference between them more precisely than their very different homes. But for Warhol home movies were a point of departure, the opening gambit in a career of publicity. His final aspiration was to inhabit the cultural apparatus of the state, to make "the movies" his home.

3

Andy Warhol: The Producer as Author

Being good in business is the most fascinating kind of art.
— Andy Warhol

Nothing Is
— Sun Ra

Stan Brakhage's theory and practice of film as categorically other than the industrial use of the medium are matched by Andy Warhol's similarly remarkable but entirely contrary project, that of taking art film ever and ever closer to Hollywood. In identifying film with the psychological and physiological processes of the individual's visual sensibility, Brakhage abjured the languages evolved by the commercial cinema; but Warhol's preoccupation with the industrial apparatus of mass fascination and with the machinery of mass perception allowed vision as an optical faculty to be transcended and distributed through the pan-sensual play of memory and desire in the operations of the culture industries at large. So while for Brakhage the critical issue was seeing, for Warhol it was being seen; in his work the construction of a personal filmic discourse is inseparable from the process of securing prominence in the discourse of others. He realized that, if in the spectacular society the logic of *esse est percipi* makes being quantifiable as publicity, then the important arena of activity is the publicity industry. So Warhol inaugurated an art practice that was fundamentally entrepreneurial; deploying filmmaking strategies in wider and wider social contexts, he negotiated an intervention in the medium as an occupation of the media.

In the early sixties cinema was still the most important of the media industries—the most popular and the most remunerative medium—and so it was the primary intersection of business and art. Warhol's entry into it was made possible by the success of his previous careers in advertising and in painting, of which his films are an entirely logical extension. If Brakhage's project recapitulated the social functions of the wilderness poet, Warhol's manipulation of the social processes that attended pictorial representation found its point of departure in the heady mix of philosophy and fashion, of skepticism and real estate, in New York pop art.

*

The simultaneous interrogation and exploitation of the media and the meditation on the elusiveness of the un-media-ted presence that characterize Warhol's films were prefigured in his early paintings of advertisements and silk-screened portraits of celebrities. His poker-faced reproduction of familiar iconography dispensed with both abstract expressionism's formal means of signifying authorial sincerity and with sincerity itself as an aesthetic criterion. Indeed it was Émile de Antonio's preference for "just a stark, outlined Coke bottle in black and white" over "a Coke bottle with Abstract Expressionist hash marks halfway up the side" (Warhol, 1980: 6) that Warhol took advantage of to maneuver his way from fashion illustration into fine art. The pop images of his initial notoriety—the soup cans, the Coke bottles, the *Red Elvis*, and the *Marilyns* of the Los Angeles and New York shows of 1962—were, however, simplified and more easily consumable versions of an earlier set of paintings done mostly in 1960. For *Make Him Want You*, *Strong Arms and Broads*, *Water Heater*, and *$199 TV*, Warhol simply projected photographs of newspaper advertisements onto canvas and filled in the outlines more or less completely with black paint.

Their severity hardly softened by the lingering hash marks and drips, these paintings floated an image in a space that was neither entirely literal nor entirely metaphoric, and so they opened themselves to the investigation of two-dimensional representation characteristic of the period. They are unusual, however, in that ontological tensions in the image generate parallel questions about the economic function of the iconography and of the paintings themselves. That play of ironies and contradictions, which in Jasper Johns, for example, is contained inside the formal structure, oscillating between the language of painting and the materials of representation, was extended to force the formal qualities of the image to confront its function in the marketplace. The vestigial signs of authorial presence are only just sufficient to differentiate the paintings from actual commercial reproduction, while the withdrawal of sensuality from the images and their insubstantiality in terms of both style and even the amount of pigment they are allowed—their meagerness as visual objects—bespeaks their theoretical severity, as if in his first outings as a "fine artist" Warhol had to purge himself of the pictorial blandishments of his former trade. For these paintings of advertisements not only narrate the migration of advertisements into paintings, but also allegorize Warhol's own entry into the world of fine art, where, with bland aplomb, he performed the reverse operation: he turned painting into advertisement.

In his subsequent paintings of consumer items and in his prints of celebrities and disasters, Warhol redeployed the tensions of the artwork's commodity function, not only as formal issues but also as components of his own marketing strategies in the art business. As before, the imagery was drawn from the popular press, but the banal water heaters and TVs gave way to movie stars, and the monochrome to strident coloration. By appropriating the preexistent publicity value of Elvis or Marilyn to the éclat of being among the first to cite such images as fine art, Warhol secured his own access to the self-generating cycles of publicity in which, along with the ease of consumption of his paintings and the surfeit of visual pleasure provided by the iconography and the representational naiveté, his fame eliminated the need for any other advertising. Rather, the problem was producing the works fast enough, and so as his imagery became indistinguishable from the media industry's, Warhol's practice as a painter approached industrial methods of production. In the prints for which he became famous, the activity of the iconography and the conditions of production are homologous, the one narrating the other.

Warhol's serigraphs do not add resolution or texture to the photographs from which they derive; neither, except in the most general way of manifesting a characteristic method, do they impose any personal inflection upon them. Instead, they extend the anonymity of the photographs by distributing responsibility in the production process over several hands, reiterating the general public production and consumption of these images in the everyday ubiquity of the media, the mass libidinal and economic investment that produces the stars who are their subjects. Similarly, Warhol's own images were themselves widely reproduced; and the initial transformation of a commercial photograph into a print in his studio was only the point of departure for a reverse movement, his print's reentry into the vocabulary and currency of popular culture. A Warhol print is thus a pivot upon which an image is retrieved from mass culture and refurbished so as to reenter the circulation process. But the authority that allows a given print to mediate between the two social processes derives purely from Warhol's control over the social and economic transactions; it neither derives from nor bestows any stronger ontological presence on the image or its subject. The multiple generations of the productive process—the initial act of photography, reproduction in the press, rephotography for the silk-screen, the stages in the silk-screening, and then the reproduction in the popular press and pop art books—further and further abstract presence until all that remains is the media icon enshrined in the reproductive process. All a given print can signify is publicity; all it can specify is its own privileged location, the social position of Art, in a series of reproductions extending endlessly in all directions.

As a moment in this self-referential signifying chain that was virtually independent of a real human body or personality, a Warhol portrait is peculiarly appropriate to the mode of existence of his subjects—movie stars and others whose self-presentation was thoroughly media-dependent. Norma Jean Baker and Merle Johnson had already been processed through several generations of self-production prior to their incarnation as Marilyn and Troy: in the coding of movie and still photography and, before that, in the assumption of an artificial name, itself preparatory to a career of role playing. Even the Elvis Warhol used was the cowboy actor, a screen image earned by his fame as a singer and one that extends the ambiguity of person and role to a doubled function in the entertainment industry. Rather than adding visual or psychological dimensionality to these images, painterly intervention such as the addition of color to black and white photographs merely echoes the simplification inherent in media reproduction; in *Marilyn Monroe* (1964), for example, the blond hair, red lips, and green eyelids—the same signifiers by which de Kooning distinguished *Marilyn Monroe* in his rows of anonymous *Woman* paintings—reinscribe the artifice of the public image. By further draining presence from his images of media personalities, Warhol became one of the few artists in the century for whom portraiture could be a major preoccupation.[1] From Picasso to de Kooning the problem of representation and the difficulty of narrating either a stable personality or the relationship between personality and public appearance had caused the sitter's image to be lost behind the flurry of painterly activity; but Warhol's lack of interest in the presence of an authentic identity solved both aspects of the problem with a single stroke. Slippage between sitter and image, between individual and role, or between subject and representation is impossible when all are incarnate only as disturbances on the screen of media attention. Similarly, that difficulty of believing in the value of the social role allotted to the subject, which has been proposed as the cause of the decline in public portraiture since Gericault (Berger, 1974: 38–39), disappears when the social role is simply existence as a media image and when media existence is the limit of conceivable ambition. When the media image is its own justification, the flattening of fleshly or psychic depth is the sign of the portrait's success. To expect something more than the notation of commodity status to be precipitated in the moment of stillness that the print snatches from the infinite duplication of the image is to indulge a nostalgia for an edenic moment before media, a hypothetical past when people were supposed to exist.

The same withdrawal of authenticity organizes the production process, for despite its genealogy in the workshop system of pre-Romantic painting and in Duchamp's conceptualism,[2] Warhol's use of amanuenses in the mass production of serigraphed multiples took the rejection of the painterly signature to a new extreme. And while production was never entirely mechanical, responsibility was often carelessly and arbitrarily distributed, with Warhol's own eye giving way to the undifferentiated activity of Factory hands. Any irregularity in the production process gave only a spurious distinction to a given print, but far from causing the aura of the prints to wither, Warhol's multiple production capitalized it. He instated his rejection of all the activities that had traditionally asserted the authorship of the individual artist as itself the sign of authenticity. Withdrawing his own participation even beyond the conceptualist outpost of the artist's role as the instigator of a perceptual process— which he did when with summary wit he *bought* the idea for his money paintings from Muriel Latow—he elevated his administrative control over Factory production and his entrepreneurial control over marketing to the status of artwork, while still retaining for himself the social, historical, and financial rewards of authorship. This contradiction between socialized production and private ownership—the defining contradiction of capitalism itself—is the origin of all the vertiginous double binds in which Warhol can satirize

1 Robert Rosenblum notes that Warhol "succeeded virtually single-handed in the early 1960's in resurrecting from near extinction that endangered species of grand-style portraiture" (Rosenblum, 1979: 9).

2 Duchamp himself was one of the first to recognize Warhol's relevance to what was soon to be called the "de-materialization" of art: "If a man takes fifty Campbell Soup cans and puts them on a canvas, it is not the retinal image which concerns us. What interests us is the concept that wants to put fifty Campbell Soup cans on a canvas" (cited in Green, 1966: 229).

3 The following is only one of several equally plausible schematizations of the phases of Warhol's filmmaking career:

a. Silent, black and white, unedited 100′ rolls with minimal motion in the profilmic and none by the camera, for example, *Eat, Sleep, Empire, Blow Job,* and *Henry Geldzahler* (1963–64).

b. The addition of sound and some camera movement (zooms and pans), some in-camera editing of 1,200′ rolls, and scripting by Ronald Tavel, for example, *Vinyl, Screen Test #2, The Life of Juanita Castro, My Hustler,* and *Hedy* (1965). This period culminates with *The Chelsea Girls* and the segments of * * * * (FOUR STARS) (1966), by which time Warhol was experimenting with multi-screen projection and mixed-media presentation, often using his films to accompany the Velvet Underground in the Exploding Plastic Inevitable.

c. Color features with varying proportions of scripting and improvised dialogue, for example, *Bike Boy, Nude Restaurant, Lonesome Cowboys* (1967), and *Blue Movie* (1968).

d. Features produced in collaboration with Paul Morrissey (previously Warhol's cameraman for about two years), for example, *Flesh* (1969), *Trash* (1970), *Women in Revolt (Sex)* (1971), *Heat* (1972), and *Frankenstein* (1974). Typically, Morrissey is credited as director and Warhol as producer, though Warhol himself directed *L'Amour* and photographed *Women in Revolt (Sex)*. He simply "presented" the Carlo Ponti Company's production of *Frankenstein*.

These categories are a simplification of the filmography in Bourdon (1971). The most complete filmography up to 1967 is in Koch (1973), itself an extension of Mekas (n.d.). For films after 1967, which Koch lists simply as "The Films of Paul Morrissey," see the Warhol/Morrissey filmography in J. Taylor (1975). Koch also contains extensive descriptions of many films, some of which, like *Haircut*, have never been released.

both consumer society and humanist indictments of it, even while manipulating it for his own profit. In fact, so tight was his play with such contradictions that if he did not succeed in raising the stakes to the point where the only "really real" Warhol was a "fake" one, at least he got them to where the question would seem naive if expressed in other than financial terms. Who fried the chicken was not important; the name on the franchise was.

Anomalous among the early portraits is "Portrait of Ethel Scull" (1963), in which the subject largely lacked the celebrity status that was elsewhere the point of departure for the marketing process. Here the art object bestowed its glamor on the sitter. Allowed access to Warhol's attention by her husband's investment in his work, Mrs. Scull enters history as "a Warhol," and so valorized she attains parity with Marilyn, Elvis, and Jackie, by whose side she returns our look from the museum wall or coffee table. The portrait is also unusual in that Warhol used original photographs. He took Ms. Scull to a slot-machine photo booth, where from her physiognomy, her hair style and her couture she composed a series of self-images. The mirror there was a stage and behind the mirror-stage was a camera. Yet whether she is primping her hair, resting her hand on her chin, or merely sporting her sunglasses, the thirty-five poses all seem to be quoted from fashion magazines, a repertoire of glances and gestures derived from model images, a lexicon of possible selves presented to her own gaze for approval and endorsement. They are all stills from the movie of Ethel Scull.

Taking place in the same year as the Ethel Scull portrait, Warhol's transition to movie-making proper was entirely logical. Albeit in a highly idiosyncratic and profitable fashion, he had taken painting to what was for him the most summary of the many impasses it confronted; it had become boring. Though painting in the mid-sixties did have a higher public visibility than ever before, its public dissemination largely depended on other media. However glamorous and remunerative it was, the movies were more so. But fine art had given Warhol financial independence; in place of other independent filmmakers' impoverished struggles with bit jobs in the industry and enervating scuffles for patronage, Warhol had an easy affluence and as much publicity and social access as he could want. Having secured the attention of the media, he was now free to explore the nature of that attention as it inhered in what was still the most popular art.

Warhol's career as a filmmaker contains so many abrupt lurches into new directions and shifts to different scales of production that description of it in terms of a single expressive urgency is as difficult as organizing it in standard generic categories.[3] Its only continuity appears to be that of discontinuity, its only coherence that of fracture. But all the singular achievements as well as the desultory, incompleted projects that lie between the silent rising and falling of John Giorno's abdomen in *Sleep* in 1963 and the logo "Presented by Andy Warhol" splashed across the ads for the Carlo Ponti Company's production of *Frankenstein* in 1974 do suggest a trajectory of which Warhol's own distinction between "the period where we made movies just to make them" and a subsequent decision to make "feature length movies that regular theaters would want to show" (Warhol, 1980: 251–52) is as just an anatomy as any. Though the caesural pivot that both joins and separates the autotelic art and the commercial enterprises is difficult to place—does it lie after *Empire*? or *The Chelsea Girls*? or *Lonesome Cowboys*? or *Trash*?—certainly a general distinction between an early Warhol and a late Warhol can be elaborated in both formal and biographical terms. It corresponds to an interest in increasingly sophisticated technological investments, to the shift from private Factory showings to public exhibition, and to an engagement with the grammar of industrial cinema and with scripting, fiction, and narrative as commonly understood. Valerie Solanis's attempt on Warhol's life falls into place as a historical marker, for although *Flesh* had been planned previously, it was during Warhol's incapacitation that Paul Morrissey wrote and directed it. After Warhol's recovery and the move to the new Factory, production and distribution were more professionally organized, and Warhol largely abandoned the social milieu that had previously sustained him.

The products of the two periods have, of course, been differently evaluated; critics with allegiance to the avant-garde find, for example, that after *The Chelsea Girls* (1966) Warhol "quickly faded as a significant film-maker" (Sitney, 1979: 371), or that "something absolutely grotesque happened to Warhol's two finest gifts: his visual intelligence and his taste. It was simply this: Degradation" (Koch, 1973: 100). Those with investment in feature film see the opposite development—for example, that Warhol came "of age as a film-maker . . . around the time that his collaboration with Paul Morrissey began" (J. Taylor, 1975: 137). Such a categorical distinction between different Warhols is a precondition of the valorization of one over the other and of a biographical narrative in which either a good artist sold out to the media or an elitist, pretentious one became popularly accessible. But any use of essentialist concepts of pure and commercial art to distinguish parallel functions within Warhol's filmmaking has to be qualified by his continuous subversion of the grounds upon which such a categorical distinction could be based. The larger story of Warhol's whole career, in which each period was no more than an episode, calls into question the thematics upon which both depend.

Preceded by highly successful careers in advertising and fine art, Warhol's filmmaking period was followed by other ventures in mass media manipulation and self-promotion that included publishing an extravagant fanzine and various forms of autobiography. Throughout, even in his activities as a pure celebrity, the same tensions and the same interdependence between art and business are present. Appearing in retrospect as primarily a strategic maneuver in the work of his life in the media in general, his career as a filmmaker spans the two most polemically opposed modes of production of the time—the underground and the industry; but it is also unified, both

3.1 Andy Warhol, "Portrait of Ethel Scull" (detail)

in itself and with the whole career, in its continuous attention to the functions of the media. In a project of progressively expanding the parameters of the apparatus he was able to control, he both engaged the commercial medium and, in a series of meta-filmic and meta-cinematic strategies, analyzed the conditions of that engagement. His investigation of the technological and social mechanisms of the recording apparatus—originally the processes of photography and eventually extending from the camera per se to the media industry as a whole—runs parallel to the industrialization of his mode of film production. The thematic and iconographic explorations simultaneously accompany and reproduce the replacement of artisanal production by a division of labor in which the different stages in the production process—writing, acting, shooting, and editing—are distributed. Warhol delegated more and more responsibility until, in some of the late films, he was no more than a name attached to a product completed essentially without participation on his part other than the marshaling of production expenses and publicity.

In the expansion of his activity from being the operator of a camera to being the operator of an industry, his erasure of authorship—his most characteristic authorial gesture—was recontextualized ac-

3.2 Joe Dallesandro, star of *Flesh*, *Trash*, *Heat*, *Frankenstein*, and other films (publicity photo)

cording to the requirements of the different spheres. But in each his formal organization of the art object was inseparable from his organization of its social insertion. It is this continuity in his role as a *producer*, which, according to one definition, is "a combination of shrewd businessman, tough taskmaster, prudent cost accountant, flexible diplomat, and creative visionary" (Katz, 1979: 933), that allows the homologies among the style, content, and social location of his work, even as they change, to be specified as thoroughly as in the case of Brakhage.

*

Even though Warhol was immediately recognized with a *Film Culture* award when he began making films, the antipathy between his work and prevailing taste, his "fierce indifference" to the contemporary avant-garde (Sitney, 1979: 372), produced a perplexity that continued through subsequent commentary.

> Strange things have been going on lately at the Film-Makers' Showcase. Anti-film-makers are taking over. Andy Warhol serials brought the Pop Movie into existence. Is Andy Warhol really making movies, or is he playing a joke on us?—this is the talk of the town. To show a man sleeping, is this a movie? A three-minute kiss by Naomi Levine, is this art of kissing or art of cinema? (Mekas, 1972: 109)

In the context of Brakhage's heavily worked, personally assertive montages, Warhol's minimization of content, his empty prolongation of duration, and his refusal to intervene in the filmic or the profilmic seemed mere gestures of provocation, at best warmed-over dada and at worst opportunism. As early as 1964, Jonas Mekas saw Brakhage and Warhol as the "two extremes" of cinema (Mekas, 1972: 158) and, as if magically to heal a rupture that could shatter the underground film community, he elaborated a story in which, after initially rejecting them when seen at 24 frames per second, Brakhage came to appreciate Warhol's films by viewing them at 16 frames per second.

Eventually, Warhol's formal strategies were recognized as more than the careerist negation of previous priorities, and Sitney, finding in an early work like *Sleep* three of the four defining characteristics of structural film (the fixed frame, loop printing, and the freeze frame which emphasized the grain and flattened the image), nominated him as a "major precursor" of it (1979: 371).[4] Foregrounding its own reductionism, Warhol's technique drew attention to the separate constituents of film, both those it used and those it excluded, allowing the fundamental cinematic conditions he isolated to be registered phenomenologically. His films' extended duration, together with their minimized sensory output, could produce perceptual changes in the spectator, sometimes as extreme as a trance; Warhol himself reputedly was wont to bliss out when watching his own work.[5]

But refusal to submit oneself experientially to the films did not

4 In a similar vein Malcolm Le Grice notes as primarily important Warhol's inauguration of a one-to-one equivalence between shooting and screening times (Le Grice, 1977: 94), unfortunately arguing this by reference to films like *Sleep* which, in fact, substantially extended screen time, not only through freeze frames and loop printing, but also through screening at 16 frames per second footage shot at 24.

5 Ronald Tavel reports that Warhol "would sit and watch [films like *Couch*] with such contentment that I felt I was in the presence of a Buddhist who had achieved the desired transcendent state" (cited in Koch, 1973: 41). Jonas Mekas describes a presumably similar "period of aesthetic weightlessness" produced in him by watching *Sleep* (Mekas, n.d.: 144).

preclude recognition of the play of their conceptual conundrums.[6] So, even though in and of themselves Warhol's films lacked any Brechtian engagement with the political functions of the mass cinema, in semiological studies of film grammar, his compositional strategies could be rewritten as theoretical probes into the language of the medium: stationary camera as investigation of the relationship between on- and off-screen space; end-flares as attention to material substrate; arbitrary zooms and strobe cutting as alienation devices. At its most ingenious, the reading of Warhol's work as essentially without content other than the specifically filmic allowed the hero of *Empire* to be understood "primarily as a device by which to present the full range of tones from black to white" (Battcock, 1967: 234). The building itself was neither so unrecognizable as to demand identification nor one from which any aesthetic stimulation could be gained; it was rather "simply a big nothing" (ibid.). Oblivious to the sexual pun and to the irony that the symbolic home of corporate capitalism and of the communications industry had at last been centered as the subject of the longest movie ever made, such a formalism was only one response to Warhol's self-effacement.

The other response was the opposite, to read Warhol's work as the means to the unhindered passage of content, and so to construct a documentarist Warhol, valuable precisely for his depiction of an otherwise unrepresented social milieu. Citing Victor Hugo as a parallel, Mekas was struck by "the uniqueness of the world presented

3.3 Empire

6 Paul Arthur has explored the implications of the unusual degree to which verbal reiteration has replaced optical experience in reference to *Empire* (Arthur, 1978: 5–6).

... and the monumental thoroughness with which it is presented" (Mekas, n.d.: 139). Even though it picked up both on *noir* currents in the industry and on underground currents going back to Lionel Rogosin's *On the Bowery* (1956), Kenneth Anger's *Fireworks* (1947), and especially the work of the group around Jack Smith, the extensiveness of Warhol's documentation of sexual deviants, drug users, and petty criminals was unprecedented, and it opened the way for the mass media interest in such milieus, as instanced by jaundiced industrial melodramas like *Midnight Cowboy* (1968). What distinguishes Warhol from his predecessors and successors is his disinterest in moral or narrative inflection; his willingness to allow marginal subcultures entry into the process of documentation is paralleled by paratactical formal structures that make no place for authorial possession of them. Its ingenuousness aside, Warhol's refusal to censor, to censure, or even to create hierarchies bespeaks a toleration, simultaneously ethical and aesthetic, that inheres in all his most characteristic gestures—his collapse of the distinctions between surface and depth, between life and art, between reality and artifice, and between high society and the underworld: "I only wanted to find great people and let them be themselves and talk about what they usually talked about and I'd film them for a certain length of time and that would be the movie" (Warhol, 1980: 110).

The supposition that Warhol democratically documents people "being themselves" provided the basis for the endemic supposition that his cinema was voyeuristic.[7] While the metaphor usefully recognizes the camera's often uninflected stare at irregular sexual practices, the more general notion it implies—that Warhol's was a form of direct cinema, without significant determination of the profilmic by the cinematic apparatus—is entirely misleading. It runs aground not only, like other absolute realisms, on its elision of the mediation of the apparatus and of generic and formal codes, but also, and more crucially, on the nature of the profilmic. For rather than unfolding in ignorance of the camera's presence or unaffected by it, the spectacle in Warhol's films is produced for and *by* the camera. Only if you are unconscious (*Sleep*) or a building (*Empire*) can you be unaware of media attention in Warhol's world. Otherwise, as the recording apparatus mechanically transforms life into art, it constitutes the space of its attention as a theater of self-presentation. Since the people in the profilmic are always trying to accommodate themselves to the demands of the camera, always conducting themselves in full recognition of the apparatus as both recording technology and as a potential avenue to fame, the defining condition of voyeurism—"repetitive looking at *unsuspecting* people" (*Diagnostic and Statistical Manual*, 1980: 272, emphasis added)—is precluded. That metaphor has to be reversed, re-contained in an antithetical coupling in which the self-conscious profilmic subject, narcissistically exhibiting himself or herself as a means of attracting attention, is complemented by a camera whose power lies in its threat to look away. Far from affirming the possibility of cinéma vérité, Warhol mordantly exposes the fallaciousness of both the social psychology

7 The fullest elaboration of Warhol's voyeurism is Koch (1973): for example, "Even more than it does most movies, voyeurism dominates all Warhol's early films and defines their aesthetic" (ibid.: 42). Despite his extensive use of the metaphor, Koch does recognize that the reverse is also true: for example, "That was Warhol's gift—he made everybody in his world watched. And what is being watched has a meaning, even if it's only the meaning of being watched" (ibid.: 6).

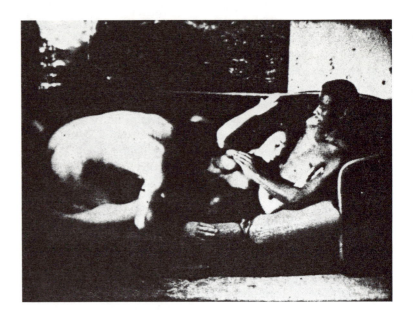

3.4 *Couch*: Gerard Malanga, Kate Heli-
czer, and Rufus Collins

8 Encapsulating both the function
of the documentary urge and the
limitations of the voyeur metaphor,
Warhol himself made this process
explicit in reference to audio recording: "The acquisition of my tape recorder really finished whatever emotional life I might have had, but I
was glad to see it go. Nothing was
ever a problem again, because a
problem just meant a good tape,
and when a problem transforms itself into a good tape it's not a problem any more. An interesting problem was an interesting tape.
Everybody knew that and performed for the tape. You couldn't
tell which problems were real and
which problems were exaggerated
for the tape. Better yet, the people
telling you the problems couldn't
decide any more if they were really
having the problems or if they were
just performing" (Warhol, 1975:
26–27).

on which its assumptions are based and the cinematic codes produced to implement them.[8] His is thus a meta-cinema, an inquiry
into the mechanisms of the inscription of the individual into the apparatus and into the way such inscription has been historically organized. In it the spectator is revealed as being as much a function
of the camera as are the actors. As Warhol opens these latter to their
own repressed self-consciousness, similarly he opens up implications of the spectator's role.

Though Warhol's elaboration of these issues proceded irregu-
larly, it can be schematized generally as having three main stages:
(1) an investigation of the process of being photographed and of
being made the object of film, (2) the construction and fragmentation of artificial selves by means of roles appropriated from film history or metaphorically related in some other way to Hollywood,
and (3) the representation of exhibitionism and spectatorship in the
narratives of feature films which themselves approach Hollywood's
formal and economic terrain. The photographic apparatus has
throughout a double role; on the one hand it is the means of reproduction, and on the other it is the signifer of mass industrial reproduction, both metaphor and metonym for Hollywood, holding out
the promise of mass consumption and thus the means of negotiating
a private event into a public spectacle. It promises the transformation of an individual into a star.

The earliest films—and often the process of shooting was so privileged that much of the footage was never shown or even assembled
into completed artworks—simply isolated a single figure before the
camera. *Eat*, *Henry Geldzahler*, *Blow Job*, and *The Thirteen Most
Beautiful Women*, through the sections of *The Thirteen Most Beautiful Boys* and *Fifty Fantastics and Fifty Personalities*—as well as the

100′ rolls of Factory visitors—shot by Billy Name, are film portraits that do not document their subjects' ability to manifest an autonomous, unified self so much as narrate their anxious response to the process of being photographed. The camera is a presence in whose regard and against whose silence the sitter must construct himself. As it makes performance inevitable, it constitutes being as performance. The simple activities proffered as the subject of documentation are insufficient fully to engage the sitter and merely establish an alternative area of attention, momentarily allowing self-consciousness to slip away. The sitter oscillates between his activity and awareness of the context in which it is taking place. In *Eat*, for instance, Robert Indiana's eyes focus on the mushroom, then rove around the room seeking to avoid the very place where they must eventually come to rest. The situation is that of psychoanalysis; the camera is the silent analyst who has abandoned the subject to the necessity of his fantastic self-projection. But unlike parallel situations later in video portraiture, in which the immediate mirror-like feedback of the monitor allows the negotiation and renegotiation of the narcissistic image to the point of its stability, allowing the "fragmented body-image" to assume a "form of its totality," even to assume "the armour of an alienating identity" (Lacan, 1977: 5),[9] here film supplies only the implication of observance, displacing its documentation and proof to the future moment of projection.

Alone in the anxiety caused by the knowledge of being observed but denied access to the results of that observation, the subject must construct himself in the mental mirrors of his self-image or his recollection of previous photography. Only in unusual instances is the narcissistic self-absorption sufficiently strong to allow the presence of the camera to be transcended in unembarrassed direct address; Eric Emerson in *The Chelsea Girls*, for example, is able to taunt both camera and spectator, daring them to look away: "I don't have anything to say so I'll just sit and groove on myself. . . . Do you ever just groove on *your* body?" More typically in this mode, since there is no second person within the diegesis with whom the subject may exchange glances, and since closure cannot be achieved auditorily, the spasmodic profilmic look is held in suspension until completed by eye contact with the camera. It then reappears as direct eye contact with the spectator, defining the latter in a single position rather than positioning and repositioning him in a diegesis fabricated from multiple points of view. Condemned to a binary off/on relationship with the sitter, the spectator is implicated in the anxiety of the profilmic; the sitter will either meet the spectator's look or refuse it, recreating in inverse terms the therapeutic tension of the original shooting. We are alternately scrutinized by Robert Indiana and rejected by him, even as we alternately scrutinize and reject him in boredom.

Though these moments when the spectator's self-consciousness catches its own trace in the sitter's do subvert illusionism, they are logically distinct from instances when the materiality of the medium itself is exposed—different, for example, from the white flares

9 Lacking video's "mirror," Warhol's cinema approaches more closely the therapeutic situation that Jacques Lacan describes in "The Function of Language in Psychoanalysis," a text used by Rosalind Krauss to distinguish between the modernist reflexive foregrounding of attention to the medium and the post-modernist "psychological condition of the self split and doubled by the mirror-reflection of synchronous feedback" (Krauss, 1976: 55). Though Warhol's cinema lacks synchronous feedback, it approximates the therapeutic situation even more closely than does video, in which the monitor allows for the closure of the mirror stage. In Warhol's shooting situation, the role of the therapist, who is present but also in his silence absent, is re-created in the silent presence of the camera and of the people around the set (often including press invited precisely to exacerbate the self-consciousness of the performers), neither of whom could furnish catoptric security.

which every four minutes signal the end of a 100′ roll. As Warhol elaborated on the former issues, he pursued not the structuralist investigation of film materials but the complication of the experience of people in the profilmic, exploring the tensions between an implied though never fully realized autonomous identity for them and the inflection of it in their experience of the medium. Two main processes that enforce the fabrication of an identity overlap: the dynamics of improvised social interaction before the camera and the requirements of more or less fictional situations, of narrative and hence of characterization. The latter eventually allowed confrontation with the conventions of role playing and with the vocabulary of acting, and so provided the vehicle for an approach to Hollywood as a historical and economic institution.

The rudimentary doubling present in the juxtaposition of Robert Indiana, the eater of the mushroom, against a Robert Indiana unqualified by the specific task—the distinction between his function

3.5 *Eat*: Robert Indiana

as the subject of a narrative and his being merely a documented presence—was initially extended by the introduction into the pro-filmic of a second actor. But both the personae assumed in the fictional narratives and the more consistent if not more real personae the actor assumed in everyday life remained unstable. Consequently, the drama of the Warhol narratives, even through the most "commercial" of the Morrissey collaborations, resides in the interplay between the different levels of artifice in any one actor/character as much as in the interaction between the separate characters, even though each is the means of production of the other. Up to *The Chelsea Girls* and *Four Stars*, the primary interest lay in people assuming roles; subsequently, as genre and narrative provided more stable fictional frames, it lay in people falling out of them.

Of the lexicon of modes of persona-assumption juxtaposed in *The Chelsea Girls*, one extreme is the minimal degree of self-dramatization instanced by Nico, who both opens and closes the film. Unique by virtue of her star status outside the film, she denotes by her beauty a role intrinsically double as both herself and the form of public desire invested in the media image. All she has to do is manifest that image by being present and beautiful. So in the first reel, though she often gazes vacantly into the camera, she is sufficiently occupied with trimming her hair, only occasionally breaking her narcissistic engrossment in her own image in the mirror to pour a glass of milk or attend to her child. In the last reel, her activity is even further reduced and, apart from briefly holding a light meter, all she does is cease weeping and enter a trance-like state of total self-absorption.

The other inhabitants of this desolate hotel must more aggressively attract the camera's attention, and Ondine's two reels constitute the complementary opposite of Nico's, the extreme of narrative intensity and character complexity. In his performance in the penultimate section, the ambiguities that Nico contained within the bland, minimal image are extrapolated in a vertiginous pyrotechnical display, with roles constantly being assumed and jettisoned as the fantasy moves through different strata or doubles back on its own conditions. The self-conscious assumption of a role, in which both the artificiality and the presence of the camera are flaunted, is played against an apparently genuine commitment to it. Ondine shoots methedrine in his wrist while conversing with the off-camera spectators ("I don't think I am going to say a word. . . . I'm not going to do that for this camera") and eventually settles into the role of Pope. Immediately he extends the ambiguity of his situation vis-à-vis this role by distinguishing the Pope-as-role from the Pope-as-man: "I came here to let you have a close look at the Pope . . . not as Pope but as a man . . . no different from other people." This ambiguity is immediately doubled, as his "popage" is specified as some indeterminate variant of the real Pope: "I want to be true to my flock . . . ; perverts of any kind, thieves, the rejected by society, that's who I'm Pope for."

By the time Pepper Davis comes in to confess, Ondine has extended himself through so many subtly incongruous shifts in iden-

3.6 *Blow Job*

tity that his assertion of the veracity of the confessional can be phrased only in the insubstantial terminology of media reproduction ("The cameras are rolling. This is a new kind of confessional. It's called *True Confessional*"). When his confessee attacks him ("I can't confess to you because you're such a phony. I'm not trying to be anyone"), her assertion of a stronger validity for the individual against the assumed role is both nonsensical and minatory in a world where such ontological certainty is not available. And so, rather than responding as Ondine to Davis's refusal to accept the Pope, Ondine juggles his outrage in an elaborate improvisation in a mode that condenses his two main personae. Her betrayal has undermined the conditions that made passage between his different roles possible, and so he responds simultaneously on all levels. Throwing coke into her face and slapping her, he attacks her physically rather than acting an attack on her, and his abuse amalgamates the discourse of the Pope ("You're a phony, You're a disgusting phony. May God forgive you") and that of the social group out

3.7 *The Chelsea Girls* (production still)

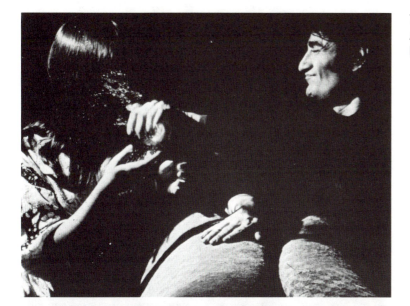

3.8–3.9 *The Chelsea Girls*: Pepper Davis and Ondine

of which the Pope was conjured ("She came up here tonight as a friend and then she tells me I'm a phony"). Apparently the outrage is felt so strongly that Ondine claims he cannot continue with the film, but even this refusal is sublated and incorporated into the film, the pretense reasserted up to the final moment when the whole event evolves into a self-valorizing reflexiveness: "This may be a *historical document*."

The more complex narratives that evolved from the one-shot nondramatic situations of the early films involved more fully artic-ulate locations instead of the Factory, a greater degree of fictional prescription, and the incorporation of the conventions of role playing. With the replacement of quasi-therapeutic acting out by acting proper, iconographic and histrionic reference to Hollywood could come into focus. And as the imitation of industrial production methods and production values eliminated the grammatical crudeness that had insistently foregrounded filmic self-consciousness, that reflexivity was relocated as an intradiegetic consideration of Hollywood, culminating in the complex intertextuality of the late films.

Though Warhol never lost sight of the commodity nature of the industrial product, the connections between the aesthetics of representation and capitalist media in general were not explicit, and the political content of his films rarely extends beyond sexual satire. When it does, as in the draft-resister section of *Nude Restaurant* or in the Hanoi Hannah sections of *The Chelsea Girls*, its forcefulness evaporates in the ironic contextualization. Without a political vocabulary, and desiring to revive rather than to undermine the movie industry, Warhol approached Hollywood at an angle; though his interest was never uncritical, and even when his films came to resemble the industrial product, his work—and the work of Paul Morrissey with which it became increasingly identified—remains essentially satirical. Though it is present in his first film, *Tarzan and Jane Regained . . . Sort of* (1963), Warhol's meditation on Hollywood replays his interest in the shifting ontologies of media reproduction up to the point at which a revival of thirties and forties cinema is orchestrated into a satire on the present state of the industry. The critique of Hollywood may be schematized in three main phases: the first entails the fragmentary appropriation of names, roles, and gestures from the golden age in narratives depicting the off-screen life of the stars (e.g., *Hedy*, *Screen Test #2*, *More Milk, Yvette*, and *Lupe*); the second consists of generic imitations (e.g., *Lonesome Cowboys*, a Western, and *Blue Movie*, a pornographic feature); and the third comprise remakes of specific films (e.g., *Heat* and *Frankenstein*).

Interest in the glamour and artifice of the screen goddesses and in camping Hollywood generally, common in homosexual subcultures, was also a common pretext for underground filmmaking, most notoriously in the group around Jack Smith.[10] Recreational dressing-up provided the basis for a parody of Hollywood in which the great stars and the great studios were mimicked in the daily life of Factory superstars. Stressing stylization over beauty, irony over engagement, theater over life,[11] this camp other world retains a subversive edge, for the colonization of fantasy by the culture industry is held in place by the self-consciousness of the artifice. The appropriation of the vocabulary of the classic movies as a means of aestheticizing everyday life certainly depends on identity confusions of the kind produced by the contradictory pleasures of the spectacle, but it is nevertheless quite distinct from the unconscious internalization of the values of the entertainment industry in passive consumption and psychic modeling. In any case, the Hollywood used by Warhol is essentially refuse, its commercial value dissipated in

10 Smith influenced Warhol enormously. Warhol filmed Smith filming *Normal Love* in 1963, and Smith acted in several films for Warhol, beginning with *Batman Dracula* in 1964.

11 These terms, summarizing the camp ethos of early sixties New York, I draw from Susan Sontag's 1964 essay "Notes on 'Camp' " (Sontag, 1966: 277–93).

countless revivals on late-night TV; the recycling appropriates this mass media debris and, in transforming it, transforms the drabness of everyday life.

The self-aggrandizement effected by Warhol's characters as they discover a fantasy self-image in imitating the mannerisms and appearance of the great stars simultaneously has the opposite effect of belittling and despoiling the stars' stature. This reciprocity, in which affection and debunking make each other possible, becomes more complex as the narrative organization and formal codes of Warhol's films begin to resemble—in however rudimentary a way—those of the Hollywood films he is critically reconsidering; always his works denigrate whatever industrial point of reference they celebrate. *Hedy*, a melodrama about the trial and death of Hedy Lamarr, for example, assaults both Hedy Lamarr and Mario Montez (the transvestite who plays her) explicitly in the plot and implicitly in the film's form. With constant verbal thrusts, the narrative follows her degradation from the surgeon's table where she is having her face lifted (Jack Smith's magnifying glass figuring intradiegetically the film's overall scrutiny), through her arrest for shoplifting, her trial and the indictment by her husbands, and her death by hemlock. Simultaneously, the stature of the historical Hedy Lamarr is eroded by the poverty of the production, the casual use of different parts of the Factory instead of locations, Warhol's undercutting of dramatic moments by his turning the camera to the walls or the floor,[12] and the obvious disparity between Montez and Lamarr. The film assaults not simply the reputation of Hedy Lamarr, but also Mario Montez's attempt to be *like* her in the double sense of playing her and himself becoming a movie star; but it is nevertheless an ordeal which earns for Montez the dignity of his death, and which allows Jack Smith's eulogy ("She was tragic and noble") in some measure to transcend irony.

Meta-generic works like *Lonesome Cowboys* and *Blue Movie* similarly foreground their refusal to reproduce key generic motifs and their desultoriness in approaching the conventions of the works they refer to. The sexual inversion of the cowboys ricochets back through all the Howard Hawks/John Wayne clichés of male bonding, eroding by caricature what is most central in them. While this quotation of generic codes differs only in degree from any new work's general acceptance of the conventions of its genre to ensure the legibility of its own innovations, it can be pushed to the point where the production as a whole becomes self-conscious. The tensions of the first silent portrait films come into play again as the players directly engage the camera and the other apparatus. The actress, Viva, is, in particular, often the means to such a dialogue between the film and its cast; she frequently verbalizes the conditions of her role and the terms of her performance of it, even as she alternately fulfills and rejects them. In *Blue Movie*, for example, she comments on both the difficulties and pleasures of acting in a pornographic film, sometimes engrossing herself in its requirements and then discussing them with her co-star or the camera: she mock-

12 Ronald Tavel has described at length Warhol's photography in *Hedy*: "As the action would move toward its most dramatic, move toward its point, its shattering, unbearable thing, the camera eye would move away, the camera eye would become bored with the action, with the story, with the problem of the star, klepto-mania and so forth, and would begin to explore the ceiling of the Factory. Well, I was just wiped out. I said this is just like something else. Beautiful. Horrible in terms of the script. . . . And that's why I always tell people that argue about why they're not called Tavel's films instead of Warhol's films. I say, well, go see *Hedy*" (cited in Koch, 1973: 75).

3.10 *Lonesome Cowboys*

3.11 *Lonesome Cowboys*: The rape

ingly accuses Louis Waldon of being disgusting for exposing his genitals "right in front of this lens," and all through the sex play she winks and smiles at the camera/spectator.

The generic debasement instanced by the tawdry sexuality and low production values establishes these films as anti-art, deliberately vulgar gestures of negation toward the commercial cinema, in the way that *Sleep* scorned the underground. Even *Blue Movie* subverts its genre, the pornographic art film, by taking its conventions to what at the time were unacceptable extremes of explicitness. Similarly, *Flesh* or *Trash*, strings of sexual encounters spaced by desultory narrative interludes but essentially without other dramatic rhythm, merely adds a little interest in character to the structural

3.12 *Lonesome Cowboys*: Viva

form of feature pornography that Warhol had accepted as early as *Couch* five years before. They affront commercial expectations as much by retarding the narrative in prolonged visual scrutiny of their stars as by their salacious subject matter. Here the investigation of role playing opens up into a double critique of Hollywood, in which a social element and a thematic/formal element make each other possible: the revival of the star system of the thirties allows the process of visual consumption to be foregrounded. The mixture of satire and affection in the invocation of "the movies" is subsumed in what is at once a dramatization and a valorization of the use of the medium for extravagant self-presentation.

Given Warhol's interest in the politics of glamour, his revival of the star system of the classic cinema and its characteristic histrionic modes was entirely logical, even if it did take place at a time when Hollywood was elsewhere being rewritten as a director's cinema. The range of histrionic modes produced during the transition from the mannered, gestured styles inherited from stage melodrama and the silents to the close identification between actor and role that subsequently culminated in the Actor's Studio Method had allowed acting in the thirties self-consciously to "acknowledge its own abstraction" and "enjoy its dissimilarity to existential modes of behaviour" (Affron, 1977: 6–7) in a way exactly appropriate to the intricate ambiguities of the self-presentation of transvestites and male prostitutes—the characteristic subjects of Warhol's late films. The unstable relationship between actor and role in these films extends Warhol's previous interest in relaying already simulated identities through further levels of artifice. As Stephen Koch has pointed out, both the denial of anatomical reality in the transvestite and the separation of self from body employed by the hustler to distinguish himself from his johns produce a confusion in sexual identity: "Sexuality is the pivot of a conundrum about being and appearing"

(Koch, 1973: 122). In the Warhol world of surfaces, multiple reproduction, and sexual disguise, let alone in the world of his films, any such polarization of reality and appearance cannot be sustained, but it does provide the basis for a more or less consistent and recognizable acting style; the actor neither fully inhabits the role nor creates any constant distance from it by, for example, quoting it in the Brechtian manner. The fitful and often tangential engagement of the role jeopardizes its authority, leaving it constantly on the point of disintegrating, even though it is equally axiomatic that the actor revealed in the gaps can never be fully independent of the persona, never authentically himself.

In the case of Joe Dallesandro, the distance between himself and his body, isolated as an object of visual consumption and of promised though always deferred physical consumption for the audience and the john, produces the extreme passiveness of both his role as a stud and his style as an actor. The sexual performance he provides

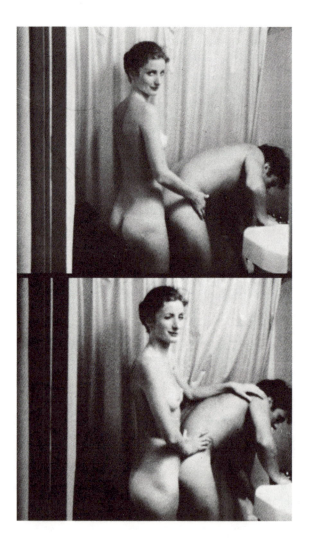

3.13 *Blue Movie*: Viva and Louis Waldon

for his johns and the acting performance he provides for his films' audience are both characterized by his absence, his failure; it is only his ability to make other people look at him and his willingness to endure their gaze that allow his activity in either area. Like the Hollywood heroine, he can never look, only be looked at, a fact that *Flesh* emphasizes right up to the final scene, in which his attention and gaze are at last attracted by the "lesbian" embraces of his wife and her lover. Like the infinitely more complex multiplication of gazes in the mirror in which Paul America watches himself being watched by Ed MacDermott in the second reel of *My Hustler*, the scene in *Flesh* in which Maurice Bradell pays Dallesandro simply to strike erotic poses is an especially articulate version of such scenarios of scopophilia, in which the spectator's, the camera's, and the performer's gazes coincide upon his body. Reduced to an object of visual consumption, he enacts this function both *in* the film and *for* the film, producing moments of metaphoric reflexivity when his relation to the film viewer is figured intradiegetically. Dallesandro's dramatic situation restates the use the film makes of him; while *Flesh* is the vehicle for his stardom, it is itself pimped by Morrissey ("Produced by Andy Warhol") to the audience. In the economics of spectatorship, each of us is the industry's john and Bradell our proxy.

For Dallesandro and the other hustlers, the female role of being looked at entails their absence from their bodies and so produces a minimalist style of acting in which—like Nico—they are never fully present except as visual objects; for the transvestites, on the other hand, as for Ondine, the need is to maximize rather than minimize their presence. Their acting consequently is a hyperbolic, highly gestural pastiche of fragments of different codes of femininity, the interaction between the different degrees of it and the various vocabularies for it being the source of multiple narrative ironies. Probably *Women in Revolt* (*Sex*) contains the fullest spectrum of such interactions among the different caricature feminists: Jackie Curtis as the schoolma'am, Candy Darling as the lesbian socialite, and Holly Woodlawn as the lusting "heterosexual" backslider. But even here, where the social satire is as strong as anywhere, it is routed through satire on the state of the movie industry. Though it may be the occasion for comedic interludes involving a producer and a columnist, Candy Darling's attempt to become a Hollywood star while there is still a Hollywood to star in invokes a Hollywood that now exists only as her performance and acting reincarnate it. The desire of biological males to become females is reproduced as the desire of women to become stars, and the career of Candy Darling in *Women in Revolt* (*Sex*) is again only the fullest embodiment of the condition reaching back to Mario Montez, the appropriation of thirties' glamour as the means of becoming both star and female.

The hustler and transvestite roles are wittily juxtaposed in a single scene in *Flesh* in which on one side of a room Joe Dallesandro is being blown by Geri Miller and on the other Jackie Curtis and Candy Darling are reading old Hollywood fanzines, mentally re-

3.14 *My Hustler*: Ed MacDermott and
Paul America

casting themselves in the image of Joan Crawford. Orally consumed
by Miller, Dallesandro is visually consumed by Curtis and Darling.
With his back to the camera he looks away from everyone, presenting his face in profile, upon which may be read the effect of Miller's
ministrations, themselves, as in *Blow Job*, out of sight. Although in
the production still both groups of characters are in frame at the
same time, in the film itself they are not; the camera pans or cuts
from one side of the scene to the other so that, as in the twin-screen
projections, one side is placed in competition with the other, the
exchange of glances passing from screen to screen, from the image
of the subject of visual consumption to the image of the object of
visual consumption, a doubled relay dramatizing the real and the
fantasy roles within spectatorship.

Just as his first paintings, differentiated only by brush strokes
from the advertisements they depicted, made both themselves and
their relation to their subjects ironic, Warhol's late films move to a
place in the popular culture adjacent to Hollywood, yet they reserve
a formal and an economic difference from the dominant industry.
Even at his most commercial and despite his scorn for the "artiness"
of Warhol's early films, Morrissey retained the key tropes of their
formal vocabulary: the long take and the uninflected gaze of the

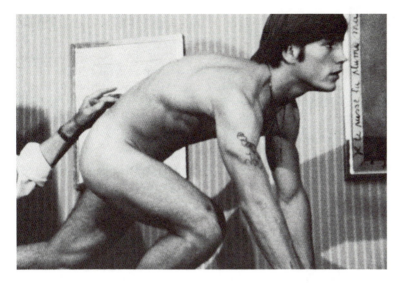

3.15 *Flesh*: Joe Dallesandro

camera, its movement restricted to pans and zooms, which together construct the coherent spatial and temporal frame inside which the actors mobilize the interplay between the various levels of their roles. Since cuts are not bridged by sound continuity, or scenes broken down into shot/counter shot codes, orthodox editing that would nest close-ups inside masters and suture the spectator inside reconstituted diegetic space and time is impossible. In place of that optical and ideological incorporation, the spectator is stranded upon his or her self-consciousness. And so, while Warhol's celebrated reinvention of the history of motion pictures did produce some striking parallels in his ontogenetic recapitulation (though none more crisp than that between *Kiss*, his first released film, and

3.16 *Flesh* (production still)

the eponymous Edison short), the approach to Hollywood grammar and the modes of audience involvement register an institutional migration whose controlling level is economic and social. In addition to the different filmic strategies set in motion, several other material concomitants of this relocation from the art world through the underground film subculture and into the wider public realm of industrial culture and pure publicity are important, especially the constitution of the audience and the nature of authorship.

The move from amateur, domestic projection at the Factory to public commercial screenings—first at the Cinematheque and then at the Regency Theater, where *The Chelsea Girls* provided Warhol with his first popular and financial success—and eventually to suburban theaters produced—even as it was produced by—a quantitative and a qualitative transformation in the terms by which the audience was constituted. Though even the earliest films had distinct subcultural functions—sexual advertising, for instance, or the flattery of patrons—their public audience was essentially nonexistent, a largely theoretical implication of the performing situation and the technology of reproduction. Many of the films were never shown, shown only during parties at the Factory when other things were going on, or shown as part of multiple sensoria like the Exploding Plastic Inevitable; or they were screened publicly and the audience walked out. Reflecting the primacy of shooting over exhibition in Warhol's early cinema, his audience was first merely a fictional construct allowing the camera to signify spectatorship and so produce anxiety and exhibitionism in the profilmic, and second the means by which the fact that Warhol's films were essentially unwatchable and denied all the activities of which spectatorship was supposed to consist could be put into public circulation.

As a de facto audience materialized, drawn at first by the scandal and then by the figuration of scandalousness in pornography, and as changing public attitudes to sexual experimentation allowed the films to be exhibited in public theaters, the audience's actual presence and optical engagement accorded the films certification as a pop phenomenon in the publicity apparatus of consumer society. For only a genuinely popular audience could open the full register of the star roles and fully mobilize the ambiguities within them. As the agent of perception became the general public, the actors entered the world of magazine stories, talk-show appearances, and conversational references; they became part of the vocabulary of public intercourse and so achieved existence in the media at large. The disparity between fantasy and reality, set in motion in the early appropriations of Hollywood iconography, was bridged as stardom became a habitation rather than a pretense, an actuality rather than an artifice. The audience for any specific film and, in fact, any specific spectator activity both were subordinate to the-audience-in-general, the subject of the communications industry as whole.

This redefinition of the audience throughout Warhol's development from transactions in the medium of film to transactions in the social and economic systems of cinema and beyond—in the media—

complements parallel continuities and displacements in Warhol's own activity. Though his professional status as an artist or film-maker was predicated on his ability to compose visual phenomena, his optical and technical skills were only the point of origin for his manipulation of entrepreneurial possibilities in the public contexts in which these visual events existed.

The various stages of Warhol's formal and thematic preoccupations run parallel to varying modalities of his role in his films' production. Although marked by substantial differences, the developments in his work as a producer essentially extend—again from *medium* to *media*—the scope of a limited repertoire of operations that can be summarized as his systematic withdrawal of authorial presence as the means of asserting control over production and proprietorship of its fruits. Until structural film, most other underground filmmakers understood their engagement with the medium as the heroic inscription of self in films generically defined as personal. But Warhol chose to forego both highly idiosyncratic work on the film material and the creation of a personal vision of the world, and then to proffer these refusals as the rationale for ownership. The managerial project—the assumption of the industrial division of labor, his increasing delegation of responsibility, and his reservation of his own activity largely to the administration of what became virtually a mini-corporation diversified through all areas of the culture industry—that accompanied his migration from art film to feature production thus in essence extended the formal and thematic concerns of his first films, even as his eventual intradiegetic attention to the history and forms of Hollywood enabled the narrative elaboration of his earliest obsessions.

As his control of the profilmic space expanded into control of the public space of mass cultural consumption, Warhol acquired the power of impeding access to the cinematic apparatus, of making performance invisible and thus nonexistent. His idiosyncratic strategies of *own*-ing, then, were also strategies of exclusion: the stationary camera excluded off-screen space; the moving camera allowed him to reject different areas in the profilmic; later, twin and multi-screen projection forced different films to compete with each other; and, in the feature films, he was able to deny stardom to all but the few he admitted into the public arena of self-exhibition, the film. Finally the films themselves were withdrawn and made unavailable, and all that remained was sheer reputation, fame, publicity. His installation of himself as a device for securing public attention, a device for mediating between a product and the public, began as a feature of style to end as a marketing strategy. To this extent all his investigations on film of the play between the profilmic and the apparatus are autobiographical allegories; they all dramatize his career in the media.

An episode in his lifelong engagement with the media at large, Warhol's investigation of the condition of being in the attention of film was a means of securing his own prominence in the media. Like his previous move from the world of advertising to that of fine art, his social and economic empowerment was facilitated as much by contemporary changes in the relation of the art and film worlds to the needs and possibilities of an increasingly information-producing and consumption-dependent capitalism as by his own peculiar visual ability and historical sense; but his manipulation of the moment of consumer capitalism by artwork was uniquely successful. Other painters and sculptors of the period effected changes in the formal concerns and social location of underground film, but even the most entrepreneurial among them, like Michael Snow, never had any impact outside the art world. Warhol's medium was the media itself, his business was the production of art; and the metaphor of the producer specifies his achievement in appropriate industrial terms.

Although producers have only rarely been considered *auteurs* (Val Lewton is a conspicuous exception, along with Mark Hellinger, Dore Schary, and, of course, in the sixties, Roger Corman), Warhol showed how that function controlled and determined all others in the communications industry. In doing so, he called into question the rhetoric of romantic authorship, clarifying film as commodity production writing itself as textual production. He thus brought into visibility what such romantic rhetoric had obscured: that making film is a social and material act taking place in history. His genius was to arrange it so that the "creative visionary" and the "shrewd businessman" in their joint operations consistently ratified the other's activity. But even as he did so he reserved that space—a narrow one finally, but a space nevertheless—from which the entire operation could be illuminated by its own self-consciousness. As the title of his first film suggested, Hollywood was "regained" . . . but only "sort of."

Underground Film: Leaping from the Grave

4

Perhaps it is not possible to rescue cinema from its
living grave? It is after all a black art
                            of shadows and passing illusions.
— Stan Vanderbeek

What is going to be made and seen in the next ten years would cause
your grandfather to leap from the grave.
— Ron Rice

Film and the Beat Generation

Of the independent productions of the late fifties, two films in
particular, *Shadows* by John Cassavetes and *Pull My Daisy* by Robert Frank and Alfred Leslie, marked the appearance of a cinema significantly different from that organized around studio-produced
narrative features. Each won a *Film Culture* award, in 1959 and
1960 respectively, and the award citations speak in similar terms
to the freshness and vigor of the elements of cinéma vérité each contained, and to their potential for revitalizing the traumatized American industrial cinema: *Shadows* displayed an "improvisation,
spontaneity, and free inspiration that are almost entirely lost in
most films from an excess of professionalism," and *Daisy*'s "modernity and its honesty, its sincerity and its humility, its imagination
and its humor, its freshness, and its truth [were] without comparison in our last year's pompous cinematic production" (cited in Sitney, 1970: 423–24). Turning away from historical reconstructions
and other spectacular fifties genres and focusing on their producers'
daily lives in contemporary New York, both films were populated
by existentialist intellectuals and struggling artists—standard countercultural types of the period, such as jazz musicians, painters,
writers, and, in *Daisy*, even a railroad man: the Beat Generation.

Only two years had passed since the publication of the book that
gave that generation its self-image, and like *On the Road*, whose all
but verbatim transcription of the exploits of beatniks prefigured a
decade of nonfiction novels, both films approach the status as well
as the style of the cinéma vérité documentary, positing the primacy
of everyday life in the work of art, even as they invoke the beat
priority of the aestheticization of the quotidian. But, unlike MGM's
version of Jack Kerouac's *The Subterraneans*, released the next year,
and all the beatnik exploitation films that followed *Bucket of Blood*

and *Beat Girl*, these were not mass-market films made by a studio about the beat subculture. They came not from Hollywood but from the milieus they depicted, and they were produced by people who were themselves as disaffected as the beats with both the film industry and American society as a whole. Though neither is an underground film in the sense that will be argued here—in fact, it is their different positions vis-à-vis the beat aesthetic that enable us to clarify what underground film entailed—still both forayed into the territory that the underground was discovering. Deriving from strong currents of extra-studio attempts to develop a film culture more responsive to the pressing issues of American life, both films made it clear that the crisis in cinema could not be solved without substantial reorganization of the conditions of industrial production.

In the late fifties filmmakers in New York, particularly, had been seeking alternatives to the sclerotic industry. The most significant of many attempts to organize independent production was The Group, formed in 1960 as an affiliation of twenty-three independent producers, directors, actors, and theater managers, including Shirley Clarke, Lionel Rogosin, Peter Bogdanovich, Robert Frank, Alfred Leslie, Adolfas Mekas, Émile de Antonio, Bert Stein, Ben Carruthers, Argus Speare Juilliard, and Gregory Markopoulos. They were called together by Jonas Mekas and by a stage and film producer, Lewis Allen. In their manifesto, "The First Statement of the New American Cinema Group," published in *Film Culture* in the summer of 1961, they indicted the "official cinema."

The official cinema all over the world is running out of breath. It is morally corrupt, aesthetically obsolete, thematically superficial, temperamentally boring. Even the seemingly worthwhile

4.1 *The Subterraneans*

films, those that lay claim to high moral and aesthetic standards and have been accepted as such by critics and the public alike, reveal the decay of the Product Film. The very slickness of their execution has become a perversion covering the falsity of their themes, their lack of sensitivity, their lack of style. (Sitney, 1970: 80)

Presenting itself as the confluence of substantial but previously sporadic and uncoordinated manifestations of new filmmaking, the group invoked the European New Waves in attacking the Hollywood production and distribution systems and their attendant aesthetic criteria. The statement argued against producers, distributors, and investors; against censorship; against existing methods of financing; and, citing *Shadows* and *Daisy* as evidence, against the "Budget Myth" that good films could not be produced for $20,000 to $25,000. As an alternative, plans were made to establish the group's own cooperative distribution center, a support fund, and its own film festival as a forum for the New Cinema from all over the world. The group also intended to renegotiate union salaries. The manifesto ended by specifying the one basic difference between the group and "organizations such as 'United Artists' " (an ironic choice, given the fact that UA had itself originated as a cooperative alternative to established studios): "We are not joining together to make money. We are joining together to make films."

Despite this conclusion, they asserted the project's commercial viability; their claim that "paradoxically, low budget films give a higher profit margin than big-budget films" suggested that, qualitative considerations aside, the group did not envisage using the medium substantially differently from the way Hollywood did. To be sure, their films were to be better than those produced in Hollywood, more serious, honest, mature, or responsible—or any other of those qualities that the underground so joyfully rejected—but they were to be made according to the industrial model of professional production and public consumption.

Though independent feature production of this kind outside the studios did continue through the sixties, projects like that of the New American Cinema Group failed to crystallize into a self-sustaining mode of production or to produce a socially viable formal vocabulary. Even those of the group who continued to make films, most importantly Émile de Antonio, Shirley Clarke, and Jonas and Adolfas Mekas, did so only by abandoning its quasi-industrial premises. Without a base either in the industry or in the social energy of the period, the project they promised lacked a cultural or ideological constituency. Instead of inaugurating a reformed industrial practice, American cinema came back to life by inventing an extra-industrial and, in fact, an anti-industrial use of the medium; for this *Pull My Daisy*, but not *Shadows*, provided a model.

Soon after these two films were exhibited, Parker Tyler wrote an article in *Film Culture*—the most significant film journal of the time—entitled "For *Shadows*, Against *Pull My Daisy*." While rec-

4.2 John Cassavetes, *Shadows*: Rupert
Crosse, Hugh Hurd, and Lelia Goldoni

ognizing their common superficial resemblance to documentary, he
argued that *Daisy*'s "pretensions are futile and unfresh, far removed
from life's center," whereas *Shadows*, despite obviously gauche and
unnecessary scenes like that in the Museum of Modern Art sculpture garden or in the literary party (both of which were added in the
second version),[1] had "the courage to reveal human depths raw
with controversy" and was "fresher . . . and close to life's center"
(Tyler, 1962: 32). Tyler's preference for *Shadows* is unanswerable
on its own terms: compared not only with *Daisy* but even with less
sentimental quasi-documentaries like Ben Maddow's *The Savage
Eye* of the same year, let alone with anything in the industrial cinema, *Shadows* was vigorously innovative in paring down generic,
histrionic, and photographic conventions. The loosely episodic
story of struggling jazz musicians and white intellectuals, whose climax is the distress caused by a case of mistaken racial identity, is
distinguished by abrupt shifts in mood, both between scenes and
within them; by its general avoidance of stock character types
(though often it is difficult to know whether Ben Carruthers's parody of the James Dean hipster is a function of the actor or the role);
by its indirect sidling up to moments of thematic tension and dramatic release that produces an angular, fragmented narrative; and
by its refusal to resolve its narrative premises in an emotionally satisfying but unrealistic closure. The maturity of its approach to racial
and other social tensions is thus corroborated in the economy and
immediacy of its style, a humanist translation of social issues into
psychodrama that reinvigorates the codes of the acted, narrative,
realist fiction film.

These same priorities and techniques also mark the social and
aesthetic limitations of Cassavetes' project; the compromises and
dissimulation they entail make viable the film's commodity function
but discredit the existential authenticity it claims. The restriction of

1 Throughout I refer only to the
second version of *Shadows*, which is
apparently, in ways germane to the
present discussion, inferior to the
first. See Mekas (1972: 10–11).

4.3–4.4 John Cassavetes, *Shadows*: Lelia Goldoni and Anthony Ray

improvisation and profilmic play to the simulation of dramatic characters in an essentially orthodox plot and unified diegesis, however vigorous these may be, does not investigate alternatives to the conventions of the industrial feature and its received social functions, but only re-legitimizes them. In this, the film is in contradiction with the ideology of the subculture it explores and from which

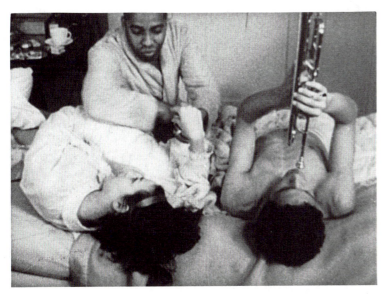

4.5 John Cassavetes, *Shadows*: Lelia Goldoni, Hugh Hurd, and Ben Carruthers

it derives its interest, and also with its own partial appropriation of the beat priorities, the aesthetic elaboration of the real-life experiences of its participants. The close identification between actor and role, in which the actors' use of their own names implies that the situations they rehearse are personally felt rather than merely professionally assumed, is supposed to empower their fictional interaction with the added energy and credibility of the quasi-therapeutic working through of real-life relationships. This primary conceit is, however, disastrously exposed at precisely the moment when it is called into play to justify the film's claim to significance as an honest confrontation of real racial tensions, its "close[ness] to life's center."

Shadows' structural center and thematic peripeteia is the horrified revulsion of the White male, Tony, on discovering that Lelia, the apparently White woman he has been dating, is in fact Black, the sister of Black jazz musicians. But, as did MGM in casting Leslie Caron as Mardou Fox in *The Subterraneans*, Cassavetes chose a White actress for the role of the Black woman. Demolishing the pseudo-existentialist, documentarist pretensions of the drama and generating entirely spurious narrative tensions, his prevarication is compounded by the absurd expectation that anyone could believe Lelia Goldoni to be Black or accept that the plot should hinge on such a flimsy deception. The casting choice pre-empts any comprehension of how the discovery of Lelia's feigned Blackness could so traumatize Tony, and so short-circuits any statement the film might make about racism. The refusal to attempt to represent what the film invokes as its most explosive ethical and aesthetic crux is finally a political equivocation. Reenacting the pandemic exploitation of Black women, the film's manipulation of the audience at exactly the point when its vaunted authenticity most calls for validation exposes the fraudulence of its premises. Similarly, its outrage that a skilled jazz musician is reduced to introducing floozies in a nightclub, its lingering on the sexploitation movie marquees in Times Square, and its other gestures of liberal social commentary, as well as its conspicuous stylistic traits—graininess, hand-held camera, and extreme close-ups, articulated respectively as realism, spontaneity, and psychological probing—all collapse back into the formal strategies of the feature film.

Despite its location on the edge of the beat world, *Shadows* was "not part of the Beat da-da-da" (Tyler, 1962: 29) but essentially only "just another Hollywood film" (Mekas, 1972: 10). Paving the way for Cassavetes' Hollywood career, it made use of production values sufficiently different from the industrial norm and it appropriated just enough of the counterculture to provide an edge of novelty, but in neither case was it so different that it called into question the industrial feature or its social function.

Pull My Daisy on the other hand was very much "part of the Beat da-da-da." Narrated by Jack Kerouac and derived from his unproduced play *The Beat Generation*, about Neal Cassady's home, it featured Allen Ginsberg and Gregory Corso, lacking of the most

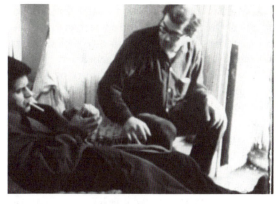
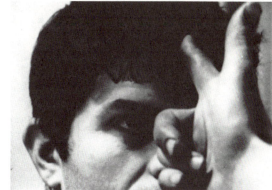

4.6–4.10 Robert Frank, *Pull My Daisy*

important beat writers only William Burroughs. Of the other play-ers, Larry Rivers was a prominent painter, as were Alfred Leslie, the director, and Alice Neal, who played the bishop's mother. Robert Frank, the film's photographer, had recently published his cele-brated book of photographs, *The Americans*.[2] Beat motifs like spontaneous poetry performance, modern jazz, reference to Bud-dhism, smoking marijuana, and homosexual bonding, as well as the bohemian artistic life of New York's lower East Side, are promi-nent, and for a commercial film it is an unusually thorough and coherent instance of subcultural representation. It begins to articu-

2 *The Americans*, Frank's spectacu-lar photographic documentation of a typically beat cross-country jour-ney, had an introduction by Ker-ouac, and the second edition in 1969 contained a page of frame en-largements from *Daisy*.

late beat ethics and aesthetics filmically, using beat values not to renovate the conventions of the narrative feature but to create alternatives to it. This is not to say that *Daisy* is in any real sense an improvised film. It derived from a script, it was rehearsed, and the released half-hour film was edited out of thirty hours of footage shot. Even Kerouac's apparently spontaneous voice-over was a composite of three separate takes. The film was produced as a commodity, financed by Wall Street investors at a time when beatniks were a popular fad and could be expected to produce a return. Despite these involvements, its disassembling of the conventions of narrative and character made both filmic and profilmic available to the possibilities of a new cinema.

Elements of a plot, one that allegorizes the impact of the beats on American society at large, remain; during a single day a nuclear family consisting of a woman, her child, and her railroadman husband is invaded and disrupted by a pair of beery beatniks, a bishop, and finally jazz musicians. The beatniks and the musicians gather round the husband and press him first to expel the bishop and then to leave his wife and his home for an entirely male night on the town. But this narrative is only fitfully and indirectly implied; it neither imposes its economy upon the film nor contains the profilmic activity or its filmic reproduction. The characters assimilate to their dramatic roles in differing degrees, ranging from the "method" identification of Delphine Seyrig with her role as the wife—complete with the enactment of anxiety and anger—to the *in propriae personae* play of Ginsberg and Corso around the self-conscious aestheticization and dramatization of what are basically their own characters. In *Shadows* improvisation is a superior form of acting, the fabrication of a consistent and autonomous though still spurious authenticity; *Daisy* prefigures Warhol's relentless anatomization of the inauthenticity of self-representation by recognizing that improvisation is a condition of being, and that identity is only an artifice. And rather than knitting the various self-fabrications into a homogenous and unified diegesis, the film allows each to float erratically, only sporadically and fragmentarily anchoring the others.

Whereas the innovation of *Shadows* was the discovery of an economy that tightened the actors' identification with their role to the point that each gesture and glance asserted a troubled specificity, *Daisy*'s is one of profligacy, a careless expenditure, an embrace of *sterility*[3] in which the predictive or retrospective signification of any action is confounded in the exercise of the present. Narrative climaxes like Gregory Corso's confrontation with the bishop or Milo's quarrel with his wife have not been prepared for, they are unintegrated and unresolved; and the film casually cuts away in unmotivated interpolations whose origins or functions are not specified. De-centered and only loosely structured, it distributes the authorship of its action casually among the participants rather than constraining them to the singleness of pre-extant narrative necessity. As Kerouac summarily remarks, "These guys aren't paying any attention . . . they're just blowing."

3 The term is Lyotard's (Lyotard, 1978) and is used to specify those movements in film that are not reengaged by other movements in its economy; existing only for their own pleasure, they thus occur at the expense of the whole and jeopardize it.

The plurality of this narrative is reproduced visually in the composition and camera movement, which maintain the apartment interior in a constant flux, continually rearranging it by pans that pull it into new patterns of depth and new planes, new patterns of unbalanced interpenetration of domestic space and artist's studio, and continually fluctuating, highly chiaroscurist patterns of black masses and everyday objects. Like the commentary of the *benshi* in Japanese film, Kerouac's voice-over maintains the spectacle at a distance, preempting the suture of lip-sync and ensuring that the scenes will be contemplated rather than entered; the narration's lack of authority in explaining the multiple goings-on cannot meld the visuals into a single, unified audio-visual diegesis, but only multiply their inconclusiveness which, aided by the fragmentary jazz track, spins off only fresh possibilities of irresolution.

Without itself fully achieving a beat aesthetic, *Daisy* recognizes the terms of such; cutting into the conventions of dramatic narrative, it clears the ground upon which, subsequently, such values could be more thoroughly elaborated. The jazz music which is its unifying device and narrative climax is thus also its closest formal analogue. Like the melody in the modern jazz solo, conventions of character and narrative are only a point of departure, to be mutilated, transformed, invoked, and occasionally touched on. For the spectator they are always to be glimpsed and inferred rather than read directly. Thus, *Daisy*'s aesthetic is at least partially one of negation; the rejection of the novelistic is the point of departure for an art of refusal and transgression which, like dada, challenges the premise that art is more ordered than life. As Tyler elsewhere noted, underground films were always "curiously 'documentary' " in that at least they "document the traditional social activity of making life itself into a work of art" (Tyler, 1969: 69). As such a "documentary," *Pull My Daisy* is a premonition of a properly beat film, heralding, though itself only partially developing, a new kind of activity in the profilmic, new criteria in the filmic, and eventually a new use for film—all consonant with beat aesthetics: the rescue of cinema from the grave.[4]

The first major instance of the breakdown of the postwar consensus, the Beat Generation marked the beginning of a continuous current of bohemianism that lasted into the seventies, a counterculture whose various names—beat, hipster, and eventually hippie—masked a continuity in its attitude to social involvement and social change. The beats did produce critiques of mainstream society—of its lack of spontaneity or joy, its conformity and repressiveness, its moribundity, and especially its cold-war militarism—which were not that different from the contemporary sociological commentary that developed in the wake of David Riesman's concept of "other-directedness" in *The Lonely Crowd* (1950). But the dominant beat response aimed not to change American society so much as to disengage from it in acts of individual rebellion. Suffering "not from political apathy but from political antipathy" (Polsky, 1969: 156), the beats were anti-political rather than merely apolitical, believing

4 On countercultures and subcultures generally, see especially Clarke et al. (1976). Though it is entirely uncritical, Roszak (1969) is the classic apologia. I generally follow his lead in reserving the term "counterculture" for those primarily White, middle-class, quietist attempts to disengage from dominant society, distinct from the politically activist social organizations that grew up around the civil rights struggle and Vietnam War protest. Though written as early as 1957, Kenneth Rexroth's essay, "Disengagement: The Art of the Beat Generation" (Rexroth, 1957), remains the best single piece on the beats, followed by Lawrence Lipton's "Disaffiliation: The Way of the Beat Generation" (Lipton, 1959: 149–50). The various novels and poetry of the beats themselves remain the authorized versions of beat life, but the sociological studies of the New York beat scene by Polsky (Polsky, 1969) and the San Francisco scene by Rigney and Smith (Rigney and Smith, 1961), as well as Lipton's recollections of Venice West (Lipton, 1959: 70–89) and Partridge's work on the hippies (Partridge, 1973), give voice to those elements in the subcultures that were not themselves literarily productive. Newfield (1966) is especially useful in placing the beats in the context of subsequent youth cultures.

Unlike structural social distinctions, specifically class, the sequence of countercultures that began with the beats cannot be defined exactly. Like other middle-class formations, it was not a clearly articulated social grouping so much as a "diffuse counter-culture *milieu*" (Clarke et al., 1976: 60)—a cluster of ideological predispositions assumed by an unspecifiable number of people with varying degrees of thoroughness and commitment and a life style inhabited for a greater or lesser period. The full-time beats—and even that notion is something of a contradiction, since all but the hardest core were obliged to work at some point—estimated by Polsky to be no fewer than two thousand in New York (Polsky, 1969: 174), lived out a social renunciation that was diffused, with varying degrees of purity, through adjacent groups and

that any systematic attempt to reconstruct society as a whole by rationally derived and progressively implemented programs could only reproduce the materialism and instrumentalism that made modern civilization, in Allen Ginsberg's term, a Moloch devouring its own children.

Circumscribed as much by its own ancestry in the traditions of populist transcendentalism as by the paranoia of the cold war, the beat revolt was aesthetic, romantically proposing a revolution of consciousness in art as the origin of social renovation. Illuminated by the crystal euphoria of LSD in the mid-sixties, this radical idealism eventually looked to spontaneous spiritual transformation rather than concrete social action. Ken Kesey's proposal that the only way to end the Vietnam War was for everybody to look at it "and turn your backs and say . . . Fuck it" (Wolfe, 1968: 199) is only a particularly terse example of a wider rejection of the political as such, whose counterweight was the liberation of consciousness summarized in Timothy Leary's advice to "Turn on, Tune in, and Drop out." But as it passed from an entirely underground phenomenon into a wider cultural possibility, beat quietism revealed the social possibilities of its ethic of individualism, demonstrating that the aesthetic could provide the basis for a minority culture of general social potential. Though it was commonly the metaphor, the agent, and the arena of dissent, art was inseparable at all these points from the construction of alternative social formations. The film production of the beats was no exception; it too was primarily an aesthetic movement whose functions and priorities were social.

The period of the underground film can be reasonably dated from *Pull My Daisy* in 1959 to the run of *The Chelsea Girls* at the Cinema Rendezvous on West 57th Street, New York, in the summer of 1966—the last and the most scandalous of a series of dramatic eruptions of the underground into the attention of the general public. That year, riots in Chicago, New York, and Watts and organized resistance to the war revealed the inadequacy of the social disengagement that had sustained underground film, while a year later *Wavelength* brought formal interests of a quite different order to bear upon the non-industrial use of the medium. The alternative practices of film that flourished in this time are unmeasureable: the modulation of underground film into home movies on the one hand and the industrial exploitation of underground film's energy on the other allow for no exact generic definition in formal terms, even as the essentially amateur basis of production and the irregular methods of distribution and preservation provide no dependable basis for enumeration. It is unlikely that Sheldon Renan's estimate in the spring of 1966 that "fantastic numbers of people [were] producing personal 'art films' " (Renan, 1967: 18) will be improved upon.[5] Though some categorizations are possible—the use of 8 or 16mm rather than 35mm, for example—and though subgeneric formal clusters can be isolated, still the term *underground* invokes not a set of formal qualities, as do the earlier *experimental* and the later *structural,* so much as a method of production.

eventually, by means of both beat cultural production and mainstream media interest, through society at large. For a model analysis of the interrelation between aesthetics and social subcultures, see Hebdige (1979).

The relation between the beat subculture and underground film is most fully elaborated by Parker Tyler (1969), who recognizes the function of film in producing the social organization: "It *encourages* beatnik expressions through its practical rule of universal tolerance" (ibid.: 32). See also T. K. Alexander (1967) for the relation between underground film and West Coast counterculture. Though here we distinguish underground film from mass media representation of beats, elements of the beat image were set in motion by Hollywood, not only in the fifties films about rebellious youth like Laslo Benedek's *The Wild One* (1953) or Nicholas Ray's *Rebel Without A Cause* (1953), but also in film noir. Kerouac mentions Dane Clark, John Garfield, and Humphrey Bogart as the first actors to portray beats on the screen (Kerouac, 1959: 42).

5 In 1955 Jonas Mekas estimated that there were forty art filmmakers in New York City and perhaps four hundred throughout the country. See Mekas (1955: 16).

Definitions are risky, for the underground film is nothing less than an *explosion* of cinematic styles, forms, and directions. If it can be called a genre, it is a genre that can be defined only by a cataloging of the individual works assigned to it. The film medium is rich with possibilities, and the underground film-maker has widely explored these possibilities, with the result that there are almost as many different kinds of underground films as there are underground film-makers.

The underground film *is* a certain kind of film. It is a film conceived and made essentially by one person and is a *personal statement* by that person. It is a film that dissents radically in form, or in technique, or in content, or perhaps in all three. It is usually made for very little money, frequently under a thousand dollars, and its exhibition is outside commercial film channels. (Renan, 1967: 17)

Along with their controlling reference to personal expressiveness, Renan's remarks are notable for the oppositional nature of their definitions.[6] His emphasis on the heterogeneity of underground films, their dissent in matters of technique and content, and their exhibition outside usual channels suggests a surprising continuity between his assessment and the first use of the term "underground film" by Manny Farber. In his essay on films that played "an anti-art role in Hollywood," Farber celebrated the "huge amount of un-prized second-gear celluloid" produced by the "true masters of the male action film—such soldier-cowboy-gangster directors as Raoul Walsh, Howard Hawks, William Wellman, William Kieghley, the early pre-*Stagecoach* John Ford, Anthony Mann" (Farber, 1957: 432). These, the B pictures in which *auteur* theorists would discover directorial authorship, were, he suggested, distinguished by their vigor and unpretentiousness, as if in the forties these Hollywood directors had contested a decadent industry from the inside in the way the underground proper subsequently did from the outside.

In its early use after Farber, "underground" referred not to a film's style but to its provenance; in 1961, for instance, Stan Vanderbeek wrote of "The Cinema Delimina—Films from the Underground" (Vanderbeek, 1961), and in a May 1963 *Village Voice* review, Jonas Mekas pinpointed "the real revolution in cinema today," noting four films (*The Queen of Sheba Meets the Atom Man, Flaming Creatures, Little Stabs at Happiness*, and *Blonde Cobra*) among the movies that had "appeared from the underground" (Mekas, 1972: 85). Whereas Renan, in the movement's ripeness, speaks of underground films, both Vanderbeek and Mekas, when the movement was underway but still far from popular, invoke a social origin; they speak of films *from* the underground, a source whose clandestine nature is made explicit by Vanderbeek's subsequent reference to artists, poets, and experimentalists who were obliged to work as if they were "secret members of the underground" (Vanderbeek, 1961: 8).

The term's original resonances were, then, thoroughly political.[7]

6 For surveys of the categories of underground film, see note 7 below and the various articles by Jonas Mekas discussed below. The heterogeneity of production was often theorized as marking its distinctively American individualism, for example, "the main characteristic of this body of work is that it defies any of the convenient means of definition and classification. The American artist has always been resistant to organized movements or defined schools" (Thurston, 1961: 32).

7 Contemporary accounts of underground film in the popular press tended, more or less sensationally, to stress the coincidence of formal infractions of orthodox film grammar and parallel moral and social transgressions, interpreting the latter either as evidence of the film-makers' degeneracy or as their social criticism. Some examples: In "The Coming of Age of the X-Film," in the men's magazine *Cavalier*, Rudy Franchi fulfilled the obligations of his title by placing the underground in the context of "art-cum-sex" films from Europe, but he did give a relatively sympathetic account of Vanderbeek and Breer before coming to Brakhage, then supposedly at work on an eight hour and forty minute version of *Sirius Remembered*, and Kenneth Anger, whose *Inauguration of the Pleasure Dome* was promised as making "even the most gruesome skin-flick seem tame" (Franchi, 1962: 85). Less sympathetically, Pete Hamill reported for *The Saturday Evening Post* on *lumpen* harassment of Jonas Mekas while he was filming *Guns of the Trees* (" 'Beatniks,' growled one beefy longshoreman as he poked his head in the car, 'Looka the beatniks looking at the boidie.' . . . One dockwalloper playfully jabbed the tip of a knife against one of the men") before summarizing other beatnik films after Robert Frank "broke the dike" (Hamill, 1963: 82). In an interested if condescending column in 1963 that noted the expulsion of the Monday Night

Film-Makers' Cooperative screenings from the Bleecker Street Cinema, *The New Yorker* reported that the productions of the underground cinema ranged "from 'poetic' color and motion studies to blunt documentary denunciations of Society and the Bomb, but most share a total disdain for the traditional manner of storytelling on film, and also for the 'self-consciously arty' experimental films of the twenties and thirties" ("Cinema Underground," 1963: 17). All these articles stressed the filmmakers' poverty and police harassment, but they also recognized the emergence of a substantial audience. As late as 1966 in a piece in *Status*, nominally on the "Underground Movie World" but essentially on Warhol, Eugene Boe could still propose that "underground signifies Cinema of the Preposterous, pornographic films masquerading as art . . . or films that are far-out, unintelligible and oppressively boring" (Boe, 1966: 71). Throughout the early sixties Brendan Gill in *The New Yorker* reviewed the underground intelligently and sympathetically (*Scorpio Rising* was "a strong and, despite its unpleasant subject matter, beautiful movie. . . . [It] justifies the notion of an underground" [Gill, 1966: 131]). So, too, though to a lesser extent, did Robert Hatch in *The Nation*.

Of an entirely different caliber were articles by Harris Dienstfrey in *Commentary* (Dienstfrey, 1962) and Ken Kelman in *The Nation* (Kelman, 1964), both of which stressed the heterogeneity of the movement. The former, a judicious yet sympathetic account of the New American Cinema and its relations to the European New Waves, discussed the "growing number of important and exciting documentaries, shorts, and features being made outside the aesthetic and monetary confines of Hollywood" (Dienstfrey, 1962: 495), including *Daisy* and *Shadows* and films by Morris Engel, Dan Drasin, Lionel Rogosin, and Jonas Mekas. Dienstfrey argued that these films (again *from* the underground) represented "the politics of the nonpolitical" (ibid.: 499) and were especially concerned with racial issues and with religion and personal salvation. Kelman's article, still one of

Its most recent prior currency had seen Dostoyevskian alienation transformed into the existential commitment of civilian resistance to European fascism in World War II, but then subsequently inflected by the tenebrous resonances of a criminal underworld or communist subversion. Its derivation, before that, from "the domain of political and military activity" noted by Tyler (1969: 2) inevitably suggests the complex interdependence of aesthetic and political radicalism—the problem that had dogged the master metaphor of the avant-garde itself since its inception in the immediate aftermath of the French Revolution. And while the appropriation of such a genealogy to an alternative film practice may measure an aspiration as much as an achievement, still the onomastic assumption clearly signals the presence of some social urgency in the aesthetic desire. The displacement of such previous terms as "poetic" and "experimental" indicates, then, not simply a formal development inside a tradition whose social location is constant (as, for example, the formal innovations of the contemporaneous *Nouvelle Vague* sustained the continuity of the French film industry) but rather an attempt to involve the medium in new social relationships and in serving new social needs. In this, as in other areas of contemporary cultural production, the referential model was the modern jazz musician; his art practice and its role in society was considered exemplary.

From Jack Kerouac's empathic nostalgia for "the Denver colored section" in *On the Road*, later cited with such approval by Eldridge Cleaver (Cleaver, 1968: 72), to Norman Mailer's essay on the criminal hipster, *The White Negro*, Black Americans occupied a privileged position in the beat imagination, their heavily stereotyped vitality, sexuality, and intuitiveness supposed to be both racially intrinsic and preserved by their exclusion from the mainstream. Their psychic and sensual liberation and their social marginality were compounded in the idealized figure of the jazz musician. Mythologized as richly promiscuous in both sex and narcotics, with art his way of life, the post-bebop musician represented the mediation of personal and social values into an aesthetic, whose formal qualities were produced by and themselves reproduced the liberation of the self.

The only major art form other than film to develop in the United States since the destruction of the indigenous peoples, Afro-American music has been the single most important means of sustaining the ideal of a noncapitalist cultural practice. Although spirituals, blues, rags, swing, and other forms of Black music were eventually appropriated by the dominant musical industry as the means to its own renewal, still the amalgamation of distinctly African tonalities and rhythms with European structures allowed the preservation of at least some vestige of the African uses of music. Serving both to articulate group identity and to help resist the psychic effects of exploitation and social disenfranchisement, Black music minimized the distinction between producer and consumer, valorized collective improvisation, and stressed its functionalism as the expression of an entire way of life, "of the Negro's peculiar way of looking at the world" (Baraka, 1967: 19): a way of being in the world.

The music that inspired the beat generation was itself, then, closely identified with social protest. The specific rhythmic and harmonic innovations of the bop revolution against the big-band music that had been at least partly developed by Whites and whose commercial rewards were largely monopolized by Whites—its use of extremely fast tempos and an evenly divided beat with emphasis on the offbeat and a new use of altered and substitute chords—carried both social and musical implications. The extreme technical virtuosity of bop and its production as communal innovation in a very limited social circle (for the first few years, essentially in one nightclub, Minton's in Harlem) attest to the increased confidence and pride of Black musicians and their disaffection with the roles assigned them in the swing orchestras. The bop musicians "created a language, a dress, a music, and a high which were closed unto themselves and allowed them to one-up the rest of the world. The bebop era was the first time that the black ego was expressed in America with self-assurance."[8]

Bop's extension of musical form as the basis for subcultural identity supplied the beats with a radically innovative model for literary practice. Valorized over and against the completed artifact, the improvisational energy and quasi-physical intensity of the process of composition broke the hold of bourgeois, European-oriented, academic literary standards in espousal of populist and third-world spiritual traditions. Artistic creation became an act of psychic wholeness and ecstasy, a model and source of social renewal and the vehicle of social dissent. So while Kerouac's summary formulation of such a practice also owes a good deal to Buddhism's cognate stress on attentiveness to the present as a meditational discipline, his categorical rejection of both preconception and any secondary process of rationalization or correction is explicitly modeled on the jazz musician's strategies for tapping the unconscious roots of creativity.

> Time being of the essence in the purity of speech, sketching language is undisturbed flow from the mind of personal secret idea-words, *blowing* (as per jazz musician) on subject of image. . . . Begin not from preconceived idea of what to say about image but from jewel center of interest in subject of image at *moment* of writing, and write outwards swimming in sea of language to peripheral release and exhaustion—Do not afterthink except for poetic or P.S. reasons. Never afterthink to "improve" or defray impressions, as, the best writing is always the most painful personal wrung-out tossed from cradle warm protective mind—tap from yourself the song of yourself, *blow!— now!—your* way is your only way. (Kerouac, 1958: 72–73)[9]

Devaluing the well-wrought, self-contained artifact, Kerouac rediscovered writing as a process of self-revelation and performance. Ginsberg's use of Whitman's strophic line is similarly to be under-

the best on underground film, argues it as a release of energies in response to the joint repressiveness of American society and Hollywood. Comparing it to the Schoenbergian revolution in music, more radical than and superior to the European New Waves, he sees it as comprising various strategies of psychic restoration. In this "spiritual medium," Kelman distinguishes three main categories: films of "outright social criticism and protest"; "films of liberation, films which suggest, mainly through anarchic fantasy, the possibilities of the human spirit in its socially uncorrupted state"; and "mythically oriented" films created "out of a need to fill our rationalistic void" (Kelman, 1964: 492–93).

8 Spellman (1970: 193). See also Baraka (1967: 23); Collier (1979: 360); and Kofsky (1970: 31). Though it seems indisputable that bop manifested the social and musical protest of the musicians themselves, including as Sidney Finkelstein argued in the forties, their "protest against monopoly control of music and the commodity-like exploitation of the musicians" (Finkelstein, 1948: 233), attempts to link it to the Black community as a whole have difficulty negotiating its status as an elite, an avant-gardist, and eventually, in the innovations of the sixties, an art music. Frank Kofsky, rejecting as a "vulgar empiricism" the argument that the mass of Black people did not support avant-garde jazz (Kofsky, 1970: 23), successfully demonstrated both the presence of distinctly Black and anti-commodity features in avant-garde jazz and the responsiveness of many musicians to the Black nationalism of the sixties, but he failed to demonstrate the music's availability to Black people in general or its political utility. This failure is especially problematic since it elides the much more substantial role of soul, a commodity music, in consolidating a Black identity in the sixties. The most eloquent account of the function of music in Black America remains Baraka (1963).

9 Compare: "Jack had often told Allen that he identified more with musical geniuses like Bud Powell, Charlie Parker, Billie Holiday, Les-

ter Young, Gerry Mulligan and The-
lonius Monk than he did with any
established literary scene, and of all
the books he ever wrote, *Mexico
City Blues* is most directly related to
jazz. Bop was to Kerouac a new art
form that had broken through to eloquence. His own method of spontaneous composition was meant to
do the same thing with words that
he heard bop musicians doing with
their instruments. When Miles
Davis played, Kerouac heard his
trumpet sounding long sentences
like Marcel Proust" (Charters,
1973: 220). And: "For the holy barbarians jazz music is both a therapeutic and a sacred ritual. . . .
Knowing the language of jazz, its
musical language, and sharing it
with others in a closed company of
the initiated, is perfectly in keeping
with its secret religious character.
. . . It is also a music of protest"
(Lipton, 1959: 212). In arguing the
importance of Charlie Parker, Kenneth Rexroth compared him to Dy-
lan Thomas, "two great dead juve-
nile delinquents—the heroes of the
post-war generation"; for both, the
creative act was the only defense
against "the ruin of the world"
(Rexroth, 1957: 29).

10 Especially important here is the
relation of film to painting and
sculpture, discussed below, and to
theater. The intermedia form, happenings, is the place where many of
these developments come together,
and a virtual subgenre of underground film derives from quasi-the-
atrical forms. It includes the use of
film projection in happenings, such
as Robert Whitman's experiments,
culminating in 1965 at the First
New York Theater Rally with the
projection upon a translucent
shower curtain of a life-sized image
of a woman taking a shower; the
more or less straight documentation
of happenings, such as Vernon Zimmerman's *Scarface and Aphrodite*,
photographed from a shortened version of Oldenberg's happening,
Gayety (Renan, 1967: 27); and
films in which the aesthetic of happenings bleeds over into the documentation of them. Many of the *Ru-
kus Films* and other films by Red
Grooms and Rudy Burckhardt fall
into this last category. See Kirby
(1969) for a survey of the use of film

stood as more than an academic disagreement with the formal
priorities of New Criticism; it made writing at moments of high
psychic intensity (the occasion of the composition of "Howl") possible, and it made writing a means of access to such intensity. His
amalgamation of Olson's use of the breath as a unit of composition
with Williams's insistence on natural speech, salted again with a
dash of Buddhist existentialism ("First thought, best thought"),
subsequently extended poetry beyond such heightened *sartori* moments to become coextensive with a transfigured consciousness;
spoken directly into a tape recorder, the poems registered the ingress
of the total perceptual and eventually historical and social fields.
Gary Snyder's location of writing in the phenomenology of perception and William Burroughs's cut-up mixes of drug visions with arbitrary media input are likewise primarily strategies for reorganizing consciousness, only secondarily translating into formal qualities
of the artifact.

Underground film was the parallel in that medium to the beat
attempt to re-create in writing the aesthetic and social functions of
jazz. As such, it was distinct from the documentation of jazz performance; though jazz sound tracks and the depiction of jazz musicians were, from *Shadows* through Michael Snow's *New York Ear
and Eye Control* (1964), common methods of collecting the resonances of beat culture and signifying the underground, even after
that function had been taken over by rock music, jazz could still be
invoked to signal "high" culture. But such intradiegetic use of the
jazz musician and of Black culture generally was merely preliminary
to the generation of filmic equivalents for jazz, propaedeutic to innovations by which film could become the occasion for the collective improvisation of a minority culture and the vehicle for individual expressiveness within that subculture's social and aesthetic
requirements.

The institution of the process of composition as the essential aesthetic event was not, of course, unique to poetry or jazz. In all fields
of postwar American art, the modernist paradigm was being challenged by assaults on boundaries between genres, between media,
between art and non-art, and between art and life, and often in a
way that called into question the fetishism of the commodity art
object. John Cage's assertion that his compositions were not objects
but "occasions for experience" (Cage, 1961: 31) and Harold Rosenberg's observation that in gestural expressionism the canvas began to appear "as an arena in which to act. . . . What was to go on
the canvas was not a picture but an event" (Rosenberg, 1959: 25)
characterize the aspiration of music, painting, dance, poetry, and
theater as well as of a whole range of intermediary forms. Film,
where as Eisenstein remarked all arts meet, was a primary nexus for
these developments.[10] Its hegemony in cultural production as a
whole made it the privileged arena in which the issues confronting
art in general were worked through, not least of all the master question—the relation of art to commerce, to industrial mass culture.
Although political significance was claimed for these formal devel-

opments in all mediums, usually by means of symptomatic analogies between the two spheres,[11] the actual political effect was ambiguous.

On the one hand, the repression of a materialist analysis of society and culture drained the potential for critical resistance in beat aestheticism, leaving it vulnerable to eventual assimilation and commodification by the culture industries. On the other hand, disengagement from the symbolic forms of capitalism and the subordination of the manufacture of commodities to an autotelic art practice sustained the possibility of alternative culture and alternative social forms, a second dimension in both life and art. Rather than argue the absolute truth of one or the other of these positions, it is more useful to recognize how both simultaneously produced in underground film the contradictions of all culture that occurs under conditions of systemic alienation. And nowhere are these contradictions more intense than in the relation of beat culture to the media industries.

Given the centrality of artistic activity in the beats' self-definition, the inconsistencies in the mixture of affection and distaste, of nostalgia and utopianism, in their attitude to contemporary society could only be exacerbated when brought to bear upon the communications industries. Even as they attacked the press for commercializing and destroying the subculture, for excoriating it even as they turned it into a spectacle, the beat writers and certainly the earliest beat filmmakers aspired to popularize it themselves and so secure commercial careers. The impossibility of categorically distinguishing a genuine beat culture from its penumbral dissolution into the general glare of media illumination and the ersatz imitations produced there surrounded the production of underground film and remains as the context for commentary on it.

Its overall project may, then, be summarized as follows: to open out the entire practice of cinema as a sphere of countercultural activity. The three phases of the cinematic process—the profilmic, the filmic, and the theater of projection—were retrieved from the instrumentality of the industrial process and made available as the occasion for relatively autonomous and self-validating performance: "a new, radically inspired revision of the home movie" (Tyler, 1969: 40). As the construction of events before the camera, the activities of shooting and editing film, and finally its projection were instituted as occasions for individual and group creativity in subcultural ritual, the inherited conditions of film and the cinema were challenged; and in the search for the codes of an authentically beat film language and for a progressive practice of cinema, the material nature of the medium itself was pushed to new limits. Alternative cinematic institutions of production, distribution, and consumption, which largely determined the functions of the films, were established, and alternative means of mediating between the physical and the mental machineries of cinema were developed in alternative criticism and theory.[12]

But inscribed within this search for an autonomous cinema of so-

in the new theater. The existential or the ludic basis of much underground profilmic overlaps extensively with developments in radical theater of the period, especially with attempts to liberate the space of theater for real-life uses and to make the performance group itself a therapeutic social microcosm. Documentation of such theater is continuous from Jonas Mekas's *The Brig* (1964) to Sheldon Rochlin's *Paradise Now* (1970), which documents The Living Theater, and Brian De Palma, Robert Fiore, and Bruce Rubin's *Dionysus '69* (1969), which documents The Theater Group. Ronald Tavel, who wrote for both the Theater of the Ridiculous and for Andy Warhol, is an instance of a more formal entry of theater into underground film.

11 See, for example, Dick Higgins's argument for the intrinsic utility of intermedia in a period when, "approaching the dawn of a classless society," compartmentalized approaches to social problems were no longer relevant (Higgins, 1969: 11).

12 Here, in place of a more precise history, are some dates: Maya Deren rents the Provincetown Playhouse in New York for a one-night show of her first three films (1946); subsequently, Amos Vogel uses the same theater as a base for "Cinema 16" presentations of documentary and experimental films, eventually developing a distributional outlet; Frank Stauffacher organizes "Art In Cinema" screenings and symposiums at the San Francisco Museum of Art (1947); *Film Culture* is founded (1955); Robert Pike founds the Creative Film society in Los Angeles for independent distribution (1957); Jonas Mekas organizes screenings at the Charles Street Theater in New York (1960); the New York Film-Makers' Cooperative is founded, guaranteeing distribution to any filmmaker who submits a print (1962) ("Its impact was immediate: an audience was suddenly available to filmmakers who had been working, unheard of in many cases, for several years" [Curtis, 1971: 155]); Bruce Baillie founds Canyon Cinema (1962); the Third Experimental Film Festival takes place at Knokke-Le Zoute, Belgium in 1964.

cial authenticity freed from the compromises of the industry runs the contrary project, the need to engage the other two spheres of determination, the dominant society and the dominant cinema. The form of underground film as subcultural production is, then, also determined by its functions as "protest" film and as intertextual dialogues with Hollywood; even at its most liberated, these functions are found. We will examine both movements, but as an exemplary case of both the filmic achievements of the underground and the implementation of critical, distributional, and exhibitional apparatuses appropriate to the new social relationships that the formal innovations depended on, we will first consider the career of Jonas Mekas, who lived as clearly as anyone the historical evolution of underground film, and who, as much as any other single person, helped to bring its social energies to fruition.

Making Us More Radiant: Jonas Mekas

All things that are clear make us more radiant.
— Jonas Mekas

In no career are the trials and the triumphs of alternative cinema more completely exemplified than in that of Jonas Mekas; in his endeavors as a filmmaker, a theorist, a critic, an archivist, an exhibitor, a distributor, a tireless publicist, and in many cases a self-sacrificing financier of other filmmakers, this self-styled "raving maniac of cinema" was the underground's nurturing genius. He also produced one of the few filmic modes that entirely fulfills its aesthetic and ethical program, even as he led the way in creating the institutions necessary for its survival. Without *Film Culture*, without the Film-Makers' Cooperative, without Anthology Film Archives, in all of which he played a major role, the social elaboration of the perceptual and imaginative renewals provided to the individual by the new film would have remained a dream. Conversely, as the independent cinema became the vehicle of his psychic, artistic, social, and professional lives, it enabled him to integrate them all, to assuage his alienation, and eventually to find a second homeland.

As a displaced person, a war refugee from central Europe, Mekas inherited in an extreme form the American artist's characteristic anxiety about origins. His familial and national deracination was compounded by an equally tortuous migration between mediums, from writing to film. Though he was a well-known poet in his native Lithuania, with various kinds of experience in publishing, his interest in film moved him to buy a camera and begin shooting in an amateur fashion almost as soon as he arrived in the United States. But his earliest prominence came from his editorship of the journal *Film Culture*, which he founded in January 1955, and subsequently from the much greater circulation of his column in *The Village Voice*. At the same time as these attempts to bridge writing and film, Mekas began to "write films," that is, to write screenplays and shoot them. But the crucial illumination that prompted his break-

4.11 Jonas Mekas in his *Lost Lost Lost*
(sequence shot in 1949)

through to writing *in* film, to one of the most thoroughly articulate forms of *caméra stylo*, was his realization that his chief work was the film of his life—even though his filmic autobiography radically calls into question the thematics of Romantic authorship from which it derives.

JONAS MEKAS: CRITIC

Mekas's essays between the mid-fifties and the mid-sixties document his discovery of a concept of alternative cinema and of a place for him in it. Initially promoting a reformist industrial practice based on the European New Waves and disparaging the underground, he eventually recognized the latter as the properly American alternative and hailed its more radically innovative, anti-industrial project. Though the beat/existential values of spontaneity, improvisation, and sincerity dominate his ideas from the beginning, the appearance of a vigorous counterculture in the early sixties increasingly enabled him to theorize a film form adequate or correlative to those values, and to understand how they could inform the filmic as well as the profilmic performance. His development can be traced in three of the articles he wrote for *Film Culture*: "The Experimental Film in America" (1955), "Cinema of the New Generation" (1960), and "Notes on the New American Cinema" (1962).

In the first article, Mekas was looking for a cinema to span the gap between Hollywood and the experimental film, some serious yet broadly populist form responsive to "the middle, the largest area, the whole human reality, sung by the poets and painted on canvas from time immemorial" (Mekas, 1955: 17). His attitude toward the avant-garde was, consequently, equivocal. His notorious attack on its preoccupation with homosexuality, for example, was not an attack on deviance per se so much as the expression of his desire that art should be related to the whole society rather than to "exceptional abnormalities." Similarly, although he clearly admitted a non-industrial use for the medium and recognized filmmakers who were interested in it "primarily as an art form" and who used the camera in the way that previously a young poet would have used a typewriter, he attacked the "adolescent character" of the film poem. But the argument was again equivocal, for he understood that character to be a reflection of the agonies of adolescence as much as an immature use of the medium; if the hero of *The Way to Shadow Garden* by the young Stan Brakhage seemed like "a poetic version of a modern zombie," it was because the film was attempting to express such a psychological condition.

By 1960 Brakhage and the other adolescents were growing up. In the second article, Mekas could see a "coming generation—a generation in the bud . . . that will create an author's cinema in America" (Mekas, 1960: 7). Inspired by the Free Cinema in Britain and the French New Wave and isolated in New York from the Hollywood independents, the members of this new generation were already setting up alternative exhibition spaces like The Bleecker Street Cinema and coming together as a force in production. Mekas's list of these members was the same as that of the New American Cinema group, and its exemplary productions were the first version of *Shadows* and *Pull My Daisy*, films that he found spoke for and emerged from the new generation, and whose relationship to it was more important than their technical qualities considered in the abstract. He lauded *Daisy* as the "only truly 'beat' film" in its expression of the new generation's "unconscious and spontaneous rejection of the middle-class way" (ibid.: 14), and he found it truthful despite its apparent nonsense: "There is no lie, no pretension, no moralizing in it" (ibid.). Its qualities characterized the new cinema in general; governed solely by intuition, it was inevitably sincere, and its authors' sincerity made it "not an esthetic but primarily an ethical movement" (ibid.: 18–19).

This crucial link between the emergent subcultures and their filmic equivalent essentially completed Mekas's position. In the 1962 essay, the social function was his major, rather than an ancillary, concern. He no longer needed to situate the new cinema by reference to the European New Waves for, as rubrics from Shelley and de Kooning made clear, in the new cinema film was only secondarily the manufacture of a product and not at all the manufacture of a commodity. Rather, it was identified with life; like painting for de Kooning, it was "a way of living today, a style of living" (Mekas, 1962: 6). Greeting the maturation of the new generation, Mekas presented a historical overview of the forms of the new cinema—low-budget feature, improvisation, new documentary, social protest films, and even Brakhage, Breer, and Menken, the "pure poets" of the cinema—and concluded by pointing to the political and social value of the new movement. Again he emphasized it as an ethical movement, "only secondarily an aesthetic one" (ibid.: 14), whose function was to encourage disobedience, disengagement, and rebellion. Both in protesting the priorities of mainstream society and in promulgating a humanist conception of dissident art, Mekas's eloquence was entirely within the Romantic tradition.

> With man's soul being squeezed out in all the four corners of the world today, when governments are encroaching upon his personal being with the huge machinery of bureaucracy, war and mass communication, [the American artist] feels that the only way to preserve man is to encourage his sense of rebellion, his sense of disobedience, even at the cost of open anarchy and nihilism. The entire landscape of human thought as it is accepted publicly in the Western world, has to be turned over. All public ideologies, values, and ways of life must be doubted, attacked. "Smell it and get high, maybe we'll all get the answer that way! Don't give up the ship!" exclaims Allen Ginsberg. Yes, the artist is getting high on the death of his civilization, breathing in its poisonous gases. And yes, our art is "confused" and all that jazz, jazz, jazz, (taylor mead). But we refuse to con-

tinue the Big Lie of Culture. To the new artist the fate of man is more important than the fate of art, more important than the temporary confusions of art. You criticize our work from a purist, formalistic and classicist point of view. But we say to you: What's the use of cinema if man's soul goes rotten? (Ibid.: 14).

Though Mekas continued to write favorably in his *Village Voice* columns of Antonioni and especially of Godard, the New Wave idea of a middle ground where thematic seriousness and aesthetic integrity would meet popular accessibility had essentially disappeared. Instead of welcoming an experimental commercial film like *Last Year at Marienbad*, he noticed its inferiority to the work of "the pure experimental film poets" (Mekas, [1962] 1972: 54). By the middle of the decade, he had abandoned reconciliation of the industry and the underground for a polarization that allowed a Manny Farber–like appreciation of the unpretentious entertainment films of the old-school Hollywood directors, while rejecting the art film and everything between the extremes: "*Variety* says there are about two hundred low-budget 'art' movies waiting for distribution. I have seen a good number of them, and the best ones are dogs. American cinema remains in Hollywood and the New York underground" (ibid.: 120).

The replacement of the earlier ideal of a morally responsible, aesthetically adventurous, reformed industrial cinema by the aggressively subversive, disengaged underground was, on the one hand, the sign of a social failure, the absence of any progressive, reformist movement with sufficient power to challenge the corporate state, a failure which Vietnam would clarify and exacerbate, resulting in the extreme polarization of the last years of the sixties. On the other hand, it marked a social success, the consolidation of subcultures around film practices fundamentally different from industrial production, and even of a degree of popular interest in them; Mekas's February 1964 *Village Voice* column that berated the American "art" film, for example, also noted the opening of the 55th Street Playhouse in New York as the first theater devoted exclusively to showing experimental and avant-garde film. This new non-commodity film culture is both documented and demonstrated in Mekas's own films; if his career as an underground filmmaker was until the early seventies overshadowed by the reputation of his other activities, the knowledge he acquired in these activities supplied the radiant lucidity of his own films, the underground's most summary achievement.

Jonas Mekas: Filmmaker

Mekas's filmmaking recapitulated the stages of his theory in discovering how spontaneity, presentness, and similar values could be enacted in the profilmic and then in the filmic. His first completed project, *Guns of the Trees* (1961), an essay in the populist American art film mode, joined underground formal motifs to the format and accessibility of the industrial feature. Structurally a trance film, it is framed by shots of Mekas himself lifting his attention from the poems of Shelley and from his typewriter to gaze through a window. What he sees (or writes or imagines, for the correspondence between these is already implied) is a narrative in which the conflicts of the authorial persona are displaced into the struggles of four main protagonists, a White couple and a Black couple, following the suicide of one of their friends. This fourfold ego analysis, common in Blake and other radical Romantics, anatomizes beat ideology into its critical and its restorative components. Adolfas and Frances, the White couple, carry the burden of the largely European existential guilt and protest, and they lament the meaninglessness of life in the alien urban landscapes they inhabit. Ben and Argus, the Black couple, are capable of play, spontaneity, and intimacy, and so embody the beat answer to this ennui. Though Ben suffers through endless existentialist debates and unsuccessful attempts to find employment in business, he and Argus have access to a love that, even if only in their domestic isolation, provides solace from the surrounding alienation; appropriately, Argus is pregnant.

Reflecting Mekas's situation as an alien caught in a cold war which allows him neither homeland nor political belief, the historical condition in which these characters all live is imaged both naturalistically and surrealistically. Long tracking shots through the urban wasteland and junkyards and scenes of protestors in Washington Square, one carrying a sign—"Both Sides Are Wrong"—that summarizes the film's beat anti-politics, are glossed by a recurrent motif, recruited from the theater of the absurd, of businessmen who moan mechanically as they wander through a wasteland of cabbage fields. Though *Guns'* plot is somewhat retarded, elaborated meta-

4.12 Jonas Mekas, *Guns of the Trees*

4.13–4.14 Jonas Mekas, *Guns of the Trees*

phorically, and made difficult in an exemplary formalist way by these visual digressions as well as by sonic metaphors (the arbitrary interpolation of sirens, or Allen Ginsberg reading his poetry), the film is essentially a linear, illusionist narrative; whatever alternative values it invokes are presented intradiegetically, especially in the intimacy of Ben and Argus. Neither the unusually extended and irregular camera movements nor the fantasy or memory shots that briefly dissolve the camera's objectivity cohere sufficiently to allow film style to mark an alternative aesthetic. The insistence of its existentialist protest aside, the film is a conventional independent feature.

Between this fictional, acted work and the immanentist mode of his *Diaries*, Mekas filmed (and his brother Adolfas edited) The Liv-

4.15 Jonas Mekas, *Guns of the Trees*

ing Theater's production of Kenneth Brown's play, *The Brig* (1964). The play was itself a landmark in a theatrical tradition that, especially after the translation of Artaud in 1958 and the production of Jack Gelber's *The Connection* in 1959, intertwined with and indeed nourished underground film. The rejection of character in preference for the performers' self-presentation in theater that "was something" rather than "about something" was itself informed by the beat imperative to situate art in the tensions of everyday life. In ensembles like The Living Theater, the theatrical performance extended the quasi-therapeutic social environment of an ongoing collectivity, a social unit akin to those that developed underground film.

Since it reproduces Brown's play, Mekas's *The Brig* is a fiction film; but his decision to shoot the play as if he were in an actual brig minimized his moment-to-moment control over the profilmic, moving the work toward the conditions of a cinéma vérité documentary. Using several cameras in sequence and with only occasional interruptions for magazine changes, he photographed the play in an almost continuous run-through that demanded the concentration of all his faculties in the process of shooting.

> My intention wasn't to show the play in its entirety but to catch as much of the action as my "reporter" eyes could. This kind of shooting required an exhausting concentration of body and eye. I had to operate the camera; I had to keep out of the cast's way; I had to look for what was said; I had to make instantaneous decisions about my movements and the camera movements, knowing that there was no time for thinking or reflecting; there was no time for reshooting, no time for mistakes: I was a circus man on a tightrope high in the air. All my senses were stretched to the point of breaking. (Mekas, 1972: 191)

Directed by his immediate perception of the play, his documentation of it situated him within its physical and psychic intensity. And though both the play and the film suggest that the brig is a metaphor for modern society, the indictment of dehumanizing institutions is balanced by the celebration of beat values that both performances—Mekas's and the actors'—emphasize.

In making the apparatus the means to and the mediator of present vision, the long takes of *The Brig* produce a constantly questing camera. Its attempts to hold onto the point of greatest energy in the profilmic and to frame the presently significant visual event opened the way stylistically and functionally to the tropes that define Mekas's mature films, in which visual and even somatic attentiveness to the process of shooting is extended to encompass the social relations that intersect there. In his film diaries, the film work breaks free from its function of recording anterior or exterior aesthetic events, even those as redolent of psychological and social significance and as thoroughly integrated into the lives of its producers as the events in *The Brig*. Two aspects of the new genre are especially important: (1) the separate phases of the production process are retrieved for their own pleasure and away from instrumentality in the manufacture of an artifact, whether that of the studios or of independent feature projects like *Guns of the Trees*, and (2) the Romantic quest for authenticity, conducted in and through the agencies of both film and cinema, is discovered as the essential practice of the medium.

During the sixties Mekas began to edit the footage that he had been shooting in a casual but apparently regular fashion since the third week after his arrival in the United States. Three hours of material shot since 1964 were released in 1968 as *Diaries, Notes and Sketches (Walden)*. Similar "notes" taken during a journey back to

4.16 Jonas Mekas, *The Brig*

his homeland in the summer of 1971 were edited into *Reminiscences of a Journey to Lithuania*, and in 1976 two and a half hours of material collected between 1949 and 1963 were edited and released as *Lost Lost Lost*. Despite the tremendous stylistic diversity of this footage, there is a clear development in Mekas's use of the camera. Initially, even when hand-held, the camera imitates studio technique; it is either stationary or granted only one-dimensional pans. Gradually the rigidity of the quasi-industrial language loosens, shots become shorter, and the camera is allowed a gestural mobility, until by the mid-sixties sharp bursts of action—with single-framing and somatically responsive and often frenetically irregular camera movement—are fully articulated as his signature style. The two key tropes of this style, the short, real-time investigation of a single scene (the vignettes in *Diaries*, the "Rabbit Shit Haiku" in *Lost Lost Lost*, the "Glimpses" in *Reminiscences*) and the rapid single-framed scan between them, are both predicated on the use of the camera as the dynamic agent of vision rather than as the recorder of perception independently established.

Though the rapid single-framed scans may be extended through an entire sequence as a continuous and otherwise uninflected synecdochic mode, most often they function as a search for significant material—as runs through the visual environment to find the set pieces examined more extensively. Each sequence contains, then, the traces of the chronology of the shifts of Mekas's attention as he scans the profilmic scene, as well as his accommodation to its changes; as each micro-narrative unfolds, the frame is in constant motion, with continual adjustments in the zoom, the camera position, the focus, or the exposure being dictated by psychic or visual responses. The particularities of film stock, processing, and projection apparatus aside, this procedure preserves the optical phenomenology of shooting; perception is circumscribed by what may be seen through the camera, while whatever is not immanent in it and mediated through it never appears. So Mekas can claim that when he was successful, he was able to inflect the documentation according to his subjectivity at the time of shooting. The program notes for *Diaries*, for example, argue that a successful film diary integrates optical registration and emotional affect.

> To keep a film (camera) diary, is to react (with your camera) immediately, now, this instant: either you get it now, or you don't get it at all. To go back and shoot it later, it would mean restaging, be it events or feelings. To get it now, as it happens, demands the total mastery of one's tools (in this case, Bolex): it has to register the reality to which I react and also it has to register my state of feeling (and all the memories) as I react. Which also means, that I had to do all the structuring (editing) right there, during the shooting, in the camera. All footage that you'll see in the Diaries is exactly as it came out from the camera: there was no way of achieving it in the editing rooms without destroying its form and content. (*Film-Makers' Cooperative Catalogue*, 1975: 178)

These remarks parallel Kerouac's insistence on responsiveness to the present moment of composition, and even more than Brakhage, Mekas does use the camera as a means of visual "*blowing* (as per jazz musician)," which permits him precisely to begin the process of composition "from jewel center of interest in subject of image at *moment* of writing" rather than from "preconceived idea of what to say about image." Indeed, at certain moments, usually but not always ones of crucial intensity, the camera is allowed its autonomous vision; Mekas will shoot without looking through the camera, holding it at waist level or even swinging it through the air so that it may gather what his eye cannot. This privileging of shooting, by which it becomes the documentation of the interaction of subjectivity with the external world, interdicts any subsequent modification of the "writing" so secured—no "afterthinking" in Kerouac's terms. Because the film preserves the pristine impression of time and place captured in shooting, unadulterated by the interpositions of consciousness subsequent to it, a collection of such takes—a film diary—records both the phenomenal world made present to the filmmaker and the development of his filmic apprehension of it; superimposed upon the narrative of the growth of the artist's mind, the *topos* of post-Romantic autobiography, is the narrative of the growth of "the mastery of [his] tools," and eventually the cinema they entail.

That autobiographical narrative can be reconstructed from readings of the technicalities of focus, camera movement, and exposure in the separate sections of the *Diaries*. But it is also sedimented in the considerably broader development of his styles, each of which carries a different implication for the proper use of the apparatus, each of which allegorizes a different cinema. In such a totalized form of Mekas's biography, *Diaries, Notes and Sketches* will have pride of place; here he fully achieved a shooting technique sufficiently subtle to allow the registration of the phenomenology of the moment of vision, and with that he fully disentangled from previous conceptions of film the realization that precisely the assemblage of the first-person footage constituted his authentic image. But in many ways even more interesting than the *Diaries* is *Lost Lost Lost*—the re-created autobiography of the period between Mekas's arrival in the United States and his participation in the underground—which documents the different practices of film he essayed before finding his own mode.

The six-reel film is divided into three, roughly equal sections. The first two reels record the tedium of the defensively self-contained refugee community, trapped in a recollected past and a continually deferred return to Lithuania. Though the community has political meetings and other occasions of fellowship organized around births, deaths, and marriages, essentially its life is held in suspension. It is not until Mekas rejects this stasis and leaves Brooklyn that, in the last two reels, he is able to make a new life for himself, first in the attempts to make independent features and eventually in the Manhattan avant-garde, even though to do so he has to recapitulate the severance of national and racial ties and give up the dream of returning to his original home. Retrospectively assembling fragments from the defeats and dead ends that terminated his attempts to reform the commercial feature film, *Lost Lost Lost* both depicts and embodies his emancipation from industrial production and its presuppositions about the proper use of the medium. His discovery of the identity of—the possibility of identifying—the artistic with the personal redeems the failures of his previous life and art; and the central beat priority of an aestheticized daily life provides the ethical basis for the production of the artist's autobiography—the portrait of the artist—as the work of art. *Lost Lost Lost* thus argues a myth of loss and renewal in which the psychic desolation of expatriation is overcome by self-discovery in art and in the company of fellow artists. The classical instances of this modern version of the primary Western myth are the Romantic autobiographies—Wordsworth's *Prelude* and Coleridge's *Biographia Literaria*—and like these Mekas's affirms art as the essential human activity. But unlike these, his affirmation of autobiography is undermined by a virtually unrelieved skepticism about art's ability to retrieve the past, and it is socially realigned by the recognition that even Romantic authorship is the activity of a community rather than an individual subject.

Like *Reminiscences*, *Lost Lost Lost* drafts conventional Romantic motifs such as the church, the countryside, and music to signify the restoration of emotional well-being. But the master metaphor is the creation of an alternative film practice; underground film rises as the phoenix of perceptual, psychic, and social rebirth, and its vision nourishes an alternative community. The Lithuanian exiles and even Mekas's brother, Adolfas, who accompanied him to Manhattan and into the attempt to develop an alternative feature industry (the film contains documentation of Adolfas's independent feature of 1963, *Hallelujah the Hills*) are replaced in the last section by Ken Jacobs and two young women, Debbie and Barbara (Rubin). In the last reel these four people appear as a social microcosm who organize their lives around the rituals of shooting film and the other activities of the alternative cinema—the Film-makers' Cooperative, *Film Culture*, and film conferences. The achievement of this community is dramatized on two excursions they make, one to the Flaherty Film Seminar in September 1963 and one to the beach at Stony Brook which ends the film. The first breakthrough comes at the Flaherty Seminar.

After meeting outside the Film-makers' Coop, the four drive up to Battleboro to a cinéma vérité retrospective, taking with them prints of *Blonde Cobra* and *Flaming Creatures*, two of the already notorious "Baudelairean" underground films which only four months before Mekas had greeted in the *Village Voice* as marking the supersession of the realist school by the cinema of disengagement. But the seminar rejects the new kind of cinema truth, and those who bear it have to sleep outside the conference center in their cars. On awakening Mekas and Jacobs both shoot a good deal of footage; short takes show the women stepping out of the cars and walking around in the fields, and Mekas smiling at the rising sun. Since both men had cameras, there are several shots of each of them shooting, including two of Mekas swinging his camera at arm's length over the grass; these shots retrospectively explain the visionary gleam of a previous Brakhage-like rush of almost unreadable flowers and grass across the screen. The sequence is accompanied by Mekas's voice-over announcing that on this occasion he felt close to the earth and a part of the morning, and then, immediately before we see him taking his camera out from under a blanket which he has draped around him like a cowl, he announces, "It was very quiet, like in a church and we were the monks of the order of cinema."

Although this reconciliation with the natural world and the emergence into a new day of cinema is specified by the voice-over at the much later date when Mekas edited the footage, its constituents are all present in the visual track: the community of the four friends, the use of the camera to document their being-in-the-present, their vocation of introducing the new cinema to the outside world, and the new shooting style which replaces industrial grammar with an improvisatory spontaneity that at its extreme allows the random activity of the apparatus itself to generate its own vision. The epiphany is reaffirmed in the visit to the beach at Stony Brook, where it is underlined by profilmic metaphors such as Salvador Dali demonstrating the sights that can be obtained by the free manipulation of op art overlays and uninhibited women who swim fully clothed in the ocean because it is "their way of doing things." The baptismal implications are ratified by a reprise of the religious music of Battleboro and by Mekas's recollection that "it was like being in a church" with all their troubles washed away by the waves. Ironically recalling the visits to Stony Brook with the Lithuanian exiles ten years earlier, the film concludes, then, by affirming the community of the independent cinema and the priority of the diary film as its privileged vehicle, and by celebrating the signature style of his own practice. Finally—however grudgingly—Mekas can admit, "We had a good time."

This achievement commandeers the narrative of *Lost Lost Lost*, providing the criteria by which Mekas's previous practices may retroactively be comprehended. His discovery of the autobiographical cinema allows him to recognize as autobiography the fractured, scattered forms his commitment to cinema as the agency of his life has taken. As the diverse practices he has engaged take their place in this autobiography, the meaning of the discontinuity, of the false leads as much as his triumphs, becomes clear. The vanquished cinemas are the antagonists the hero has defeated, and their negative significance is the terrain upon which the epic journey has been pursued. In scrutinizing these previous attempts at film, the diverse footage that he "happened" to have shot and preserved, *Lost Lost Lost* passes through the various possibilities for film in the fifties and sixties, clarifying the social contexts of the technical develop-

4.17–4.18 *Lost Lost Lost*: Jonas Mekas
and Ken Jacobs, "monks of the order of
cinema."

ments and perceptual processes they brought into being. That characteristic of autobiographical film inevitably to constitute "a reflection on the nature of cinema, and often on its ambiguous
associations with language" (Sitney, 1977: 63) here appears as the
account of interdependence between the language of film and the
social organizations of cinema, the site of Mekas's singular achievement.

The filmic fragments and misdirections this one assembles are le-
gion: the film's first images of Adolfas and Jonas playing with the
camera, gagging for it, and investigating its possibilities with Mé-
liès-type prestidigitation tricks such as making a bottle appear in a
magician's hand; a series of Lumière-like *vues* of the immigrant

4.19–4.20 *Lost Lost Lost:* Jonas Mekas,
Debbie, and Barbara at Stony Brook

community and New York City, which depict Mekas's loneliness in
shots of him walking down deserted streets; footage from an attempted anti-war movie in which Adolfas appears as a Nazi soldier;
footage of several gatherings of the Lithuanian community, whose
greater formality suggests it is perhaps a historical record made for
use after the return to Lithuania; fragments, outtakes, and test shots
from other movies; amateur footage of Jonas and Adolfas writing
movie scripts; footage of Mekas directing actors and a cameraman;
fragments of an uncompleted trance film in which a young woman
imagines the death of her husband in a car accident, followed by her
first-person vision of the accident that fulfills her dream; a series of
aperçus, "Rabbit Shit Haikus," made during the shooting of *Hallelujah the Hills* (that typically discover some numinous moment

4.21 *Lost Lost Lost*: Adolfas and Jonas Mekas

in phenomenal reality, a peculiarly plangent scene in nature—Mekas playing his accordion in the snow—or in the movies—Ed Emshwiller acting the devil—and that often contain some pattern of tension between two shots—a shot of Emshwiller focusing a camera followed by the shot he takes—or use a simple camera technique to relate two planes within a single shot: a close-up on a window, for example, is suddenly replaced by an abrupt focus-pull that reveals a rural scene outside); and footage of Mekas shot by Ken Jacobs at the Flaherty Seminar and during the excursion to Stony Brook, along with the footage shot by Mekas himself on the same occasions.

Distended through this fractured, macaronic assemblage are transitions and evolutions of many kinds. As Mekas discovers his place in the underground, the limited camera vocabulary of the formal historical documentation and essayed fictional features of the first reels are progressively personalized, and in the uninhibited spontaneity of the Battleboro and Stony Brook scenes the shooting style approaches the gestural, kinetic handwriting of *Diaries*. The variety of registers of professionalism implied by the different shooting styles is matched in the profilmic in the range of ways in which people perform for the camera, a range in which "real" acting appears as only one of many modes of self-dramatization. But as well as announcing formal developments, the chronology of these different film modes also traces different functions for film. Produced by different groups of people with different relations to and around the apparatus, they designate a spectrum of historically determinate positions in respect to the film industry. Mekas's odyssey through the early practices to the underground cinema and its aesthetics of disengagement, the plot of *Lost Lost Lost*, is represented *in* the film, in the narrative of the discovery of the Coop community; but it is also

4.22–4.23 *Lost Lost Lost:* The immigrant community

manifested *by* the coming into existence of *Lost Lost Lost*, in the breakthrough to the formal criteria that can authorize as a self-sufficient and autonomous work the assemblage of these otherwise incommensurate fragments. The film narrates the inauguration of a cinema, the only cinema, which could allow it to come into being. A sequence late in the third reel illustrates the terms of this breakthrough, whose summary form is the redemption of the detritus of industrial cinema in the personal.

Shot, so an intertitle indicates, by Charles Levine, the sequence documents Mekas directing a scene from *Guns of the Trees*. The footage, which with flares, jump cuts, and repeats, appears to be unedited, details several practice runs with the dolly and finally the actual filming of the scene, though Levine's camera cuts away from the actors to Mekas, biting his lip as he watches the performance. Such meta-filmic interludes are a staple of sixties film; since this one depicts a dolly shot, it recalls the opening of *Contempt* as much as anything in the underground. But where Godard retains the industrial use of the apparatus even while animadverting on its constraints, Mekas includes documentation of the industrial mode only to cue attention to the present film's rejection of it. Marginalized as an amateur appendage to another, more real event whose commercial success alone could render it significant, Levine's footage, in its existence outside *Lost Lost Lost*, was torn across an axial tension between *énonciation* and *énoncé*, between the laboriously rehearsed artifice of the industrial language and the spontaneous and unrevised documentation of it. In its inclusion in *Lost Lost Lost*, this hierarchy is canceled, and the social tension between the cinema Levine's footage depicts and the cinema it itself implies is displaced narratively into Mekas's biography, where it is sublated in what is presently that biography's culmination—the making of *Lost Lost Lost*. This film's depiction of Mekas's participation in the birth of the new cinema gathers into itself all his previous practices according to the autobiographical aesthetic of filmmaking that the new cinema made possible. And as the new film emerges into the new

4.24–4.25 *Lost Lost Lost*: Jonas Mekas directing *Guns of the Trees*

cinema, it clears the way for the shooting practice of the *Diaries* in full consciousness of its social authority.

Yet *Lost Lost Lost*'s assembly of these fragments is not without its defeats and disappointments. While it is not properly dialogic in that the fruitless practices are contained within the thematic and formal hegemony of the mature mode, it is nevertheless as a whole as discontinuous as the projects from which it was drawn were incomplete. It may—finally, tentatively, and provisionally—claim transcendence, but even here it also manifests fracture and the impossibility of organic or totalizing unity being located in an individual ego. This impossibility is especially powerful and especially plangent as it becomes apparent during editing. While editing is the point at which the acceptance of the role of the failed forays in Mekas's career allows *Lost Lost Lost* to be constructed out of them, it is also the point at which the viability of the film autobiography as a means of rediscovering the past is most fearfully questioned. Rather than celebrating the redemption of the past, the voice-over can only describe the failure of these fragments to make the past presently comprehensible or even available. Even supplemented by stills and intertitles, the re-viewing is the occasion of virtually unrelieved despair and confusion, parallel indeed to the initial loss of the Lithuanian homeland. Mekas can regularly recall his desire "to be the recording eye . . . the camera historian of exile," but the records do not yield the past. And while the poetry of the commentary frames the visuals, giving voice to their muteness, still the tracks slip from one another into contradiction. As he chants an unrelievedly maudlin litany of loneliness and loss, Mekas reveals himself as an unreliable interpreter of images preserved from a life that is, in any case, no longer his own. In one glaring instance, he asserts that a particularly trying winter in New York saw them with nothing to eat except miserable sandwiches and coffee, while the exactly synchronized image track shows a party scene with a woman toasting the camera. Continuing the trail of ruptures produced by the forcible yoking of heterogenous fragments, such openings undermine the voice on the sound track and hold it apart from the lost self it contemplates in the visuals.

But if the fragments it stores are not those of the reconstructed Romantic subject, neither are they entirely impotent to arrest the ruinous loss of the past. *Lost Lost Lost*'s recognition of the joy of Battleboro and Stony Brook relieves what would otherwise have been a spectacle as unreal as a dream of a film. But in doing so this recognition points again to it own social origins; Mekas's hard-won final assertion that "*We* had a good time" reminds us again that what was achieved was cinema. This achievement, represented as we have argued in the film, is also attested by the juxtaposition in its climactic moments of first-person footage from several sources. Throughout, *Lost Lost Lost* alternates between different kinds of sights of Mekas—those he had and those others had of him—tempering the dominant autobiographical mode and the first-person seeing, and framing its subjectivity with the testimony of other eyes. This distributed authorship reaches its apogee at the points when Mekas's own perceptual and social breakthroughs take place, at Battleboro and Stony Brook. In these instances, the film has recourse equally to footage shot by the two friends. Especially important is the double ending, two apparently unedited long takes, first Jacobs's footage, then Mekas's own. For its climax, then, the film juxtaposes sights of Mekas with what he saw, the vision of Jacobs with Jacobs's vision. Here the film moves from improvisation to group improvisation, from collaboration to communal practice. It is perhaps as far as film can go.

Mekas's work to form a counter cinema was not without its own aporias and certainly not without critics; it was attacked continuously with great wit by Jack Smith, for example, on the grounds that even the independent institutions delivered Dionysian energies back into the repressive social functions exemplified by the archive and the museum. Smith's argument raises the crucial issue of the institutionalization of dissent in the administration of countercultures into the hegemonic order; but it is finally coherent only at the point of social despair. Nowhere is the beat answer to that despair—the construction of alternative communities based upon art and the communal aestheticization of daily life that transformed it into political practice—more generously or luminously realized than in Mekas's example, not only in his films but also in the alternative cinema they document and implement.

Underground Cinema

Practise is Art.
— William Blake

Growing variously from New York and from San Francisco's North Beach scene, the history of underground film was shaped by the history of the bohemian subcultures and the shifts in their ideological and aesthetic principles. Wide use of hallucinogenic drugs and the replacement of jazz by rock music as the chief countercultural focus, on the one hand, and politicization around civil rights and the Vietnam War, on the other, were the most important of these influences, and indeed the war virtually ended underground film by polarizing the youth cultures and discrediting aesthetic disengagement. While one edge of the underground cinema only indirectly generalized the social implications of its emphasis on personal vision, by far the majority of underground films were essentially documentaries of these subcultures. Works as formally and socially diverse as *Triptych in Four Parts* (Larry Jordan, 1958), *Flaming Creatures* (Jack Smith, 1963), *Lurk* (Rudy Burckhardt, 1965), *S.F. Trips Festival, An Opening* (Ben Van Meter, 1966), *Inauguration of the Pleasure Dome* (Kenneth Anger, 1966), *The Chelsea Girls* (Andy Warhol, 1966), *Kirsa Nicholina* (Gunvor Nelson, 1970), and *July '71 in San Francisco, Living at Beach Street, Working at Canyon Cinema, Swimming in the Valley of the Moon* (Peter Hutton, 1971) are all instances of minority social groups representing themselves, and in them the ideological and the economic, the filmic and the cinematic, are mutually determining.

Important though this *prise de la parole* was, self-documentation only provisionally encompasses the innovations of underground film. Representation, even self-representation, is a bourgeois aesthetic value, and the transformation of *activities*—singing, writing, dancing, and the like—first into objects, then into marketable objects, is the form taken by art in capitalist societies. Though it was made possible by the desire to take control of the apparatus, to produce rather than merely consume film, the radical innovation of the underground exceeded this function by inventing film as practice rather than as manufacture. And so, while the specificity of underground film initially appears as the conjunction of beat subject matter and a style that reproduces its values—the constitution of the *énonciation* by the conditions of the *énoncé*—that conjunction is only the form of appearance of innovations prior to it, the de-instrumentalization of the production process and its institution as the site where alternative values might be produced and enacted. The invention of filmmaking as performance, as activity—the institution of "to film" as a transitive verb complete apart from its object—marks the utopian aspiration of the underground, the point where it simultaneously confronted the medium's material nature and the capitalist use with which it had been identified historically. Of the spaces opened up to their autoteleology in this "greening" of the apparatus, three are primary: that of the profilmic, that of the filmic, and that of projection. In each case the innovations of the underground reorganize the hermeneutic process; it becomes not the discovery of the order of the film as an object or even as idealized cognition, but rather the recovery of the activity which the film traces but does not necessarily represent.

PRACTICE IN THE PROFILMIC: RON RICE ET AL.

So we made movies of the anti-orgies.
— Don DeLillo

Imitating jazz's identification of composition and performance, the underground inaugurated the profilmic as the site for improvisation rather than merely for the assumption of pre-scripted roles in dramatic narratives. Though the underground sought both spontaneity and authenticity and, in the lives of the performers, a more substantially relevant subject matter, the real life it documented was in no sense the unselfconscious reality hypothesized in naive versions of cinéma vérité. The rituals into which the conventions of the well-made plot and sustained characterization were shredded and dispersed always involved a high degree of artifice. As an aestheticism in which the real was constructed, if only fragmentarily and ungrammatically, out of the language of Hollywood, beat existentialism presupposed ludic self-dramatization. Fantasy, play, and theatricality were the elements of its heightening of daily life and nowhere more critically than in sexuality, where transvestism, emerging from the strong current of homosexuality in beat culture, summarizes both the extreme of self-fabrication and a more general emphasis on sexual unconventionality. Indeed, in sexual license a social transgression becomes the basis for the formal transgression of publicly sanctioned filmic codes and at the same time a privileged vehicle of social protest. In this cinema of moral and social aberration, of sensual deviance and excess, the formal sterility that accompanies both narcotic immobility and hyperactivity (Lyotard, 1978) allows areas of signification to spill out and be experienced hedonistically, for themselves rather than within a narrative economy.

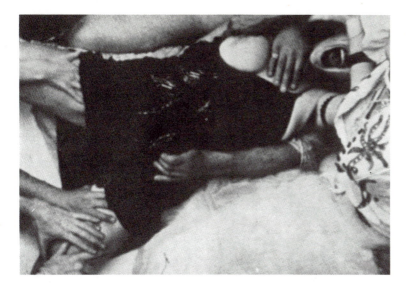

4.26 Jack Smith, *Flaming Creatures*

In the *Village Voice* review of 1963 noted previously, Mekas characterized the four films he singled out as Baudelairean—Ron Rice's *The Queen of Sheba Meets the Atom Man*, Jack Smith's *Flaming Creatures*, Ken Jacob's *Little Stabs at Happiness*, and the Jacobs, Smith, and Fleischner collaboration, *Blonde Cobra*—as revealing "a world of flowers of evil, of illuminations, of torn and tortured flesh; a poetry which is at once beautiful and terrible, good and evil, delicate and dirty" (Mekas, 1972: 85). Others fit the mold equally well—Barbara Rubin's *Christmas On Earth*, for example, or, on the West Coast, *Fireworks* and later films by Kenneth Anger. But the four Mekas mentioned have survived as classic instances in which the forbidden behavior in the profilmic found an appropriate correlative in parallel formal infractions of orthodox film grammar. The most notorious, *Flaming Creatures*, which was refused exhibition in the 1963 Knokke-Le Zoute festival, proscribed as obscene in the New York courts, and eventually withdrawn from public exhibition by its maker, clinched the popular association between the underground and sexual irregularity; in it action and character and even distinctions between the sexes dissolve so completely that the film approaches the condition of a quasi-abstract textural virtuoso performance. But the processes of the mode can be clarified in the less complete disengagement from industrial norms seen in the work of Ron Rice; here the innovations stand out in relief against the remnants of what they are in the process of discarding.

The Flower Thief (1960), Rice's first excursion in the beat mode, extended the surrealist, quasi-picaresque tradition developed in San Francisco in the late forties by Sidney Peterson. In it Taylor Mead's peripatetics marked, according to P. Adams Sitney, "the purest expression of the Beat sensibility in cinema" (Sitney, 1979: 313). Recapitulating the key beat motifs of transcontinental travel by car and train, of Mexico and marijuana, *Senseless* (1962) came close to

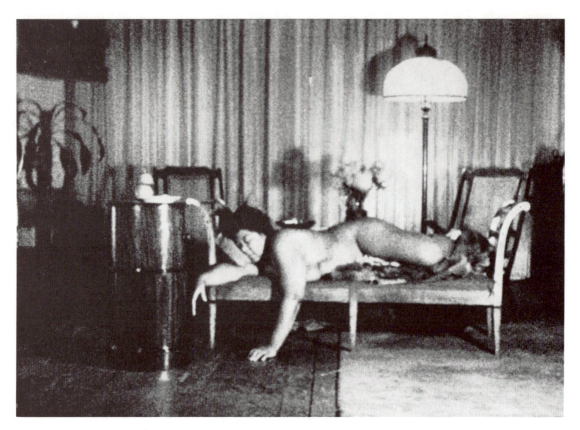

4.27 Ron Rice, *The Queen of Sheba*
Meets the Atom Man: Winifred Bryan

being a film equivalent to *On The Road*. But *The Queen of Sheba Meets the Atom Man*, left incomplete at the time of Rice's death and subsequently put together by Howard Evengam in 1965–67, is especially interesting in that the constant tendency toward chaos and frustration in the profilmic activity overflows into the structure of the film itself. As social refuse, metaphorically associated with garbage, its players are outside the economies of hegemonic society and its narrative forms. The film does retain references to previous avant-garde genres like the city poem, and to traditional beat motifs like the relation between a Black woman and a White man, but only to mutilate them. Its chaotic *mise en scène* and its frustrated and frustrating structure produce a negative articulation of its bohemian inhabitants by consistently defeating and refusing even those expectations that it internally generates.

Broadly farcical with an Aristophanaic buoyancy, *Sheba* unwinds in interior scenes in which Taylor Mead and the more or less undressed Winifred Bryan are grotesquely displayed in cacophonous tableaux of total disarray, enmeshed in furniture, props, and costumes, with a stuffed bear and other junk strewn across their bodies in chaotically unstructured compositions. Often these are shot from above, but, unlike the similar shot at the beginning of *Pull My Daisy*, for example, which allowed for an aerial mapping, the wide

4.28–4.32 Ron Rice, *The Queen of Sheba Meets the Atom Man*: Winifred Bryan, Taylor Mead, and Jack Smith

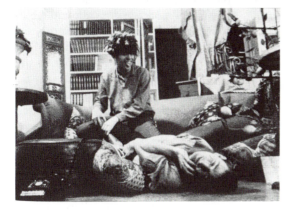

lens used here only distorts the scene further. The point of departure for these comic scenes is the unusual physical characteristics of Mead and Bryan and their incongruous relationship: the puny, rubbery, and totally uncoordinated Atom Man is simultaneously drawn to and intimidated by the massive bulk and voracious appetites of the African Queen. In her strolls through the city streets and parks and especially in a sequence in which she takes a ferry ride in a dense fog, Bryan establishes for herself a strong and plangent dignity; but in the interiors she is an almost amorphous mass of flowing flesh which fills or engulfs whatever it encounters, capable not really of shifting but only of being redistributed in more and more grotesque shapes. Typically in the underground and on its edges, in *Shadows*, for example, or in *Guns of the Trees*, White male/Black female relationships are manipulated within a humanistic frame of reference, used to display a beat rejection of social prejudice. But Rice refuses to engage liberal polemics. The friendship the two display as together they stare into department store windows or stand in the lobbies of alien commercial buildings rides not on a proposed similarity beneath their different skin colors but on a categorical dissimilarity. Bryan stuggles with a plethora of desires which Mead is simply uninterested in satisfying, refusing even to countenance her massive sexuality.

Given a typically beat homosexual inflection with the appearance of Jack Smith as an alternative interest for Mead, this sexual disjunction is a central motif around which parallel infractions and incongruities in both the diegesis and the form of the film are (dis)organized. Mead's chaplinesque, anarchic improvisations with a variety of incidental trash—encounters with drugs (a ten-gallon can of heroin), with technology (he finally fixes a television by planting its antenna on his head), and with junk foods of all kinds—are self-contained without narrative links, though the monstrous props do ensure a continuity of mood. His improvisations are roughly alternated with exterior scenes in which he and Bryan together wander through the streets and parks of Manhattan. Without developing narrative momentum, the parallel montage does allow the film to extend itself paratactically by building up patterns of antithesis. But since they do not organize any play of expectation and recollection or other tensions of plot, these patterns do not generate the possibility of thematic resolution and narrative closure; all they do is produce a series of false climaxes that are simply stacked one on top of another. The film expands itself unpredictably in alternating waves of intensity and lack; boring sections in which interest seeps away are suddenly revitalized by flashes of Mead's humor or Smith's manic gibberish.

While Rice emphasizes the chaos of the interior *mise en scène* by using strikingly off-angle shots, reproducing compositionally the startling disarray of the profilmic, in general beat values are confined to the characters' desultory escapades and to the refusal of any strong architectural or thematic underpinning for them. The camera is mostly neutral and there is no trick photography, no layering of multiple superimpositions to produce the sumptuous textures, colors, and rhythms of the later *Chumlum* (1964). *Sheba* is distinguished filmically only by the looseness and irresolution of its structure, and by its refusal to engage a purposive narrative form. The emphasis on the activity of the profilmic implies for it an unusual priority in the total cinematic economy that is incommensurate with the commodity function Rice himself imagined for the film, though quite in keeping with his failure to finish it. Rather than the means of producing footage whose real function lies elsewhere, the camera and the general implication of cinema authorize the self-sufficiency of the profilmic activity; they frame a self-regarding play that, more concerned with its own pleasure than the audience's, constitutes what Sidney Peterson designated an *activist* cinema.[13] As the process of shooting generates a self-validating sufficiency in the play of the profilmic, it appropriates from the moment of projection and its commercial uses a greater share of the function of the film. By opening up as potentially autotelic a stage in the production process that is customarily instrumentalized, it makes visible the rationalization by which film's dependence on separate manufacturing processes and the temporal displacements entailed in its production obliges it to recapitulate the division of labor characteristic of industrialization in general.

Such a manipulation of the presence and implications of the apparatus is not intrinsically incompatible with commercial intentions. Self-conscious address to the camera is, of course, a dominant trope of commercial television, where it had developed fully articulate conventions by the fifties. Rice himself expected a career in an industry revitalized by his films, and Warhol became commercially viable by tapping these very charges of narcissistic self-consciousness. Indeed, as profilmic improvisation developed its own grammar of interacting with the camera to complete a vocabulary of histrionic reflexivity, it provided the basis for both the acting of the New Hollywood and the conventions of sixties comedy in general. On the other hand, even in these instances, the foregrounding or rupturing of the continuity of the filmic established the basis for the critique, eventually a political critique, of illusionist cinema. The reflexive features that develop from such self-consciousness will be considered separately as a quasi-autonomous genre, the art film. But here, before moving to underground innovations in the filmic, we must briefly remark on one instance in which the demolition of industrial grammar in profilmic improvisation is thoroughly enacted in the filmic, the remarkable *Blonde Cobra*.

With its depiction of homosexual bohemians communally improvising roles in a generally moribund end-of-the-world atmosphere figured by the frame of New York as a cemetery, *Blonde Cobra* is a prototypical beatnik film. A "Merz-film" mixing deviance and despair with a quintessentially underground flippancy, it was produced communally with Ken Jacobs editing Bob Fleischner's footage and Jack Smith's audio tapes. It is also a dialogue with the industry, a confession *in extremis* of belief in the popular movies of the thirties and forties. The interior *mise en scène* clearly derives from the Arabian/South seas Maria Montez movies (like Robert Siodmak's *Cobra Woman* of which it is a catastrophic remake), and the sequence in which Jerry Sims stabs a man is only the fullest of several invocations of film noir. But if such references attest to the degree to which the vocabularies of fantastic self-projection are supplied by Hollywood, they also denote nostalgia for an era of innocence. That innocence must presently be replaced by a self-con-

13 "There is an element of comedy in film itself, in the very process of filmmaking. . . . This leads to an *activist* attitude toward film among those who are able to enjoy making it. Which is probably why film-makers are so unsatisfactory to critics whose literary instincts lead them to be more interested in what films are about than in what they are. . . . Given the *activist* approach, the tendency to exploit the intrinsic and often misleading comical-diabolical attributes of the medium is almost overwhelming. . . . New and perhaps unintended subjects emerge. Narration succumbs to the comic devices of inconsequence and illogic, and story becomes something that should have been lost with *The Great Train Robbery* but wasn't" (Peterson, 1963: 28–29).

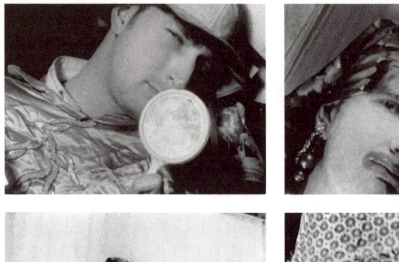

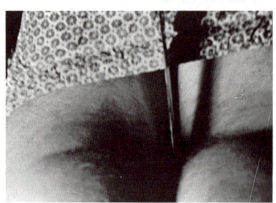

4.33–4.36 *Blonde Cobra*: Jack Smith

scious negation so acute that it all but prevents the film from coming into being. Like Tinguely's *Hommage à New York* the year before, *Blonde Cobra* is primarily a mechanism for self-destruction. While he allows Smith the improvisation of the visual and sound tracks, as editor Jacobs seems to have disassembled rather than assembled Fleischner's footage so as to demolish the conventions of narrative. Visuals and sound are largely, but not systematically, mutually exclusive; Smith's two monologues about the dream of Madame Nescience and his childhood oblige the spectator to improvise visuals out of extended episodes of blank leader. Elsewhere, the visuals are deliberately formless; they carry no narrative and no rhythm that suggests formal development. The whole "turgid dream" is constantly on the point of collapsing back into the mass media detritus from which, like some bedraggled monster from a lost lagoon, it only partially emerges. The effect of its obdurate narcissism is perfectly summarized by Smith's comments: "What went wrong?" and "Let's call the whole thing off."

The primacy of the negative, the subtractive, and the anxiogenic sets the limit to the form of the film in another way, for when the mode of a film is negation, then the practice of cinema becomes abnegation. The dada anti-art gesture that constitutes the film as anti-unified and anti-organic does so in the play between those elements of it that are present and those that depend on these vestigial presences only to make apparent their own absence. *Blonde Cobra*'s minimalism and meagerness, its aggressive imperfection, stand, then, as the recognition that the social permeation of commercial film is so total that non-commodity culture can only consist of the private reorganization of fragments of the mass cultural product, and that the only response to the hegemony of the industrial practice capable of integrity is the denial of the medium itself. The coherent anti-film includes only as much implication of film-as-such as its negation of it may body forth. For its authority, as Cage remarked, film had "to find a way for it to include invisibility" (Cage, 1970: 116). Here such an inversion discovers the complete register of the contradictions that surround the desire to make an authentic film. *Blonde Cobra* looks like the worst film ever made; that is the condition of its excellence.

The broken berm *Blonde Cobra* hacked from the scarp of the industry is at best a negative celebration of cinema; so precipitous was the decline around it that its affirmation had to be marginal, contingent upon the narrowness of its reservation. The mood it represents was complemented by the more typical underground conventions, which responded to industrial styles not by thinning them to the point of virtual depletion as does *Blonde Cobra* and other Jacobs films, but by intensifying them, multiplying them into a bebop frenetic density and richness. Brakhage with his barrages of superimpositions and multiple cuts that amass an overpowering optical energy is the prototypical instance of the manufacture of the filmic equivalent not of diminished but of expanded vision. With the growing popularity of hallucinogens, the tropes of Brakhage's mode made their way even into commercial film like Roger Corman's *The Trip* (1967), where they were taken as simulating and even inducing psychedelic consciousness.

Innovations in this area of "expanded cinema" span two primary poles: the development of a film style and content that had some direct relationship to meditational practice or visionary experience and the development of viewing situations in which consumption of film and other manipulations of light were integrated into social situations more dynamic than those of the conventional theater. Transcendence of the rationalized ego in inventions of cinema as religious experience was facilitated by rituals in which such private perceptions could be experienced socially. Though neither of these developments was without its aporias, in their separate and occasionally overlapping ways they mark a significant incursion into the constraints of commodity cinema. The work of Jordan Belson and Ben Van Meter may be taken to illustrate them.[14]

PRACTICE IN THE FILMIC: JORDAN BELSON

Asian religions were almost as important as jazz in beat aesthetics. Buddhism's subordination of dogma to meditational practices that integrated mental and physical disciplines was crucial in the

14 The best source of information on "expanded cinema" is Gene Youngblood's book of that title (Youngblood, 1970). The celebration of the supposed reciprocation between psychedelic drugs and technological innovation was especially a West Coast phenomena, but see Mekas (1972: 118, 145) for parallels in the New York underground. Noting how expanded cinema had been anticipated during the period of the historical avant-garde, Wollen cites Van Doesburg: "The spectator space will become part of the film space. The separation of 'projection surface' is abolished. The spectator will no longer observe the film, like a theatrical presentation, but will participate in it optically and acoustically" (Wollen, 1982: 94). See also Wolfe (1968) for descriptions of California psychedelic events, including the Trips Festival discussed below.

15 Since he so thoroughly reproduces the euphoric rhetoric of the
period and its assumptions, Gene
Youngblood remains the most interesting critic of Belson; his position is
summarized in the suggestion that
"by bringing together Eastern theology, Western science, and con-
sciousness-expanding drugs, Belson
predates the front ranks of the avant
garde today" (Youngblood, 1970:
159). P. Adams Sitney has no problem in repeating this evaluation,
even though he replaces the techno-
euphoria with an aesthetic absolut-
ism; Belson's "personal cinema
delineates the mechanisms of transcendence in the rhetoric of abstrac-
tionism" (Sitney, 1979: 265).
Within the avant-garde tradition,
Belson and what became theorized
as a West Coast psychedelic school
suffered most as hard-core structur-
alists tried to shatter the Romantic
line; Malcolm Le Grice's assessment—"not significantly different in
kind to the car chase in *The French
Connection*" (Le Grice, 1977: 83)—
is the least reasonable of these.

beat critique of post-enlightenment ideologies of progress, materialism, and ego-affirmation, and because it was unincriminated by
association with modern institutions, it could supply the basis for a
social ethic. Eventually, widespread commercialization depleted
countercultural use of Asian religions as a model for translating the
perceptual transformations caused by hallucinogens into utopian
social programs; still, varying levels of filmic innovations and even
forms of resistance to mass marketing were sustained through these
religions. Buddhism was especially valuable for filmmakers, since its
emphasis on vision in meditation made it possible for spiritual functions to be adapted directly from it to film and made film easily
adaptable to these functions. Especially on the West Coast, where
Asian religions had currency on many cultural levels, the received
tradition of graphic abstract film was tuned to religious uses, despite
continuing tensions between the formal and mystical sources. In the
work of James Whitney and Jordan Belson, the tradition of Mary
Ellen Bute, Douglas Crockwell, and Oskar Fischinger, who used abstract film as visual music, is extended to allow reference to interior
or transcendental realities (though Fischinger himself was not without mystical interests). Proposing graphic, aural, and rhythmic
equivalence with expanded states of consciousness, Belson's films
present themselves as objects of meditational attention.

Belson's earliest films were single-frame animations, strongly influenced by the work of Fischinger and the Whitneys, which he saw
at the Art in Cinema Series in San Francisco in 1947. The switch to
the real-time photography of his mature mode was facilitated by his
collaboration with the electronic music composer Henry Jacobs in
the Vortex concerts at the Morrison Planetarium from 1957 to
1960, where the star machine, aurora borealis machines, shooting
stars, and the other resources allowed him to develop many of his
rhetorical motifs, as well as supplying a model of the synaesthetic
interchange between sound and vision. *Allures* (1961), the culmination of this phase, depends heavily on the movement of geomet-
rical shapes of uniformly colored light in a black field, and where
spatial depth is suggested it is usually by means of superimposed
symmetrical grids. This formal material is interspersed with cos-
mological imagery, most prominently with a strongly centered sun
that is sequentially filled with different colors. After abandoning
film for several years in the early sixties to study Hatha Yoga, Belson
returned with *Re-Entry* (1964) and a sequence of films, including
Phenomena (1965), *Samadhi* (1967), *Cosmos* (1969), *Momentum*
(1969), *World* (1970), *Meditation* (1971), and *Chakra* (1972),
which simulate the experience of meditation. Though their man-
dalic imagery is prefigured by James Whitney's *Yantra* (1955) and
Lapis (1966), these constitute Belson's achievement, a film practice
in which kinaesthetic optical effects are both produced in response
to the visual and visionary experience of altered states of consciousness and used to achieve them.[15]

In these films the primarily two-dimensional screen and the geo-
metric forms of the graphic tradition are replaced by a quasi-illu-

sionist interstellar space, in which light is an almost palpable though diffuse presence, often independent of the organic, nebulous shapes and forms upon which it falls. Some images seem to designate or at least refer to natural phenomena like clouds, rain, or planets, and rather than being split into discrete phases with different optical maneuvers, they are continuously structured by progressive visual and aural pulses. Though the compositions are frequently de-centered and asymmetrical, still they recur to and strongly foreground circular shapes that invoke both the physical eye and cosmic space, affirming a series of metaphors—of the voyage through outer space as a voyage through inner space, or of optical vision as spiritual vision, for example—that are common in religious thought, the very concept of the Heavens being summary.

Samadhi, for example, a five-minute, unsigned work, begins with the explosion of the light blue pseudo-oriental letters of its title into white dust in a pulsating, convolving mass of cloud-like forms. Washed over in multicolored, constantly changing light, these congeal into a circular, centered ball. After this prelude, the film settles into a roughly regular rhythmic alternation between more or less strongly articulated circular forms and an all-over field from which they are gathered and to which they return. First, a revolving but irregular blue sphere containing internally refracted white light ac-

129
Underground Film

4.37–4.40 Jordan Belson, *Samadhi*

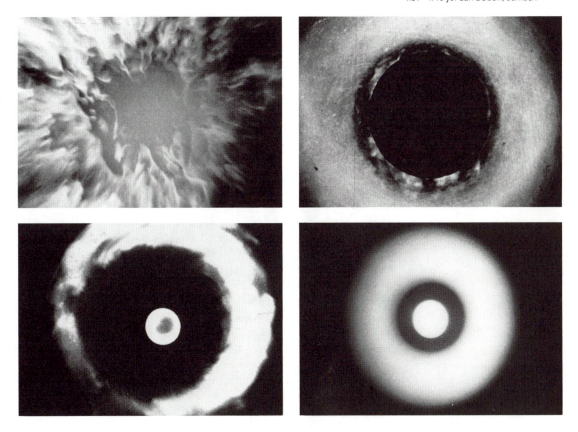

quires clear symmetrical outlines as it passes through reds and greens, eventually coming to resemble a rotating red planet. A figure/ground switch in coloration transforms it into a blue eyeball in a red eye, then into a burning sun, and then back to a black eyeball in a white field. As this sphere passes through other colors, its clarity dissolves into the initial blue form and then into an indefinite blue and green field. From this emerge several concentric rings in different shades of red which, constantly imploding and exploding into each other, alternately fill the frame, pushing themselves out beyond the screen, or retreat into deep space as sharp planetary forms. These lose their clarity in a largely yellow and then white all-over pulse. Strongly articulated blue circles emerge from a point of white light, rapidly transubstantiating into one another as they surge out from the surface of the screen. They dissolve into a smoky, amorphous space, through which a traveling white sphere englobes and becomes transparent to illuminate anamorphically distorted landscapes. The sphere becomes diffused into a field of white and blue, from which the earlier revolving skeins of blue light emerge and into which they finally disappear. After the opening, the film is cyclically, or perhaps serially, organized; without structural crisis or resolution, it appears as a fragment from an infinite spatial and temporal field. Nodes of energy crystallize, then fall away, as if in its rhythmic interchange between the biological and the empyrean the film embodies the experience of *samadhi*, a Sanskrit word meaning the meditational state of calm concentration where subject-object dualisms are transcended.

Belson records that *Samadhi* marked an unusual coincidence of his meditational and filmmaking practices—"the only one in which I actually caught up with the film and ran alongside of it for just a moment" (cited in Youngblood, 1970: 174)—a relation between film and the artist's spiritual life that epitomizes a religious rather than a mercantile use of the medium. His work stands, then, as a negation of the bourgeois era in art—a revival of a pre-secular as well as a pre-industrial practice—which is especially notable since it was effected in one of the media of mechanical reproduction that destroyed cultic values. Despite the political occlusions such projects depend on (and these were, if anything, overemphasized as varieties of structuralism proposed the demystification of filmic presence as the precondition for understanding its political function) and although its peculiarly pleasurable sensuality was quite easily amenable to commercial usage (and, in fact, Belson himself occasionally did special effects for Hollywood), his use of the medium in devotional practice remains salutary. Rather than attempting to evade his spirituality or justify it by translating its transcendental vocabulary into a therapeutic one, it may stand as a utopian aspiration in which austere meticulousness in the fabrication of visionary splendor, however compromised, instances a model emancipation from the surrounding cinema, a "beautiful image of liberation" (Marcuse, 1978: 6).

Just as easily as it may sustain a libidinal refusal preliminary to social contestation, however, such an affirmation of the radical autonomy of the spiritual may be co-opted back into the cultural conditions it seeks to escape. Neither the use of the meditational vocabulary per se nor the narration of the quest for a perceptual breakthrough to the pure light of samadhic consciousness leads with any surety to progressive social action, even if the hunger they speak to is among its preconditions. Such radical subjectivity, however, becomes reactionary when it uncritically incorporates within itself elements of the conditions it should seek to transcend. The association of spiritual quests with contemporary technological developments, especially the space industry, which so readily supplied a context for the interplanetary vocabulary, was a common instance of such a lack of historical understanding. The failure to distinguish between the cosmic imagery and the political implications of the U.S. space program—which, as well as everything else, is a failure of religious thought, a failure to distinguish between the transcendental and the mundane—often circumscribed the liberating potential of the spiritual, containing it in the apparatus of the very repression that engendered its urgency.

Such a Fullerian naiveté, common in counterculture techno-euphoria, is most clear in Belson's successors, in John Stehura's *Cybernetik 5.3* (1969), for example, in which the visionary eye is the mediator between subatomic revolutions, their isomorphic counterparts in the celestial sphere, and tribal gatherings down below, or in Scott Bartlett's *Moon 69* (1969), which identifies the Apollo space program as a religious quest. Beginning with a chorus of astronauts reading from Genesis, it intersperses solarized images of space modules, astronauts, and even banks of television consoles monitoring the space voyage with a similarly solarized shot of an Indian philosopher talking about unity in the cosmos, building up to a flicker climax underscored by rapidly accelerating pulses of sound in which a rocket takeoff is simulated. Belson himself never allowed the spiritual endeavor to become mere valorizing resonance around a naive ode to expansionist military capitalism in this manner; but traces of such contradictions are present even in his work, in the rocket take-

4.41–4.42 Scott Bartlett, *Moon 69*

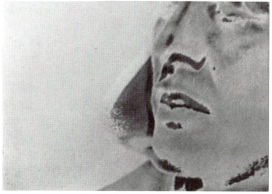

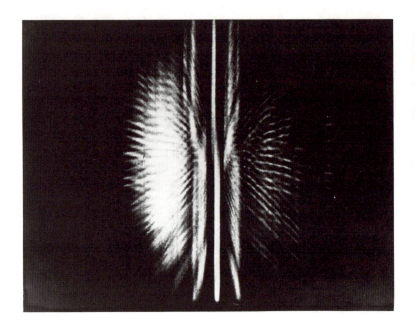

4.43 Jordan Belson, *Re-Entry*

off at the beginning of *Momentum*, for instance, and especially in *Re-Entry*, a crucial work marking his own re-entry back into film-making. This latter takes space travel for its dominant metaphor and iconography, using John Glenn's earth orbit as the vehicle for a visual reproduction of the Tibetan concept of the *bardo*, and using Glenn's voice on the sound track. Vestiges of the symmetrical mechanical imagery that was later replaced by the nebulous forms are made to suggest space technology. Banks of red and yellow lights seem to resemble either an airport or the underside of a fleet of planes; similar phases structure the film in the manner of *Moon 69*, especially *Re-Entry*'s climactic section which simulates movement through space to arrive at a perfect circle in a black space, a cosmic tunnel down which the camera looks into the light.

Belson himself maintained an aloof distance from the mid-sixties explosion of expanded cinema events, insisting that his films be shown separately in highly controlled situations and refusing to join the Canyon Co-op or to participate in hippie social rituals. Clear parallels remain, however, between the implications of his work and the various multimedia events of the period 1966–68. His use of film as a component in religious practice and his relocation of its representational capacity from the natural to the psycho-spiritual world entailed subversion of its commodity function; in the light shows such de-instrumentalization of production and transformation of the functions of consumption are recapitulated in a social form, but also extended so that projection itself becomes the site of creativity where the somatic passivity of theatrical consumption is replaced by ecstatic engagement.

In adopting from oil painting and bourgeois theater the quattro-cento perspective, monocular point of view, and other conventions for the illusionist representation of the material world that allowed it to supply the vicarious possession essential to commodity specta-cle, film became an accomplice to the other apparatuses of sensory fragmentation and reification of the modern world. The enforced physical immobility of the spectator within fixed seating furthered the separation of vision and hearing from the activity of the whole body. The extreme of this rationalization, itself only a material re-fraction of the post-Kantian reification of art in general, was reached not in the commercial cinema but in Peter Kubelka's view-ing booths at the original Anthology Film Archives. Each "a *ma-chine for film viewing*" (Sitney, 1975: vii), immobilized and impris-oned the spectator as a monadic visual consumer, repressing even the social interaction allowed in the commercial theater (let alone the amorous play which has been its great redeeming function). In-terrupting the history of cinema as authority and discipline, the multimedia light show discovered itself in a dance against somatic repression.

In the late sixties, a spectrum of events and environments shat-

4.44 Cinema of Anthology Film Ar-chives . . . "a machine for film viewing."

tered the parameters of cinema: institutional extravaganzas like the multi-screen constructions at the New York World's Fair and the Montreal Expo '67, John Cage and Ronald Nameth's HSPCHD event at the University of Illinois in 1969, and Jud Yalkut's presentation of *Festival Mix* at the University of Cincinnati in 1968; more genuinely subcultural festivals including the Single Wing Turquoise Bird performances in Los Angeles, the many equivalents in San Francisco that followed from Henry Jacobs and Jordan Belson's Vortex concerts between 1957 and 1960, and Andy Warhol's Exploding Plastic Inevitable in New York; Ken Jacobs's projected light and shadow manipulations and light sculpture by individual artists such as James Turrell and Robert Irwin; and more popular versions of similar effects in concert halls or in the neighborhood psychedelic discothèque. In their different ways, all of these produced transformations of optical experience that mediated between parallel expansions in both the mental and social theaters.

In place of the confining rectangle of the film frame and the closure of narrative or even the terminal truncations of the abstract film, light shows offered a three-dimensional visual field, matrixed neither spatially nor temporally, which dispersed rather than unified subjectivity. The various mixes of representational and abstract imagery, the diversity, irregularity, and overlapping of the projection surfaces, the different rhythms of the different projection apparatuses, the mix of predetermined and aleatory effects, and the free mobility of the participant all combined in a continuously transforming, enveloping, pan-sensual experience that could be entered and exited at will, a circumambient theater of light and sound that strove never to be distinct or distinguishable from the interior projection of hallucination. The work of Belson opened up a passage between images of the natural and the supernatural worlds; similarly, in the psychedelic festivals the transformation of visual reality, in the intermix of concrete and abstract and in the suspension of the logical, narrative, or metonymic relations between images, both derived from and constituted psychedelic reality and its re-vision of ordinary reality. Such festivals, then, were not merely occasions when images of hippies were returned to them, though the self-representation of the alternative culture remained centrally important; they were also occasions when the terms of that culture were discovered, practiced, and elaborated, the means by which it constituted itself.

This opening of the optical field, and the conceptual and kinetic liberation of the spectator within it, was often construed as either analogous to or premonitory of some paradigmatic genetic shift in which the engineering of consciousness would parallel developments in the electronic communications industries—an instance of "man's ongoing historical drive to manifest his consciousness outside of his mind" (Youngblood, 1970: 41), for example. Since they omitted consideration of the political control of the new technologies, such expectations were naively collusive; but their utopian decentralization did, to some extent, inform social relations within the

4.45 Ben Van Meter (upper left) and Roger Hillyard (lower right) doing liquid projection at the Avalon Ballroom, 1966

events themselves. In the performances of the Single Wing Turquoise Bird, for example, and in the Fillmore and Avalon Ballroom events, projection was instituted as collective improvisation; at the latter up to six people at the same time had control over several projectors of different gauges, as well as liquid projectors, banks of slide projectors, strobes, and spotlights. All equipment could be spontaneously manipulated to interact with the music; projectors thus became instruments that could be *played*,[16] apparatuses through which the projectionists could interact with each other, collectively composing visual events in response to the present of projection.

Like other countercultural rituals, the innovations of the light shows were contained within the economic operations of mainstream society; nevertheless, they did permit a temporary modification of the social relations of film production. The non-hierarchical distribution of authorship in cultural production, demanded by hippie ideology, may rarely have been implemented as material prac-

16 The idea of "playing" visual instruments of one kind or another has several antecedents, including Lazlo's "color piano" and Thomas Wilfred's "color organ." According to Hans Richter, the Russian, Rosinee, demonstrated in 1925 "an instrument with which colors and forms could be freely and voluntarily moved and changed" that was used in entr'actes in playhouses to show "sequences of abstract forms in pure colors" (Richter, 1947: 21). Improvising visual effects in response to music was also a feature of John Whitney's early methods; he drew on an oil bath so as to coordinate visuals with prerecorded music: "So I would rehearse two or three riffs of a piece, plan it more or less spontaneously right there and then shoot it" (Whitney, 1980: 217). In the same essay, which looks forward to real-time visual composition through computer technology, Whitney also records a proposal made in the early fifties to use various manipulation techniques on video cameras: "Then we'd perform a real-time graphic experience as an ensemble" (ibid.). Not until Morgan Fisher's *Projection Instructions* (1976) would projection again be creative rather than merely mechanical, but by then the projectionist, like the audience, would have reverted to monadic isolation.

tice, and light shows were largely supplied to the audience by film-makers and light-show artists, just as the social event was the entrepreneurial appropriation of what ideally should have been a communal social activity. But still there remained a greater degree of communalism in film production here than in any other cinema. The distinctions between artist and audience were challenged on several levels. The activity of the projectionists was only one item in a total event which, to a much greater extent than in orthodox theaters, presupposed active participation by the audience; rather than manifesting in other spheres the categorical producer/consumer relationships, filmmakers were more like surrogates for or proxy agents of the community; and the values, optical and social, enacted in the visual displays were communally produced and experienced as subcultural self-representation. Just as the dadaists made films for their soirées, Ben Van Meter, for instance, would shoot footage in Haight-Ashbury during the week and show it on Saturday night at the Fillmore with people in the audience frequently recognizing themselves on the screens. If only to a degree that allows for perception of an ideal rather than its thorough exemplification, such subcultural self-production was in effect collective documentation, a public form of the diary film in which the apparatus was used by a community to document itself for itself—for its own self-recognition and subsequent elaboration as a community.

Though this expanded cinema is event-specific, traces of it remain in several films—in Ronald Nameth's documentation, *Andy Warhol's Exploding Plastic Inevitable* (1966), and in Ben Van Meter's *S.F. Trips Festival, An Opening* (1966). Held in late January 1966, the Trips Festival was an entrepreneurial assembling of previous innovations in mixed media performance, notably Ken Kesey's Acid Tests. For each of the festival's three nights, Van Meter exposed the same four 100′ rolls, sometimes using his hand as a traveling matte and varying exposure and focus so that images on each of the three levels of superimposition are continually in the process of emerging from and dissolving back into each other. The spectacular and maximally visual diegesis fabricated in the film is thus a collage, collapsing spatial and temporal distinctions into a continuous perceptual flow that identifies the people in the film with the environment and the event. Personal differences, certainly as constitutive of bounded egos, are subsumed in the synaesthesia of the collectivity in which dancers, musicians, filmmakers, spectators, people of all races—all are performers, permeated by the fractured luminescence of the hall and suffused by the light of old movies, educational slides, and strobe lights that is projected all over its interior.

In this stream of visual and acoustical images, the continuous interpenetration and displacement of one by another engages the spectator's attention simultaneously on different layers of superimposed vision. The film simulates the perceptions of people under the influence of psychedelics, and so produces a documentary which in its own historical moment was formally and ideologically consonant with the festival rather than in contradiction to it. This corre-

4.46–4.48 Ben Van Meter, *S.F. Trips Festival, An Opening*

spondence between *énoncé* and *énonciation* depends in large part upon the film's function. Though now it must be rented and projected under the same conditions as any other film, originally it was projected as a component in other, subsequent light shows, itself playing a part in generating an environment like the one it documents. Instead of being either displaced from its subcultural location or obliged to enter into social transactions antithetical to it, the film participated in developing and reproducing the rituals of the subculture.[17]

The Idea of Practice: Cinema beyond Film

As they allow the activities of production their own meaning and pleasure, over and above their instrumentality in the manufacture of the commodity object, these practices nevertheless open out into psychic, discursive, symbolic, and other modes of engagement with the film industry. In them Hollywood is recognized as the source and repository of the myths of American society, but also as the embodiment of the dominant role of the communications industries in the array of institutions that constitute the modern world. The former, the critique of specific qualities of the commercial cinema,

17 A similarly important counter-culture documentary is Kelly Hart's *Nowsreal*. A Digger, Hart made the film for free showings, and while on one level it is merely a loose compilation of hippie activities—practicing yoga, dancing in the park, burning money—on another it too articulates its own other functions in the subculture, specifically in respect to issues of spectatorship and financing. The film's final sequence, for example, which builds up to a rapid, eventually single-frame, parallel montage of a sunset imposed upon a young woman belly-dancing, intercuts shots of businessmen in the street as if they were watching the dancer. Whereas in similar shots at the beginning of the film they had been hostile, now they appear to applaud the dancer as if they had changed during the film. Similarly, its frequent references to money—demands for free housing, money being burned, the Diggers giving away free food—all foreground its own rejection of commodity status and so articulate its non-exploitative relation to the counterculture it documents.

informs the underground's self-production as an alternative to Hollywood and also as an intertextual dialogue with it. But as an introduction to this confrontation we may take note of the possibility that the latter—the role of the movies in general, the movies as an idea distinct from any specific product in the collectively imagined symbolic economy—may be appropriated as the vehicle for fantasy reenactment or even as the metaphor ordering the revolutions of everyday life. Thus filmmaking may become a partially dematerialized ritual, the site of symbolic operations. The most complete vision of such an activity is depicted by Dennis Hopper in *The Last Movie*, in which Peruvian villagers use straw cameras in a ritual exorcism of a Hollywood film crew. A similarly exemplary case at one of the most luminous moments of the counterculture is that of Ken Kesey and the Merry Pranksters.[18]

As LSD turned Kesey away from the rational and the conceptual and toward the intuitive, the numinous, and the nonverbal, so writing, the medium of his celebrity, increasingly appeared a function of obsolete states of consciousness. It was therefore abandoned for film, putatively an intrinsically more visionary medium, more compatible with the experience of psychedelics since it operated on a more primary psychic level, and one whose mass popularity would make it more useful in effecting social changes. Kesey's own first acid trip had derived part of its visual vocabulary from Hollywood—he had seen "waves of white desert movie sand dunes each one with MGM shadow longshot of the ominous A-rab coming up over the next crest" (Wolfe, 1968: 42)—and his ambition was to provide a model in a film of his own by which such industrial determination of the furthest reaches of the psyche could be supplanted by images more germane to the ethics of LSD and the social changes it implied. He therefore redefined himself as a movie director, his friends as movie producers and movie technicians, and reported to the press that he was engaged on a vast experimental movie, *Intrepid Traveller and His Merry Pranksters Leave in Search of a Cool Place*.

Like other underground films, this one would communicate countercultural values to the outside world, both through the trip it documented and also through the manner of that documentation.

> The Pranksters spent much of the fall of 1964, and the winter, and the early spring of 1965, working on . . . The Movie. They had about forty-five hours of color film from the bus trip, and once they got to going over it, it was a monster. Kesey had high hopes for the film, on every level. It was the world's first acid film, taken under conditions of total spontaneity barreling through the heartlands of America, recording all *now*, in the moment. The current fantasy was . . . a total breakthrough in terms of expression . . . but also something that would amaze and delight many multitudes, a movie that could be shown commercially as well as in the esoteric world of the heads. But The Movie was a monster, as I say. The sheer labor and tedium

18 All information on Kesey derives from Tom Wolfe's account (Wolfe, 1968).

in editing forty-five hours of film was unbelievable. And besides
. . . much of the film was out of focus. Hagen, like everybody
else, had been soaring half the time, and the bouncing of the
bus hadn't helped especially—*but that was the trip!* Still . . .
Also, there were very few establishing shots, shots showing
where the bus was when this or that took place. But who needs
that old Hollywood thing of long shot, medium shot, closeup,
and the careful cuts and wipes and pans and dolly in and dolly
out, the old bullshit. (Ibid.: 137–38)

Pushing the beat aesthetic of present-ness in the shooting process to
an extreme, the film's form so thoroughly reproduced the psychedelic experience that it left behind the possibilities of even making a
finished product, let alone one capable of being widely circulated.
Kesey failed to understand that the utopian imperative of psychedelics could not achieve mass currency except as neutralized and re-
contained in commodity culture (and, in fact, the *Intrepid Traveller*
project was preempted by the sanitized imitation, *The Magical Mystery Tour*). But this failure was a function of a larger critical failure,
Kesey's inability to distinguish between the liberating potential of
the *idea* of the movies, radically reconceptualized as the interaction
of separate subjectivities, and the proto-fascist control of mass subjectivity by the entertainment industries. Thus in Kesey's practice
the process of shooting the film, as either an autotelic act or as the
formalization of alternative optical and social experience, modu-
lates into a more comprehensive psychic strategy in which the conceptualization of reality as a movie and oneself as its director transcends the need for actual film production. It is in this more
extensive recourse to the medium as a metaphor for consciousness
and a model for behavior that the potentialities of "acid" filmmaking extend out to include all phenomenal experience and then all
reality as a projection of a director's own ego and consciousness.

Kesey took the idea that in one's life one lives out a script—a
metaphor common in the culturally adjacent transactional analysis
therapy—and grounded it in the biology of perception. Because of
the lag in the nervous system, all sensory registration of experience
is necessarily displaced: "We are all of us doomed to spend our lives
watching a *movie* of our lives—we are always acting on what has
just finished happening" (ibid.: 145). Since our lives are movies in
which we act a role, social relationships become a jockeying for
dominance between rival subjective realities, a collision of different
movies. Crucial confrontations, as with the police, for example, are
determined not by rational or physical strength, but by psychic maneuvers in which each participant attempts to incorporate the
others in his or her own perceptual gestalt, thus demonstrating his
or her own "movie" as more comprehensive and potent than those
it confronts.

Having successfully included even the Hell's Angels in their
movie, the Pranksters moved from local confrontations to public
ones, to Acid Tests—where, as at the Trips Festival, movies proper

were only one element in a multi-sensual array of total psychologi-cal incorporation—and even beyond these to the mass media at large. As Warhol demonstrated, the ultimate movie in a mediated society was to incorporate the whole world into your trip, just as the ultimate trip was to incorporate the whole world into your movie. Hence the apogee of Kesey's project occurred when the pub-licity about the acid test graduation mobilized the San Francisco media about him: "They've got the whole town in their movie by now" (ibid.: 382). But it was also his final failure. Despite his no-toriety, his control of the media was temporary; he was outdis-tanced, as he was in the manufacture of the actual trip movie, by a superior movie, the Beatles'. Their ability to control media attention circumscribed his own; they were powerful enough to refuse the invitation to his ranch, for their movie included his, and he had to go to see them. His disgust at the Beatles concert, where the band appeared as a cancerous head that had lost control of the public body that mindlessly worshiped it, marked his own psychological and social failure, as well as the failure of his critical intelligence. But it also marked the historical termination of the cultural hege-mony of the medium he had chosen as the vehicle and the metaphor for his social mission. By 1966 the movies' power to demand and manipulate the libidinal investment of the youth cultures had been purloined. Rock music was a bigger movie than the movies.

Underground Intertextuality

It is a general illumination which bathes all the other colors and modifies their particularity.
— Karl Marx

The de-instrumentalization of the various processes of cinema in the re-creation of profilmic performance, shooting, editing, distri-bution, and consumption as autotelic practices follows from the project of creating an alternative to Hollywood rather than from any desire to reform it. The expropriation of the apparatus from the corporation and the redefinition of its uses is the signal achievement of underground film, categorically more significant than its formal innovations, though inseparable from such as their precondition. This radical significance is, however, misunderstood if it is assumed that these functions allowed complete emancipation from the values and history of the industry or were achieved spontaneously as prac-tices springing fully formed *ex nihil* or from an autonomous avant-garde tradition. Stan Brakhage clarified his mature mode only after an apprenticeship in narrative forms that, he claimed, were in-formed by Griffith's tropes; and even the meditational cinema of James Whitney or Jordan Belson has its origins in a graphic cinema fully integrated with the industry. Its father figure, Oskar Fisch-inger, was brought to the United States by Paramount, and he worked in Hollywood whenever he could; similarly, John Whit-ney's own contribution to the titles for *Vertigo* is only the best known instance of the regular commercial use of his innovations.

These and other artists, both in the underground and in even
more recalcitrant cinemas to which we shall attend, do, however,
stand as limits in the total field of film production. Between them
and the routine output of the industry lies the spectrum of production more or less affiliated with the industry in general, the range of
practices maintaining various kinds of intercourse with Hollywood
as both a stylistic matrix and an exemplary mode of production.
The underground's opposition to Hollywood was accompanied by
dialogues with it, which make clear that while the underground may
have been inspired and stylistically nourished by extra-industrial
priorities, by other art forms, and preeminently by social developments, the most significant determinant upon it was Hollywood itself.

The complex intertextuality of independent film's reference to the
industry in the filmic is also enacted in the material realms of production, distribution, and consumption. A full materialist taxonomy would clarify the relation between all the various alternative
modes of production and the industry, and the evolution of new
working methods, ranging from the use of friends through more
formal arrangements such as film schools, then nonunion crews,
and so forth, up to the point at which so-called independent production is carried on under the industry's wing. Similarly, the area
of consumption would be broken down to clarify intermediate situations between the points of absolute non-distribution and industrial distribution. Locations on this gradational scale include authorial withholding (for example, the early films of Warhol and the
films of Jack Smith, Gregory Markopoulos, and Barbara Rubin)
and repression by the police and the courts; domestic screenings (in
the lofts of the lower East Side in Manhattan for the works of Smith,
Rice, and Warhol, or in Brakhage's living room, or in Ernest Callen-
bach's garden in the early days of Canyon Cinema); the more formal screening societies, where underground film often was interspersed with old Hollywood films; and film festivals of various
kinds.

No more than the films themselves, these practices are not reducible to a synchronic field; they do not mark stable positions in some
absolute, transhistorical table of possible modes. In general, underground cinema migrated from essentially domestic exhibition
through special theatrical showings and eventually into the museum
and classroom and the occasional commercial outlet, even as motifs
innovated in the underground were constantly finding their way
into fringe Hollywood productions and from there to the films of
the major studios. All these influences and determinations have their
own histories, and together they compose the institutional history
of the avant-garde and the history of its own realization both as
other to the industry and as a means of production for the industry
itself. Although we will not record these histories here, we will examine the overt presence of Hollywood in the filmic of the avant-
garde. The history of this penetration and incorporation is not simply a history of formal, filmic relationships, for it always intersects

4.49–4.51 Stan Vanderbeek, *Science Friction*

with the other historical function of the underground, the critique of contemporary society in protest film.

By the late fifties the realization that macro-political issues—the cold war, for example, or institutional racism—were not separable from the priorities of consumer society in general was widespread. Given the received hegemony of Hollywood in mass culture, any critique of American society inevitably returned to it, discovering the logical and the formal basis of a satirical genre that proposed the mass media as both symptom and cause of cultural decadence. This underground protest genre is exemplified by the collages of Stan Vanderbeek.

In his *Science Friction* (1959), for example, the debris from print advertising and the popular press functions simultaneously in two ways. On the one hand, it is the major source of imagery by which the satire on the confrontational aspect of the cold war, the arms race, and modern technology in general is articulated; on the other, it is itself the object of satire, the manifestation of a logical connection between the materialistic obsessions of advertising and the permeation of the texture of everyday life by technological overdevelopment. Newspapers themselves turn into missiles, and rockets are constructed out of pictures of the tail fins of fifties automobiles. In one set piece, a TV screen is the frame through which pass two women comparing the brightness of underwear they have washed, a man injecting a brain with a huge hypodermic needle, a Wild West comic, a handgun, a movie cowboy, a collage of brassiere ads, a young woman in a prom dress, and a boxing glove punching out a policeman; a finger switches the set off, but almost immediately the screen is shattered by a rocket. The industrialization and indeed the militarization of everyday life is similarly figured in a later section in which all the appurtenances of a "house-beautiful" cutout of a fifties "nuclear" family home are transformed into missiles. Images of a cigarette lighter, a pen, a dessert glass, a fork, the family cat, and even a medieval Madonna turn into rockets, and then, as a man reads the headline "4 Ton Atlas Missile Put Into Orbit," a rocket crashes into his home, leading to a finale in which magazine images of the architecture of the entire West, the Capitol, the Washington Monument, and the Statue of Liberty all take off in phallic aggression.

Such a double valency in mass media images is similarly exploited in dialogues with Hollywood, which are implemented in two forms: in the intradiegetic reenactment of the characteristic narrative structures, histrionic modes, and other vocabularies of the commercial feature, which Warhol most thoroughly explored, and in collage modification of fragments of industrial films—modification which is either less systematic than the subsequent manipulations of structural film or systematic in relation to thematic issues rather than to the materials of the medium. Usually, the two forms of incorporation were pursued separately. The former, in the Kuchar-Smith-Warhol tradition, continues down through John Waters to dissolve into B-picture genres; the latter, the more classically modernist collage tradition, follows from Joseph Cornell but was especially important on the West Coast, where it continued through the seventies in Pat O'Neill's elaborate image modifications of found footage and in Chick Strand's collages like *Loose Ends*. The analysis of Hollywood's role in modern capitalism is more specific in the explicitly engaged cinema into which the underground developed in the last half of the decade, but, opening the way for that politicization, underground film constantly referred to the production of the inauthenticity of everyday life by the inauthenticity of the commercial cinema. The polarization of the alternative and the commercial cinemas only rarely allowed the films of the former to generate their own specificity; more typically, it resulted in a homogenized mix of affection and disparagement with irony as its central structural device. The films of the Kuchar Brothers, Kenneth Anger, Bruce Conner, and Bruce Baillie represent four different situations with respect to Hollywood, four kinds of social and eventually political criticism mediated via reference to commercial film.

THE CRITIQUE OF AUTHENTICITY: THE KUCHARS

The early 16mm works of the Kuchar brothers are amateur reconstructions of the vocabulary of Hollywood B pictures of the forties and fifties, especially of Douglas Sirk's melodramas and Roger Corman's horror films. The parallels between these "pop" films and pop painting is direct (and, in fact, Warhol's middle period owes much to them): first, authorship is inscribed not in the narrative or the imagery so much as in the self-consciously domestic manufacture; second, in the quotation of industrial motifs, affection is indistinguishable from a self-conscious distancing that suggests but always short-circuits explicit criticism; and third, signification hovers between the generic stock and the hypothetical real life outside film that the diegesis invokes but never asserts. Any moment in a Kuchar film—a grimace, a pose, a stabbing, a lighting effect, or a costume—can never have presence as itself; it can only be the point at which the absence of any extratextual experience sufficient to legitimize its emotional claims intersects with the absence of production values or acting skills sufficient to secure an image of professional quality. The one-dimensional emotions set in play—love, hate, desire, and despair—evoke their industrial models; but they are so exaggerated and artificial, either so rapidly impacted upon each other or separated by such torpid interludes of posing, and juxtaposed with so little regard for thematic, psychological, or even narrative continuity, that they simultaneously abort claims they make. Yet the obvious quotation of emotions, the mixture of over- and under-acting, and the artificiality of the profilmic are never sufficient entirely to discredit the narrative. The films always reserve their own seriousness at some level, and so always preserve some degree of thematic urgency. The oscillation between lampoon and emulation strategically preempts the unequivocal affirmation of either; the authentic can be present in neither art nor nature, film nor life, but only glimpsed, fragmentarily, in the practice that slips desperately between them.

The similarity between accidental incompetence and the deliberate subversion of industrial codes is itself present in the Hollywood sources, where the Corman Z movie, for example, stands in something of the same relation to the films of the major studios that a Kuchar film stands in relation to the Z movie. Since the sixties this critical double bind has provided the basis for a self-consciously produced genre of "bad" movies, and for a reevaluation of older directors like Edward D. Wood, Jr., and Oscar Micheaux which has elevated them from bad to "bad." In this tradition the simultaneous engagement and discrediting of a generic discourse undermines all statements made within it. Consequently, ever more exaggerated or sensationalist effects are needed in order to buttress action and prevent its receding into mere generic misquotation. Divine eating dog shit in *Pink Flamingoes* will probably remain the limiting instance of reaching to visceral extremes for anchorage, though parallel quests for pure affect are common in both pornography and films of violence, and indeed throughout post-modern culture. The destabilizing of meaning and the evaporation of presence from the filmic sign tend to strand the Kuchars' films on portentous but facile propositions about either art (It cannot represent life) or reality (It is

4.52–4.56 Mike Kuchar, *Sins of the Fleshapoids*

irrational); or they may cue allegorical readings through the narratives to the implications of the conditions of their production in such a way that the formal disparity between a Kuchar film and its Hollywood model subtends some more general extratextual thematic proposition.

The narrative logic of Mike Kuchar's *Sins of the Fleshapoids* (1965), for example, joins with the formal mobilization of depleted signs to produce a critique of both the authority of Hollywood and the underground's claims to filmic authenticity. In this allegory of the distant future, humans rest secure in ease and plenty through the labor of a race of anthropomorphic robots. But as the humans

4.57 Mike Kuchar, *Sins of the Fleshapoids*

lapse into luxurious decadence, these androids (to use the term of Philip K. Dick, who more thoroughly investigated similar issues in his fictions of the early sixties) discover within themselves the capacity for human emotions. They begin to fall in love, and then to rebel against their human masters. The narrative is maintained on a skittish, unstable edge by the interspersal of incompetence with melodrama in the acting, by the contradiction between the implied opulence of the sets and their improvised dime-store tackiness, by the haphazard synthesis of the detritus of cultures spanning from the Middle Ages to the distant future (which allows moments of inspired incongruity—a male whore wearing ancient Greek clothes and eating a Clark Bar or wearing a football uniform), and by the garish, soft-core comic book emotional vocabulary. But despite the deprecation of its own mode and of most of its crises, still the film retains moments of pathos, especially in the closing scenes as the love of the robots comes to fruition in the birth of a baby robot.

This interpenetration of the real and the artificial—rather than the primacy of one or the other or the opposition between them—is validated by the narrative logic. While the humans float in a limbo of greed and unresolved homosexual narcissism, it is the fleshapoids, indeterminate mixes of the human and the mechanical, of the mechanical asserting its right to the fullness of feeling previously reserved by nature to the human, who seize upon love, destroy the humans, and begin to reproduce. Rather than expressing fear of the mechanical other or nostalgically locating true emotions in the pre-technological past, the film envisages the assumption of the human by the machine, the assumption of the authentic by the synthetic—a symbiosis that then valorizes the film's own artifice. Its distance from the "natural" worlds of both Hollywood and real life, which previously appeared as a deficiency in production values or as a disconcerting lack of thematic seriousness, retrospectively appears as the only legitimacy possible in a bastardized world. Like the fleshapoids themselves, *Sins of the Fleshapoids* is a robot hybrid, affirming its own condition as the only available propriety.

Readings of this kind depend upon a subtext that constantly inserts the fact of the film's domestic production and the disparity between its flaws and the glamorous surface of the Hollywood film as a register of the values its narrative implies. In other Kuchar works, this use of form as an index of an amateur mode of production and as a metaphor for represented content is amplified to the point where the dominance of the reflexive element over the mimetic makes the process of filmmaking itself the site of meaning. *I, an Actress* (1977), for example, a much later film by George Kuchar which simply documents his attempt to teach a young woman to act a melodramatic love scene, refers only to film production. But *Hold Me While I'm Naked* (1966), his second 16mm work and one that also uses the film-within-a-film motif, is an especially interesting dramatization of the motives and conditions of its own production and of its own potential function.

The roughly assembled elements of a plot—Kuchar himself playing a director who is shooting a soft-core art film, the defection of his leading lady, and the failure of his attempts to find a replacement—gesture toward a narrative and establish at least the possibility of analogies between the film as a whole and the film whose beginning it documents. But the boundaries between the two dissolve; the initial sequential nature of the represented narrative falls apart into a non-narrative montage that plays the director's actual frustrations against the erotic plenitude that he imagines and created in the initial scenes, and that (perhaps) is experienced by his actors in real life. This blending of levels of reality reaches a climax in a late sequence in which first the original actress and then her replacement make torrid love with their boyfriends in the shower, and which culminates in Kuchar himself, the director of the film, getting into his own shower dressed in women's clothes and banging his head on the wall in frustration. Here the derivation of the separate shots and the different filmic contexts they imply are thoroughly confused. The scenes that Kuchar as the fictional director imagines are not distinguishable from either the memories or the desires of the Kuchar who makes *Hold Me While I'm Naked*.

But even as these ontological conflations subvert the distinction of the film from the life it would on some level like to represent, they also narratively suggest the cinematic continuity between them by invoking the possibility of a career in the cinema for these amateur

4.58–4.63 George Kuchar, *Hold Me While I'm Naked*

cinephiles. The vicarious possession of the object of his desire—his actress's body—that directing a film allows (itself the premonition of the audience's similarly vicarious consumption of that object) is matched in the rewards promised by participation in the social and economic enterprises of the movies. In an early scene the lead actress is trapped behind a wire fence, and the director urges her on with promises to make her a star, which presumably would allow both her and him to escape the prison of the Bronx, the drabness of the world outside *The Movies* that is figured in the shots of the wintery seas of rooftops and TV antennae and the interiors of Kuchar's mother's home.

The possibility that amateur filmmaking will supply Kuchar with erotic satisfaction or commercial success is, of course, finally denied. The narrative of sexual frustration from which he never escapes is reciprocated by the film's insistent formal deficiencies: the repeated takes; the end-holes; the saturated, one-dimensional colors; and the grotesquely exaggerated metaphors. But though the film fails on all these levels, certain promises remain alongside the negative implications of the oxymoronic superimposition, Hollywood in the Bronx. As an allegory of an amateur reconstruction of an industrial practice that itself uses an amateur reconstruction of an industrial language, it must recount a failure. But in doing so still it evidences its own success. At the end of the movie, when all George has is his mother's burnt dinner, he begrudgingly affirms, "There's a lot of things in life worth living for, isn't there?" If the reply to this is anything but a resounding "No!" it can only be because one of those things is the pleasure of making underground films like this.

FILM THAT CANNOT BE ONE: KENNETH ANGER

The structural irony engendered by an independent film practice's reference to its industrial other reaches its apogee in the work of Kenneth Anger. Rather than merely referring to Hollywood, it argues itself as a thesis on the duplicity of all cinema, industrial and independent alike. All the crisscrossing of relations between dominant society and the counterculture, between hegemonic and oppositional film, as well as these areas separately, are proposed as either intrinsically double or capable of being raised to duplicity by the power of the artist's vision. The "passionate union of opposites" required by the "True Magick of Horus" pervades both the objects of Anger's attention and the process of his scrutiny, recurring in homologous sexual, social, cultural, and aesthetic vocabularies in a myth that purports to explain both the individual psyche and the structure of contemporary history. Anger finds his energies in a variety of natural, psychic, and subcultural locations; his vocabulary successively enlists the sexual fantasy of *Fireworks* (1947), the homosexual motorcycle and customized car subcultures of *Scorpio Rising* (1963) and *Kustom Kar Kommandos* (1965), the explicitly magical *Inauguration of the Pleasure Dome* (1966) and *Invocation of My Demon Brother* (1969), and finally the transhistorical natural forces evoked in *Lucifer Rising* (1966–80). But the historical matrix of each film is specified, either by the chronological fix of mass cultural references or by more explicitly historical figurations, of which the Vietnam helicopters that run as a continuous though only rarely visible subtext through *Invocation of My Demon Brother* is the most highly charged. Anger's oeuvre is in the fullest sense religious, and no less so for being a critique of Western religion in the alter-

4.64 Kenneth Anger, *Inauguration of the Pleasure Dome*

native tradition made available to him by the writings of Alastair Crowley.

The hero of Anger's myth is Lucifer, the Light God rather than the devil of Christian slander, who is present in all his films; each of them contains "a figure or a moment . . . which is my 'Lucifer' moment" (cited in Haller, 1980: 8). Lucifer is, however, only gradually discovered by Anger; he is invoked in *Invocation of My Demon Brother* and finally represented in the summary form of the myth in *Lucifer Rising* itself. Since both logically and historically Lucifer exists as contrary—his message is that "the Key of Joy is Disobedience" (ibid.: 8)—he is thoroughly ambivalent. His intrinsic polyvalence is constructed as multiple and oppositional by virtue of its subversion of Christianity's obsessive one-dimensional distinctions between good and evil. As in the tradition of Romantic Satanism, Lucifer's manifestation in a repressive society demands his continual self-deconstruction. Since he must resist being ossified into a new pantheon, as static and moribund as what he comes to destroy, he oscillates mercurially between himself and his opposite, and he does so in a filmic form that constantly eradicates its own alternative formulations.

Thus Lucifer inhabits Anger's cinema as both the figure of its mythology and its basis as formal practice and material event. As an

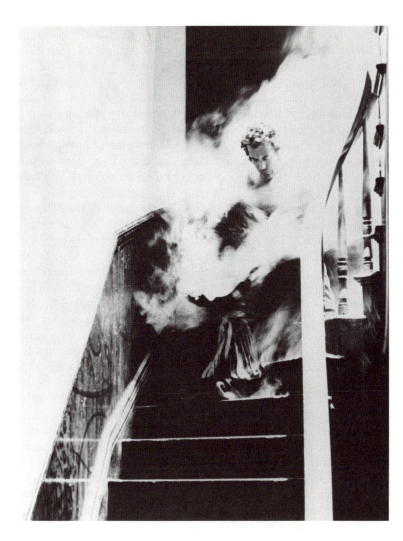

4.65 Kenneth Anger, *Invocation of My Demon Brother*

agent of Lucifer, Anger documents magic, and his practice is itself magic; his lifework is MAGICK, the cinematograph is his Magical Weapon, and his films are a Magick Lantern Cycle (Sitney, 1979: 122), all illuminating Lucifer and illuminated by him. And as the essence of film which is itself intrinsically double, visible only in the alternation between light and darkness, between itself and its absence, Luciferian cinema takes form in the space between itself and its opposite, the dark commercial cinema. Its assertion of its own independence necessitates the constant foregrounding of its opposite, the ground and context of its dependency. Since Lucifer is also partially manifest in the evil of cinema in general that Anger seeks to exorcise, he thus rises in the play of ironic disturbances by which each image signals the instability of its signification, its approach and retreat in respect both to itself and to its other, the mass media in general. For even as it proposes itself as the subversive alternative to Hollywood, Anger's cinema is constantly traversed by Hollywood, "both his matrix and the adversary" (Sitney, 1979: 94–95).

The role in Max Reinhardt's *A Midsummer Night's Dream* that Anger's grandmother, a studio costumer, obtained for him when he was a child began a continuous fascination with the ambiguous energies of the media, especially as they live in the stars. This preoccupation is everywhere apparent: in a very early plan to make a movie about the stars and their homes; in his collection of Hollywood memorabilia; in his notorious encyclopedia of gossip about the stars' sex lives, *Hollywood Babylon*; in the costumes of *Puce Moment*; in *Scorpio Rising*'s collages of *The Wild One*, *The Road to Jerusalem*, and the Mickey Rooney clip; and in the fragments of unrecognizable features that appear in *Inauguration of the Pleasure Dome* and *Lucifer Rising*. Even the cars in *Kustom Kar Kommandos* remind him of "an American cult-object of an earlier year, Mae West in her 'Diamond Lil' impersonations of the Thirties" (cited in Sitney, 1979: 125). Since it reiterates Hollywood's place in the vocabulary of our consciousness and unconscious, Anger's cinema is available for all the pleasures of nostalgia and fantasy; but his use of Hollywood's stories also turns them reflexively so that they are made to dramatize Hollywood's role in modern society. The stars' own real-life careers create a vast mythology of the present that illustrates the ambiguities of industrial culture as such and their own part in it. Their sybaritic excesses and libidinal transgressions—always punished by a ghastly death—embody the demonic energy that is Anger's obsession; they figure an ongoing dialectic, ultimately of metaphysical reach but which received its first and exemplary historical manifestation in the sexual excess and codic plurality of Babylon.

As the modern re-creation of that indulgence, "Hollywood Babylon" begins when Griffith makes a simulacrum of Babylon with "fat phallic columns . . . , improbable priests adoring Istar . . . , warriors and wantons, noblemen carousing with courtesans" (Anger, 1965: 2). If *Hollywood Babylon*'s description of Belshazzar's orgy sounds as much like outtakes from *Inauguration of the Pleasure Dome* as it does anything in *Intolerance* (for Anger makes Griffith over into his own image as thoroughly as does Brakhage in *Film Biographies*), it is because Anger's films reiterate the duality of Hollywood's social life. There is a direct continuity from the reality of Babylon behind the appearance of Hollywood—"a New Babylon whose evil influence revealed the legendary depravity of the old" (ibid.: 11)—to Anger's own themes of the actuality of demonic energy beneath the repression of everyday life. His own dramas are therefore contextualized and given meaning by the epic debauchery of Hollywood—which was diagnosed by none other than Alastair Crowley himself, with exactly Anger's blend of outrage and pleasure, as "the cinema crowd of cocaine-crazed sexual lunatics" (cited in Anger, 1965: 9)—but also are defined against it. For it is precisely Hollywood's failure to live up to its past excess that makes Anger's cinema both necessary and possible. Joe Dallesandro's pilgrimage to the destroyed Fox Studios at the beginning of *Heat* and Warhol's attempt to re-create the Golden Age are prefigured by Anger's own speculations at the end of *Hollywood Babylon* as to whether Jayne Mansfield, who had "made Scandal her career" and so assures us that "the Hollywood Way of Life is still a good one" (ibid.: 271), will renew the industry.

Such a renewal could only take place in independent film, because by the mid-sixties Hollywood's role in nurturing the collective mythology was being assumed by television and popular music; thus, alongside Mansfield as the basis for Anger's hopes at the end of *Hollywood Babylon* stands Elvis Presley, "the first 'dirty star' in a long time" (ibid.: 270). Indeed, Anger's historical insight is marked by his early recognition that rock-and-roll embodied the age's demonic energies and cultural potency, and by his attempt to appropriate it, especially in the image of Mick Jagger, who himself trafficked in the sexual double-ness that informs Anger's own vocabulary of the demonic. These motifs and strategies are all fully present in *Scorpio Rising*, and although it is a thanatotic excerpt from the erotic master myth—in Anger's own words "a death mirror held up to American culture" (cited in Haller, 1980: 8)—it is at the same time a film about a love generation. Celebrating even as it satirizes the counterculture, it oscillates in self-perpetuating ironies that solemnize the banal even while pushing its own most solemn affirmations to the edge of absurdity. *Scorpio Rising*'s critique of its hero is doubly articulated; the narrative accumulation of the popular cultural motifs that define him is reiterated in a similarly ambiguous formal assimilation of fragments from commercial films and music.

Though intercut images of Hitler imply that Scorpio's cult is fascist and his command destructive, in general the associations that accrue around him are unstable. The central ambiguity is sexual. By superimposing homosexual and female implications on the hyperbolic masculinity of the image of the motorcyclist, Anger destabilizes it but also valorizes it as the embodiment of a sexuality which cannot be unified or identified with itself. Around this indeterminacy, an entire lexicon of cultural icons is reinterpreted. As in the myth as a whole, the complementary projects of undermining received meanings and introducing semantic multiplicity to maintain the subversion of any unequivocal system of signification make the text itself irretrievably ambiguous, for even previously stable images are set in conflict with themselves and their own ironic errancy is released by their contact with the semantic duplicity of the central myth. Marlon Brando's machismo becomes a narcissistic posing, an easily imitated repertoire of melodramatic gestures, while Christ, even as he supplies Scorpio with connotations of being a martyr and a scapegoat, is first belittled by association with the party goers and eventually, by means of the animated image of him inserted into the eyes of the skull, equated with Hitler.

The comprehensive form of Anger's refusal to allow these ironic patterns to find stability in a moral system immune to aesthetic subversion is the film's overall attitude to popular culture; the juxta-

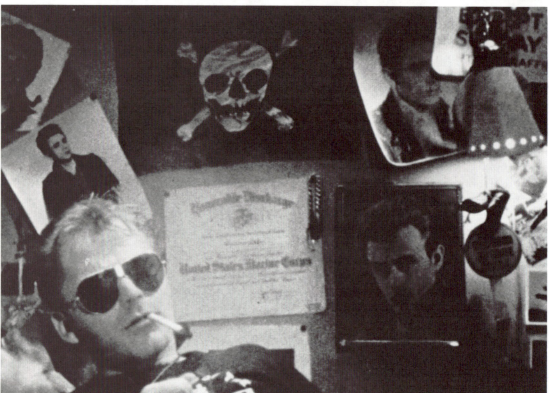

4.66–4.68 Kenneth Anger, *Scorpio Rising*

position of the best and the worst of pop songs makes for a pervading ambiguity and polyvalence in any given image. As with Warhol's invocation of classic screen stars, references to media icons both aggrandize and belittle; Scorpio is on the one hand ennobled by the mythic rhetoric of pop music's fantasy context, but every "Devil in Disguise" or "Wipe Out" resonance is undercut—for example, by "Wind up Doll" as the motorcycle is initially assembled, and, at the most vulnerable point as the epic hero is completing his armoring, by "She Wore Blue Velvet." Similarly, the comic strip images of boyish affection that suggest Scorpio's homosexual-

 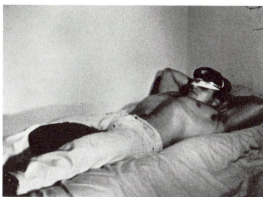

 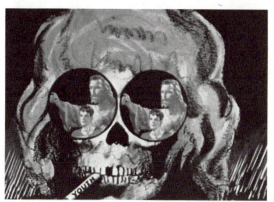

4.69–4.72 Kenneth Anger, *Scorpio Rising*

ity trivialize what is elsewhere presented in epic proportions. On the other hand, the film does embrace the massive energy of its music and propose itself as the filmic form of that energy.

The constant interchange in the filmic between the film itself and pop culture is replayed in *Scorpio Rising*'s own relation to the commercial cinema. Whatever debt it owed to the entertainment business, it returned; it was substantially responsible for refashioning the motorcycle genre for such late sixties uses of it as *Easy Rider* (which also mimics its structural use of pop music), and, indeed, not simply middlebrow kitsch like Federico Fellini's films but more serious work like Nicholas Roeg's *Performance* clearly derive from Anger. These formal interrelationships are complemented by the film's own penetration of mass culture. Of all underground films, *Scorpio Rising* secured most notoriety and the widest circulation, and, much more than any other, it became itself a pop cultural item. The traditional capability of collage to speak what cannot be directly said—here, most obviously, the revised models of sexuality—becomes thus a cinematic as well as a filmic function, and the actual footage of Brando and the actual pop songs, as well as being intra-diegetic markers that internally restructure signs, are the means by which the restored signs can be socially negotiated. They allow the social critique some currency outside the homosexual, underground, or demonic subcultures.

Though *Scorpio Rising* is unusual in Anger's oeuvre by virtue of the amount of incorporated material, still the interpolated fragments and other appropriations remain embedded in his own footage and are clearly placed by it. In his other films the collage functions are more entirely subordinate to the autonomous diegesis. His use of collage does, however, provide a bridge to a more thoroughly, and on occasions a totally, collage cinema in San Francisco, where a strong "funk" tradition preserved a populist surrealism, quite distinct from the reflexive modernism of New York.

A Filmmaker: Bruce Conner

Since their component tesserae never conceal their sources, Bruce Conner's film mosaics are insistently reflexive; as they foreground the fact of their fabrication, the pattern of extratextual reference they begin to suggest is always headed off or made to detour through reference to either the nature of their source material or the implications of the mass media in general. The internal logic of *A Movie* comes finally to settle on propositions about the reality Hollywood constructs, specifically its particular combination of violence and male-oriented eroticism. Conner's editing techniques, which fracture expected continuity in the illogical juxtaposition of incommensurate fragments, estrange the imagery, so that the collage rises to a second degree of defamiliarization to draw attention to its own techniques. Thus *A Movie* is a representative example of the medium, a plenary instance that quotes all the essential components of a movie; but it is also a meta-movie, an anatomy of all previous movies that clarifies their method of operation. On the other hand, since the imagery is never entirely arbitrary, never merely a vehicle for filmic effects, and since its literalism and referentiality are never entirely effaced, the reflexiveness of *A Movie* remains distinct from the abstract self-reference of structural film.

These tensions between abstraction and literality, between refer-

4.73–4.74 Bruce Conner, A Movie

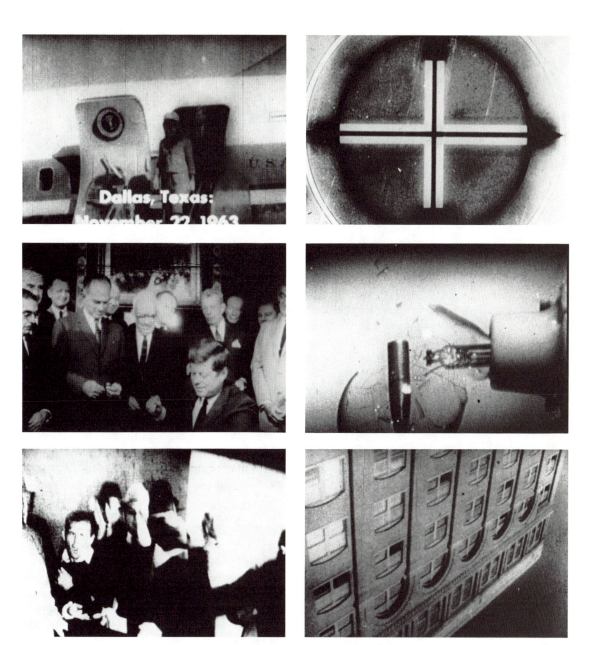

4.75–4.80 Bruce Conner, *Report*

ence to the medium and reference to the world, are especially crucial in *Report* (1967), since the film is at least in part a hyperbolic demonstration of the presence of the very tensions that it finds in its source material. Although its subject is the assassination of President Kennedy, its real purpose is to indict the media and its role in the American way of life, even implying that the corporate interests manifested in the media are complicit in Kennedy's death. If it is an elegy for Kennedy, its plangency arises from the irony that an elegy for such a figure of the media can only be constructed from the detritus of the cultural wasteland in which he perished.

4.81–4.82 Bruce Conner, *Report*

The primary object of analysis is the television report of the assassination, the murder of Lee Harvey Oswald, and Kennedy's funeral. The dominant strategy is the subjection of this news footage to a series of exemplary formalist modifications—"the action is continually interrupted; the author repeatedly goes backwards or leaps forward" (Shklovsky, 1965: 27)—which, even as they draw attention to the object hood of the present film, also echo the media presentation of the event; it is constantly and more or less fragmentarily played over and over as it was in public broadcasts in the weeks after the assassination. Yet no matter how many times it is shown, how laboriously it is broken down, the footage cannot reveal the process of Kennedy's death. Like the Zapruder footage, the ostensible documentation may be subjected to an extended scrutiny, but it can never be made to give up the truth. Ironically, the only time we even see Oswald is when *he* is being shot, as if at one of the film's crucial moments the roles are reversed and the assassin can be seen only as the victim. Even the Dallas book depository is visible only upside down and in negative. All that remains, all that can be made present, is the television coverage; the film is a report not of the assassination, but of the mass media use of the assassination.

But if filmic analysis cannot reconstruct an authoritative narrative of the assassination, by using the methods of *Cosmic Ray* and *A Movie* it can force the account to reveal its own nature and even to make implications outside the textual system. By splitting the signs, by wrenching fragments out of their syntagmatic chains, and by displacing and inverting the received syntagmatic and paradigmatic locations of the fragments, *Report* obliges them to reveal what their seamless institutional closure allows them to repress. Such "poetic" functions can be predominantly connotative, inflecting the event with emotional resonances, such as the countdown "crosswires" that force the pun on film-shot and gunshot, the anxiogenic suppression of the visuals during the early voice-over account of the shooting, or the brief flash of "Finish" leader that disintegrates into invisibility as Kennedy is rushed to the hospital. Or they can attempt a more vigorous denotative explicitness, as do, for example, the elaboration of a mass media context around Kennedy through the collage association between him and the bull that is the matador's victim; the audio reference to the car doors flying open coupled with the commercial showing the refrigerator doors opening; and especially the culminating IBM image in which the secretary pressing the SELL button terminates the film and, by implication, Kennedy himself.

The structural irony of *Report*, which finds the intrinsic ambiguity of montage reciprocated in the oscillation between direct social criticism and the reflexive manipulation of strictly filmic possibilities that is Conner's signature, speaks for the mixed heritage of underground film and the mixed motives of the underground as a whole. Yet the film's lucid synthesis of aesthetic and political progressivism punctuates a phase in film history. *Report* was not completed until 1967, four years after Kennedy's death; while the interim period had seen the intensification of both imperialist projects abroad and domestic resistance to them, it had also made it possible for beat aestheticism to be qualitatively intensified in a film practice that severed reflexivity from all social reference. The same year as *Report*, Michael Snow's *Wavelength* revealed the emergence of structural film, and while Parker Tyler is right to note that it too is still a "pad" film (Tyler, 1969: 173), it is also one that marked the end of the beat tradition, the finale to a social history. On the other hand, the formation of New York Newsreel the following year would make it clear that changing social conditions demanded that the protest film be radically energized. Before we turn to these two streams into which the underground split, it is appropriate to consider as its coda—as a summary of the different aspects of its projects and as one of its greatest achievements—the work of Bruce Baillie, and in particular the film that documented the changes which made the underground project no longer feasible, *Quixote*.

CODA: BRUCE BAILLIE's *Quixote*

Shot and taped in 1964–65 but not finally edited until 1968 (Arthur, 1979a: 32), *Quixote* spans the period of rapidly increased politicization, especially the Black espousal of confrontation and violence and the systematic and similarly violent opposition to the Vietnam War. Although the extreme forms that this dissent eventually took are not depicted in the film, they are implied in the scenes of Black protesters in New York and in the collages of Vietnam imagery, as indeed is the issue that would eventually supersede them, women's liberation. And so the journey from the West to the East that is *Quixote*'s structuring motif also leads from a rural spring into a winter of ominously severe urban discontent.

The antipodes of this journey recur in a series of parallel antitheses that allow the extensively heterogeneous mass of visual and aural images of contemporary American life to be organized both chronologically and synchronically. The compositional method is that of the juxtaposition of contrasting motifs: within the frame of

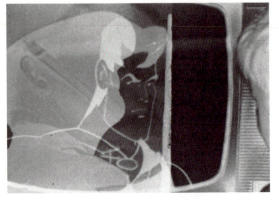

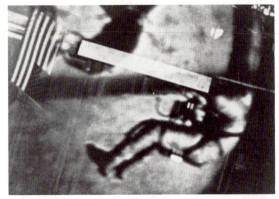

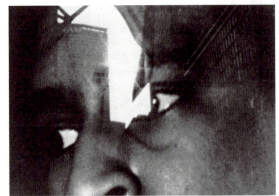

4.83–4.87 Bruce Baillie, *Quixote*

a single diegesis (the migrant worker outlined against the smoking power plant); through collision editing (the adobe ruins and young Indian girls supplanted by industrial machinery gouging the earth); and through the constantly shifting superimpositions that are the film's dominant stylistic trait and rhetorical strategy—the location of its characteristic precise, sensuous rhythms and textures. Foregrounded by several devices, especially the use of color, and occupying the film's chronological and thematic center are recurrent image clusters in which the remnants of the pre-colonial past—its geography, its fauna, and especially the richness of its aboriginal cultures—coalesce, fragments of an Indian summer shored against the ruin of the modern metropolis.

As in *Mass for the Dakota Sioux*, whose social analysis *Quixote* extends, this indigenous culture is presented as a prelapsarian ideal, falling before industrialism, urban blight, the mass media, and war. The protagonist of *Quixote*, however, is not the Indian of *Mass* but a movie spaceman, himself a creature of the media whose mobility, vision, and indeed very existence is contingent on modern technology. The utopian perspective of the pre-capitalist past is no longer even vicariously available to be the film's subject; that life can now be present only as an object, idealized but also framed and reified, artificially sustained on the reservation or in the form of the aged, broken contemporary Indians in the midwestern diner. In *Mass* the aboriginal past had been recalled by a real, if dying, person; now it is a construct, touristically visited in detours the film makes in its journey to a present whose Third World preoccupation is of a different order. Now the utopian alternative is Vietnam, which like the domestic Third World is ravaged by the technology of corporate capital. But whereas the Indians of the West could be known or at least seen directly, Vietnam is knowable only indirectly, through television—the "latest Vietnam Report," as an advertising logo announces it over images of the war.

The densely impacted collages of the final sections of the film, in which battle footage floats over Wall Street, a naked woman retreats before the policeman's billy, and the hard hat sneeringly overlooks the Black protesters, and into which the anguished face of a woman in superimposition regularly rises, is a clear indictment of the racism, the sexism, the political violence, and the material obsession of capitalist society. The connection between the corporation and Vietnam is made clear, and though *Quixote* is not as explicit as is the collage of war films and television commercials that form the parallel climax to *Mass*, still its attention to the media's representation of the war strongly hints at its role in the ideological consensus that allows the economic imperialism of which Vietnam is one result.

4.88–4.89 Bruce Baillie, *Quixote*

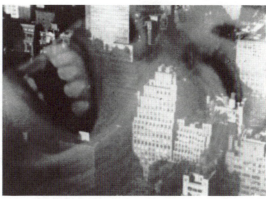

The final shot, in which a short, color close-up of the face of an Asian woman washed in red light replaces the black and white shots of New York, thus gathers the film's recurrent themes, but rather than resolving them it can only point to an undefined future. For that final shot is thoroughly ambiguous; though a small movement at its very end in which the woman appears to place her hand on a man's shoulder finally suggests that the extreme emotion reflected in her face is sexual ecstasy, it could equally well be extreme pain. The shot recalls a series of similarly ambiguous black and white shots of a woman's face that have almost subliminally been floated in under the dominant images at several points: a grimacing face juxtaposed with shots of a woman looking at herself in the mirror, a profile of a model superimposed over a female acrobat displayed before a bright light, and a woman's face briefly glimpsed in the section about the civil rights protesters. As a reprise of these, the final shot brings to completion a subtext of woman as spectacle and commodity that has hovered throughout. But it also brings together the central color sections dealing with "red" Indians and the later imagery from Vietnam, closing the film with a reminder that both the technologically underdeveloped Indians and the Asians—and even perhaps the earth that is their common mother—are *in extremis*, with the red marking blood, or communism, or both. And while the image's summary implications are probably of the Third World being *fucked* by American technology, the very ambivalence

4.90 Bruce Baillie, *Quixote*

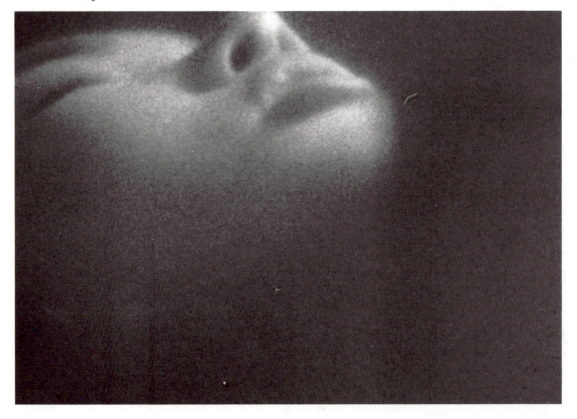

of that verb allows for the possibility that on some level it can also
signify a utopian alternative to the blight documented in the body
of the film, a future transformation of that rape into a more happy
copulation.

The placing of the Asian woman as the film's concluding metaphor can also be read as an allegory of cinema, for, like all collage
images, alongside its own literal content it also signifies the specific
media system of its provenance. It may not be too whimsical, then,
to see hailed in this representation a future cinema, one in which the
radical implications of *Quixote* and the underground would be followed to their logical conclusion, as if Baillie felt a premonition of
a cinema of the cinematically disenfranchised, a Third World feminist cinema . . . perhaps even Christine Choy and Third World
Newsreel. But before we turn to this political cinema, we may note
that even as its direct social address derives from work like Baillie's,
it goes beyond it; it transcends even as it extends innovations such
as his. *Quixote* thus marks both the limitations and the achievements of underground film, and so makes clear the cinematic implications of the ambiguity of its final image.

In *Quixote* Baillie uses the techniques of underground film to explore the inflections of a personal vision with a subtlety and precision equaled only by the work of his film correspondent, Stan Brakhage, but his explicitly political inflection of those techniques was
radically innovative. His orchestration of a film vocabulary in
which sensuous attention to minute local textures is combined with
an overall rhythmic sweep, and his use of this method to register the
world of public affairs, is on the one hand testament to the flexibility and resourcefulness of that underground cinema, its providing
the individual with access to the arena of social commentary. It also
marks, on the other hand, a limit noticeable initially in the very virtues of the "poetic" method, for the obverse of its subtlety and in-
direction is its inability to speak explicitly about the role of Hollywood, of Wall Street, of Vietnam. This inability marks not just the
limitation of underground film, but also the social and historical
limits of underground cinema. The significance of Baillie's style is
thus double: it is a means of marshaling images to articulate a critique of a social degeneration, and its own formal properties represent values alternative to that degradation. The precision of his perception, the subtle analytic cues of his rhythms, and the virtuoso
orchestration of an extended register of sensual tonalities of film not
only stand *against* the commercial film and television and their political complicity, but also stand *with* the counterculture and its representative, here the American Indian. The aesthetic qualities of
Quixote thus allegorize social values, mythic richness, ecological
sensitivity, even technological primitiveness; its aesthetic is completely a politics and vice versa. Its method is that of the poet—of
associational implications, of connotation, of the play of significance, sensitivity, and seriousness . . . "a cinema which . . . has been
liberated by poetry."

If this epithet summarizes the aesthetic ambition of underground
film and the political implications of its aesthetic, its source also

suggests a critique of the idealism of the underground revolt. The remark comes, of course, from Godard's attack on the underground, which in *Wind from the East* he decries as "a cinema which thinks it is liberated. A drug cinema. A sex cinema. A cinema which claims it has been liberated by poetry, art. A cinema without taboos, except the class struggle" (Godard, 1972: 164). Godard's accusation that the underground cinema's idealist basis not only precluded a materialist understanding and analysis of modern society and the industrial cinema's role within it, but, in fact, made it a class cinema, "the flunkey of Nixon-Paramount, the flunkey of imperialism," comes of course blinkered with his own ignorance; but more important here than the question of either the justness of Godard's summary or the coherence of his own alternative is its illumination of the difference between political and cinematic conditions in the United States and in France.

Quixote and *Wind from the East* are in many ways similar: both are concerned with U.S imperialism and both attack the commercial feature as the agent of that imperialism; both are simultaneously westerns and anti-westerns that invert generic orthodoxy by apotheosizing the Indian. For Godard, the Indian's claim of power for the working class is the third term that allows passage between the otherwise discrete diegetic levels of the western and the strike, and so, as in *Quixote*, the Indian becomes the emblem of the Third World as a whole. But Godard's sacrifice of the pleasures of narrative illusionist film to the rigors of the self-critical didactic essay and his subordination of cinema to politics along the lines of Dziga Vertov's realization that "it is impossible for a film to exist outside the context of the class system," and that "the actual production of films is only of secondary importance" (ibid.: 124) allow him to make discursively explicit what Baillie can only imply. Godard's rejection of the conventions of the feature, his mutilation of the filmstrip, and his attempt to negate cinema are all theorized as components in what aspired to be a vanguard attack not just on cinema, but on the state itself. It is the frontal nature of that attack, not its urgency and certainly not its own viability as a cinematic alternative (for *Wind from the East* marked a terminal contradiction in Godard's own quest for political integrity), that marks a position the underground could not occupy. The social possibilities upon which its utopian aestheticism had been constructed and from which it emerged had passed, their project broken apart.

As filmmakers responded to the increasingly urgent and volatile political situation of the late sixties by addressing specific political issues and joining with more militant subcultures, the balance between the aesthetic and the existential that allowed the making of art to be both self-validating and the central ritual in a countercultural revolt became increasingly fragile. Under the stress of increasing militancy, the coincidence of the aesthetic and the social components that had sustained that balance split; by a process of specialization, itself responsive to the new social possibilities that allowed dissident energies to be mobilized in new ways, the main direction of alternative film forked. That aspect of it with personal and institutional ties to the art world, especially the New York art world, continued to investigate the formal and material properties of film, whereas that aspect that had evolved with more militant social groups subordinated concern with filmic processes to the possibility of cinematic participation in violent political contestation. It is to the latter that we now turn.

5

Political Film/Radical Cinema: From Dissent to Revolution

Don't tell me to shut up. I got a right to speak. I need to speak to defend myself.
— Bobby Seale

The war is language.
— Allen Ginsberg

Representation: On Film/In Cinema

They cannot represent themselves; they must be represented.
— Marx

Bobby Seale's demand to speak for himself, in his own words and not those of his White co-defendants at the Chicago Conspiracy trial, recognized that discourse is itself political activity, not merely its mirror. As industrial production has become increasingly the production of information, political power has lodged more and more in the apparatuses of ideology, and media events have themselves become substantially the activity of the political process. And as the practice of politics has become a matter of the deployment of the media, access to the means of representation has become a crucial component in minority struggle. The revolt that the media reported in their accounts of war protesters and police in Chicago was itself engaged in the media, literally in the attempts both sides made to ensure the promulgation of one version of it rather than another, and also symbolically in their agreeing that the war in Vietnam would partially be lost or won on the domestic television screen. The war that was observed in the living room was also fought there.

Seale's further insistence that he be tried separately from the White radicals presaged the concomitant disadvantages of such a radically asserted difference. The very success of the various dissident activist groups in securing their own right to speech by establishing alternative media systems created the risk that their concerted attack on the state would be dispersed, and that their separate discourses would disappear in a babble of competing idiolects. For in extending and reorienting the project of the underground, radical film took the medium to people with no previous tradition of access to it. As the social dehiscences of the last half of the decade revealed the remoteness of the conditions that had allowed the beats their articulation of their own subcultural identity as aesthetic revolt, Blacks and students, soldiers and women stepped in to sustain the underground's desire. But they did so separately; their various attempts at self-representation on film and in cinema and their individual contestations of the establishment media never amalgamated into a unified opposition.

Unbroken both socially and aesthetically, the lines from the underground to radical film saw the protest films of the early civil rights and nuclear disarmament movements become entirely agitational. The role, pointed out by Staughton Lynd, that the beat writers had had in helping "young people to take the first groping steps toward a psychological freedom from convention," which found political expression in the sixties (Lynd, 1969: 6), has direct parallels in alternative filmmaking. In one of the first accounts of independent militant filmmaking, Jonas Mekas claimed that there was "no difference between the avant-garde film and the avant-garde newsreel" (Mekas, 1968: 40), suggesting the structural continuity that links films about beatnik life with the similarly amateur documentation of more activist subcultures. The films of peace marches and civil protest, such as Lenny Lipton's *We Shall March Again* (1965), Jerry Abrams's *Be-In* (1967), Anthony Reveaux's *Peace March* (1967), David Ringo's *March on the Pentagon* (1968), and Saul Levine's *New Left Note* (1969–75), and the collectivization of such individual efforts in the various Newsreels all document minority cultural activity essentially for in-house use in a way analogous to the films of Ron Rice or Ben Van Meter. Not even insistently anti-political filmmakers were unaffected; Stan Brakhage's *23rd Psalm Branch*, Andy Warhol's *The Chelsea Girls*, and Paul Sharits's

5.1 Anthony Reveaux, *Peace March*

Piece Mandala/End War all instance, as early as 1966, inflections of idealist aesthetics by anxiety about the war.

The continuity between the beat/hippie and the militant cinemas is exemplified by a film like Leonard Henny's *The Resistance* (1968)—which is concerned as much with communal eating and yoga, dancing in the streets, and the San Francisco Mime Troupe as it is with news reports from Vietnam and protest against the war—and especially by *New Left Note*, a meta-cinematic meditation on the relationship between counterculture aesthetics and activist politics. Constructed from extended sequences of extremely rapid parallel montage of documentary footage of anti-war, Black liberation, and women's movement activity on the one hand and television broadcasts of the war and of Nixon's speeches about it on the other, *New Left Note* also foregrounds solid color frames, end-holes, splice-bars, and other stylistic devices from the repertoire of Brakhage. But instead of terminating the film in impasse or contradiction, these tropes reinforce its analysis of the practice of politics. The energy and violence of the filmic activity (particularly the extreme agitation of the montage and the sustained splice-bars which, as often as every second frame, score the representation) complement the political energy and violence the film engages and restate the problem of perception as a political rather than merely an optical or phenomenological issue. The difficulty of seeing through the film to a clear image of either the war or the peace movement represents the film's own alterity to both the war and the news media's use of it. All the manifest work on the film and the pain and estrangement it involves thus articulate its formal and functional differences from illusionist, mass media representations.

Though its success in integrating advanced filmic strategies with radical political activity makes *New Left Note* anomalous though not unique, it and the other films from the politicized counterculture do make clear the origin in underground film of the later, more confrontational cinemas. Indeed, the beats' innovation of a performative film practice in place of the reified industrial commodity film object provided a model, not the only one to be sure but a potent one, for the creation of a cinema of radical praxis out of what began as simply a contestation of representations. The history of the beats' progressive amalgamation is similarly recapitulated in the film practices around the Movement, with individual efforts only the point of departure for group and institutional engagements.[1] New York Newsreel, for example, the most important of the Movement production and distribution organizations, emerged directly from the underground. Its first meeting in December 1967 took place at the Film-Makers' Cooperative, and Jonas Mekas printed the initial manifesto in his *Village Voice* column (Mekas, 1972: 305–6), greeting it in his summary of 1968 as "the most important new development in the American Cinema" (ibid.: 326).

Reflecting the historical drift and swirl of the vocabularies in which both alienation and community were experienced, such continuities between the underground and the militant political film-

1 Nichols notes that "Newsreel's nucleus of founding members had been 'experimental' or independent filmmakers and they had friendships and connections with various members of the underground," and that the underground had shown the feasibility of noncommercial, anti-Hollywood filmmaking (Nichols, 1972: 60–61).

5.2 Saul Levine, *New Left Note*

making of the late sixties are only surface manifestations of the more fundamental continuity in the attempts to develop alternative systems of production and distribution. Demonstrating alternative film's contingency upon an alternative cinema, the underground's reorganization of the social relations set in motion by the medium was intrinsically political, even if its innovations did not contribute to a successful redistribution of power nationally. The more properly political cinema, radical beyond simply its minimization of exploitative relations among those whom it involved, made these innovations the basis for a more aggressive contestation of the structures and operations of capitalism. As they used film to call into question the social relations within the state as a whole, radical filmmakers found themselves face to face with the local recapitulation of those relations within the filmmaking group. Conversely, when such mal-distributions of power among classes, races, and sexes and between filmmakers and the public were confronted and overcome, the reformed practice of filmmaking provided a prototype for general social reform, the new cinema a model for a new society.

Nothing distinguishes the New Left from the Old Left—particularly in the United States—more than the fact that in the sixties the popular unavailability of materialist analyses of the state and of resistance based on class consciousness coincided with outbreaks of dissent that called into question the basic principles of Marxism. The central theoretical issue became what, in a celebrated letter to the *New Left Review*, C. Wright Mills formulated as "the problem of the historical agency of change, of the social and institutional means of structural change" (Mills, 1969: 21), for even as the working class appeared less and less likely to fulfill its role, other groups appeared on the vacant stage of history.[2]

Until late in the decade when the women's movement came into prominence with the formation of the National Organization for Women (NOW) in 1966 and the development of anti-sexist self-criticism in radical cadres, two domestic oppositions were especially important: that of Blacks—and other people of color who formulated nationalist movements in their pattern—and that of White radicals, mostly of privileged backgrounds, especially students—Mills's "young intelligentsia" (ibid.: 23). With the Blacks typically a year or so in advance of the students, these contestations accelerated and intensified after the mid-sixties, and in each case increasing militance accompanied increased attention to materialist social theory. The Black movement abandoned integrationist nonviolence for the nationalist militancy of Black Power, developed in 1966 after the murder of Malcolm X and the foundation of the Black Panther Party. Displaced from their role in the civil rights movement, White students broke with liberal reformists to follow French neo-Marxists in theorizing themselves as a revolutionary class and, more aggressively, to contest the Vietnam War.

Sixties politics were shaped by these more or less separate oppositions and attempts to make alliances between them, by struggles

2 For histories of the New Left, see Lynd (1969); Sale (1973); Unger (1974); and especially Young (1977). More subjective, biographical, or autobiographical accounts such as Powers (1971), Stern (1975), and Alpert (1981) provide a personal sense of the social tensions of the period, especially during the militancy of the last years of the Movement.

for power within such alliances, and by the purging of aberrant factions. The foundation of Students for a Democratic Society (SDS) in 1959, the Student Nonviolent Coordinating Committee (SNCC) in 1960, and the Congress of Racial Equality (CORE) in 1961, Malcolm's split from the Muslims in 1964, SDS's dropping of its communist exclusion clause in 1965, the entry of the Progressive Labor Party into SDS and the expulsion of Whites from SNCC in 1966, the coalition between the Black Panthers and the Peace and Freedom Party in 1968, the splintering of SDS into Marxist-Leninist, Weathermen, and Revolutionary Youth Movement factions in 1969 and its disintegration the next year—all these are crucial gathering points in the swirl and eddy of affiliation and counter-affiliation that are summarized in the coalition of dissent that came together in the late sixties, only to fall apart by 1972. The premise for this coalition was the realization that the Vietnam War was no more an aberration in an otherwise benign system than Mississippi was; rather, it was the necessary imperialist expression of corporate capitalism, "the mirror of America."[3]

This perception made it possible for discrete areas of dissent to be rethought as aspects of a single historical undertaking. Understanding the structural unity of the Los Angeles riots, the peasant revolution in Vietnam, and the Free Speech movement at Berkeley, radicals could think of themselves as part of a worldwide revolutionary struggle; by 1965 "peasants throughout the world, ghettoized Negroes and other poor people in America, and middle-class American youth" ("A Statement on Civil Disobedience": 46) all appeared to be part of the same movement. Correspondingly, after Black Power used Franz Fanon to develop I. F. Stone's proposition that the condition of Black people in the United States was "a unique case of colonialism, an instance of internal imperialism, an underdeveloped people in our very midst,"[4] the equation of domestic minority racial groups with the Vietnamese allowed some rapprochement between Blacks and White radicals, a reengagement, though on quite different terms, of the early sixties alliances. So the notion of a unified and militant Third World resistance, initially occupying the place of the absent theory of an international working class but, especially as the Black Panthers formulated themselves in socialist rather than racial terms, eventually coexisting with it, became a metaphor within which the actions of ethnic minorities in the United States as well as other marginalized groups, such as prisoners, students, and eventually women, could be understood as an internationally coordinated assault on American capitalist, racist, and finally patriarchal imperialism.

Produced by and producing this political history, radical film reflected its surges of amalgamation and collapse. As the practice of more or less autonomous subcultures, minority and special interest groups, and issue-oriented social movements, it was only occasionally or partially able to span the projects of several factions or to maintain long-term strategies above and beyond immediate needs. Rich, multiple, ambitious, and frequently pragmatic and provi-

3 The phrasing here is that of the Vietnam Day Committee's "A Statement On Civil Disobedience," but the analysis was popularly announced first by Carl Oglesby in his address to the November 1965 March on Washington to End the War in Vietnam. See Oglesby (1965: 44).

4 *The New York Review of Books* (18 August 1966: 10), cited in Carmichael and Hamilton (1967: 3).

sional, American political film reciprocated the splintered social field, thus contrasting with both post-1968 European attempts to reconstruct the culturally hegemonic commercial feature and the native tradition of radical political filmmaking—the Film and Photo League of the thirties. Reproducing the labor orientation and pro-Soviet line of its sponsor, The Cinema Bureau of the International Union of the Revolutionary Theater, the Film and Photo League had aimed "to produce documentary film reflecting the lives and struggles of the American worker . . . [and] . . . to spread and popularize the great artistic and revolutionary Soviet production" ("Workers Films in New York": 37). Until its energy began to seep away into Hollywood or the various New Deal–sponsored projects like Pare Lorentz's *The Plow that Broke the Plains* (1936), the Film and Photo League had worked from a class analysis of American society as a whole, even though in doing so it too may have been haunted by an absence of widespread class consciousness (W. Alexander, 1981: 45). The possibility of Marxism providing such a theoretical infrastructure in the sixties came as late to cultural practice as it did to politics. But when, in the period of ultra-leftism between 1969 and 1972, it did influence filmmaking, it did so decisively in the form of a Maoism that led the most progressive filmmakers to integrate themselves into the communities they aspired to serve and to produce films that focused on specific local issues, on subsections of the working class rather than on issues affecting the proletariat as a class. *Break and Enter* (1970), New York Newsreel's film about the reclamation by a New York City Puerto Rican community of homes appropriated for urban renewal, and *Lincoln Hospital* (1970), Third World Newsreel's film about hospital workers, exemplify this emphasis. Not until the mid-seventies did Newsreel make films with a more extensive analytic base (e.g., *Controlling Interest*).

But until that Maoist phase in Newsreel and well after it in the Movement generally, most considerations of film naively privileged pragmatism over theoretical correctness. As late as 1969, for instance, Robert Kramer argued that the absence of a clearly defined, single revolutionary class in the United States made the idea of a "correct line" for radical film production "a bankrupt formulation" (Kramer, 1969: 28). Whether or not the diversity of dissent made this true, certainly the fact that different interests were uneasily held together in an acephalous but energetic resistance did not invalidate cultural work premised on their structural congruity. In any case, American resistance to cultural theory, notably to European structural-Marxist theories of ideology, left the Movement without a critical theory of the media and of Hollywood.[5]

In the absence of such a theory, public affection for the movies sustained a chauvinist nostalgia, a mirage of populist integrity and American innocence. The correspondences between the form, ideological function, and social insertion of the commercial feature remained largely invisible, as did the industrial function of Hollywood and its role in ideological reproduction. The tardiness with

5 Notable exceptions include Irwin Silber's columns in *The Guardian*, four of which were collected in Silber (1970), and, for film, the journal *Cinéaste*. Founded in 1967 as non-sectarian, it quickly became engaged; for example, by its third issue in 1967 it featured an article on *Made in U.S.A.* next to a review of *The Chelsea Girls*.

which the interdependence of Hollywood's aesthetic and commercial functions was recognized meant that only rarely was commercial film understood in the context of the other systems of imperialism. The Movement was consequently a ready mark for the aestheticized, de-contextualized violence of youth-culture films of the late sixties—films such as *Bonnie and Clyde*, *Wild in the Streets*, *The Wild Bunch*, and *Easy Rider*—as well as for the pseudo-political thrillers imported from Europe, especially the work of Costa-Gavras.[6] Forced to the edge of the cultural field and to the edge of radical politics, the characteristic American political film emerged from subcultures that had previously been as disenfranchised cinematically as they had been politically.

Without the power to represent themselves, Blacks, leftists, students, and women had, like the peasant proprietors Marx noticed in nineteenth-century France, been entirely represented by others. In their attempt to acquire media power of their own, to manipulate cinema instead of being manipulated by it (Enzensberger, 1974: 104), homologies inversely parallel to those that structure Hollywood recurred. Subject and agency of representation as well as method of representation were all interdetermining. The realization that control of the means of production and distribution of images set the limits to the discourse these images could serve revealed that contestation of the ideological perspectives of the established media necessitated contestation of those media as institutions and as practices. Accurate representation on film demanded adequate representation in cinema—and the construction of new cinemas.

The most useful provisional schematization of the total field of political film classifies together, on the one hand, the films made by the various minority and special interest groups on their own behalf and, on the other, the films made about them or for them by the establishment and industrial media. Such groups may be categorized structurally (the working class); by function (GIs, prisoners, students); by race (Blacks, Native Americans, Latinos); by gender or sexual preference (women, homosexuals); or by issues (the war, the environment, drugs). In the student section, for example, Newsreel's *Columbia Revolt* and *San Francisco State: On Strike* confront *The Strawberry Statement* and *Zabriskie Point*; in the Black section *Nothing But A Man* and *The Murder of Fred Hampton* face *Guess Who's Coming to Dinner* and *Shaft*; in the Native American section *Intrepid Shadows*, *A Navajo Weaver*, and the other films made by the Navajo under the guidance of Sol Worth stand against *A Man Called Horse* and *Soldier Blue*; in the GI section *Winter Soldier* and Newsreel's *Army* are matched with *The Green Berets*, and so on.

Such a taxonomy of binary oppositions between dominant and minority cultural production has all the limitations of parallel models of the representation of the beats and the counterculture. But it retains utility in illuminating the absences within the total schematization. Areas where film production is only minimally present or not present at all allow considerations about political

6 See Gitlin (1980: 197–202) on the relation between these films and the militancy of the Movement in the late sixties.

film to be recast in terms of the preconditions of alternative cinema. The scarcity of films about working-class life, self-sufficient women, or the actual conditions in prisons, in the ghetto, or on the reservation constitutes both filmic and social absences. These absences are of two kinds: those areas into which the dominant cinema could not enter without coming into contradiction with itself and those areas in which alternative cinemas were not able to establish themselves.

While the entertainment industry's approach to polemical topics varies according to conditions outside its own control, still the incompatibility of certain topics with the entertainment function produces anathemas fully as rigorous as the proscriptions of the Hays code. Admission into a commercial film of any social discontent that cannot be recuperated into final affirmation of the status quo, or the omission of accepted motifs (the woman-as-commodity, the Indian-as-savage, or the finally honest police system), sets that film into contradiction with the ideological and psychological preconditions of its function as entertainment, sets text against context. Marking the historically variable limits of the medium as capitalist industry, the boundary between possible and impossible industrial films is always process, constantly being readjusted to accommodate simultaneously the institutionalization of new social need and the industry's own need in each new film for that degree of transgression and novelty upon which constantly renewed consumption depends. (Indeed, one of the histories of sixties cinema is that of Hollywood's discovery of a way of dealing profitably with contemporary politics.) Similarly, the boundary between possible and impossible alternative cinemas is determined by the flux of the continuous social redistribution of power. But general social power, which always determines access to the medium and to systems of distribution, is always mediated through the history of the situation of the specific social group in respect to cinema.

In the case of most minority groups, certainly those that are working class, the received cinematic tradition is entirely one of consumption. Excluded by their overall class situation from control of the means of production, they are the least capable of securing their own representation. The difficulties of their appropriating and de-industrializing the apparatus for popular use marks the coincidence of their economic and cultural determination. The expense of even 16mm equipment—let alone the costs and logistical problems of creating alternative distribution mechanisms and viewing centers—especially when compared to the cheapness and even the profitability of equivalent items in other forms of cultural expression, combines with a history of subjection to the film industry—the history of hegemonic film as industry—and forms a boundary that can be crossed only with great difficulty.

Though within the working class the conditions of access to cinema vary and in each case must be specified against the other priorities of the group in question, there are certain limits to the possibility of minority groups using film. Of these the most extreme is absolute cinematic disenfranchisement.[7] In the case of prisoners, for example, economic deprivation and political impotence are inversely matched by the material preconditions of cinema; at such extremes, the homologies are direct: no social power, no cinema. Since such disenfranchised groups were thought to be primary to social change in the sixties—were supposed to inhabit an intrinsically revolutionary situation even if their consciousness were not revolutionary[8]—they represented a special challenge to radical film; indeed, it is with at least the partial access to cinema for the most disenfranchised group—Third World women prisoners—that this account will conclude. But even and especially here, since cinematic traditions do not spontaneously create themselves *ex nihil*, alternative cinemas are built less on films made by members of minority groups than on films made by others about them and on their behalf. The radical filmmakers' (Maoist) task became that of identifying with the working class or some subsection of it, either by assisting disenfranchised groups to develop cinemas of their own or by integrating themselves within the group they attempted to serve.

Even though Newsreel's decision "to provide an alternative to the limited and biased coverage of television news" (Mekas, 1972: 305) summarizes sixties' attempts to wrest control of representation from the industrial media, still the model of simple alterity in which industrial and radical film, each without internal contradiction, stand in absolute mutual opposition has to be qualified to accommodate the range of intermediate positions occupied by works neither entirely of the subculture nor of the establishment, and also instances when dissidence was expressed within the established media, either through allegorical displacement of contemporary issues or through other means of "partially dismantling the system from within."[9] The infiltration and reorientation of established media apparatuses, which liberals proposed as more feasible than the construction of separate media systems, became less viable after about 1966, when Black nationalism and militant opposition to the war obliged the liberal press to condemn domestic dissent. But even after this time, any assumption of a monolithic homogeneity in the mass media was countermanded by the media's own dependence on popular opinion and other ramifications of its commercial imperatives.

The sensationalization of radical politics provided the mass media with ready-made mechanisms of audience attraction, central to both the industrialization of television news and Hollywood's renewal in the late sixties by a tardy and largely spurious injection of the youth culture. MGM's *The Strawberry Statement* (1970), which not only plagiarizes Newsreel's *Columbia Revolt* but also exploits the excitement of the student rebellion, coloring it with countercultural cliché but effacing its internal logic, is only the most blatant of a whole range of expropriations of dissent. Despite this kind of cooptation, the mass media itself became to some extent the site of contestation; television's role in further discrediting the war after public opinion swung against it and the pursuit of Watergate by the

7 The political determination of representation received a classic figuration in Emile de Antonio's *Underground*, in which the fugitive members of the Weather Underground spoke concealed behind a heavy scrim. Through de Antonio's agency they were allowed a marginal presence in cinema, though representation per se was proscribed.

8 "Underneath the conservative popular base is the substratum of the outcasts and outsiders, the exploited and persecuted of other races and other colors, the unemployed and the unemployable. They exist outside the democratic process; their life is the most immediate and the most real need for ending intolerable conditions and institutions. Thus their opposition is revolutionary even if their consciousness is not" (Marcuse, 1964: 256).

9 Comolli and Narboni (1971: 33). Formalist taxonomies such as this, which claim the possibility of intra-institutional dissent, have to be supplemented by materialist investigation of the internal structures of the institutions in question. Recent research suggests that the mechanisms that ensure conformity are largely informal rather than directly coercive. See Gurevitch et al. (1982: 18) for a review of this literature. When a particular subject matter is too polemical to be treated directly by institutional media, the social anxieties involved are often projected allegorically. The Vietnam War was thus subject to numerous rewritings, often in terms that involved domestic Third World groups, though the latter were themselves frequently treated elliptically. Stanley Kubrick's *Spartacus* (1960), for example, portrays a rebellion of slaves in Roman times more sympathetically than any direct treatment of the civil rights struggle could have done at that time.

10 Gitlin distinguishes five stages in the formation of a symbiotic relationship between the Movement and the mass media: (1) the period between 1960 and 1965 when there was no coverage; (2) an initially sympathetic treatment of a new student left after the Berkeley Free Speech movement; (3) more extended coverage after the 1965 March on Washington, but with increasing disparagement and de-legitimization; (4) the growth of an "adversary symbiosis" in which the left attempted to turn the media's negative coverage to its own advantage, for example, by using it to publicize the burning of draft cards; and (5) the flood of new recruits, attracted by media coverage, into SDS, which transformed its internal organization (Gitlin, 1980: 25–31). He also notes six stages in the media's effect on the Movement's subsequent history: (1) "generating a membership surge"; (2) "certifying leaders and converting leadership to celebrity"; (3) "inflating rhetoric and militancy"; (4) "elevating a moderate alternative"; (5) "contracting the movement's experience of time and helping encapsulate it"; and (6) "amplifying and containing the movement's messages at the same time" (ibid.: 128–29).

press are symptomatic of a limited autonomy. And while the established media did feed off radical media work, sanitizing it and stripping it of its subversiveness, still in several key processes the Movement depended upon the media and became itself part of the general mass-mediated culture. The media's need for the spectacular images and formal innovations that radicals and their culture supplied was matched by the Movement's own need for publicity, both for recruitment purposes and to bring its demands to the attention of the public.

In Todd Gitlin's analysis of the relationship between SDS and the media, what he calls the "grammar of [their] interaction" (Gitlin, 1980: 22) has a history in which the different use made of one by the other forestalls the simple indictment of media attention for destroying SDS, despite the continuous hindrance and adversity.[10] Though the status of even a "relatively autonomous practice" overstates its freedom from the imperatives of the corporate state, the media was sufficiently in flux that dissidents could engage it, either by attempting to radicalize it from within or by using it against itself. But this necessary engagement of the industrial media is always being transformed into its opposite and reclaimed as the media's own operations; the descent of "media freaking" (Hoffman, 1969: 46) into celebrity mongering, or the failure of the Yippies to develop any social base despite their ability to cut through the sclerotic academic left and capture the imagination of the young, marks only the hyperbolic extension of conditions inherent in all modern radical activity. The continual process of disengagement and reengagement, negation and re-appropriation, pervades all political activity, since it pervades all being in the thoroughly mediated life of the modern world. And just as in daily life we struggle to discover the political form of our relation to the media, so political activity itself struggles within its own spectacularization.

This ubiquitous self-consciousness, by which all authenticity was thought to have evaporated from public life to be replaced by "pseudo-events," was lamented by a phylum of social critics from Boorstin (1961) to Brustein (1971), but whatever its other implications the realization that politics had become a form of theater and theater a form of politics made it clear that the semiological issue of representation was always a function of the social conditions that control dissemination. The size and density of the media jungle was the context that forced the redefinition of the task of the guerrilla artist as one of institutional intervention—the construction of counter-systems that challenged the industrial cinema and the industrial use of dominant cinema. Here we examine three such projects, separating for clarity three main levels upon which contestation was engaged and the limits of cinema they reached: the attempted appropriation of the apparatus to develop a Black cinema; the innovation of alternative film languages in challenges to the discourses by which the war in Vietnam was purveyed; and the development of new social relations around the practice of cinema, as well as the representation of them in radical film.

mourn for us soldout and chained to devilpictures.
— Amiri Baraka

The integral role of Black arts in creating the cultural and national identity that nourished the civil rights and Black Power movements can hardly be overestimated. Though in instances like post-Coltrane jazz, the popular and indeed revolutionary aspirations of the most avant-garde artists may have outstripped their social base,[11] in general Black dance, theater, writing, and music combined aesthetic and political vanguardism in cultural practices whose origins in popular traditions were reciprocated by their availability for popular use. Distinguishing Black art from that of other races, the similarities and frequent interdependencies between achievements in these different mediums made possible the definition of a specifically Black aesthetic, even as the clarification of the African origins of Afro-American culture made available pragmatic conceptions of art of the kind that have been suppressed by idealist aesthetics in the West since culture became commodified.

The Black aesthetics of the late sixties transcended the split within the Black movement between cultural nationalism and the materialist understanding of the situation of racial minorities within capitalist social formations. They were radical, not because they invoked ironic inversions, stylistic switches undetectable from the outside, subversive adaptations of hegemonic forms, or other formal qualities that reflected ghetto life (though they certainly presupposed these), but because they stressed a populist functionalism.

> Tradition teaches us, Leopold Senghor tells us, that all African art has at least three characteristics: that is, it is functional, collective and committing or committed. . . . And by no mere coincidence we find that the criteria is not only valid, but inspiring. That is why we say that all Black art, irregardless of any technical requirements, must have three basic characteristics which make it revolutionary. In brief, it must be functional, collective and committing. . . . Black art must expose the enemy, praise the people and support the revolution. (Karenga, 1972: 32)

Given the privileged position that, since Lenin, the cinema has occupied in pragmatic aesthetics, it would not have been illogical to anticipate a large investment in the cinema by Black artists in the sixties and the development of film as a Black art, one capable of participating in the creation of a revolutionary Black subject committed to political struggle. But apart from one or two notable exceptions, film played a marginal role in the Black movement, and, if anything, the sixties marked the culmination of the decline of the Black cinema, whether it be defined rigorously in terms of Black control over all stages of production or more generally so as to recognize any Black participation or responsiveness to Black needs.[12] The failure of Black people to develop a film practice responsive to

11 Though even here the lack of a mass Black audience for avant-garde jazz does not discredit other political functions. Kofsky, who has argued the relationship between Black nationalism and modern jazz most thoroughly, quotes Archie Shepp as claiming that jazz is "anti-war, it is opposed to Viet Nam; it is for Cuba; it is for the liberation of the people" (Kofsky, 1970: 64). While this assertion may better represent the feelings of the musicians than it does the concrete function of the music, still in its resistance to commodification and its modernist pursuit of its formal possibilities, jazz came closer than any other art form to reconciling negation with commitment.

12 In the most extensive collection of essays from the period defining the Black aesthetic (Gayle, 1972), not only is there no section on film, but film is mentioned only three times, in each case to note the absence of a satisfactory Black film. Most commentators prefer to reserve the term "Black Cinema" for productions entirely controlled by Blacks, but they admit the unfeasibility of doing so. On Black film as genre, see especially Cripps (1978: 1–13) and Murray (1973: xi–xv). In addition to providing the best account of the independent Black feature industry of the twenties and thirties, Cripps also records the extraordinary case of the traveling preacher, Eloise Gist: "She ranged over the South during the great Depression, spreading her revivalist faith through motion pictures shot only for the specific narrow purpose defined by her own faith and spirit. Nowhere from script to screen did any white hand intrude, or any white eye observe. Neither white financing in the beginning nor white appreciation at the end affected her pristine black fundamentalism. Her films were naive, technically primitive, literal depictions of black Southern religious folklore that brought faith to life, much as an illuminated manuscript gave visual life to Christian lore in the Middle Ages" (Cripps, 1978: 4). Cripps is interested naturally in Gist's work as the best examples of "pure" Black films; this purity notwith-

their political needs directly reflects the intrinsic conditions of the medium and its hegemonic use, and it does so in a way that makes that failure exemplary for a materialist understanding of film and of minority cultural interventions generally.

On the one hand, the double integration of the dominant film industry into the institutions of the capitalist state—the contribution of its narrative and formal codes to bourgeois ideological reproduction and its own economic determination as itself a capitalist enterprise—allowed only one role for the proletariat, that of consumer. The industrial function ensured that the lack of representation of Blacks in the cinema would be reciprocated by their lack of representation in film; the imprisonment of Black people as consumers of commodity film culture reproduced their imprisonment in the proletariat.

On the other hand, traditional Black cultural practices were both outside the institutions of cinema and also, characteristically, antipathetic to the conditions of film. As Amiri Baraka pointed out, only those nonmaterial aspects of African culture, "music, dance, religion [that] do not have *artifacts* as their end product" (Baraka, 1963: 16),[13] survived the diaspora and slavery. When these performing arts entered into industrial production, Blacks did successfully engage technology—in popular song, for example. But the general unfamiliarity of film technology and its antipathy to their cultural traditions reinforced the general difficulty the proletariat has in obtaining access to the means of industrial commodity production, making it especially difficult for Blacks to break through that fetishization of advanced technology by which Hollywood naturalizes the industrial practice. It would not have been impossible for Black filmmakers to inflect an avant-garde practice of their own with Black motifs or qualities, and thereby to inscribe blackness as a filmic function (as indeed the underground so often had done and as Bill Gunn did to some extent with the anomalous *Ganja and Hess* in 1970); but to make such an endeavor the focus or vehicle of popular resistance would have meant repeating the beats' attempts to wrest a community practice out of industrial functions, at a time of great political urgency and without the resources of a subculture in which film was the privileged medium or in which independent distribution was feasible.

Not until the increased Black enrollment in higher education in the seventies did an ongoing independent Black cinema emerge in university and semi-academic milieus; the work of UCLA film school graduates like Haille Gerima (*Bush Mama*, 1975), Larry Clark (*Passing Through*, 1977), Charles Burnett (*Killer of Sheep*, 1977), Ben Caldwell (*I and I: An African Allegory*, 1977), and Julie Dash (*Four Women*, 1978) typifies the independent momentum and social responsibility attained by what was initially an artificially nursed practice. But, ironically, the increased enrollment of Black students in film schools that generated this alternative film culture followed from the same liberal thrust that had destroyed the only previous instance of a genuinely Black cinema. The liberal commit-

standing, Gist's appropriation of the medium for devotional practice and her total integration of it into a life's work is unequaled in recorded film history, though it is approached by the utopian functionalism that history allowed to Vertov.

Though Clyde Taylor claims that a "new black cinema was born out of the black arts movement of the 1960's" (C. Taylor, n.d.: 46), all the examples he gives are from the mid- to late seventies, which substantiates my claim that independent Black film developed from the educational reforms produced by the Black movement rather than from the movement itself. In addition to the films discussed below, mention must be made of the remarkable *Finally Got the News* (Black Star Productions, 1970), "the only radical film of the sixties which was made under the direct control of revolutionary working class blacks with the specific purpose of radicalizing other black workers" (Georgakas, 1973: 2).

13 Compare with Baraka's essay "Hunting is Not Those Heads on the Wall" (reprinted in Baraka, 1966), in which he elaborates the distinction between art-as-artifact and art-as-process.

ment to integration that continued the anti-racist rhetoric of the World War II era did produce an increase in the visibility and participation of Black people in the industry; and an industrial genre of Black problem pictures through the mid-sixties, from *A Raisin in the Sun* (1961) and *To Kill A Mockingbird* (1963) to *Guess Who's Coming to Dinner* (1967), preached a reform of race relations on a personal if not a systemic basis. But the gains made as a result of NAACP and government pressure to bring Blacks into the mainstream destroyed what before the war had been a sizable Black feature industry which, though almost invariably White-financed, was still Black-controlled and in some cases entirely Black-operated for the exclusive patronage of Black people.[14] With the failure of the independent Black production companies after the thirties, subsequent Black cinema was White-funded and almost entirely White-written and White-directed. In this independent cinema two groups, corresponding to the liberal integrationist and the radical separatist phases of the Black movement, may be distinguished.

The first group developed from the social intersections between the beat subcultures and Black bohemianism, from the attempts by the underground to model film practices on jazz,[15] and from the reformist milieu of the New American Cinema Group; this group of films is best illustrated by Shirley Clarke's *The Cool World* and Michael Roemer and Robert Young's *Nothing But A Man*, both of 1964. The sensitivity and courage of these new-realist dramatizations of Black life in the urban North and the rural South, respectively, exhibit the liberal hope of changing social injustice through knowledge and good will. Clarke's use of cinéma vérité strategies— hand-held camera, cutaway shots to details of the environment, rapid and unpredictable editing—for what is mostly a staged drama allows her to texture her story of a Harlem teenager's fall into crime with both the energy and the aimlessness of slum life. The more extended narrative of *Nothing But A Man* details a young Black laborer's attempt to maintain his marriage in the face of systemic and apparently ineluctable racism that attacks all aspects of his life—racism in the prejudice of his bride's middle-class parents, in the virtually complete disintegration of Black family life, and especially in employment, which can be secured only at the price of abject self-negation. Largely unsentimental and free from studio stereotypes, the film demonstrates how racism is useful for capitalism, and how it produces sexual violence. In its final depiction of the hero's determination not to allow social forces to destroy his resolution, it looks forward to the Black militance of the next years. Both films fairly represent the prison walls around the Black community, the absence of social opportunity for people trapped in the ghetto, and the psychic damage these inflict. In both, the White world appears as a suffocating horizon peopled by gargoyle caricatures, imprisoning an accurately but sympathetically portrayed Black world that includes models of dignified and courageous Black people. *Nothing But A Man* is especially anomalous—and, in fact, virtually unique—in portraying a Black woman with respect.

14 See especially Cripps (1978: 13–63). Mapp (1972) excludes from his discussion as atypical Black films by Black producers (The Birth of a Race Company, Ebony Pictures, and even Oscar Micheaux), but otherwise his is an exhaustive inventory of the changing portrayal of Blacks by Hollywood and by independent White productions. Save only *A Raisin in the Sun* (1961), *Nothing But A Man* (1964), and *The Learning Tree* (1969), he records unrelieved failure to treat everyday Black life with seriousness or dignity, and especially to address the issues of the Black movement.

15 Although the tradition of the representation of Blacks by the underground goes back through Ron Rice's *The Queen of Sheba Meets the Atom Man* (1963), Jonas Mekas's *Guns of the Trees* (1961), and John Cassavetes' *Shadows* (1959) to Lionel Rogosin's *Come Back, Africa* (1959) and Sidney Meyers's *The Quiet One* (1948), throughout Blacks are typically used as metaphors for White desires or fears. Even an instance of substantial Black control over the profilmic, such as Shirley Clarke's *Portrait of Jason* (1967), sensationalizes and spectacularizes its subject. Still, together with its use of Black music, the underground's representation of Black people made it a major moment in Black cinema; its reproduction in the medium of film of the formal and social qualities of jazz is even more significant in indicating the terms by which a popular Black film could have been developed, given a different situation for the medium in Black society generally. The link between the bohemian underground and the lost Black cinema is, of course, Amiri Baraka; if his *Dutchman* (1967), made in England, had been a popular Black success, some of the energy of the revitalized Black theater might have gone into film.

5.3–5.5 Shirley Clarke, *The Cool World*

Despite their real achievements, both films remain refinements, however more subtle and courageous, of the problem films of the late fifties,[16] their formal limits reproducing the limits of their liberal ideology. They strain the industry's narrative and representational codes, but they cannot pass beyond them any more than they can conceive of alternatives to humanist appeals on behalf of the social plight of the Black people they present as sensitive and courageous but essentially impotent and condemned. They cannot envisage structural social change any more than they can envisage the transcendence of the illusionist narrative film. The importance for the civil rights legislation of the mid-sixties (the Civil Rights Bill of 1964 and the Voting Rights Act of 1965) of the liberal social currents from which these films emerged cannot be overestimated; but the year after they were released, riots in Los Angeles, New York, and Newark and the assassination of Malcolm X revealed a social urgency they could not address.

With the failure of reform to keep pace with the explosion of desire after 1964, integrationist demands and nonviolence gave way to the nationalist aspirations of SNCC and Stokely Carmichael, and to the anti-racialist, revolutionary program of the Black Panther Party. As liberal reformism was left behind, films like *The Cool World* and *Nothing But A Man* were no longer ideologically or formally possible. Increasingly militant action demanded the speedy

16 Though, as Mapp notes, Clarke recycles the same stereotypes about Blacks—the vicious criminal, the absent father, the petty thief, the stud—that populate the most racist films (Mapp, 1972: 94–95).

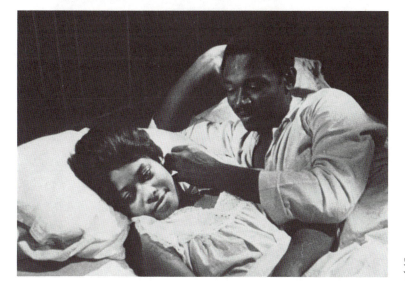

5.6–5.7 Michael Roemer and Robert Young, *Nothing But A Man*

circulation and mass accessibility of the newsreel documentary, but like the Black community at large, the Black Power leaders had neither experience in filmmaking nor access to means of production and distribution. So, continuing a tradition that began with *Troublemakers* (1966), Norman Fruchter and Robert Machover's film about community organizing in the Newark ghetto, radical Black films in the era of the assassination of Martin Luther King, Jr., the publication of Eldridge Cleaver's *Soul on Ice*, and riots throughout the country were made by radical White filmmakers.

Exemplary of this tradition was the collaboration of San Francisco Newsreel with the Oakland Black Panther Party on three films (*Black Panther*, 1968; *Mayday*, 1969; and *Interview with Bobby*

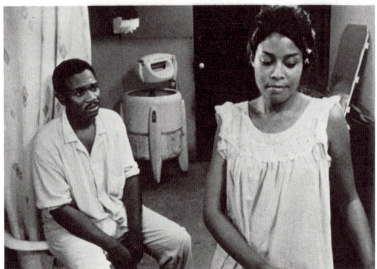

5.8–5.9 Michael Roemer and Robert
Young, *Nothing But A Man*

Seale, 1969); the Los Angeles Newsreel's (finally aborted) project,
Breakfast For Children; Third World Newsreel's early seventies
films about Black prisoners (*Teach Our Children*, 1973, and *In the
Event Anyone Disappears*, 1974); and various ad hoc productions
of a similar documentary/agitational nature, such as Leonard Hen-
ney's *Black Power, We're Goin' Survive America* (1968) and the
collaboration of Stewart Bird and Peter Gessner with the League of
Black Revolutionary Workers that produced *Finally Got the News*
(1970). Working on such films typically proved educational for the
White filmmakers: for example, making *Black Panther* radicalized
San Francisco Newsreel and turned it away from the counterculture
toward Marxist-Leninism, while later the integration of Third
World Newsreel within the proletariat approached the conditions

of a truly popular practice. Of the films made by White radicals in cooperation with the Black Panthers, the most substantial were *The Black Panthers: A Report* (1968), Agnes Varda's documentation of Black protest during the imprisonment and trial of Huey Newton on a charge of murdering an Oakland policeman, and *The Murder of Fred Hampton* (1971), Mike Gray Associates' documentation of the Chicago Panthers that focused on the murder of two of them by the Chicago police.

Both films attempt to explain and vindicate the Panthers, and apart from a single voice-over remark by Varda noting that the Panthers want Newton freed "without even raising the question of his possible guilt," both are entirely without qualification or assessment of the justice of the Panthers' cause, of the correctness of their methods, or of the fact of the police program to eradicate them. This is not to say that either film emerges directly from the processes of Panther political activity or that either allows an absolutely unmediated transmission of the Panther's own discourse. Despite Varda's sympathy, locutions like her claim that Stokely Carmichael is "the leader of all Afro-Americans," as well as being incorrect, ring with a cultural unfamiliarity that in other aspects of the film—for example, the awkwardness in interview technique, a touristic lingering on an item of dress or mannerism—tends to objectify Black people, almost producing them as the exotic natives of an ethnographic documentary. While the makers of *Fred Hampton* are closer to the Panthers, the film's poor sound quality, its grainy images, and its generally low production values interpose a scrim between the Panthers and their audience—though this impediment can translate into a suggestion of financial exigency that reciprocates the Panther's own economic marginality. These interventions are, however, minor, and by and large both films are successful attempts by White radicals to make themselves, their skills, and their access to the apparatus the vehicle for a discourse that is essentially the Panther's own; they are the means by which the Panthers can obtain a presence in alternative cinema or a voice in the media at large which by themselves they would not be able to secure. Since their audiences, comprising immediately adjacent groups in the Black community, White American radicals, and Third World sympathizers in general, were predisposed to be sympathetic, the filmmakers' task was as far as possible to allow the Panthers to speak for themselves. Thus their speeches—at rallies, in conversation among themselves, and also in direct address to the camera—make up the bulk of the films, supplying both their ideological stance and their formal organization.

In *The Black Panthers*, an interview with Newton in jail supplies a center of authority from which radiate other ratifying discourses—those of Eldridge Cleaver and Stokely Carmichael at a rally in Newton's support, of lesser known figures from the Oakland community, of more or less casual presences at the rally, and finally of Varda herself. In support of these mutually corroborating speeches, the film produces illustrative images. For example, the recitation of the 10 Point Plan, almost a generic convention of Panther films which, as in Newsreel's *Black Panther*, usually is simply inserted while the camera tours the ghetto streets, is here formally integrated. At the "Free Huey" rally that the film concentrates on, Bill Brent, a captain in the party from Oakland, introduces himself. This provides the motive for a survey of Oakland with voice-over information about its size and population, the nature of its police force, and the formation of the Panthers up to Newton's arrest. Returning to the rally, the camera allows Brent to provide details of the incarceration of Newton, who is himself introduced in a jail interview. His complaint that prison officials intercept his reading materials includes mention of Mao's writings, which prompts a series of cutaways revealing young people at the rally reading the *Little Red Book*. Back in the cell, the camera records Newton describing some of the features of the party: that it is a Marxist-Leninist program, and that its members are practical revolutionaries who identify with the armed struggle of colonized people throughout the world. Then the film returns to the rally for a speech by Stokely Carmichael about the war being waged upon Blacks in the United States. The camera picks out Brent again in the crowd to allow him to explain the 10 Point Plan, but his recitation is interrupted by cutaways to community people who extend his references: a young woman discusses his demands for education; when he comes to draft exemption for Blacks, several young men amplify his remarks;

5.10 Agnes Varda, *The Black Panthers*: Huey Newton

5.11 Agnes Varda, *The Black Panthers*: Stokely Carmichael and Eldridge Cleaver

5.12 Agnes Varda, *The Black Panthers*: Bill Brent

and when he demands the release of all Blacks in jails, the camera returns to Newton's jail cell. As well as providing the editorial logic for a densely textured and thematically coherent film, this constant interweaving of many voices, each explaining the Panther position with illustrative and corroborative material from their constituency, produces ideological consistency. The Panther spokespeople are seen to speak with the voice of the community, accurately representing its interests, and, conversely, the community is seen as deriving its own self-consciousness from the Panthers' analysis.

With almost no voice-over narration, *Fred Hampton* is constructed from inter-Panther dialogue and direct address by Panthers; it admits non-Panther discourse only to discredit that discourse. The first part of the film is built up around situations inside

5.13 Agnes Varda, *The Black Panthers*

5.14 Agnes Varda, *The Black Panthers*:
Kathleen Cleaver

the Black community—speeches at rallies, meetings between Panthers and representatives of other groups, visits to a Panther breakfast program, and a community medical center—but after this community is violated by the murders of Hampton and Panther Defense Captain Mark Clark, the diegesis is similarly penetrated by the mendacious discourse of the establishment. The press conferences held by State's Attorney Edward V. Hanrahan, the accounts of the shootout in the *Chicago Tribune*, and the inconsistent accounts of the police officers involved are all as much in conflict with each other as with the evidence the Panthers produce, and they are totally discredited by a federal grand jury. The ease with which the Panthers prove their propositions verifies their argument that the state is set to destroy Black dissidents, demonstrates the accuracy of their so-

State's Attorney Edward V. Hanrahan

5.15–5.17 Mike Gray, *The Murder of Fred Hampton*

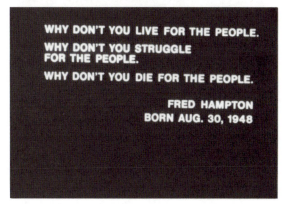

WHY DON'T YOU LIVE FOR THE PEOPLE.

WHY DON'T YOU STRUGGLE
FOR THE PEOPLE.

WHY DON'T YOU DIE FOR THE PEOPLE.

FRED HAMPTON
BORN AUG. 30, 1948

cial analysis, and so justifies Hampton's own exhortations that his audience "live for the people . . . struggle for the people . . . die for the people."

One film liberating Huey Newton's discourse from incarceration and the other redeeming Fred Hampton's from the murderers' guns, neither can be faulted for infidelity to the Panther position; making it their own, they gave it a public dissemination wider than the limited circulation of the Panther's public speeches and the *Black Panther* newspaper, and more honest and sympathetic than the version of the Panthers sensationalized by the media. Where the films became problematical—and the reason for their unpopularity on the left and within sectors of the Black community[17]—was their failure to confront the contradictions of the Panther's position, especially as these were duplicated and exaggerated in the sensationalized, reified Panther image constructed in the mass media.

Although the Panthers' class analysis of the situation of Blacks and their identification of the Black struggle with Third World liberation were superior to rival analyses by cultural nationalists and liberal integrationists, their assumption of a Leninist vanguard role and their decision to militarize resistance to the state finally destroyed them. Whether or not American Blacks constituted a colonized society, without the resources of the Vietnamese or the Algerians, they were not to throw off the *colon* by Vietnamese or

17 *The Murder of Fred Hampton* was especially unpopular; invoking Godard's distinction between radical filmmaking and the filming of radical politics, *Cinéaste* suggested that "in its portrayal and advocacy of revolutionaries as gun-slinging, death-defying desperadoes [it] will thus be seriously counter-productive" (Crowdus, n.d.: 51). Godard, incidentally, warmly recommended Varda's film at showings of his own, very different treatment of the Panthers, *One Plus One*—a film which itself depicts the Panthers as gun-slinging desperadoes.

Algerian methods; the promulgation through the media of the image of the urban guerrilla, quite eclipsing the breakfast and education programs, only ensured that the Panthers' most adventurist gestures, but not their legitimate grievances, were brought to public attention. So while the various African revivals, the leather jackets and the dark glasses, and all the other accoutrements of the outlaw uniform distinguished Panther militancy from the integrationist programs of the civil rights period and stimulated recruitment by providing a role-model alternative to the self-deprecation that Fanon and Freire both diagnosed as the essential mechanism of oppression, the audacity corresponded to no viable method of achieving political power. The para-military posture simply polarized public response to the point where the White community's fear and the state's anger permitted a systematic, illegal police offensive against them.

Like Fred Hampton's prediction that he would not die by slipping on a piece of ice but in the service of the people, the aggression and paranoia of the Panthers' rhetoric could be validated only by the destruction of its speakers. Thus both films appropriately emphasize the fury that the police reserved for *images* of the Panthers; Varda's, for example, ends with a shot of the Panthers' devastated Oakland headquarters and dwells on posters of Newton riddled by police bullets. But neither is capable of critical attention to the social function of those images or of self-critical attention to their own role in the dissemination of those images. In their inability to deal with the disparity between the claims of the Panthers' image and their actual political potential, *The Black Panthers: A Report* and *The Murder of Fred Hampton* participate in their errors; their spectacularization of the Panthers did nothing to avert the group's destruction. The failure of these films to negotiate the contradictions in such highly politicized representation is all the more striking since it prefigures

5.18 Agnes Varda, *The Black Panthers*

parallel ambiguities in a slightly later industrial genre—one that exploited a debased form of Black militancy to preempt a genuinely Black cinema—blaxploitation.

The financial success of Ossie Davis's *Cotton Comes to Harlem* in 1970 spawned a plethora of generic remakes aimed specifically at the Black market: the western was represented by Sidney Poitier's *Buck and the Preacher* (1972), for example, and the musical by *Lady Sings the Blues* (1972). The most successful of these was the gangster movie. This new film noir featured a Black, urban outlaw hero—usually a drug dealer and a pimp—pitted against the Mafia and a corrupt White police force. A sister genre mobilized an equally ferocious heroine who, ironically, took an equally ferocious revenge on ghetto drug pushers: *Shaft* (1971), *Shaft's Big Score* (1972), *Shaft in Africa* (1973), *Across 110th Street* (1972), *Slaughter* (1972), *Slaughter's Big Rip-Off* (1973), *Superfly* (1972), *Superfly T.N.T.* (1973), *The Mack* (1973), *Trick Baby* (1973), and *Truck Turner* (1974) are representative of the former; *Coffy* (1973), *Cleopatra Jones* (1973), and *Foxy Brown* (1974) are representative of the latter. The first films in these genres were independently produced by Blacks, but they were always studio-distributed; once they proved to be financially viable the studios took control of production. *Superfly*, for instance, was independently written and financed by Blacks, with Warner Brothers purchasing it for distribution, but the sequel was produced inside the studio (Mason, 1972: 62). Though the fourteen examples mentioned above all had Black stars and extensive Black casts, ten of them were White-written, White-produced, and White-directed, with only Gordon Parks's direction of the two *Shaft* films and the first *Superfly* and Ron Neale's direction of the second *Superfly* interrupting the shut out (Klotman, 1979).

5.19 Gordon Parks, *Superfly*

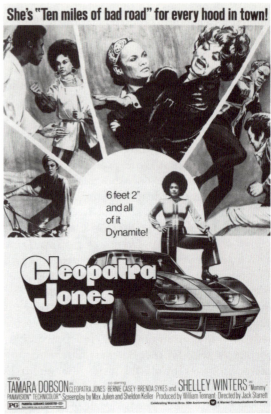

5.20 Jack Hill, *Coffy*: Pam Grier

5.21 Jack Starrett, *Cleopatra Jones*

Blaxploitation did provide the Black proletariat with something no previous film had, heroes from the community, resourceful and powerful enough to take on and defeat their predators. But the value of those role models was almost entirely countered by the films' displacement of attention away from the political analysis of the situation of Black people and from the possibilities of improving it by systemic social change. By presenting the traumas of the ghetto empirically as local criminal issues, blaxploitation spoke directly to its audience's everyday experience, but not to what determined it. The genre's conventions—the redress of wrong by the superhero vigilante rather than by community control, the portrayal of corruption as a police or Mafia aberration rather than as endemic and structural, the backhanded glorification of heavy drugs, prostitution, and other forms of self-destruction that sublimated resentment rather than channeling it in socially useful directions, and a chauvinist, macho anti-intellectualism—allowed for a vicarious release of anger in ways that challenged the power of neither the state nor its local institutions. Despite the popularity of blaxploitation, its regressiveness and its instrumentality to the bourgeois state was widely recognized in both the popular Black press (e.g., Mason, 1972) and radical film journals (e.g., Washington and Berlowitz, 1975).

While almost all blaxploitation films were entirely cynical formula productions, some remain of interest, either because, like *Across 110th Street*, they take the conventions to such hyperbolic extremes that they subvert the genre's mechanism of gratification or because, like Melvin Van Peebles's *Sweet Sweetback's Baadasss Song*, they struggle against the limitations of the genre strongly enough to rupture its ideological closures. *Sweetback* is especially illuminating since in the trials of its hero it dramatized the tensions between the genre's need to depoliticize the Black condition and Van Peebles's own political commitment—a tension that recurs on the formal level in his attempt to use strategies developed in the underground to force the industrial vocabulary toward a more authentic Black dialect. The film may be understood as a meta-generic meditation on the difficulty of making over the Hollywood film as the vehicle of a Black cinema.

Van Peebles retained the full roster of generic motifs: "a detailed and graphic social anatomy of the black underworld that established credibility; a carefully segregated point of view, which unfortunately misfired because no white character was allowed a shred of humanity; a set of symbols and gestures that bore a great freight of outlaw meaning; and a ritual of mayhem that almost orgasmically released upon the film audience the picaresque urban outlaw as a mythic black redeemer" (Cripps, 1978: 133–34). While carrying some of these conventions almost to the point of caricature (making Sweetback himself a professional stud, for example), he also attempted to align them with the politics of Black liberation. In distinct contrast to the genre's suppression of political self-consciousness demanded by the entertainment industry function (*Superfly*'s ridicule of political activists is typical), Van Pebbles makes Sweetback's response to Black Power the motive of his actions and the condition of his heroism. The implications of Sweetback's transformation from a child into a man and then from a woman into a man in the opening scenes are completed by his decision to intervene in the police attack on the radical, Moo Moo. Saving Moo Moo awakens him from his social passivity; he acquires speech and, shortly after, day breaks for the first time in the film. By jeopardizing his life for Moo Moo, he is freed from his degradation as a sexual spectacle and freed for his role as a political outlaw. His recognition that his people's future lies with the young radical is endorsed by representatives of the Black community—by the preacher, for example, who applauds him for having saved "the young bud" that the police would have picked off. First as Moo Moo's protector and then as his heir (for the end suggests that after recovering his strength in Mexico, he will return to the struggle), he receives the support of the Black community and of other racial and sexual minorities.

On the basis of such a reading Huey Newton was able to declare *Sweetback* "the first truly revolutionary Black film made" (Newton, 1972: 113)[18] and Sweetback himself "a beautiful exemplification of Black Power" (ibid.: 139). While it overstates the case and entirely ignores the film's relentless sexism, the argument is not without

18 Newton ingeniously allegorizes the film; he interprets the sex scenes as indicating Sweetback's absorption of the community's love, for example, and his silence as a space to be occupied by the voices of the audience.

5.22–5.25 Melvin Van Peebles, *Sweet Sweetback's Baadasssss Song*

some justification, for the narrative does supply a logic to the hero's growth from the renegade stud of blaxploitation to the militant of the documentary tradition, the latter role model is used as a critique of the former, and there is the suggestion that Sweetback's sexual potency carries the stigma of his political impotence. But the implications of such a *bildungsroman* form cannot be elaborated through the full register of narrative motifs. Sweetback cannot finally transcend his blaxploitation machismo; neither, despite the terroristic pretensions of his name, can Moo Moo be more than a cipher. Without charisma or initiative, he provides no politically useful role model, and his absolute dependence on Sweetback undermines all the claims for his importance. Incapable of appropriating film presence, the proffered example of Black Power is incapable of asserting himself in either aesthetic or political terms.

These thematic tensions, which subvert the militance *Sweetback* wants to endorse and cause the film to fall back into the generic codes it wants to distinguish itself from, recur in Van Peebles's attempts to expand the formal vocabulary of the commercial feature. The general absence of shot/reverse-shot patterns and other standard tropes, the often ungrammatical lighting patterns, and the grainy image—all following from the low production costs—by and large harmonize with the decrepit ghetto slums, rhyming with their decay rather than producing spectator distance. In this, as in many

of its motifs, *Sweetback* recalls contemporary independent feature
productions, especially Roger Corman's and Russ Meyer's biker
and soft-core exploitation films, but it goes well beyond these in its
assertion of authorship. Independently produced by Van Peebles
(though perhaps with completion funds from Bill Cosby [Cripps,
1978: 132]), it was also written, directed, edited, and scored by him,
and it starred him in the title role. This insistence on personal vision
links it with the underground in terms of its *auteur* control over all
stages of its production, and with the trance film especially in terms
of its structure.

Like the picaro heroes of Curtis Harrington's *Fragment of Seeking*, Kenneth Anger's *Fireworks*, or Stan Brakhage's *Reflections on
Black*, Sweetback wanders through an urban nightmare of demonic
antagonists and sexual hyperbole, seeking the resolution of psychosexual confusion. This structural subjectivity is reciprocated by
parallel formal invocations of the late sixties' psychedelic underground, especially the color solarizations, multiple superimpositions, loop printing, and other forms of image manipulation associated in Los Angeles with Pat O'Neill and Burton Gershfield (and,
in fact, some of the effects in *Sweetback* were done by a small company run by O'Neill). Used to punctuate crises like Sweetback's initial beating of the police and his sexual triumph over the motorcycle
gang leader, such optical effects skew the film toward the first person, though the subjectivity does not distinguish the artist from the
community so much as affirm the commonality of his highly
charged vision; it inscribes blackness. The same is true of the other
main stylistic trait, the construction of a phantasmagoric mosaic out
of short shots of the cityscape and brief, documentary-style interviews with people from the community; in these visual jazz riffs, the
continually moving and zooming camera creates a vertiginous run
through the ghetto that establishes the reciprocity of Sweetback's
vision with the community's. Other underground conventions that
destroy diegetic unity and narrative transparency, such as the use of
Black music and the quasi-surrealist chorus of voices that follows
Sweetback through his desert miasma, similarly fix the individual
hero, especially in his crisis, as the surrogate for a whole culture.

It is appropriate to approach *Sweetback* as psychomachy, as the
dramatization of deep psychological conflicts in which the tension
between the political and the sexual is only the summary vocabulary
for a whole series of social and libidinal bifurcations across which
the Black self in its historical uncertainty is stretched. In this trauma,
Sweetback recapitulates the condition of an entire people; but
Sweetback does not. It is set against itself in contradiction: its reenactment of the social relations of capitalist culture is at odds with
those of its avowed thematic project. As a commodity in exploitative social transactions, even Black social transactions, it does not
derive from the praxis of the community, but only from the isolated
entrepreneurial determination of a single man. His attempt to make
the production methods and marketing operations of capitalist cinema the vehicle for social reform are abrupted at the point where

5.26 Melvin Van Peebles, *Sweet Sweet-back's Baadasssss Song*

market functions enclose revolutionary desire. Unlike Black music, Black cinema could find no authentic place in the Black community, neither as popular expression nor, especially, as a model of production capable of popular imitation. As a commodity, its function is finally that of every other industrial film, every other exploitation film. *Sweetback*'s opening credits, which affirm "The Community" as its stars, speak this contradiction, for what they propose as its stars are really its marks. Concealing the commodity relations by which it works to sustain the capitalist cinema, its very celebration of blackness, of blackness given voice, is inevitably alienated, and so can do no more than preoccupy the vacant space of a genuine community culture—a Black revolutionary cinema.

The virtual absence of cinema from the most progressive social movement of the sixties must be understood as the interdependence between the establishment media's refusal to portray the radicalization of the Black movement honestly and the parallel failure of Blacks themselves to develop a film culture adequate to their needs. This relation provides a particularly clear instance of the historical and social determination of cultural production. Parallel conditions among other ethnic groups forestalled any substantial cinematic contribution to their struggles in the sixties as well. Hollywood did continue the modification of its portrayal of Native Americans that had been developing since World War II,[19] and there were a few instances of successful collaboration between independent filmmakers and Indian groups, such as that between Carol Burns and the Survival of the American Indian Association which produced the Newsreel-distributed *As Long as Rivers Run* (1971). Yet Sol Worth's remarkable 1966 experiment of introducing the apparatus to the Navajo, however fascinating the films are and however invaluable the critical perspectives on cinema that it makes available, was of little use to the Navajo themselves. Nor could collaboration

19 But these films—*A Man Called Horse* (1970), *Soldier Blue* (1970), *Tell Them Willie Boy Is Here* (1970), and *Little Big Man* (1971)—were little more than "a facelifting on the old Cowboys and Indians" (Georgakas, 1972: 32).

between White radicals and the Latin community in Newsreel films like *Los Siete* (1969), *Rompiendo Puertas (Break and Enter)* (1970), *El Pueblo Se Levanta (The People Are Rising)* (1971), and *G.I. José* (1974) produce anything with the social momentum of the Chicago Guerrilla Theater or Fresno's El Teatro Campesino or New York's Soul and Latin Theater. Apart from isolated instances, the gap between the politically disenfranchised and economically marginal ethnic minorities and the material conditions of cinema, along with the antipathy of ethnic arts to the material conditions of film, precluded any substantial role for the medium in ethnic political contestation.

Cultural traditions aside, it is clear that the virtually unalloyed commodity consumption that occupies the position of these absent ethnic cinemas is a matter of class rather than ethnicity per se. With the exception of students, women, and sexual minorities, those sixties dissident groups who theorized themselves politically, especially ethnic minorities, prisoners, and GIs, were all predominantly from the working class. Their inability to produce cinema for their own purposes should be thought of as aspects of the absence of a working-class cinema. Like its constitutive instances, this more general failure has implications for cinema as a whole, clarifying the dominant cinema's integration in capitalism—its intrinsic and inevitable reiteration of economic and social subordination and impoverishment. But these general issues also reflect the condition of the working class in this period, the repression of historical self-consciousness and materialist thought in general. By the end of the sixties a class understanding of the United States was available to inform attempts to produce a working-class cinema. But both class knowledge and proletarian film were shaped by the war in Vietnam.

Film and the War: Representing Vietnam

The document, then, is no longer for history an inert material through which it tries to reconstitute what men have done or said, the events of which only the trace remains; history is now trying to define within the documentary material itself unities, totalities, series, relations.
— Michel Foucault

One day at the battalion aid station in Hue a Marine with minor shrapnel wounds in his legs was waiting to get on a helicopter. . . . "I *hate* this movie," he said, and I thought, "Why not?"
— Michael Herr

For the last half of the decade the war in Vietnam was the largest single determinant of other economic, social, and cultural developments in the United States, eventually becoming the master metaphor by which they were understood. As the imperial state declared itself in the ghettos, in the streets of Chicago, and on the campuses of the rest of the country, albeit with less ferocity than in the villages of Vietnam, Blacks and war protesters came to feel themselves to be fighting alongside the Vietnamese people in the same war of liberation. When Black Power's equation of the struggles of domestic minorities with that of the Vietnamese expanded to include other marginalized groups, then the notion of a unified Third World could stand in place of the largely absent class analysis, and acts of resistance against the state, especially as they became more violent in the Weatherman period, could be thought of as parallel to the Vietnamese resistance rather than simply ancillary or subordinate to it. The Progressive Labor Party's attack on North Vietnam's participation in the Paris peace talks as a betrayal of world revolution marks the extent to which the initially hegemonic confrontation in Asia could be re-contained in the political developments it engendered. Until this point, however, the operations in the Asian theater were the parent actions from which the "two, three, many Vietnams" of Che Guevara's injunction were spawned. Each of the special interest groups—students, GIs, the Vietnamese themselves, and indeed everyone conscious of the way his or her experience of capitalism, even at the psychic level of alienation from oneself, recapitulated the situation of Third World people—had thus a "Vietnam" of his or her own, a lived experience of imperialism.

This pandemic dispersal of the Vietnam War is the context for the specific issues faced by filmmaking that sought to intervene in it, either directly, by attempting to propagandize against it, or indirectly, but no less importantly, by confronting the establishment media's complicity in the social consensus that allowed the administration to fight the war on its own terms. Consideration of the way in which even the most dissident filmmaking was incriminated, on some level or other, in the international political system of which the Vietnamese decolonization struggle was the rupture eventually produced meta-cinematic reflections that argued themselves as the only politically valid filmmaking. As their only means of negating mass media representations which, however situated ideologically, only profited from the war, they refused to allow any unmediated image of Vietnam or any film practice engaged in its purview to pass without saturating it with the evidence of its own contradictions. Carried to their logical conclusions, such meditations would call into question the possibility of even making film, and so would open the road to a refusal that could authenticate itself only by espousing silence or self-destruction, or by totally recasting the practices under which cinema could be pursued. The filmic form of appearance of these cinematic issues is the tension between image and discourse in the documentation of the war. The inflection of general problems of representation by the specific question of representing the war imposed semiological crises upon the political crises involved in the dissemination of images and in the relation between such images and the institutions producing them. Contestation of the establishment definition of the war, of what constituted "Vietnam," thus inevitably involved contestation of the methods of representing it, of the agencies of representation, and hence of the relationship between media institutions and the other institutions of state power.

That the photograph manifests a stronger existential bond with reality than do most other forms of representation is accepted even by those semiologists who are most careful to insist that ostensibly transparent referentiality is in fact produced by means of the codes of visual language.[20] And so while Brecht's remark that by itself a photograph of the Krupp ironworks does not say very much may be true, one thing it does say is that the photographer has been there. In the case of motion pictures, this *"having-been-there"* of the still photograph "gives way before a *being-there* of the thing" (Barthes, 1977: 45), but in both instances the assertion of one or another kind of presence is fundamental both to the rhetorical power of the higher levels of signification articulated by the image itself through the codes of its own legibility and to the other languages with which it is contiguous. In most sixties documentary war films, the resonances of the cinematic codes of World War II feature films that depend on this illusion of presence are amplified and directed by accompanying verbal languages—indirect speech, titles, direct speech, voice-of-God narration[21]—in which the image is encased. But even when such discursivity is not explicit, in genres like cinéma vérité that claim the aural and visual reproduction of nature as it is, the apparent iconicity only frames an intrinsic exposition. Thus presence and meaning—object and interpretation, denotation and connotation, representation and discourse—are the terms between which sequences of images argue a point of view while maintaining the semblance that their mediation is neutral, merely the articulation of what is implicit in the evidence they make present.

Bridging the pacific distance that kept the war in Asia from its production in the United States, the Vietnam War documentary exploits and compounds at two points especially the polemical assumptions of the documentary model in general: at the point where, to use Bazin's inaugurating image, a photographic "impression" (Bazin, 1967: 12) is taken from the war by light and at the point where it is delivered to the public. The transactions involved at both points were scrutinized in the period in reflexive assaults on the theory of representational documentary, but in most Vietnam War documentaries, the precariousness of these moments when reality was transformed into film and when reality was recovered from it was typically supplied by a compensating excess of affirmation, so that the vehemence with which such and such film was offered as proof or disproof of the war's justification depended upon corresponding assumptions that the derivation of its images from situations of danger and horror empowered them with a more than ordinary authority. To invoke a metaphor used in one of the most rank exploitations of the war, those images secured from the heart of darkness were held to be simultaneously beyond language and the most eloquent. It is entirely appropriate that, as if in recognition of the centrality of this model of authority in the discourse of the Vietnam War as a whole, even Hollywood, in its only contemporary attempt to deal directly with the war rather than allegorizing it or displacing it into one of its adjacent issues, recognized that the politics of the Vietnam War were inseparable from the politics of its representation.[22]

20 On this debate, see especially Eco's demonstrations of the limitations in the Peirceian concept of iconicity to refute Metz's assertion that, in its "perceptual literalness," the film image "reproduces the signified spectacle; and thus it becomes what it shows to the extent that it does not have to *signify* it" (Metz, 1974b: 75–76; Eco, 1976: 593–96).

21 The term was coined by Paul Rotha, but I take it from Nichols's taxonomy of documentary forms (Nichols, 1981: 170–208).

22 Although Hollywood's avoidance of the Vietnam War—by 1975 only four combat films had been set there (Smith, 1975: 3)—was indeed a function of the political complexities, the failure to represent accurately the Vietnamese and their position was a cinematic as well as an ideological problem that arose from the inapplicability of the anti-imperialist model of World War II and hence the inappropriateness of the codes of World War II movies. Thus, while it is an oversimplification, Julian Smith's witty summary, "Vietnam did not generate a great many films but it may have been America's first film-generated war, the first . . . war to grow out of attitudes supported, perhaps even created, by a generation of movies depicting America's military omnipotence" (ibid.: 4), correctly points to the fact that representation was only half of Hollywood's role in the war. Writing after the rush of big budget Vietnam War films of the late seventies, Gilbert Adair is able to address some of the conditions which made them so amenable to revisionist histories of the war, refurbishing for the cold-war revival the imperialist rhetoric of the sixties (Adair, 1981).

23 Like representations of the GI in general, films about the GI's experience of the war reproduce his military instrumentality in his instrumentality in the political functions of the cinemas in which he is contained; hence his own extreme disenfranchisement, his exclusion from production. On the one hand, the films made by the army for Vietnam soldiers, the Armed Forces Information Films series, and The Big Picture series (many of which are still available) and, on the other, the various films made about or on behalf of veterans opposed to the war, such as Joseph Strick's *Interviews with My Lai Veterans* or the various documentations of the Wintersoldier hearings, and films made to counter the Army's own recruiting publicity, such as Newsreel's *Army*, are necessary adjuncts to the present discussion, especially in the way they fail to deal with the ambivalent location of the GI as simultaneously the agent and the victim of imperialism. The army indoctrination/training films are an especially interesting case of the politics of representation, in which the categorical servitude of the common soldier is reproduced in his absolute cinematic disenfranchisement.

Though a fictional feature, John Wayne's *The Green Berets* (1968), made when public opinion was already swinging against American presence in Vietnam, directly addressed the obligation of the press to produce domestic consensus. It dramatized the education of a skeptical journalist who is invited by a marine captain played by Wayne himself to go to Vietnam and share the day-to-day life of the Green Berets. The journalist becomes convinced of the necessity and indeed virtue of the U.S. defense of the south from communist aggression, not through argument of the historical process or explanation of the sequence of colonial penetrations that have produced the war, but by being brought face to face with National Liberation Front (NLF) atrocities. The wrenching visceral encounters he experiences—the sight of a murdered Montagnard chief, a GI horribly killed by a bamboo skewer booby trap, and finally the NLF attack on Fort Dodge—bring the war into focus for him as an altruistic response to a worldwide communist threat that only has been obfuscated by the cant of a liberal press. Though Wayne continuously interprets this evidence to ensure that the correct implications are construed, the journalist is essentially convinced by the nature of the atrocities themselves; they are, as it were, self-explanatory, conjuring a history and an ethics out of their own material presence. Like Eric Sevareid in 1966, like Morely Safer in 1967, he goes to Vietnam *to see for himself*, and he returns to the United States determined to report the truths that firsthand observation has made plain to him. He thus enacts the model role of the documentary filmmaker, even as intradiegetically he has enacted the role of the ideal audience for such a documentary.

Like *The Green Berets*, the typical Vietnam War documentary recreates a trip to the front; its transformation of the movie theater into the theater of war depends on the effectiveness with which the audience can be made to experience phenomenally the textures and terrors of battle. The crucial nexus is the GI, and, just as in the war itself he is our surrogate, so in the film he is intermediary between us and Vietnam.[23] His experience of the war, always weightier and more authoritative than ours and circumscribing any experience we can have, is proposed as the moment of authenticity and knowledge—of authenticity as knowledge—upon which the war can be evaluated and validated, just as his sacrifice is the war's justification, the proof of its virtue. Television specials like CBS's *Christmas in Vietnam* (1965) and films like Pierre Schoendorffer's *The Anderson Platoon* (1966–67) and Eugene Jones's *A Face of War* (shot in 1966 but not released until 1968) are representative of such documentaries that propose the GI as the site of exemplary understanding.

For three months in 1966, Jones and his crew lived with a company of the Marine Corps that was unsuccessfully resisting the NLF's liberation of a small village. With as many as three cameras simultaneously, all equipped with radio microphones, the filmmakers followed the soldiers through all their activities. By virtue of the closeness of this surveillance and the crew's readiness to follow the soldiers into action, *A Face of War* does succeed in making available

5.27–5.28 John Wayne, *The Green Berets*

what is probably the most densely textured version of the GI's experience of the Vietnam War and of the day-to-day conditions under which it was fought. Jones does not fall into the obvious formal and ideological trap of structuring his presentation dramatically upon the experience of a single hero and subordinating the remainder of the company in a hierarchy around him (and to this extent the concern of the film remains the generalized experience of the GIs almost as a historically representative class); still, some of them become sufficiently familiar that the remoteness of their civilian lives from the Asian front emphasizes both the poignancy of their attempts to make sense of Vietnam and the political mediation that lies between the GIs as individuals and the GIs as agents of an imperialism of which they have no understanding or real knowledge.

Inevitably the film's highlights are the points when these contradictions are greatest; in the combat scenes the cameramen's defensive reaction to enemy attack causes the coherence of the visual and aural fields to fall apart into the energized cacophony of the recording apparatus's own contact with violence, reproducing in the enunciation the chaotic violence of the exchange of fire and the cries of pain of the wounded. The film's overall structure exploits the tension between torturous and fearful silence and these sudden eruptions of filmic and profilmic violence, with collision montage used to juxtapose the terror and destruction of battle with the soldiers' attempts to befriend the peasants. The most powerful of these rapid shifts comes in a sequence showing the GIs providing medical care to the villagers when a truck is suddenly blown up by a land mine and a number of young soldiers are killed. In the jarring unpredictability of these alternations—the suddenness with which a silent march through empty paddies can be transformed into a miasma of destruction—Jones locates the essence of the GI's experience. And by following the soldiers into the heart of battle and by so fully subjecting himself to their risks that he was twice wounded—shooting so assiduously that he himself was shot—he appropriates for his film the authenticity of their extreme jeopardy.

While this most crucial assertion of Barthes's *"having-been-*

5.29–5.31 Eugene Jones, *A Face of War*

there" does have its value, not the least of which is its unspoken but
unmistakable conclusion that the GI's are as much victims as heroes, still the fallacies of the cinéma vérité model expose its naiveté.
Its suppositious faith in the capacity of reality to reveal itself, the
basis of its humanist pathos, is discredited by the clearly staged nature of many sequences, and especially by the self-consciously plangent, high-art photography of scenes such as that of soldiers on
watch at dusk silhouetted by flares against coils of barbed wire, or
of old women weeping as these same soldiers burn their homes. This

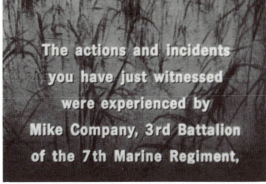

The actions and incidents you have just witnessed were experienced by Mike Company, 3rd Battalion of the 7th Marine Regiment,

5.32–5.33 Eugene Jones, *A Face of War*

implicit pleading on behalf of the military that finally only recapitulates the most egregious of the war's justifications comes to a head in the covert appropriation of World War II as a master metaphor. Most of the motifs *A Face of War* employs—the man on point listening to the jungle and waving his troop on, the chaplain's pre-battle address giving the imminent self-sacrifice a divine sanction, the football game in the mud, the communal bath in a natural pool, the smiles and gratitude of the natives, and even the birth of a baby—are recruited from Hollywood features; their silent intent is to rewrite imperialist invasion as the anti-fascist liberation of Asia from the Japanese, or of Europe from the Nazis.

As World War II supplied the model for understanding the Vietnam War, so Hollywood war movies provided the vocabulary for conducting it. Michael Herr's *Dispatches*, an attempt to write the soldiers' stories that was preempted by an artificiality that made the war for them already a movie (Herr, 1978: 188, 206), is only the most perceptive account of the war as a totally media-ted event, itself made over into the conventions of art. Such a Wildean mimetic inversion presents a particular problem for a would-be objective documentarist, for further transformations into language of an already aestheticized reality merely multiply the layers of reflexivity. What saves Herr himself from capitulation to total subjectivity and gives substance to his torrent of psychedelic flotsam is not appeal to the adequacy of any one story or to the actuality of events, for these are more bizarre than any trip; rather, it is the establishment of self-consciousness of the medium between events and any representation of them—the attention to language itself in the face of its attrition—that makes a place for understanding.[24]

Elsewhere that attrition, the dissolution of meaning into labyrinthine ironic jargon, facilitated the army's and the administration's use of the public media to present the war as non-ideological, as an apolitical, humane response to ideologically motivated aggression. Thus Jones, and in fact the establishment media at large, would have it that the intensity of the Vietnam experience was not only its own justification, it was also its own explanation. The affirmation of presence in the film image supposes a parallel aesthetic of empir-

24 Since by and large only those filmmakers who were favorably disposed to the administration's idea of the war either chose or were allowed to go to South Vietnam, there is no equivalent in film of Herr's awareness of the effect of the penetration and presence of the recording apparatus. Instead, as is argued below, the reflexive moment did not occur in American film until the object of documentation became the war at home.

icism, a repression of knowledge that can be countered only by an engagement with what it must suppress: history. As the war grew, the need for explanations of it was in no way lessened by the currency that television gave to hard-core imagery of its atrocities. Whatever value same-day footage of the bombardment of Khe Sanh or the fighting in Hue had in legitimizing the war or in authorizing an account of it became eroded by familiarity, but also by the disparity between the visceral overload and its lack of meaning. Films like *A Face of War*, which privilege the GI's trauma as the explanation of the war, were collusive with the tragedy they lamented. Suspended across the absent explanations of the historical events which produced the war, and by virtue of those absences contributing to public mendacity; they were collusive with the White House, which was able to prosecute the war for so long precisely by misrepresenting its causes.

The most important of the official apologies for the war was *Why Vietnam?* (1965), an extension of the Pentagon's World War II *Why We Fight* series. Scripted by the State Department to garner support for President Johnson's bombing of the north, its point of departure was a speech made by the president in July 1965 in which he cited a letter from "a woman in the midwest" who wanted to know why her son was in Vietnam. The answer, articulated both in Johnson's own words and in the extrapolation and commentary of a narrator, described a drama of aggression and appeasement: in the tradition of Hitler and Mussolini, Ho Chi Minh had invaded South Vietnam in a communist offensive aimed initially at the rice and the mineral industry, but with long-term ambitions stretching as far as East Pakistan. Blatantly misrepresenting history, Johnson argued in the film that Vietnam was a defensive war; the United States was simply "helping a free people to defend their sovereignty" against Ho and his plans for "a reign of terror." But his claims—Dien Ben Phieu had been a battle between communist and non-communist Vietnamese; at Geneva, Vietnam was divided into two in the pattern of Korea; there had been free elections in the south; the United States destroyers in the Gulf of Tonkin had been fired upon without provocation—are all apparently supported by documentary evidence. There is enough footage of fleeing peasants to prove the repressiveness of Ho's regime; shells with Chinese markings justify the assertion that the invasion is part of a global communist offensive; and though the enemy is as invisible in this film as he was reputed to be in the jungles of Vietnam, still the evidence of his presence is borne upon the bodies of the wounded American soldiers. Substituting for the indirect address of cinéma vérité the direct address of the narrator, and incorporating Johnson's discourse into its own even as it appropriates presidential authority, the mendacious history on the sound track closes the visual text and encloses the plenitude of meaning it is supposed to contain. In the 10,000 prints circulated throughout the country and shown to all GI's before departure to Vietnam, *Why Vietnam?* epitomizes the conjunction of a system of representation and a system of distribution—a film and a cinema—that to-

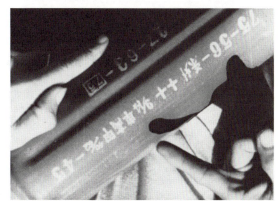

5.34–5.38 U.S. Department of Defense, *Why Vietnam?*

gether form the object radical film would have to contest. In that contestation, the representations of the Vietnamese and their methods of representation had a privileged role, one which may best be approached *via* their ideological and material absence from most Vietnam films.[25]

In *Fire in the Lake*, Frances Fitzgerald's perception that the war was a Vietnamese rather than simply an American event enabled her to collate the strategic crisis with the crisis in American misconception of the Third World in general. She suggested that the American command's absolute failure to understand the Vietnamese was

25 Cf. "From *Saigon* to *The Green Berets*, American films set in Vietnam always emphasized American characters and did not create a single important Vietnamese who is not defined through his or her relationship to Americans" (Smith, 1975: 111).

matched by the soldiers' inability even to perceive their adversaries. Ignorant of the role of the village as the pivot of Vietnamese social life, the GI was incapable of knowing how the NLF had used that role to confound the distinction between combatant and noncombatant, drawing entire sectors of South Vietnam into its ranks and redefining the conditions under which the war could be fought. "In raiding the NLF villages, the American soldiers had actually walked over the political and economic design of the Vietnamese revolution. They had looked at it, but they could not see it, for it was doubly invisible: invisible within the ground and then again invisible within their own perspective as Americans" (Fitzgerald, 1972: 192). Running like a leitmotif through both the films and the other accounts of the war, the invisibility of the Vietnamese allowed them to be everywhere but also to be everywhere absent. It was a fact not only of the military experience but also of the media activity that reenacted it; and ironically so, since the privileged role of the Vietnamese as the verminous enemy or as the vanguard of the revolutionary resistance to imperialism endowed their images—representations of them and their representations of the war—with a peculiar authority.

Such images did have several kinds of use for the administration and the army, and in fact one of the most interesting of all the films produced by the war is *Know Your Enemy—The Viet Cong* (AFIF 172), the U.S. Army's re-presentation of captured NLF footage of its own combat operations and non-military and propaganda work. In this film the army narrator, who is shown reviewing the footage, continually attempts to discredit scenes of NLF activity, for example, women and children transporting weapons on modified bicycles, casualties being met by doctors and nurses and assigned to underground hospitals, and the production of liberation newspapers—all scenes in which they appear to be proficient soldiers and fully human people—by warning the audience to remember that what they are seeing is "the Viet Cong as the Viet Cong would like to see themselves."

By and large, however, the White House and the corporate interests behind the war preferred to repress the Vietnamese's view of themselves and of the war and so reproduce in the domestic theaters that invisibility which was so devastating in Asia. Whose interests were finally served by the media's decision to follow the military in conceptualizing the Vietnamese people only as body counts is difficult to tell. The dinner-time saturation of the American psyche with what became known as " 'bang bang' coverage" (Arlen, 1969: 112) was by definition and structure piecemeal, and unable to deal in anything that could not be reduced to visual sensationalism; it probably did the administration as much harm as good, but certainly the media attempted to follow the official line. The networks regularly aired documentaries that parroted the government rationales, often under immediate direct pressure from sponsors and the White House (Barnouw, 1974: 273),[26] and they refused to show the many available documentaries that presented an opposite point of view.[27]

26 For the Nixon White House's attempt to determine media coverage of the war, see also Gitlin (1980: 277–79).

27 Films from the NLF and North Vietnam that were available in the United States were listed in "Films in Vietnam" in 1969, and also in the various Newsreel catalogues. Four had been described by Peter Gessner in *The Nation* three years earlier (Gessner, 1966). Documentation of the North had been begun in 1954 with the Soviet Union's Roman Karmen's *Vietnam* (1955). After escalation documentaries were available from both the NLF and North Vietnam, from Cuba (Santiago Alvarez's *Hanoi, Martes Trece* and *79 Primaveras* (79 *Springtimes*), from East Germany, and from Japan. Most were suppressed in the United States. For Vietnam documentaries, see especially Barnouw (1974: 262–87). Television coverage of the war is summarized by C. Hammond (1981: 194–221). Because many of the films shot in North Vietnam, such as Newsreel's *People's War* (1969), Felix Greene's *Inside North Vietnam* (1968), and Santiago Alvarez's *Hanoi, Martes Trece* (1967), tended to recapitulate the aesthetics of presence, substituting the effects of U.S. bombing—the devastation of hospitals, the rebuilding of roads and bridges by peasants, individual bomb shelters, and burying the dead—for the village patrols, the booby traps, and the NLF dead shown in the establishment documentaries, they remain empirical and subjective; Greene's, for instance, subtitled "A Personal Report," is emphatically his presentation of the North's position.

5.39 U.S. Army, *Know Your Enemy—The Viet Cong*

Felix Greene's *Inside North Vietnam* is a case in point; although CBS sponsored it and supplied Greene with stock and laboratory services in return for an option, it deemed the film unshowable (ibid.: 281). Even Walter Cronkite's celebrated expression of reservations about the war on his visit to Vietnam in February 1968 merely reflected the shift in majority opinion that had happened eight months before.

With American and world support necessary for the continuation of the war, the media became as much the site of the war as the place where it was depicted, forcing the anti-war movement to adopt tactics whose decentralization, infiltration, and other strategies had a good deal in common with the NLF. Since access to images of the NLF was always a function of social power, a mark of a position in respect to the war mediated through specific relations with the army, with the State Department, and with the media institutions, and since wherever the Vietnamese people's struggle was supported or reenacted such images were most highly prized, the way they were handled was intrinsically so important that the contest of representation was inseparable from the contestation not only of the agencies of representation, but also of the modes of representation.

In this guerrilla media war these multiple interdeterminations demanded a new relation between image and exposition, between sight and sense, such as had, in fact, been developed by the NLF.

> The Viet Cong do use films, but not widely. However, they use filmstrips quite widely. All the Viet Cong films I've seen—captured propaganda films used in South Vietnam by the Viet Cong—are *silent*. These films are *accompanied by a narration delivered by a man during the projection*. It's as if this was an illustrated lecture. In that way he can *suit his content to the current local situation*.[28]

28 The informant here was a United States Information Service (USIS) filmmaker who worked for two years in South Vietnam. He also noted that the improvisational quality of NLF films, their inevitable crudeness, gave the "impression of being the films of a revolutionary force" ("Films in Vietnam," 1969: 58). Consciously imitated for the same reason by radical filmmakers in the United States, such crudeness was ideologically loaded when assimilated with a war that culminated in a great victory over capitalist technology per se. In this respect the NLF's film *Young Puppeteers of Vietnam* is especially interesting. Showing how teenagers in liberated areas of Vietnam make puppets from bits of a downed U.S. plane and travel through the country putting on puppet shows that illustrate their resistance to the United States, the film is important in documenting the reconversion of the enemy's technology to instruments of liberation and also in documenting an art form largely supplanted by film in "advanced" societies.

This extreme revision of cinema must have been substantially determined by material conditions, by the logistics of jungle warfare, by technological exigency, and by a limited cine-literacy on the part of the audience (and in any case it is not generalizable to all NLF films, some of which were extremely sophisticated). Still, it must be understood as a decisive and programmatic reorientation of the use of the apparatus. Indeed, it is in precisely such terms—and almost certainly drawing on the Vietnamese as a model—that the concept of a "Third Cinema" was formulated. In domestic attempts to reproduce this guerrilla cinema, supplantation of spectacle and consumption by the "film act," "A MEETING—an act of anti-imperialist unity . . . [in which the] film is the pretext for dialogue, for the seeking and finding of wills" (Solanas and Gettino, 1976: 62), together with other revisions of the social relations of film, is crucial. In their integration of cinema into the liberation struggle, the Vietnamese made concomitant modifications in the filmic.

The discovery that films "offer an effective pretext for gathering an audience, in addition to the ideological message they contain," and that "the capacity for synthesis and penetration of the film image . . . makes the film far more effective than any other tool of communication" (ibid.: 53) meant that formal codes had to be reconstructed accordingly. Interposing himself like the *benshi* between the film and its audience, the NLF spokesperson inserted his discourse between the image and its self-articulation. In doing so he contained its presence inside his present-ation of it, inaugurating the possibility of a reading of the film and dispelling the unity of the diegesis into "a field of signs"[29] capable of further amplification and specification. Supplanting mimesis by the more fully articulate and situationally flexible verbal discourse, and retaining images only as subordinated illustration within that discourse, the NLF's rejection of theatricality in the reconstruction of cinema as an interactive educational and suasive process within a larger struggle against capitalism necessitated the destruction of the signifying procedures developed by capitalist cinema. The analogous American domestic guerrilla cinema developed by the Newsreels may be introduced by reference to the two most interesting attempts to engage the conditions of the discourse of liberation inside the largely unified hegemonic film text of Vietnam: Émile de Antonio's *In the Year of the Pig* (1969) and Nick Macdonald's *The Liberal War* (1972).

An intervention against the media's collusion in the administration's misrepresentation of the war, *In the Year of the Pig* differs from even establishment recognitions (like *Why Vietnam?*) that Vietnam had a history by emphasizing that history as the site of competing discourses rather than as a single unified text, a fact. The film is an assemblage of archival footage culled from East Germany, Hanoi, and the NLF offices in Prague, as well as from American companies such as ABC, UPI, and Paramount news, together with interviews with and speeches by over eighty politicians, and soldiers including Ho Chi Minh, Nguyen Huu Tho, Daniel Berrigan, Senators Wayne Morse and Everett Dirksen, Lyndon Johnson, Robert

29 Cf. "We may, in fact, consider the *benshi*'s entire discourse as a *reading* of the diegesis which was thereby designated as such and which thereby ceased to function as diegesis and became what it had in fact never ceased to be, *a field of signs*" (Burch, 1979: 79).

5.40–5.43 Émile de Antonio, *In the Year of the Pig*

McNamara, and Generals LeMay and Westmoreland, as well as interviews with scholars like Paul Mus, David Halberstam, and Jean Lacouture. In its presentation of a history of the texts of Vietnam, the film contains scenes of colonial days followed by information on the life of Ho, on the Japanese occupation, on the expulsion of the French, and finally on the stages of American involvement.

Throughout, filmic documentation is not an authoritative showing forth of the truth so much as the occasion for interpretation. Eschewing the continuity of a single narrative voice, it replaces both the self-articulation of reality and the unified text of history with a collage in which visual information destabilizes and contradicts the verbal interpretations. For example, while Hubert Humphrey claims that prisoners are not being ill-treated, we see a Vietnamese beaten and kicked, and scenes of the self-immolation of Buddhist monks are juxtaposed with Madam Nu suggesting that it is a media event, not to be taken too seriously. The apologists for the war are betrayed by their own excess—General Patton's glee that his men are a "damn good bunch of killers," for example, or Curtis LeMay and General Mark Clark talking about the soldiers as "precious commodities." Other accounts are discredited by contradictory juxtapositions. *Why Vietnam?* presented the Gulf of Tonkin incident by means of a unified narrative consisting of footage of Johnson's speech, footage of American planes strafing and bombing, and a

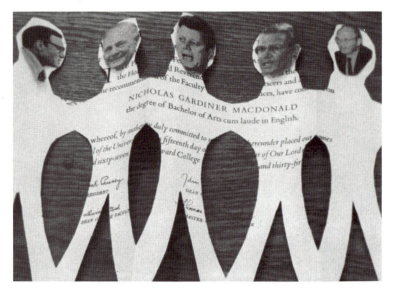

5.44–5.45 Nick Macdonald, *The Liberal War*

press conference in which, according to the omniscient voice-over that synthesized all these, "Secretary McNamara sets the record straight" by reiterating North Vietnamese provocation. In *In the Year of the Pig*, however, McNamara's flat assertion that the U.S. ships were reacting defensively to attacks on them is ruptured by testimony from a sailor from the Maddox who denies that these attacks ever took place. Setting one discourse against another, de Antonio calls into question all institutional versions of the war, especially discrediting the naive use of putative attacks on American soldiers to justify the administration's offensive. Consequently, the television network battle footage he eventually incorporates as his account moves into the present can no longer unequivocally manifest the war's propriety. His reconstruction of the history of Vietnamese liberation struggles and the competing ideological interests

5.46–5.47 Nick Macdonald, *The Liberal War*

within them reveals the sacrifice of the GIs as a consequence of political maneuvering rather than of the innate perfidy of the NLF.

Nick Macdonald's homemade film *The Liberal War* (1972) aban-
dons all pretense at realism and objectivity and, supplanting iconicity with symbolism, shifts presence away from the image to the
voice of a narrator, who claims only that his account of the invasion
of Vietnam and the genocide committed upon its peoples is "my
own view, the way I see it." That narrational exposition is an account of the origin of the war during the Kennedy administration,
in which it appears not as a mistake blundered into, but as the direct
result and indeed logical implication of liberal policies. In illustration of the successive stages of the U.S. invasion, Macdonald supplies not scenes of soldiers or refugees, but models made out of toy
soldiers and weapons, newspapers, and household bric-a-brac.

Events and conditions are illustrated diagrammatically, often by literalizing the para-metaphoric language of the war's discourses: Diem's puppet regime is represented by a hand puppet with his face stuck on it; the difficulty of extricating American troops, by toy soldiers trapped in a narrow-necked bottle; the imprisonment of peasants in the concentration camp–like strategic hamlets, by plastic figures entombed in bricks; Kennedy's repression of the press, by cutting up the *New York Times*; the domino theory, by actual dominoes; and American financial interests, by coins on the map of Vietnam. When photographic images of the war do occur, it is their material nature as cultural signifiers that is stressed rather than the plangency of the represented scene; in illustration of napalm, it is a photograph rather than actual peasants that we see burning.

In its use of footage commonly available, *The Liberal War* exposes the social implications of de Antonio's archival footage and interviews almost as much as it does those of the "bang bang" aesthetic of the networks. It thus makes possible a critique of almost all use of front-line imagery as the trace of collusion with the institutional powers that control access to Vietnam. This is not pursued or made explicit by the film, but the domestic political implications of its own artisanal minimization of the cinematic apparatus are suggested by the film's fictional setting. While clues suggest that the narrative voice is Macdonald's own, his account is displaced hundreds of years into the future, so that it appears as a historical reconstruction made in an anarchist community that has transcended Kennedy's liberalism and authoritarian centralism in general. Imaged, in shots that open and close the film, as a natural paradise cleansed of technology, this utopian future is clearly a projection of sixties ruralism and carries with it all the contradictions of such idealisms. But although the intense rationality and social systematization of the Confucian bases of rural Vietnamese society would have no place in this Walden of the future, it is also in some sense Vietnam; the hostility to the city and to the instrumentalizing of social relations, the emphasis on self-discipline and decentralization, with a *bricoleur*'s resourcefulness that can fabricate the model of the massive financial and technical complexity of the war from the odds and ends lying around the house, recapitulate the resourcefulness of the Vietnamese themselves—their ability to take apart American bombs and tanks and make such technological spillage over for their own purposes.

In Macdonald's refusal to represent the war iconically and his abstinence from imagery drenched in the presence of the military experience, a critique of the war becomes a critique of the media's use of it. The technical simplicity of his film, its articulation of its partisanship and subjectivity, its insistence on the discursiveness of historical interpretation, and its inevitable foregrounding of its own enunciation all reject the liberal languages of the war, as well as the liberal war itself. Though *The Liberal War* is not as explicit about the war's utility for the media as is *In the Year of the Pig*, in which, for example, the clear visibility of ABC microphones in interviews

5.48 Émile de Antonio, *In the Year of the Pig*

with soldiers lays bare the superimposition of station advertising upon ostensibly objective documentation, Macdonald's rejection of the technological resources and the language of the media industry allows him to project a *cinematic* alternative, displaced equally from hegemonic processes of cultural signification and from hegemonic cultural production.

Though implicit in both films' difference from the media practices that surround them, attention to their own mode of production or social location is not overt in either's critique of the communications industries. Confident and unselfconscious in their own formal mode, neither questions or even alludes to its own cinematic situation, though both were components in an alternative cinema and were used against the war. *In the Year of the Pig*, for instance, was "used as a tool by the Moratorium; it was a benefit for the Chicago Seven at the opening of their trial; the Australian anti-war movement used it as its primary film weapon" (de Antonio, n.d.: 37). Nevertheless, the films do not themselves articulate the issues of the alternative cinema. The remainder of this chapter is concerned with production that does manifest consciousness of itself as cinema and that confronts either intradiegetically or as practices of cinema not only institutional filmic codes, but also the hegemonic modes of cinematic production, consumption, and distribution. A summary of the issues of radical documentary film and a definition of the conditions under which a radical cinema could be established may be found in one of the most precise statements of the limits of the modern cinema, Jean-Luc Godard's section in Chris Marker's compilation film, *Far From Vietnam* (1967).

Far From Vietnam is compiled from several different kinds of representation of the war: Joris Ivens's footage of North Vietnam, a history of the war from the resistance to the French through the U.S. subversion of the Geneva agreements; a modified television address by General Westmoreland; interviews with the family of Norman

5.49 *Far From Vietnam*: Jean-Luc Godard

Morrison, a Quaker who immolated himself on the steps of the Capitol; collages of television and magazine journalism; and documentation of protest activities in both Europe and the United States. This displacement of the war into its repercussions throughout the world is reciprocated in the displacement of the illusionist documentary mode into varying degrees of abstraction, discursivity, and reflexiveness. The questions of where the war is and of what an appropriate cinematic response to it is do come together, however, in Godard's section, which is a pivotal and seminal moment in modern film because it articulates a termination for modern cinema.

Introduced as "Camera Eye," the segment details a situation that is, in fact, exactly antithetical to Vertov's, for where Vertov's reflexivity flowers from his confidence in the role of the filmmaker in socialist society, Godard is paralyzed by the realization that in his society the impossibility of making a film about the Vietnam War means that film in general may be no longer possible. The newsreel footage, which Godard reproduces even as he admits that it is all he would have come up with had he been a cameraman for ABC in New York or for Soviet television, is only indirectly available to him, since the North Vietnamese correctly recognized that his ideology was "a bit vague" and refused him an entry visa. Obliged to remain in Paris, he realizes that the best thing we can do for Vietnam is to let Vietnam invade us and find out what part it plays in our everyday lives. The practical implementation of such a scrutiny would be for Godard to make films for and about the French working class—from whom he is as estranged as he is from the Vietnamese. The only film he can make—this one—comprises shots of the Mitchell studio camera, interspersed with fragments of newsreel footage and of his previous attempts to deal with Vietnam (the scenes from *La Chinoise* in which Juliet Berto as a Vietnamese peasant is attacked by U.S. planes). But the industrial camera is itself the site of contradictions, and scrutiny of it summarizes the contradictions faced by the film as a whole. A beautiful object, almost erotic in its responsiveness to his manipulations, the Mitchell is typical of the American technology with which the war is fought. But its instrumentality in the war goes beyond the analogy between the precision of its gears, the accuracy of its movements, and those of the war machine; as the means of production of American and French commercial film, it is the means by which U.S. cultural imperialism has stifled Third World cinema.

A function of his previous career in the industry and of his inability at that time to imagine a feasible alternative to it, Godard's impasse did make clear the need for an alternative cinema by which mass media collusion in imperialism could be contested, even though Godard was not himself capable of inaugurating it. The same imperatives define radical American film, which in its best instances produced a revolutionary, anti-industrial cinema that decolonized production and distribution, both participating in and enacting collective political action.

Revolutionary Cinema:
From Representation to Practice

His mission is not to report but to struggle; not to play the spectator but to intervene actively.
— Walter Benjamin

Independent film's initial role in the Movement was, like that of the underground press, essentially reportorial. Radical filmmakers attempted to provide alternatives to what were felt to be politically motivated distortions in the hegemonic media (especially as brought to a head by the mendacious accounts of the 1967 March on the Pentagon) and to the late sixties cinéma vérité, which failed to engage the most pressing social issues of the time (and, in fact, most of the latter's practitioners, like Drew Associates at Time-Life, were themselves lodged in the bosom of the mass media). Whereas the underground had picked up from the surrealist and cubist avant-gardes of the twenties, political filmmaking looked back to the Soviet revolutionary cinema, and, indeed, its films were often naively constructivist in form. But its function was never merely to provide an alternative to the biased political reporting of television news. Even the most dispassionate portrayal of radical politics—and dispassion of any kind was rare—also involved self-legitimization, communications between groups, production, and crystallization of group identity and other functions beyond simply that of documentation. An early work in this tradition, like Norman Fruchter and Robert Machover's *Troublemakers* (1966), though it in fact details the failure of civil rights workers to organize a Newark ghetto, could still be used to build and boost alternative social groupings. Protest film was a form of political praxis, itself an act of contestation rather than merely the documentation of contestation taking

30 The following account of New York Newsreel and Third World Newsreel derives from Choy (n.d.), from Nichols (1972 especially, 1973, 1980), and from Newsreel (1968). For other radical filmmaking cooperatives, see the accounts of Cine Manifest in Corr and Gessner (1974), and of the Kartemquin Collective in "Filming for the City" (1975). New York Newsreel's progression through different phases toward a centralized, democratic organization and thence into crisis in the early seventies was approximately paralleled and, in fact, somewhat preceded by the internal development of the other major film-producing Newsreel, that of San Francisco. San Francisco Newsreel did, however, have a stronger relationship with organized labor and with the Black movement, specifically with the Black Panther Party, and through that an earlier and more substantial involvement with Marxism-Leninism. San Francisco was also the scene of a unique attempt to make the film-producing collective economically independent over and above income from film rentals: it instituted a work-furlough program in which, on a rotating basis, some members of the collective held income-producing jobs to support the film work of the others. The significance of these jobs has been well summarized by Nichols: "They provided income of which all but a living stipend was administered by Newsreel collectively; they formally eliminated the discrepancy between members who had to work and those who did not; and they provided important exposure to the working-class milieu in which Newsreel sought to make most of its films" (Nichols, 1973: 10).

31 For example, Peter Gessner with *Time of the Locust* (1966) and *FALN*, made in North Vietnam and Venezuela, respectively; Norman Fruchter and Robert Machover with *Troublemakers* (1966); Robert Kramer with *The Edge* (1967); and Alan Jacobs with *Alabama March* (1965).

place in other practices: in Godard's phrase, "pas spectacle, lutte!" (MacBean, 1975: 78). Even this participatory and interventionist function was not the limit of radical developments. As the socially systemic inequities of class, race, and gender were discovered and confronted within the filmmaking collectives, so filmmaking became the site of political transformations, a micro-society in which the utopian aspirations of the Movement's address to the society at large were internally and locally enacted.

The furthest radicalization of underground cinema comprised, then, a double project: to overthrow both the existing social relations within the filmmaking group and those that inserted the subculture into the dominant society. The terms in which the two areas were theorized were substantially interchangeable, with reform of the power relations within the group projected as a model for new relations between the group and society at large. Left filmmaking in the last years of the decade thus shows an increasing democratization away from a strong central authority, a Leninist vanguard, toward a Maoist distribution of power prefiguring a more thorough integration of the group in the constituency it hoped to serve. The restructuring of both social relations within film production and the relations of the film practice to society was not accomplished without intense self-consciousness and self-criticism, for the path from simply making political films to making political films *politically* had not been recently trodden. The development of the various branches of Newsreel throughout the country—in Boston, San Francisco, Los Angeles, and Chicago, as well as New York—was not entirely even; each had its own history, produced by the interaction between the filmmakers' own idiosyncrasies and the political conditions of the areas in which they worked. Still, the substantial personal interconnections, as well as the overall correspondences produced by the national nature of the terms of dissent and the use of political films as communication between different cells, meant that the same crucial issues recurred in all the collectives. New York Newsreel, the first to be founded, in general represents a sequence common to the histories of all the Newsreels: formation of alternative production and distribution systems, reorganization so as to incorporate and empower women and minorities, integration into working-class communities, and eventually an almost catastrophic crisis.[30]

Begun simply as the cooperative coordination of independent filmmakers, many of whom had already been separately documenting radical activity,[31] what was to become New York Newsreel first met on 22 December 1967, the same day that the last of the theatrical newsreels, the Universal Newsreel Service, closed. From the beginning, contestation of the hegemonic media's information was seen to entail an alternative cinema; in introducing its intention of providing "an alternative to the limited and biased coverage of television news" for events which, indicating radical changes taking place in American society, had been "consistently undermined and suppressed by the media" (cited in Mekas, 1972: 305), Newsreel's

initial statement projected the organization as a center of both production and distribution.[32] Several types of news film—"short
newsreels . . . longer, more analytic documentaries; informational
and tactical films"—were envisaged, and plans were made for non-
theatrical projection, for the encouragement of a network of other
newsreel centers throughout the country, for the distribution of foreign films, and for free distribution to community groups who could
not afford rentals.

Production was initially open, all members being free to make a
film without the group's prior approval; but the earliest newsreels
reflected the group's dominant social makeup and especially the
concerns of the original nucleus of White, male, middle-class members who, by virtue of their prior experience or their access to equipment and funds, had de facto power in the nominally open and democratic organization. Of the first thirteen films released, all but two
were concerned with the war and especially with resistance to the
draft; they documented, for example, speeches by notable resistance
spokespeople, interviews with deserters, demonstrations, and plans
for the actions at the Democratic convention. Like the activities they
depicted, these first films were by and large agitational. Containing
a minimum of analysis, the unsophisticated voice-overs were subordinate to the emotional impact designed to promote confrontation with state power. Early explanations of their purpose tended to
theorize them as analogous to acts of war. For example, Robert Kramer, one of the founders and most prominent members, explained
the raw production values in terms that point to the participation
of the filmmaker in physical confrontation as the condition of a
valid depiction of it: "Our films remind some people of battle footage: grainy, camera weaving around trying to get the material and
still not get beaten/trapped" (Newsreel, 1968: 47–48). Since these
films were not designed for a general audience, they depended less
on persuasion or explanation than on such visceral strategies or
moralistic appeals as would excite an already committed constituency to action: "You want to make films that unnerve, that shake
assumptions, that threaten, that do not soft-sell, but hopefully (an
impossible ideal) explode like grenades in people's faces, or open
minds up like a good can opener" (ibid.). The identifying Newsreel
logo introduced at this time, which flickers to the staccato chatter
of a machine gun, epitomizes these reciprocal notions of the film as
a weapon in the hands of a filmmaker engaged in physical combat;
the documentary, analytic function is conditioned by a participatory, performative one.

During 1969 this anarchic production of agitational film was increasingly questioned. Though at first no single, correct, analytic
credo or ideology was insisted upon, Newsreel revived the Film and
Photo League's practice of sending speakers with the films to lead
post-screening discussions. "How the films are presented is as important to us as the films themselves," the 1969 catalogue claimed.
"We hope you will invite NEWSREEL members to your screenings to
help present the films and to participate in audience discussions. We

32 Like the Film and Photo League
which had distributed Soviet films in
the thirties, Newsreel also distributed films from the Third World, especially from Cuba and Vietnam,
and indeed recognized this function
as being as important as its own
contestation of the representations
of these countries by the establishment media. Alternative distribution
was in general a major element in
the formation of alternative cinema
and of several other organizations
distributing radical film. America
Documentary Films, founded 1966,
distributing Third World films, and
New Day Films, founded 1971, distributing feminist films, are only two
of the best known. See Hess (1981).

want people to work with our films as catalysts for political discussions about social change in America. . . . Without these kind of discussions, our films would be incomplete" (*Newsreel Catalogue*, 1969). This use of film as a tool for consciousness raising and organizing, "a detonator or a pretext" (Solanas and Gettino, 1976: 62) subordinate to the debate it could be made to generate, produced a concomitant emphasis on theoretical investigation of a more general and less pragmatic order. With the leadership still strongly linked to university activism and still under the influence of "new-working-class" theorists, analysis in class terms or, indeed, according to any single system of categorization was not yet judged relevant (Kramer, 1969: 28). As the stress on discussion, theoretical inquiry, and organization gradually supplanted the anti-analytic interventionist urgency of Kramer's theory and of films like *No Game* (1967), which was about the Pentagon demonstration, it provided a vocabulary and a context in which the diagnosis of the macro-political situation could be applied to the micro-society of the film-making group. After 1968, and especially after SDS and the Movement as a whole fractured into increasingly violent projects like the Weathermen's attempt to precipitate domestic revolution by re-creating Vietnam in the United States, the principles that inspired such groups demanded that the terms of the revolution be lived within them.

The consequent stress on self-criticism within radical cells as a means of transforming liberal college students into socially integrated, disciplined vanguard cadres was echoed in Newsreel's own reorganization. Initially, its ultra-democracy was replaced by a more formal structure in which democratic procedures could be brought into play to secure a means of communal control. In late 1969–early 1970, this "barometric" reflection "of the thoughts and acts of a large portion of the Movement" (Nichols, 1972: 51) produced sessions of intense self-criticism. The inequalities in the roles of women and Third World members provided the conceptual leverage that dislodged the White male nucleus, allowing more radical reconsiderations that subsequently split the organization by polarizing an anti–"correct-line" faction against the advocates of stronger discipline. Recognition that there were almost no non-White members, no working-class members, and few skilled women members discredited the confrontational moralism of the earlier stance and stimulated internal reorganization. A central "operations committee" and three "work groups," responsible for Third World, high-school, and working-class films, were formed; each had a more strongly democratic internal organization than Newsreel as a whole did before 1969, and production skills were to be taught to all members. Resistant to this intense self-analysis or undermined by it, the majority of the members of the original nucleus left, and those who remained formed a collective in which the greater power of women and Third World members allowed a much closer relation with the working class. The films produced in this period, such as *The Wreck of the New York Subway* (about the fare increase in 1970) and *Lincoln Hospital* (about the attempt of staff members to run the hospital themselves), are concerned not with resistance to the Vietnam War and not with issues that were of direct national interest, but with local and domestic questions; they replaced the earlier confrontational mode and newsreel format with an analytic and organizational function. And while they were frequently neither as politically nor as artistically sophisticated as they aspired to be, nevertheless they did achieve the closer integration of the production group with the constituency it hoped to serve.

The deployment of film as a constituent of domestic struggles that were at most parallel to the war resistance rather than immediately functional within it, and the more considerable shift away from the contestation of the mass media's coverage of the macro-political arena, echoed developments in the New Left as a whole. In fact, like SDS, which split over disagreement as to which faction of the proletariat was most proper for students to align themselves with, Newsreel was traumatized by the attempt to integrate itself in revolutionary classes. The recruitment of more Third World members and their participation in film production exacerbated tensions, especially with White males, and also produced resentment among the Third World members themselves. After an unsuccessful attempt to increase Third World presence in the central operations committee, it was disbanded, and amid bitter divisions on grounds of race, gender, and class, in February 1972 New York Newsreel entered a third stage by splitting into virtually autonomous White and Third World factions.

Many of the disagreements had come to a head after a decision to make a film about the Attica prison rebellion of September 1971. Since mostly Third World prisoners had been involved, a crew was formed consisting of three White and three non-White members; further discontent reduced this crew to only two people, Christine Choy and another Third World woman, neither of whom had production skills. They nevertheless persevered, completing the film *Teach Our Children* in 1973. In the meantime, continuing crises caused the White caucus to disband, and so in April 1972 New York Newsreel became Third World Newsreel, with a membership of three. The trauma of this attrition of all experienced personnel was compounded by the theft of most of its equipment, eviction from its office premises, and mounting debt. But after a year of retrenchment, Third World Newsreel increased its membership to eight, rebuilt its production facilities, and enlarged its distribution operations to 2,000 bookings and an audience of 20,000 (Nichols, 1980: 32); and after 1974 it made films that were concerned entirely with minorities and the working class. Its commitment to the economically, socially, and cinematically disenfranchised—and throughout the seventies Newsreel was the only such collective—is nowhere more vividly marked than in the three films after *Teach Our Children* that were about prisoners and prison conditions: *In the Event Anyone Disappears* (1974), *We Demand Freedom* (1974), and *Inside Women Inside* (1978).

DON'T BE SHOCKED WHEN I
SAY I WAS IN PRISON.
YOU'RE STILL IN PRISON.
THAT'S WHAT AMERICA MEANS,
PRISON.

MALCOLM X

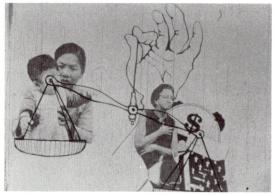

5.50–5.56 Third World Newsreel,
Teach Our Children

Teach Our Children, the Attica film, does present first-person accounts and still and motion news photography of the rebellion and the ferocity with which it was punished, but overall it is as much concerned with the condition of the poor in general as with the disproportionately large sector of it that is physically incarcerated. Indeed, rather than distinguishing prisoners against the community, it follows Malcolm X in proposing the continuity of the condition of the poor inside and outside the prisons; the Attica rebels are argued as surrogates for the community at large, their uprising an exemplarily heroic emulation of the resistance of the Third World.

Visuals thus rhyme Attica—its architecture and its prisoners—with the urban decay of the ghetto and demonstrate the similarities between the brutality of the state in each sphere. The film gives voice equally to ghetto inhabitants and to the men who took part in the rebellion, including television footage of interviews with prisoners during the uprising. These segments are supplemented with didactic interludes which introduce a larger historical context for the personal experiences that are recounted. Again, the continuity of oppression is emphasized, while a more extensive political analysis of the international operations of capitalism is provided. Montage sequences juxtapose engravings of slave ships with shots of housing projects and the prison walls, and animated sections show photographs of Nelson Rockefeller and President Nixon manipulating South America and Asia, laying bare the international forms taken by U.S. imperialism. Though the simple equation of slaves, prisoners, and the proletariat elides important differences in the structural relation of each to the economic system (Nichols, 1980: 74), demonstration of the parallels between the prisoners and the Third World, with domestic minorities located between them so as to summarize and polarize their historical options, is both a striking rhetorical maneuver and a precondition of a correct formulation of the political situation of each group. And by making clear the connections between Rockefeller and the corporate interests involved in Third World imperialism and between Rockefeller and the Attica uprising, the film fixes him as a symbolic nexus, the point where the domestic struggle reciprocates the international one.

The collage that argues these connections also has cinematic implications, for the appropriation of news photos and television footage from inside Attica uses—but also reverses—the intended significance of the images. In the establishment media they are designed to instill fear in the populace and to foment hostility against the part of the proletariat held in the jails by that part which is nominally free, thereby preventing recognition of their common interests. The film's access to these images depends on the assistance of sympathizers within the media who supply the footage, for the cost of exclusion from the state apparatus is that you can film the outside of prisons but not the inside; you can take pictures of the poor, but not of the agencies of oppression. In the context of images of the ghetto streets and of images of what the poor can film—themselves—these images do new ideological work, just as the new social order they look to (and the film's optimism is such that its final collage mixes shots of victorious Vietnamese with shots of the prisoners exercising, building their strength) entails the reorganization of all capitalist mediums and the inauguration of a new order of cinema.

Teach Our Children and Third World Newsreel's subsequent prison films form the conclusion to several histories of cinema. To the history of New York Newsreel, of left filmmaking in the sixties, and of the more general movement to liberate the cinema, they mark a limit in respect to both filmmaker and subject; both are members of previously disenfranchised groups, and the minority female filmmakers of Third World Newsreel and the Third World prisoners they made films for and about were alike in previously being most completely the victims of cinematic imperialism, most completely anathema, even for the emerging feminist cinema. Third World Newsreel's democratization of the production process, the full distribution of skills within it, the minimization of the structural distinctions between producers and consumers so as to subvert the social relations produced by the commodity film, and the use of cinema for grass-roots organizing instance a Maoist cinema, diametrically contrary to the industrial cinema on all levels. The completeness and integrity of their alterity, and the reciprocation of their ideological program in their mode of social being, allow these films a triumphant discursive directness and confidence, the fruits of their surviving the theoretical and logistical upheavals summarized in the transformation of New York into Third World Newsreel.

This achieved simplicity is all the more interesting because it contrasts markedly with the extreme self-consciousness of a good number of earlier Newsreel films, especially those produced by and around the student resistance. In these films, the ambivalent relation of political activity to the media and the similarly ambivalent situation of alternative media production in respect to the hegemonic industries together produce a recurrent intratextual reflexivity, a politicized equivalent of and heir to the underground's own filmic self-consciousness.

Radical Reflexivity

The formal self-consciousness of radical media work reflected the same social anxiety that inflamed the debates within and about the Movement itself. It took the form of a self-interrogation about the appropriation and distortion of political activity by the mass media, and about the forms by which alternative media production could non-collusively intervene.[33] A dramatized account of these tensions in a group doing political organizing and media work is provided in Robert Kramer's *Ice* (1969). This political thriller, a fictional, independent, narrative feature, is sufficiently orthodox to be generally

33 An important complement to these meta-cinematic investigations is The Pacific Street Film Collective's *Red Squad* (1972), which documents the harassment of a group of radical filmmakers by the New York Police Department's Bureau of Special Services. Using such tricks as setting up an unloaded camera in front of the FBI headquarters and, with another hidden camera, filming the FBI agents who harass the first cameraman, the film makes clear the relations of political power which underlie and inform filmic and cinematic relations, specifically the reenactment of political contestation on the level of control of representation.

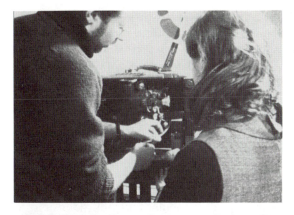

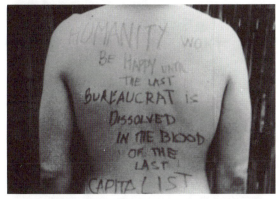

5.57–5.61 Robert Kramer, *Ice*

accessible, though it depicts film practices that in form and social use depart radically from the industrial norm.

Ostensibly set in a fascist future in which Latin America has succeeded Vietnam as the front line of resistance to U.S. imperialism, *Ice* is essentially a dramatization of the political issues of its own day and of the relation of alternative media work to those issues. The debates it depicts are those that divided the Movement at the end of the sixties: the relationship of White radicals to Blacks and to army deserters, the possibility of alliances with progressive portions of the bourgeoisie, the relation between local and national acts of resistance, and the need to replace fruitless terrorism by the coordination of all radical groups. But however political contestation is organized, it is not separable from media contestation; like Newsreel, of which Kramer was still a member,[34] the radical cell that the film depicts is a filmmaking collective as well as a political action group, and indeed its political action consists substantially of alternative media work.

The group's major political undertaking is a regional uprising, conducted as part of an attempt to build a mass movement. This does entail freeing political prisoners as well as assassination, kidnapping, and other terroristic strikes against the state. But its primary function is an attempt to communicate with the people, to publicize the weakness of the security police and the strength of the resistance. The uprising is unsuccessful, the reprisals are severe, and fear exacerbates the tensions among the survivors, though *Ice* ends with them working on a new film, trying to regroup. In the movie, the state's success in containing the offensive corresponds to the social failures of contemporary America. Kramer's refusal to escalate his allegory into fantasy by depicting a successful revolt recognizes that a mass revolutionary movement of systemic rather than issue-oriented contestation had failed to appear. But both the absence of such a movement and Kramer's inability to imagine one as a successful conclusion to the radicals' efforts call into question the appropriateness of their methods, especially of their use of media, and they do so in a way that reveals fractures in the premises of *Ice* itself.

As a dramatization of a Newsreel-like cadre, *Ice* portrays several kinds of radical film practice, all different from its own. The filmmakers themselves constantly discuss the nature of revolutionary cinema, but since *Ice* was made before the Newsreel debates of 1969–70, the questions of the distribution of power and skills and the need for ideological correctness that brought about the restructuring of New York Newsreel and Kramer's own departure from the group are glimpsed only in embryo—in the personal and psycho-sexual tensions among members of the cadre, in the absence of people of color from it, and in an unforegrounded scene in which a woman is shown being instructed in the use of a projector. The group discussions focus instead on more pragmatic issues such as formal strategies in agitational films of the kind Kramer had privileged—for example, whether a guide to the manufacture of gasoline bombs needs a diagram, or whether the sound track should contain further instructions. At the end the filmmakers are shown engaged in an experimental project in which they are trying "to get away from the reportorial thing" by using models and toys—a rocket pointed at the Third World, a robot with "Ruling Class" stenciled on its front and "Empire" on its back—much like Macdonald did in *The Liberal War*.

For the militants these issues are not merely theoretical, for agitational film is integral to their day-to-day activity and to the re-

34 Kramer shot *Ice* "with the active support and participation of other Newsreel members" (Nichols, 1972: 110), and it was listed in 1969 in Newsreel's fourth catalogue. The decision against distribution only occurred after Newsreel's reorganization; subsequently, Film-makers' Cooperative distributed it and Kramer's other features.

5.62 Robert Kramer, *Ice*: Showing guerrilla films

gional uprising. The latter's key project is the temporary takeover of a large apartment building and the education of its inhabitants. In the meetings that the radicals oblige the building's occupants to attend, they address themselves explicitly to the mass media distortions that Newsreel was specifically formed to contest; they illustrate their explanation of the political situation with films that document the resistance's success. One film, supplied by the South Texas Liberation Collective, reveals that what the government and the mass media have reported as an industrial accident was, in fact, the Collective's destruction of a U.S. military facility in which its members were aided by factory workers and Third World people. These film showings, which precisely exploit the "capacity of [formal] synthesis and [social] penetration of the film image" that Solanas and Gettino specify as fundamental to the guerrilla use of the medium (Solanas and Gettino, 1976: 53), are part of an ongoing practice. In the fashion of the fragments of the autonomous hippie cinema, the meetings and the entire uprising are themselves filmed for use in future propaganda events of the same kind.

These and several other intradiegetically presented instances of agitational media depart more radically from the conventions of the commercial feature and its mode of consumption than does *Ice* itself; nevertheless, the film's dominant mode is more self-conscious than the attempts like Costa-Gavras's *"Z"* of the previous year to introduce politics into *retardataire* illusionist narratives. Its chief tropes are the use of long takes even in dialogue scenes and a dependence on natural light that produces harsh chiaroscuro and overall graininess, both deriving from cinéma vérité via Newsreel's agitational period. The film includes direct address intertitles and voice-overs attacking examples of liberal ideology and false consciousness, as well as occasional tricks like splicing in negative footage immediately after a placard has announced that "We must negate the future." These all resemble Godard's fracturing of the diegesis, as indeed the desolated modern metropolis used as a metaphor for a totalitarian dystopia suggests *Alphaville*. *Ice* replaces focus on the linear evolution of a small group of clearly defined individuals with an episodic development that jumps from one character and phase to the next, and it maintains all the characters at a visual and psychological distance. But these deviations from industrial narrative grammar and the suture function are not sufficiently disturbing to preempt the pleasure of a general audience; *Ice* remained relatively accessible, not raising the distribution problems of the films of the *Groupe Dziga Vertov*. In fact, the disparity between its own only mildly unorthodox form and that of the more extreme media practices it portrays can be read as a critique of the directions in which Godard was moving in 1969, as well as a retrospective assessment of the domestic newsreels that Kramer had hoped would "explode like grenades in people's faces, or open minds up like a good can opener."

For whatever homage there is to Godard and whatever violence *Ice* retains to polarize its audience, Kramer's turn to a form that can mediate between the conventions of the commercial feature and the conflicting imperatives of the various radical challenges to them does represent an abjuration of film "terrorism" in favor of populist education. Its attempt to pry the general public loose from the media industry is analogous to the move to a democratic center that the narrative of *Ice* contemplates with such meager expectations. And so while the fictional entertainment film, *Ice*, itself offers a clearly different solution to the problems of political media work than the agitational, didactic practices it portrays, still the similarity between Kramer's hope for a popular audience and his radicals' hope for a popular insurrection provides the basis for a critique of the film's own viability. It is finally pessimistic about the possibility of contributing to a revolutionary movement any more successfully than Newsreel had. Even as *Ice* criticizes a cultural terrorism that itself it leaves behind, it cannot imagine for itself a more fruitful function than the one it supersedes. Its real, and in fact its only tenable, point of reference lies not in its expectation for its own intervention in the marginal theater, but in the extreme social politicization instanced by the fragments of the Vietnamese film and the Black Panther film with which it ends, and which signify the nostalgia for the increasingly remote dream of a coalition between White radicals and the Third World—the inauguration of White radicals as Third World and of their cinema as a third cinema.

Closely prefiguring Kramer's own departure from Newsreel and Newsreel's own move toward the more properly, albeit domestic, Third World concerns of the prison films of the early seventies, *Ice* dramatizes the situation under which it was produced and to this extent has much in common with the reflexive art films examined below. Its fictional nature displaces it from the documentary genre—and, indeed, the degree of reflexivity that appears in a film ostensibly about revolutionary practice is a measure of the anxiety involved in such a transition. But the consciousness of itself as film and of the relation between alternative film and the mass media it shows is not at all unusual within the newsreel tradition, in which may be found several kinds of inscriptions of the situation of cultural production in political activity. While in general cinéma vérité rationales are totally foreign to the partisan pragmatism of Newsreel's approach to its projects, some of the films are fairly circumscribed by the particular social problems they address, and in these the limit of cinematic self-consciousness is the eye contact between the camera and interviewee. But especially when they are concerned with issues of high public visibility and so are competing with other media treatments, even as their own cameras compete with and also document the range of other media apparatuses that public interest calls out, then the newsreels themselves become media events and frequently address their own situation in respect to other forms of media. In lieu of a full taxonomy of all the regions of cinema foregrounded in such self-consciousness, which would engage and extend into history the taxonomies of reflexivity undertaken in respect to structural film (see Chapter six, note 10), here the scope of such a taxonomy will rather be suggested by reference to several films which occupy strategic positions within it: Newsreel's *Columbia Revolt* (1968) and *Summer of 68* (1969) and Jon Jost's *Speaking Directly* (1974).

In those films that document events whose function is the engagement of media attention in order to publicize certain demands, political action consists of the competition for and the manipulation of information. Film documentation of the event thus becomes the extension and the realization of it; it does not become ontologically different from it. Traces of this continuity between filmic and profilmic are often present in the exposition itself, which, as it bares the codes of its own didacticism, clarifies the relations between its own guerrilla function within the total field of media production and the process of building alternatives to the political hegemony the mass media commandeers. A typical example is Newsreel's film about the student uprising at Columbia University.

The first sustained campus disruption since the 1964–65 Free Speech Movement at Berkeley, the building occupation and student strike at Columbia also marked the first major implementation of the "new-working-class" theories that had emerged in the previous two years. This new militance proposed the campus as the location of political activity and urged the use of issues such as the condition of the students or the university's contribution to the war to provoke wholesale confrontations that would radicalize students; it then similarly urged the use of campus issues to radicalize society at large. Thus, though legitimate grievances did exist at Columbia—both local issues like the university's involvement in ghetto real estate (which, in fact, sparked the events) and the national question of its participation in the Institute for Defense Analysis—the radical elements in SDS were able to exploit the administration's intransigence in relatively minor matters to politicize the student body to the point where eventually over one thousand students took part in occupations. The brutality of the New York police in expelling these students outraged liberals and generated support for a strike which closed the university for the remainder of the academic year and became a model for campus activities elsewhere.

Columbia Revolt is a vivid and vigorous documentation of the strike, with both still and motion photography of important phases within it, including extended footage taken inside the buildings during occupation. Its popularity—and along with *Black Panther* it was "the best known, the best liked early Newsreel" (Nichols, 1972: 76)—came not from the reportorial accuracy with which it contested mass media misrepresentation, but from its unqualified hortatory exposition. The film's documentary intent is contained within its propagandizing function, and so rather than simply representing the students and their action, it completes the discourse and strategy of the most militant students and continues their politicizing and polarizing outreach program. Like other subcultural self-representations, it is designed to extend its own constituency, especially by challenging competing vocabularies of group identity. Its dominant self-consciousness is then rhetorical; it foregrounds its own strategies of generating solidarity with its student audiences and of reproducing within them the analysis and activism of Columbia. Though when it was made New York Newsreel was still nonsectarian, the film is unequivocal in celebrating the rebellion. The editing and commentary argue that the administration and the students are of different classes, while the collage of students' voices on the sound track that describes the events emphasizes the sequence of crises through which the correctness of the students' pres-

5.63 Newsreel, *Columbia Revolt*

5.64–5.65 Newsreel, *Columbia Revolt*

ent position was earned. All other reference to confusion, mistakes, and intra-student dissidence is suppressed, except the opposition of the jocks, which is immediately re-contained in the larger admin-istration-student polarization. The case against the university ("hooked into servicing the corporations and hooked into servicing the war machine") and the rationale for the strike are explicitly ar-gued, and the film emphasizes those events in which the students are able to secure for themselves a space within and against corporate iniquity. By participating in the occupation of the buildings, they overcome their alienation; the authenticity they achieve in the col-lective praxis of resistance, appropriately characterized by one of the many euphoric comments on the sound track as "an electric awakening," is justly figured in the wedding of two of the students, surrounded by their new "family" inside the occupied and besieged buildings.

What self-consciousness there is in *Columbia Revolt* is largely a matter of the propagandistic single-mindedness that proceeds from its moment in the history of New Left theory, when it was widely recognized that political action as such was inseparable from the public projection of it. Apart from scattered reflexive openings like shots of press conferences and evidence of collusion between the *New York Times* and the Columbia trustees, *Columbia Revolt* does not directly address media activity. But the engagement of the news industry is explicit and dominant in *Summer of 68*, a meta-filmic meditation on the role of alternative media work in the domestic contestation of the war.

Centered on the demonstrations at the Democratic Convention in Chicago, *Summer of 68* begins, ends, and is liberally punctuated with action footage of street demonstrations and police rioting of the kind sensationalized in the popular media. The filmmakers are ambivalent about this street violence: the elation of the mass action in Chicago allowed activists to overcome privilege and feel identity with the people—to feel that they *were* the people—and this experiential transcendence of alienation, itself a premonition of a post-revolutionary social wholeness, validates the organizing done in preparation for Chicago. But the spectacle of the police riots, observed by millions of Americans and indeed the whole world, preempted attention to the real object of the protest. A narrator summarizes: "The issue of Chicago became police brutality, not the party we'd come to expose, not the war or the racism we'd come to protest. Chicago gave us a success we couldn't use and suggested the limits of any attempt to talk to the media." The ability of the press to use Chicago for its own purposes makes clear the continued need for the more mundane task of day-to-day organizing, and much of the film documents the work of activists in induction centers and GI coffeehouses near army bases. But Chicago also makes clear the need for alternative media practices to overcome the Movement's impotence in the face of the networks' exploitation. If understood as primarily a documentation of the convention, the film will seem disorganized;[35] but it is coherent when seen as an analysis of the way activist programs need to negotiate differently with different forms of media. Recognizing the Movement's vulnerability before the media industry and the naiveté of hopes that organized draft resistance will end the war, the film argues for more sophisticated attempts to organize GIs, for a more considerable opposition to the Democratic party's pursuit of the war, and especially for the production of alternative media systems that can themselves control their interventions in the mass media. Primarily, therefore, *Summer of 68* is concerned with control over the institutions that produce public information.

Immediately after the demonstrations and street fighting in Chicago with which it opens, the film cuts to an alternative film practice, a scene in which a Newsreel member is showing a Newsreel

35 Nichols, for example, argues that it lacks continuity and direction; it is "a very loose compilation of events" that "does record a major shift in New Left thinking, but without analyzing it" (Nichols, 1972: 87).

5.66–5.69 Newsreel, *Summer of 68*

film, *Boston Draft-Resistance Group*, in his own draft-resistance presentation. He introduces the film as "a portrait of reality" which the spectators may enter, a way of life alternative to the army. Continuing the theme of resistance to the war, this intradiegetically presented film comes to focus on a Cambridge organizer, Vernon Grizzard, whose activity is then taken up by the master film. Grizzard reports on a trip he made to Hanoi to receive three American prisoners released by the North Vietnamese to the peace movement. To the accompaniment of both still and motion footage, he reports on the collective self-confidence of the North Vietnamese, also noting the difficulty of photographing them "because often what I wanted to photograph was the inside of my head and I couldn't find it out there." Although Vietnam itself will not provide images satisfactory to him, still he recognizes that his trip there is itself a media event, "a propaganda act" which is both dependent on and adversary to the mass media. The Movement depends on the news media to publicize its role in the release of the prisoners; but the State Department is able to exclude Grizzard and Newsreel from the press conference, and as the media turns the event into a "Doris Day homecoming," the anti-war workers are robbed of their publicity. The activists' failure to control the way the industrial media represent and interpret them, and hence their failure to ensure that the

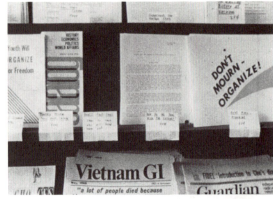

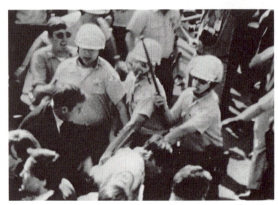

5.70–5.73 Newsreel, *Summer of 68*

correct issues are articulated, is repeated in Chicago; there, the limits of any attempt to use the mass media for the dissemination of their position are realized, and the decision is made to organize not draft resistance but GIs themselves, and to develop other media practices.

The initial narrative center for the second half of the film is a GI coffeehouse near Fort Hood in Texas, but attention quickly shifts to the alternative press, especially to the underground newspaper *Rat* and to *Vietnam Vet*, a paper produced by veterans for GIs. Subsequent scenes show Newsreel members and other independent journalists (including Jeff Shero, editor of *Rat*) successfully and on their own terms handling a press conference that publicizes the decision to go to Chicago; they refuse, for example, to discuss certain issues on the ground that while they appear logical in print, they would be inflammatory in a medium like television. Finally, the film documents an occasion when radical reporters, including a representative from Newsreel and a journalist from *The East Village Other*, disrupt and temporarily take over a Channel 13 discussion of the underground press to demonstrate "that people can act against the media and can build their own media for their own needs." This final confidence, which is followed by a return to the most exciting footage of the collective action in Chicago, also validates the film itself. Implicitly a self-justification, it testifies to Newsreel's own ongoing centrality in the peace movement and in the politics of dissent in general. In a materialist and historical rediscovery of the beat valorization of art, *Summer of 68* is finally able to reaffirm the centrality of alternative cultural practices in the struggle for a free society.

Coda: Jon Jost's *Speaking Directly*

If *Summer of 68* brings the energy and confidence of an expanding political activism to filmmaking, thereby establishing it as itself radical political practice, Jon Jost's *Speaking Directly: Some American Notes* (1974), some five years later, is a requiem for that euphoric conjunction of art and life. The draft resisters' perception of themselves *as* the people had provided the social foundation for their contestation of other media and of the state; by 1973 that confidence in alternative media activity had collapsed, along with the social vision upon which it had been based. *Speaking Directly* argues a paralyzing political impotence; responding to the dissolution of the Movement with a disillusion with filmmaking, it presents the social closure as a cinematic dead end. The reflexiveness of *Summer of 68* emerged as the film's discovery of the nature and uses of radical media work, as well as its clarification of its own possibilities and limitations and of its relation to other media systems; here, reflexiveness derives from the debilitating realization that the contradictions of political life are intrinsically the contradictions of the film medium itself.

Imprisoned for two years for refusing induction into the military, Jost worked after his release for the war resistance and assisted in the establishment of the Newsreel office in Chicago. But instead of being the inspiration for him that it was for the filmmakers who made *Summer of 68*, the convention and the subsequent confrontational militancy caused him to withdraw from political activism, and eventually, in 1972, to retreat to a small cabin in southern Oregon, where he lived with Elayne Ketchum and her child. This is the condition investigated in the film. The rural retreat, the use of the medium for self-analysis, and the synecdochical exploration of the microcosmic domestic situation as surrogate for the overall political situation are all familiar motifs in the underground; but unlike, say, Stan Brakhage's family dramas, *Speaking Directly* locates the alienation of the film's subject in contexts that are historically defined and thus explicitly political. The self-analysis is conducted through a series of binary oppositions in which what is immanent and experienced empirically is juxtaposed against what is distant and perceived only indirectly—through the agency of some other person or the media and, as such, constituted as knowledge. These binary oppositions structure the film, setting "a geography: here" (Jost's cabin in the woods) against "a geography: there" (looped footage of bombing raids over Vietnam); "people I know: directly" (photographs of or interviews with lovers, friends, and acquaintances) set against "people I know: indirectly" (photographs of Nixon and

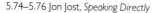

5.74–5.76 Jon Jost, *Speaking Directly*

Kissinger); Jost's sense of his own maleness against his experience of women; and finally himself as a maker of films set against "a person who watches films: you."

While neither the recognition of the discontinuities between the individual and the socially constructed events in which the individual is implicated nor the cognitive schizophrenia they produce is original, what is important is the demonstration that the contradictions of the social and political systems inevitably permeate all cinema, all film, including this one. The conceptual abyss between, for example, Jost's experience of being an American and his knowledge of what the United States is doing in Asia, and between his experience of a lover and the constitution of woman in mass media images from advertising to pornography, recur as fractures within film and as cinematic contradictions. The dynamics of a long shot in the middle of the film illustrate.

The shot begins with a view of the Oregon countryside that is radically transformed as the camera pulls back to reveal a large mirror in which, along with the initial image, we see Jost and his camera. Reading a text, Jost discusses his alienation from the social rituals of American life and from the imperial system of which Vietnam is the summary. As the camera pans through the countryside, eventually coming to rest on the almost naked body of a man scattered with fake blood, Jost suggests that however remote the

atrocities in Vietnam may seem, they were produced by us Americans, and that it behooves us to examine our own lives for traces or symptoms of them. In his self-examination he notes that his ability to make films is the sign of the privileges of his class, race, and national background—privileges that he makes further use of in his more or less exploitative treatment of his family and friends in making this film. The camera pans to reveal Ketchum operating the tape recorder that makes Jost's words available to us; it then passes back to the body and, zooming in, retrieves the original image. The reality this deep-focus long shot redeems encloses the physical one of Kracauer and the phenomenological one of Bazin in an ideological totality; by means of the spoken text and the camera movements Jost opens out the original image of rural innocence—the Western picture—to the mechanisms of its own production and the attendant social implications, and to the political reality it simultaneously signifies and defers. The context of the shot is Kent State, Jackson State, Vietnam, and at the same time the technologies of cinema—the social relations of the one duplicating those of the other.

Recurring from the cells of late sixties resistance and from their cinemas, Jost's Maoist application of political principles in domestic self-criticism discovers the power relations of the society at large repeated in all its units. The feminist analysis of the relation of the

5.81 Jon Jost, *Speaking Directly*

male to the family and of the subordination of women (which in the film is investigated more thoroughly in a series of failed attempts to provide Ketchum with her own section of the film) is as true in the process of filmmaking as it is in the world the film documents. On one level these contradictions are functions of the historically specific use of the apparatus in a late twentieth-century imperialist state, where the participation of the cinema in the ideological operations of the corporate state corroborates its own industrial function within a worldwide industrial system. From this material complicity there is no escape, even for the most dissident filmmaker. As Jost points out over a series of shots that show him surrounded by all the equipment used in making even this simple and relatively inexpensive film, his work is contingent not only upon the woman who provided the approximately two thousand dollars that it cost, or upon the other friends who lent equipment and skills, but also upon the workers in the iron mills in the United States, the gold mines in South Africa, and the camera factories in France. Any film, including this one, must be read finally as an allegory of the entire industrial system of the West that has made it possible. Imprinted on the celluloid itself by the mechanisms it passes through, and beneath the codes of the specific systems of representation and narration, there inevitably will be found the traces of the more comprehensive and determining narratives of capitalism itself, of both its civilizations and its barbarisms.

Given the absolute impossibility of any film's transcending the political implications of its context, the only logical and completely authentic path open is to repudiate film entirely. This is implied by one of Jost's acquaintances in the "People I know: Indirectly" section who, entirely logically, proposes to us in the audience that our only appropriate response to Jost's duplicity in making a film about the futility of communication and the expense of making a film is for us to lynch the filmmaker or, failing that, to burn the print or leave the theater, a suggestion he implements from the perspective of his own role by discontinuing the interview and leaving the frame. Such a course of action, a re-creation in a materialist register of the *via negativa* of the exemplary modernist silences, is, however, incoherent for the political artist whose commitment to intervention precludes simple renunciation. If contestation in the cinematic—the identification of filmmaking with the potentially revolutionary classes manifested in Third World Newsreel's orientation at exactly this time—is not possible, then consciousness of the contradictions must take the form of a critique of the filmic, specifically of representation. Here Jost's work enjoins the Godardian enterprise of filmic demystification, in which the fracture of illusionism per se implements the critique of the specific uses of illusionism in the capitalist cinema. And so, whereas the social makeup of Third World Newsreel allowed the group's consciousness of these issues to be worked through in the macro-cinematic context of the class structure of American society, for the isolated post-Romantic artist that Jost had become, consciousness of these issues had to be worked through in the film's address to the monadic and equally alienated spectator.

The final self-consciousness produced by *Speaking Directly* is the semiological one of the play of filmic signification, of the materiality of the medium, and of the nature of spectatorship. Hence the interposition of a distance between audience and screen—for example, through a long shot showing in the corner of the otherwise blank screen a stopwatch that ticks off the duration only of the spectator's attention, and through other devices such as looped sections foregrounding the grain, artificial surrogate screens, and scratches on the celluloid that fracture the processes of illusion. Though several of these devices extend, often in a feminist direction, the work of the *Groupe Dziga Vertov*, the concern with the filmic itself has an American genealogy of its own in structural film. In earlier films such as *City* (1964) and *Canyon* (1970) Jost had elaborated a purely formal self-consciousness; the amalgamation of this with a political self-consciousness produces in *Speaking Directly* an anomaly, made possible by the idiosyncratic coincidence in Jost of both the aesthetic vanguardism of the structural filmmakers and the political self-consciousness of the radicals.

Speaking Directly stands at the intersection of several film practices: in addition to its position as a critical afterword to underground solipsism (itself recapitulated in a reprise to the film in which, alongside fragments of the didactic interludes, Jost assembles a selection of sunsets, beaches, and other underground clichés) and as the summarization of the meta-cinematic concerns of radical film, it opens up the questions of the representation of women and of feminist discourse. Its forays into the problems of narrative illusionism link it with a sixties tradition of reflexive features (and, in fact, Jost subsequently escaped the impasse *Speaking Directly* records by turning to low-budget features with progressive political content). But all these practices are subsumed by its attention to filmic representation, to the material nature and processes of film and the phenomenology of spectatorship. These issues had been pursued in film's most complete modernist moment, the apotheosis of film and the repression of cinema that was the historical complement to and the dialectical other of the engaged cinema: structural film.

Pure Film

6

They were aroused by pure film.
— Alfred Hitchcock

Stella . . . wants to be Velázquez *so he paints stripes.*
— Michael Fried

"Suddenly a cinema of structure has emerged" (Sitney, 1969: 1). Clearly *something* had emerged, something quite different from and in its own way no less scandalous than the most decadent eruptions from the underground, and often as scandalous in the underground as the underground itself had been in the culture at large. But precisely what was essential in this rush of innovation or even what exactly differentiated it from the underground was less clear. Debates about the meaning and value of the term *structural film*, either in its original formulation or in more or less severely wrenching variations of it, were rivaled only by the controversy over whether there even existed a referent for it.

That structural film from the beginning should have been besieged by semantic and ontological disputes is in retrospect splendidly ironic, for the practice it designated subjected film language itself to a radical scrutiny of the kind that *structuralism* had brought to play upon language in general. The use of models drawn from post-Saussurian linguistics to question the relationship between language and some extratextual reality to which it had been supposed to refer and the overall attempt "whether reflexive or poetic . . . to reconstruct an 'object' in such a way as to manifest thereby the rules of functioning (the 'functions') of this object" (Barthes, 1972a: 214), which constituted both the methodology and the ideology of structuralism, thus entered the cinema by a happy terminological accident. For though references to structura*lism* are common in early structural film literature—everywhere in Hollis Frampton, for example (who often reads like a parallel writing of Roland Barthes in the manner of the Borgesian allegory of the *Quixote*), or in Paul Sharits's citations of Barthes's "The Structuralist Activity" in his own seminal manifesto, "Words Per Page"—structuralism has not been generally recognized as the twin enterprise of structural film and the initially most useful critical frame of reference for it. Whatever the reasons for this—and the American academic resistance to structuralism was neatly complemented by the early film semiologists' militant ignorance of the avant-garde and collusive concentration on the narrative feature[1]—the field of film and thought about

1 Metz's attribution of "numerical and social superiority" to "the *feature-length film of novelistic fiction*" allowed him to take it as normative for film semiology in general; hence his expectation that a semiotics of non-narrative film could take the form only of "discontinuous remarks on the points of difference between these films and 'ordinary' films" (Metz, 1974b: 94). While this disposition—which saw as alternative to the industrial cinema only "various experimental films, with their avalanche of gratuitous and anarchic images against a background of heterogenous percussions, capped by some overblown avantgardist text" (ibid: 225)—can be ascribed simply to his ignorance, subsequent academic repression of non-narrative film may only be understood as politically collusive, an instinctive response to the threat represented by the radical alterity of structural film's pure aestheticism.

film that "structural" now designates may most usefully be approached by means of the issues that dominated the American art world. This route will have the further advantage of eventually furnishing the terms by which both structural film and the structuralist mode of analysis it almost organically engenders may be re-contained in an understanding of their common historical determination.

The Texts

Realistic, illusionist art had dissembled the medium, using art to conceal art.
Modernism used art to call attention to art.
— Clement Greenberg

The distinction of a specifically modernist moment in the history of film is complicated beyond parallel difficulties in other media by the peculiar historical and social conditions of film's use. Its material dependence on advanced technologies deprived it of any antique or classical era, against which the character of a specifically modernist break may be gauged. Since its history is thus virtually coextensive with the high-modern period as a whole, and since its operations so appositely model the experience of the modern factory and of the modern city, it has been ubiquitously proposed as the modern art par excellence.[2]

At the cost of only minor simplification, however, it is possible to see in the first three decades of film an ontogenetic recapitulation of the itinerary followed by other media since the Renaissance that allowed it to succeed the expended forms of the realistic novel, the proscenium theater, and easel painting by appropriating from these the bases of its own representational codes. The rapid formal development that took film from its primitive stage to Griffith's fully articulate realism coincided with social and functional innovations that prohibit the duplication in film of the tacit agreement that allows histories of modern fiction or painting to be limited to their high bourgeois or specialist forms—those forms that almost by definition inhibited their own mass consumption. Such an exclusion of popular forms from even a schematic model of film cannot readily be made, and so its history appears not as an orderly linear evolution but as a quickly established and relatively consistent industrial usage, coexisting with occasional irregular alternatives. Though the dominant mode does include its own formal versions of modernism—the fracture of the visual field and the single spectatorial position in shot/counter-shot editing, for example, and the temporal and spatial dislocations involved in parallel montage—their major result was to lay the bases for the interdependent formal and ideological closures and social functions that, when completed with the advent of synchronous sound, fulfilled the mimetic dreams that had inspired the technological searches of the medium's prehistory.

Despite considerable internal variations, the form of this classic cinema is sufficiently homogenous that it may stand as the summary

2 A notable if idiosyncratic exception is Michael Fried, for whom artistic modernism is defined by its attempt to transcend or defeat the theatricality of the spectator's confrontation with the art object. Fried suggests that since "cinema escapes theater—automatically, as it were . . . even at its most experimental [it] is not a *modernist* art" (Fried, 1968: 141).

of the industrial uses of the medium against which various alternative cinemas have formed themselves. Maintaining recurrent if attenuated formal preoccupations of their own that surface in unpredictable places such as Japan in the thirties, these alternative practices are dominated by two major bursts of innovation: the twenties' European avant-gardes and the sixties' revival of them, including the various Third World cinemas of decolonization. Since we shall have occasion to consider the special way the early Soviet cinema shadows European and American independents of the sixties, the peculiarities that derive from its unique social preconditions may be temporarily set aside for a general distinction between an early twenties cubist/constructivist impulse, which became important to the U.S. avant-garde in the late sixties, and a late twenties surrealist phase which, revived by Maya Deren and sustained by Kenneth Anger, Sidney Peterson, Curtis Harrington, and eventually Stan Brakhage, was most important in the United States in the fifties and early sixties. Both phases mark the migration into film of artists from other mediums, and also the use of film to extend issues or solve crises confronted by painting, especially the representation of motion and duration in the first case and the representation of extraordinary psychological states in the second. Even if only in the use of montage to fabricate imaginary diegeses, all phases of the surrealist tradition exploit material properties specific to film. But the rejection of illusionist narrative for filmic constructions and the attempts to clarify the purely cinematic (evidenced by temporal extension and intension; loop printing; explicit reference to the processes of filming and editing, and to the filmstrip and cinematic apparatus; the non-photographic production of imagery; the use of specifically filmic devices to produce a film "language"; and the fracturing of the film frame) variously present in the work of Duchamp, Eggeling, Richter, Leger, Gance, Epstein, Kirisanov, and Seeber, as well as Vertov, ally this other tradition with the modernist critique of representation inaugurated by Cezanne and elaborated as a formal problem by the cubists and as an ideological one by Duchamp and Dada.[3]

As rediscovered and resuscitated by painters and sculptors in the very different social conditions of the United States in the sixties, this project quickly claimed priority for itself as the essential program for modernism, dated by its preeminent theorist, Clement Greenberg, from the Kantian "use of the characteristic methods of a discipline to criticize the discipline itself" (Greenberg, 1965: 193). The following summary of his position in the widely influential essay "Modernist Painting" displays an authority within which the shift from description to prescription was as subtle as it was unquestioned.

It quickly emerged that the unique and proper area of competence of each art coincided with all that was unique to the nature of its medium. The task of self-criticism became to eliminate from the effects of each art any and every effect that might

3 Thus Wollen summarizes two tendencies in filmic modernism: first, "the muting or exclusion of the non-cinematic codes;" and second, "the reduction of these codes themselves to their material—optical, photo-chemical—substrate ('material support') to the exclusion of any semantic dimension other than reference back to the material of the signifier itself" (Wollen, 1982: 197).

conceivably be borrowed from or by the medium of any other art. Thereby each art would be rendered "pure," and in its "purity" find the guarantee of its standards of quality as well as of its independence. "Purity" meant self-definition, and the enterprise of self-criticism in the arts became one of self-definition with a vengeance.

Realistic, illusionist art had dissembled the medium, using art to conceal art. Modernism used art to call attention to art. The limitations that constitute the medium of painting—the flat surface, the shape of the support, the properties of pigment—were treated by the Old Masters as negative factors that could be acknowledged only implicitly or indirectly. Modernist painting has come to regard these same limitations as positive factors that are to be acknowledged openly. (Ibid.: 194)

Though it took place in a context that included exactly the obverse project, that is, the proliferation of art activity bridging several mediums or taking place between them, the quasi-scientific demonstration of the axiomatic conditions of each medium, achieved by the elimination of its inessential conventions (typically entailing the expulsion from the art object of mimetic or discursive reference) was the paradigm within which in the sixties art was understood as an encounter with problems and issues peculiar to itself. If in this it did not entirely subordinate the retinal to the intellectual, still that Duchampian diversion took art through most of the territories that the modernist advance opened up. As a result a field of concerns was organized: the investigation of irreducible material elements, the search for axiological principles that open from the specific medium to questions about art in general, and the relation between art and criticism. But in these investigations the material quiddity discovered by the Greenbergian model was irresistibly transformed into its opposite. The theology of material presence slipped into what had formerly been its context, the critical idea, to produce conceptual art. As the spatial articulation of minimalist sculpture succeeded to painting's self-representation, it too became vulnerable to the purer statement, the enumeration of its own conditions and the description of the space it occupied. Finally, the itineraries of a self-critical art practice articulating its own cognitive horizons met the concurrent theoretical elaboration of this activity; art became one with its idea, practice merged with theory.[4]

The people who became known as structural filmmakers had strong ties to this art world, and several were already successful sculptors or painters. Though there were continuities with underground film (and both Ernie Gehr and Paul Sharits had made underground films), still structural film marks a categorical break with the aesthetic and social project of the underground.[5] It contains precise analogues to minimal art's insistence on the work's own materiality and its search for a clarified rational shape for the whole work and for its relation to its parts, even as those priorities modulate into various conceptual activities that open up the patterns of

4 Cf. "Ultimately, the repudiation of the aesthetic suggests the total elimination of the art object and its replacement by an idea for a work or by the rumor that one has been consummated—as in conceptual art. Despite the stress on the actuality of the materials used, the principle common to all classes of de-aestheticized art is that the finished product, if any, is of less significance than the procedures that brought the work into being and of which it is the trace" (Rosenberg, 1972: 29).

5 Examples of established underground filmmakers taking up the concerns of structural film are rare, Ken Jacobs being the only important instance. Brakhage's attack on structural film (Brakhage, 1978) voiced a widespread dejection and alarm among underground filmmakers, especially outside New York City. Sitney's model, which unveils structural film as the unrecognized telos of underground film, distorts both underground film and the relation of structural film to it. In fact, the distinction between structural and underground film is much clearer than the distinction between structural film and the films produced by artists as conceptual art or as documentation of conceptual art, body art, or earth art. In films like Vito Acconci's *Applications* (1970) and *See Through* (1970), John Baldessari's *Script* (1973), Bruce Nauman's *Art Makeup: Green, Black, White, Pink* (1971) and *Playing a Note on the Violin While I Am Walking Around the Studio* (1968), Robert Smithson's *Spiral Jetty* (1970), and especially Richard Serra's *Hand Catching Lead* (1968) and Serra and Joan Jonas's *Paul Revere* (1971), the boundary between film's own textual properties and the purely instrumental use of the medium is called into question.

disjunctions and identities between the work and the series of procedures that bring it into being and those that control its apprehension. This orientation took the form of a general subordination of interest in representation, especially of narrative, and a corresponding emphasis on the materials and resources of the medium, on the conditions of production and display, and on the specific kinds of signification of which film is capable.[6]

Such a generalized assumption that what is essential in structural film is its concern with materials and language—with materials as language and with language as material—is, of course, more adequate for some films than for others. But whatever differences it elides within the extensive field it delineates—between films that embody Sitney's initial characteristics and those that do not; between "formal and structural organization" (Sitney, 1979: 369); between formal film and "the new formal film" (Le Grice, 1977: 88); or even between structural and "structural/materialist" (Gidal, 1975)—still all the work that has swirled within the tow of the concept has in common a determining reflexive concern with its own nature and its own signifying capabilities that also entails an implicit critique of illusionist narrative. Like language games in Wittgenstein's analogy, the term structural film may be thought of as referring to the net of "family resemblances" that recur through films that are *related to one another in many different ways*" (Wittgenstein, 1968: 31). This is the basis upon which structural applies to both the film and the theory, for here structural film joins structuralist thought in general in the latter's characteristic "transformation of form into content, in which the form of Structuralist research . . . turns into a proposition about content: literary works are about language" (Jameson, 1972: 199); films are about film.[7]

While the realism of commercial film has often been interrupted by the foregrounding of its own procedures or formal anxieties, in the art film self-conscious concern with filmic form and especially with the difference between film and other mediums has been especially prominent. Maya Deren's imperative orientation around the material properties of the apparatus—evidenced in her claim that "if cinema is to take its place beside the others as a full-fledged art form, it must cease merely to record realities that owe nothing of their actual existence to the film instrument. Instead, it must create a total experience so much out of the very nature of the instrument as to be inseparable from its means" (Deren, 1960: 162)—reflects ongoing preoccupations with medium specificity and attempts to make the material properties of film the site of its meaning. Long before such overtly formalist essays as *My Mountain Song* (1969), Stan Brakhage was exploiting the material of the filmstrip itself metaphorically, for example, in the scratches on the film in *Reflections on Black* (1955). Warhol's minimalist investigation of filmic time and his reductionist foregrounding of separate elements in the vocabulary of film mark similar meta-filmic preoccupations. And such self-consciousness is everywhere in the earliest underground film—in Kenneth Anger's scratches in *Fireworks* (1947), in Richard Hu-

6 Cf. Arthur: "A shared position/ aspiration . . . is the rejection of a sphere of associative or metaphoric meaning as given by image-content and its interaction with organizational procedures in favor of the production of a network of relations between subject-viewer, the representation of film-material elements and shape as a function of the experience of duration" (Arthur, 1978: 6–7). Arthur's two essays on structural film (Arthur, 1978 and 1979b) most precisely locate its art-historical context, and indeed his analysis takes as its point of departure Warhol's *Empire*: "At last, the first conceptual film" (ibid.: 1978: 6). Wollen makes a useful distinction/ comparison between narrative and structural film in terms of their ontological presuppositions—a differentiation between a (Bazinian) "ontology basing itself on the possibility, inherent in the photo-chemical process, of reproducing natural objects and events without human intervention" and "the conscious exploration of the full range of properties of the photo-chemical process, and other processes involved in filmmaking" (Wollen, 1982: 194). The distinction, which is of course primary, may be traced back at least as far as Metz's distinction between two realisms: "The impression of reality *produced by the diegesis*, the universe of fiction, what is *represented* by each art, and, on the other hand, the reality of the vehicle of the representation in each art" (Metz, 1974b: 12–13).

7 Sitney's first formulation of the term "structural film" was in the article "Structural Film," published in *Film Culture* in the summer of 1969, where he listed as exemplary practitioners Tony Conrad, George Landow, Michael Snow, Hollis Frampton, Joyce Wieland, Ernie Gehr, and Paul Sharits. Proposing that theirs was "a cinema of structure where the shape of the whole film is pre-determined and simplified, and it is that shape that is the primal impression of the film," he noted three formal characteristics of structural film: "a fixed camera position, . . . the flicker effect and loop printing" (Sitney, 1969: 1). The extension of this seminal presentation in Sitney's *Visionary Film* ([1974]

1979) retains the formalist definitions but endows structural film with a quasi-spiritual motivation that enables him to situate it as the logical culmination of the visionary tradition through its capacity, not simply to record, but to induce extraordinary states of consciousness: "The structural film approaches the condition of meditation and evokes states of consciousness without mediation; that is with the sole mediation of the camera" (Sitney, 1979: 370). For a critical overview of Sitney's and subsequent theory, see Arthur (1979b). Other significant contributions to the debate are Maciunas (1970); Le Grice (1972); Gidal (1975); and Arthur (1978).

Complaints such as Le Grice's observation that "Sitney's use of the term 'structural,' to cover what he makes it cover, is totally misleading and does not help the perception or understanding of any of the films which he puts into the category" (Le Grice, 1972: 79) are not without justification, for Sitney did not himself theorize what he called structural film in terms that recognized or even were cognate with structuralism. The concept of structure, however, was already well established, in ways analogous to Sitney's use of it, in New York art criticism—as for example, in "Primary Structures," the first major exhibition of minimal art, which was held at the Jewish Museum in 1966, or in Lucy Lippard's rejection of the term "minimal art" for "primary structures" in the catalog introduction "10 Structurists in 20 Paragraphs" (Lippard, 1978)—though Arthur (1979b: 132, n. 3) reports that Sitney was unaware of art-critical writing on minimalism when he wrote the original essay. The present argument—that the film practice referred to by Sitney and subsequently marshaled by his sobriquet is ideologically and methodologically cognate with structuralism—thus conjoins what were initially two distinct terminologies. For an overview of earlier attempts to negotiate between the film practice and the theory, see James (1978). The first substantial attempt to bring the two into some mutually enlightening focus was Peter Wollen's two articles "The Two Avant-Gardes" (1975) and " 'Ontol-

go's multiple superimpositions in *Melodic Inversion* (1958), in Bruce Conner's morphemic analysis of the grammar of the Hollywood film in *A Movie* (1957), and of course in Deren's own work.

But filmic reflexiveness can be traced back before Deren, to that remarkable meta-cinematic address to the difference between the industry and its own amateur production, Florey and Vorkapich's *Life and Death of 9413—A Hollywood Extra* (1928), and so to the twenties avant-gardes. The search for an entirely literal film language or for an unselfconscious cinema goes further and further back through the archaeology of the early cinema, past the reflexive audience confrontation and the movable shot in *The Great Train Robbery*, past the almost schematic analysis of illusion in *Uncle Josh at the Moving Picture Show*, and so to the premonition of Warhol in the earliest preserved film, *John Rice–May Irwin Kiss*. Eventually the search falls away in the filmstrips of Muybridge, in the enumeration of the components of a possible cinema, and in the speculations in which the idea of film was first broached, the first conceptual film created.

Though this history precludes any simple polarization between reflexive and non-reflexive film, or between ironic and literal, materialist and illusionist, or any of the other distinctions that the modernist paradigm resorts to, nevertheless the reflexive imperative did intensify in the mid-sixties, not so much to align an already extant avant-garde cinema into reciprocity with other mediums, but rather to provide the matrix for an essentially new cinema. Its foundations had been lain by the Fluxus artists,[8] who by 1966 had produced a program of radical filmic reductions: George Brecht's *Entry-Exit*, in which a plain white wall with the word ENTRANCE on it gradually darkens to black then lightens to pure white revealing the word EXIT; George Maciunas's *10 Feet*, the projection of ten feet of clear leader; James Riddle's *Nine Minutes*, in which crudely stenciled numbers interrupt the black background every minute; and Nam June Paik's *Zen for Film*. As this last reveals the continuous formication of the apparently empty white screen, it draws attention to the fact of light projection and to film as the arbiter of duration—only to jeopardize these absolutes simultaneously by the constant phenomenological exchange it produces. All these films are in their different ways varieties of "first films"[9] in which this or that single element in the total register of the codes of filmic signification has been isolated, set into lonely self-display.

In the last half of the decade such a minimalist aesthetic produced a body of films, each of which more or less systematically concentrated on a restricted number of filmic codes. Though not always with the single-minded rigor of the best Fluxfilms, they variously emphasized the material nature of film and the separate stages in the production processes—from script, through editing and projection, to reception by the audience. Thus: flicker films, and preeminently Tony Conrad's *The Flicker* (1966), are *about* the optical effects of rapidly alternating monochrome frames; Michael Snow's *Wavelength* (1967), *Back-Forth* (1969), and *La Région Centrale*

6.1 Edwin S. Porter, *Uncle Josh at the Moving Picture Show*

(1971) are *about* the effects of camera zoom, panning, and 360-degree rotation; Barry Gerson's films are *about* the ambiguous space between legibility and abstraction and thus draw attention to the dependence of representation on focus, framing, camera angle, and so forth; Larry Gottheim's *Barn Rushes* (1971), which documents several shooting runs past the same object under different light conditions and using different film stocks, is *about* filmic reproduction; J. J. Murphy's *Print Generation* (1973–74) is *about* reprinting and so *about* the photographic image; Anthony McCall's *Line Describing a Cone* (1973) and subsequent films that articulate the projector beam three-dimensionally are *about* the sculptural properties of film projection; Ernie Gehr's *History* is *about* the grain of the film as it is illuminated by light leaking through a sprocket hole in the printer. And on through the list, it is possible to map out a periodic table of all structural films, all possible structural films, by positing a film constructed to manifest each moment in an atomized model of the entire cinematic process.[10]

The predictive limitations of such a project lie not in the limitlessness of the cinematic, but rather in the fact that structural film is rarely this "purely" abstract. While represented imagery may on occasion be arbitrary ("probably any 'content' is valid"—Sharits, 1972: 27), essentially a vehicle upon which purely filmic effects can be demonstrated and filmic variations played, it is always specific and, in fact, usually has some material or semantic quality that makes it specifically appropriate to or allegorical of the material operations performed on it. Thus the three-dimensional retreat of the corridor centered in Gehr's *Serene Velocity* produces in the two dimensions of the filmstrip the symmetrical frame that allows the effects of the apparently superimposed exposures taken at different focal lengths their special force. The alternation of black and white frames in *The Flicker* hyperbolically reiterates the nictitation of the

ogy' and 'Materialism' in Film" (1976), both reprinted in Wollen (1982), though Sitney recognized as early as 1974, in the first edition of *Visionary Film*, that "the theory of the structural cinema has its historical origins" in Russian formalism (Sitney, 1979: 365) and was himself by that date using Shklovsky extensively.

8 George Maciunas, the leader of the Fluxus group, immediately proposed alternative schematizations, and also provided extensive documentation of films predating Sitney's examples. See Maciunas (1970: 349).

9 Cf. Michael Snow on Ernie Gehr's *History*: "At last, the first film" (*Film-Makers' Cooperative Catalogue*, 1975: 98).

10 Such an undertaking has been sketched twice by Malcolm Le Grice. The first time he isolated the following categories: (1) "Concerns which derive from the camera: its limitations and extensive capacities as a time-base photographic recording apparatus"; (2) "Concerns which derive from the editing process and its abstraction into conceptual, concrete relationships of elements"; (3) "Concerns which derive from the mechanism of the eye and particularities of perception"; (4) "Concerns which derive from printing, processing, re-filming and re-copying procedures; exploration of transformations possible in selective copying and modification of the ma-

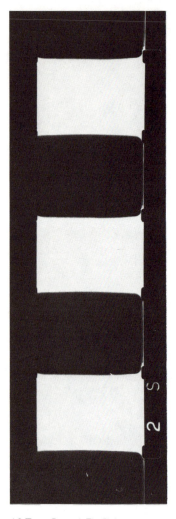

6.2 Tony Conrad, *The Flicker*

apparatus and the alternation of light and darkness that is the medium's constitutive condition. And the opening and closing of the shutters of the sign in Bill Brand's *Moment* (1972) visually parallel the progressively briefer sections into which the film record of the sign's operations are broken. The increasing number of layers of footage of coursing water in Sharits's *S:TREAM:S:S:ECTION: S:ECTION:S:S:ECTIONED* rhymes with the progressively proliferating, rippling scratches into the surface of the emulsion.

Such films are, then, precisely experimental; rather than reproducing established formal conventions each develops principles of construction peculiar to the specific area of the filmic process it designs or to the conjunction of the filmic and the specific imagery it confronts. Since each is therefore a *hapax*, its unique form determined by its particular enterprise, each is by definition successful, for the quasi-scientific model of operations—everywhere latent, but perhaps best summarized in Sharits's notion of "cinematics," "a cinema of exploration . . . which has the thrust at its every point of opening up for continual reexamination its premises and objects of research" (Sharits, 1978: 44)—is satisfied by the completion of the procedures the film adopts a priori as the form of its operations. While theoretically this implies the evacuation of aesthetic criteria as previously understood, in practice any impulse toward such a scientism, for which the fulfillment of predetermined protocols is intrinsically self-justifying, is re-contained as itself one element in a field of mutually ironizing processes. Structural film thus typically operates in the wake of Romantic art's need to distinguish itself from science while simultaneously incorporating it.

The high-modernist reworking of these imperatives was the New Criticism, and, as in that theory of literature, the dominant trope of structural film is irony—in fact, to invoke one summary formulation of this aesthetic, "Irony as a Principle of Structure."

> Irony, then, in this further sense, is not only an acknowledgement of the pressures of a context. Invulnerability to irony is the stability of a context in which the internal pressures balance and mutually support each other. The stability is like that of the arch: the very forces which are calculated to drag the stones to the ground actually provide the principle of support—a principle in which thrust and counterthrust become the means of stability.[11] (Brooks, 1971: 1043–44)

Structural film proceeds by elaborating such internal tensions: form against content; part against whole; presence against discourse; materials against representation; object-text against meta-text; motion against stasis; black and white against color; sound against silence; frame-line against uncalibrated celluloid, and so on.[12] As it does so it implies criteria for evaluation different from those of experimental science, criteria that valorize an object as well-wrought to the extent that these internal pressures do indeed "balance and mutually support each other." The successful film is not one that with whatever rhetorical embellishment makes reference to the world—

terial"; (5) "Concerns which derive from the physical nature of film"; (6) "Concerns which derive from the properties of the projection apparatus and the fundamental components of sequential image projection"; (7) "Concern with duration as a concrete dimension"; and (8) "Concern with the semantics of image and with the construction of meaning through 'language' systems" (Le Grice, 1972: 80–83). A similar taxonomy underlies his more extensively illustrated and intensively argued survey of North American and European "formal" cinema (Le Grice, 1977).

11 See Weinbren (1979) for a reading of the ways in which several films generated by predetermined

for such content itself is included in the array of mutually canceling figures—but one that sets in play the maximum number of such encounters, that thickens the text with reference from one part to another, that maximizes its metaphorical restatement of itself. So alongside the conceptual precision and impeccable lucidity of minimal films lies another aesthetic, in which the apparent simplification is merely the clearing away of debris that impedes perception of complex operations which otherwise would go unnoticed. The minimal always implies its opposite and complement, the encyclopedic. Some examples:

6.3 Michael Snow, *Wavelength*

GEORGE LANDOW'S *Film in which there appear sprocket holes, edge lettering, dirt particles etc.* (1966)

This simplest of films, a throwaway fragment of standard negative control set (the strip of film showing the head and shoulders of a woman that lab technicians use to adjust color balance) printed over and over again, may appear as only "a found object extended to a simple structure . . . the essence of minimal cinema" (Sitney, 1979: 390). In fact, *Film in which* . . . orchestrates superimposed strata of filmic codes and material properties in such a way that any given datum's assertion of itself as presence on one level simultaneously draws attention to its illusoriness on another. The matrix for these ontological paradoxes is the several generations of filmic events present in one form or another in any given projection. The most crucial of these generations are (1) the original looping of the found footage, (2) the first completed copy of *Film in which* . . . that recorded the passage of this loop through the printer, and (3) the specific condition of the release print which at any given moment contains the traces of its previous projections. Playing amid this clathrate history of passages through various apparatuses are patterns of mutually ironizing formal propositions that invert the hierarchy of codes that customarily make film comprehensible.

Primary among these inversions is structuralism's formalist subordination of reference to text, the subordination of the represented image to the materials of its presentation. The representation of the female model does engage issues of spectatorship that are continuous with the dominant issues of the film: for instance, her profession is to be looked at, but here she will alternately be overlooked by and look at us; the rhythm of her blinking is one of the signifiers of the mechanism of the film's construction and the source of its characteristic pulse; and though she may look like the Dragon Lady, she is in fact only China Girl. A phantom of industrial cinema, an object of the attention of technicians but customarily withheld from the audience, she is now, like the dust she will gather, for the first time made insistently present to our attention. Because of these correspondences, the image content is not entirely arbitrary. Yet, if for no other reason than the explicit cuing provided by the title, we are prompted to put the image content aside, to see it as primarily the vehicle upon which the true content of the film may register and

procedures produce an ironic distance between themselves and their paradigm.

12 Once the implications of a structure supported by such mutually ironizing antinomies have been established, they can be made to serve an infinite series of sublations. Thus the uncritical spontaneity that trivializes the films of Michael Snow (the suppositious kinesthetic kick at the end of *La Région Centrale*, the arbitrary coloration in *Wavelength*, the unsystematized camera movement in *Back-Forth*) can be theorized as one area of activity to be "balanced" by another characterized by more intelligent control. Hence Regina Cornwell can speak of the "double direction" of *Wavelength* in which "the evocative, expressive, and apparently arbitrary [are] balanced with the exploratory and analytical" (Cornwell, 1980: 67).

6.4 George Landow, *Film in which . . .*

accumulate. Consequently, the film's major tension becomes the competition for our attention between that image and the formal and material effects it carries, between seeing it and seeing through it. Understanding *Film in which* . . . entails conceptualizing the fact of loop printing, and then discriminating between that part of the optical information which refers to an initial profilmic scene and that which refers only to filmic processes.

This latter narrative, Sharits's "higher drama," involves a return to what is customarily repressed, to the concealed mechanisms by which film imagery is produced (the sprocket holes and the color scale) and the overlooked processes of projection recorded in the dust and scratches. But the distinction can only heuristically be phrased as being between illusion and reality, for in the first perfect print of *Film in which* . . . , the structuring tensions between photography and material presence are sublated in the more abstract distinction between the re-photography of previously photographed images and the photography of the material of the filmstrip. Mocked and rejected, that primary tension nevertheless returns in the difference between this ideally pristine *Film in which* . . . and any subsequent experience of it, when the processes of projection will have recapitulated the action that made it in the first place. Any actual projection will juxtapose the dust and scratches *represented* in *Film in which* . . .—the primary accumulation—with their capitalization in the dust and scratches materially present in the specific print, accumulated in the "loops" of its previous projections. And just as the film has already taught us to look *through* the represented imagery to the purely filmic processes, now it requires us similarly to look through the film to isolate the specificity of the state of the present print, to distinguish between the illusion of dust and scratches and the unmediated prehension of dust and scratches themselves.

If we thus see in any present projection the sediment of the film's work in previous projections, we may also look forward to a more substantially complete print; for as it restructures cinematic hierarchies, reorganizing the consumption phase as also the production phase, *Film in which* . . . holds out the promise of ever more intense versions of itself. These will accumulate more and more content until the final showing when, collapsing under the ravages of its previous projections, the material inscription so severe, the dust and scratches so thick, the film will fall out of the gate, perhaps allowing a glimpse of what it has so far been obliged to conceal, its own edge numbers and sprocket holes.

KEN JACOBS'S *Tom, Tom, the Piper's Son* (1969)

Though the image content of the object-text in *Film in which* . . . does have specific properties that allow it to be conducted into the film's dominant concerns, the representational thrust of the original fragment is largely subsumed by the effects performed upon it. The stability of the image through the loopings and through the ravaging of its material vehicle supplies the ostinato in reference to which other activities are clarified. *Tom, Tom, the Piper's Son* is structurally similar in that a given piece of found footage, a ten-minute short of the same name attributed to Billy Bitzer, is serially re-presented; but in this case the re-presentation takes different forms (forwards, backwards, different speeds, focusing on one character or another or on this or that area of the film frame) which decompose the original and allow for the separate scrutiny of the various mechanisms of signification of both the filmic codes and the photo-chemical materials that support them. Indeed, just as one year later in an entirely analogous project Roland Barthes's *S/Z* would break open Balzac's *Sarrasine* with "a minor earthquake" to rewrite it as a modernist textuality, here Jacobs's meta-filmic scrutiny of the object-text discovers not a stable meaning, but only multiplicity and change, a text centrifugally dispersed, constantly reformulating itself in new configurations.

In these terms *Tom, Tom* is a post-structuralist rather than a structuralist film, a critical essay that does not reduce its object-text to a single, simple structure but opens it to its own difference. Comprising semi-autonomous tableaux—long takes shot with a stationary camera—the 1905 short antedates Griffith's grammatical tropes and so occupies a status more primarily iconic even than Balzac; Jacobs discovers there the textual multiplicity Barthes later described in *Sarrasine*.

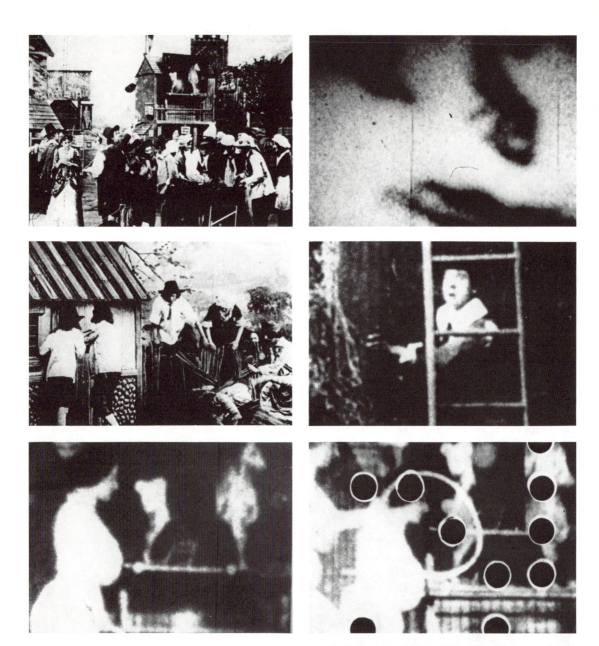

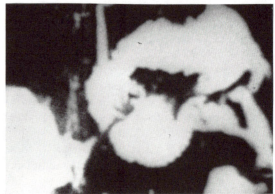

6.5–6.11 Ken Jacobs, *Tom, Tom, the Piper's Son*

In this ideal text, the networks are many and interact, without any one of them being able to surpass the rest; this text is a galaxy of signifiers, not a structure of signifieds; it has no beginning; it is reversible; we gain access to it by several entrances, none of which can be authoritatively declared to be the main one; the codes it mobilizes extend *as far as the eye can reach*, they are indeterminable . . . , the systems of meaning can take over this absolutely plural text, but their number is never closed, based as it is on the infinity of language. (Barthes, 1974: 5–6)

Jacobs's method of operations is very similar to Barthes's: opening up the object-text's various codes—of acting, of character continuity through a plot, of the projection apparatus, of the grain of film. Like other contemporary rewritings of primitive cinema as more modern than classic realism (e.g., Burch, 1979: 61–67)—and indeed like Barthes's entire model of the transitive reading of "writerly texts"—Jacobs's critical practice is simultaneously an archeological discovery of elements buried in the original and a construction which makes over this work as a point of departure, *pretext*, for something new of his own. The decomposition that fractures the flowing continuity of the signifiers of the Bitzer short brings into visibility effects that its visual cacophony conceals: a pickpocket stealing a handkerchief, a woman stuck in the hole of a fence, and a hundred other moments when attention alights upon a face, a gesture, or a pose that is otherwise unnoticed in the vigor of Bitzer's all-over visual field, which had not been simplified by the visually prescriptive grammar of suture. Jacobs's refilming is a rewriting that conjures new narratives; by selecting this or that character for closer scrutiny, this or that event for reorganization, even reversing the original, he is able to discover in its story an anthology of new plots.

But the de-constructive scrutiny brought to bear upon these depicted instances does not redeem their extratextual provenance; the closer the film is examined, the more the narrative detail it can be made to yield gives way before its opposite; the film passes over the threshold of its grain to generate bizarre Rorschach-like configurations in the abstract patterns of emulsion and reflected light. It asserts as its most crucial content the processes by which the literality of darkness and light is made to signify, and the processes which turn the density of grain into representation and discourse. Working in the middle space between materiality and illusion, it displays as its content the processes of its own coming into being, issues that it also represents in the variously interpolated shots of the projector lamp, shadows on the wall of the workroom, and sections of clear leader that fracture even the continuity of its interrogations.

Morgan Fisher's *Production Stills* (1970)

Though Laurence Sterne, Victor Shklovsky's model, did himself invoke the physical properties of the book in *Tristram Shandy*, the

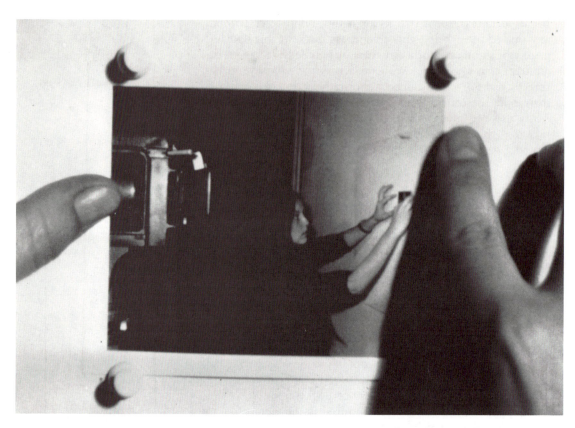

6.12–6.15 Morgan Fisher, *Production
Stills*

Russian Formalists conceptualized what they understood as the essential activity of art, the "laying bare" of technique, in reference to "literariness" and the distinction between literary and ordinary language. They thus theorized it in formal rather than material terms, and in the formalist-structuralist tradition the materiality of the text was largely ignored until the late sixties. Such a suppression of attention to the material means of production has never been as easy with respect to film, and, in fact, even commercial film has often been concerned with the social processes of production (the lives of film people), though not with the codes of filmic enunciation. *Production Stills* is such a documentation of its own material manufacture, employing still photography as the intermediary device of its reflexivity. While it develops meticulous procedures for bringing the two modes of photography—still and motion—to bear upon each other, it also calls its own premises into question with great wit.

Production Stills opens with what appears to be clear leader, and apparently before the visuals proper have begun, voices are heard: "perfect," "good balance." When a polaroid still photograph, showing a sound stage with a camera crew and a Mitchell pointing at a white wall, is pinned into this space, it reveals the screen of projection as the intradiegetic field of that camera's attention. The comments heard previously are retrospectively interpreted as referring to the photograph we now see, and we quickly realize (or presume, for the film is never able finally to validate what it apparently records) that the polaroid still depicts the apparatus that is producing the present film by photographing the white wall and whatever is placed upon it and by recording the live sound. The protocols for the remainder of the film become clear, and indeed subsequent photographs do depict the environment, the machines and the workers that make the film.

The procedures of the film are enclosed by the 400', 16mm roll and by the eight exposures on the roll of polaroid film; in fact, accommodating the latter to the temporal constraints of the former—making sure that all eight exposures are made before the movie film runs out—gives the film a narrative tension that further dramatizes its internal architecture. Its structure and content depend on the material conditions of the two photographic processes; *Production Stills* represents and is determined by nothing other than the means of its own production. A *uroboros*, it engages only itself, it remains within itself, and it terminates itself. While the film does document its own integrity in remaining within this entirely self-referential and consistently predetermined procedure, recourse to the polaroid as the mediating agency of self-documentation ironically plays one half of the system of the apparatus against the other. The technological disparity between the 16mm and the polaroid methods of photography allows for typical formalist reflexive conundrums to be conjured around their specificity. What, for example, becomes of the mutually exclusive definitions of frame, shot, and film when the entire film is a single shot virtually of eight single frames? Or, how can we accommodate the generational regressions and contradictions in scale that multiply vertiginously as we watch (represented in this film) fingers placing inside the holding pins a still photograph of a young woman pinning in the same position on the wall and in the camera's field (what we presume is) the still we have just finished watching!

So while on the one hand the film respects the priority of motion over still photography, and indeed elaborates it through a series of parallel opposites (motion versus still, color versus black and white, sound versus silent), the polaroid and the less privileged terms associated with it are not entirely reducible to that hierarchy. The former may have generational primacy, both in the general sense by which "the *having-been-there* [of still photography] gives way before a *being-there* of the thing [in film]" (Barthes, 1977: 45) and in the sense that the film (or a print from it) is present at the moment of projection, while the stills are merely "re-presented." And the movie apparatus resonates with the glamor of professional production, signaling "the media," while the polaroid camera is only a domestic toy. But this priority does not extend throughout the production, and, in fact, the film is slave, not master, to the stills. Its self-scrutiny is entirely dependent upon the catoptric ability of the stills to let the film's apparatus see itself. Without them the Mitchell could shoot only the white wall, producing a film which would be indistinguishable from clear leader, and so unable to document itself for either itself or the spectator. The only motion and the only color we see—these two attributes being markers that ostensibly assert the primacy of the film—are the fingers that slide the successive stills into the thumbtacks. Being otherwise entirely still and in black and white, the film manifests not its own qualities but those of the polaroid. Nor is it able to be coterminous with its own processes, for, like the stills in Hollis Frampton's *nostalgia*, the stills we see here are always one phase behind the present; they depict the apparatus, not as it is present in the moment of filming, but as it was some time ago. Only the audio, which is largely a description of the still photography, is present to itself, synchronous with its own recording; but while it can document the filmic apparatus, it too is incapable of documenting itself, of producing the sound of recording.

*

Though their predetermining procedural basis remains simple, these films nevertheless proliferate metaphoric extensions and displacements of filmic events so thickly that they tend toward discursive multiplicity, toward assembling sets of axiological conditions that are in other works mobilized singly. As such they tend toward the dialectical complement of modernist minimalism, toward a film encyclopedia, which rather than limiting itself to a single item in the set of filmic codes attempts to mobilize more and more of them in more and more combinations—a last film rather than a first. So, for example, Michael Snow, in *"Rameau's Nephew" by Diderot (Thanx to Dennis Young) by Wilma Shoen* (1974), justifies his labyrinthine title (itself acknowledging the *Encyclopedists*) by assem-

bling an exhausting array of permutations of sound/image relations.
Each of the twenty-five films that compose this array manifests a different combination of sound and image, ranging from synchrony to forcible, arbitrary juxtaposition, and playing on the effects produced by the reduction of the multi-locational origins of sound in the profilmic to the single source in film projection. While other artists rarely attempt Snow's range, that urge to complete the set of all possible effects in a limited number of parameters recurs frequently in structural film, with Paul Sharits's *Analytic Studies* series (1972–76) and Bill Brand's *Rate of Change* (1972) examples of the long and the short ends of the impulse. But the filmmaker for whom the idea of the total film provided the ruling aesthetic principle was Hollis Frampton.

THAT PART OF FILM WE CALL HOLLIS FRAMPTON

Polymath of enormous cultural range and erudition, Hollis Frampton pursued both the analytic principles of modernist reflexivity and the synthesis from them of the encyclopedic meta-text of the kind that haunted his masters, Ezra Pound (at whose feet in St. Elizabeths he sat) and Flaubert. In his exemplary career, Frampton's various attempts to establish "the irreducible axioms of that part of thought we call the art of film" (Frampton, 1983: 62–63)—the frame, the plausibility of photographic illusion, and, perhaps, narrative—are articulated in comprehensive clusters that more and more closely approach a summary statement of "a complete tradition from nothing more than the most obvious material limits of the total film machine." In his effort to describe this endeavor—nothing less than the structuralist attempt to reconcile *parole* with *langue*—the same metaphor comes to Frampton's mind as to Shklovsky's; the problem is "analogous to that of the Knight's Tour in chess" (ibid.: 116). Distinct from any historiographical undertaking, which is responsible for every actual film ever made, the *metahistorical* project is a rational reconstruction of an ideal history, establishing a model order for the medium. Privileging neither motion nor narrative (and in this respect Frampton's catholicity contrasts with contemporary cine-semiology's attempt to derive the language of film solely from that of the commercial feature), his conceptualization of the proper activity of the filmmaker and the now logically inseparable film theorist performs that quintessentially structuralist realignment, the 90-degree shift by which the diachronous extension of film's actual history is collapsed into the synchronous schematization of its total formal and material possibilities. Like Eliot's "tradition," Frampton's too requires "movement of energy in all directions" (ibid.: 74). The result, then, is neither Saussure's slice through the present state of the system nor the historian's account of what has been, but rather the poet's consideration of what may be and should be. Here the motive for filmmaking is found, for the metahistorian will inevitably encounter spaces, like the space of semiology itself in Saussure's original speculations, where certain

6.16 Hollis Frampton, *Information*

texts do not yet exist, even though logically they should; "then it is his duty to make them" (ibid.: 113).

After an apprenticeship in the foundations of the art—still photography, the construction of the "isolated frame taken out of the infinite cinema" (ibid.: 111)—Frampton began a series of minimalist mobilizations of a restricted number of filmic effects. They range from *Information* (1966), in his own words a "hypothetical 'first film' for a synthetic tradition constructed from scratch on reasonable principles, given: (1) camera; (2) raw stock; (3) a single bare light bulb" (*Film-Makers' Cooperative Catalogue*, 1975: 88), to *Artificial Light* (1969) in which a single shot is successively treated to a variety of filmic maneuvers: reversed, in negative, tinted, with parts bleached out, scratched, vertically split and inverted, and so on. In the works of his maturity, *Zorns Lemma* (1970), *Hapax Legomena* (1972), and the unfinished *Magellan*, the strategies of such minimalist probes were combined as semi-autonomous components of assemblages in which the separate concerns of each overlap, generating patterns of parallelisms and contrasts that travel throughout the set.

In *Hapax Legomena*, a cycle of seven films, the relation between sound and image that is initially made problematical in the asynchrony of *nostalgia* is fed through a range of different kinds of combination, including the visual presentation of the verbal script in *Poetic Justice* and the metrical editing distortions in *Critical Mass*. Similarly, the issues of framing, already brought into question in *nostalgia*, are foregrounded in the manual modifications visible in *Travelling Matte* and in the broken white line that internally frames *Special Effects*. While such internal ligatures lattice the cycle of films to contain the temporality of its unfolding within the synchrony of the model of filmic effects that it constructs, diachronous meanings and extratextual references are not entirely excluded; like the similar sequence by which different technologies are emphasized in *Zorns Lemma, Hapax Legomena*'s passage from still photographs through film proper to video allegorizes both the history of the apparatus and Frampton's own autobiographical recapitulation of that history. Such extratextual references or the literal content of the imagery, however, rarely strain the formalist reflexivity; real life is, rather, appropriated by the film to allow it its own work. Frampton's early photographic series, *Ways to Purity*, made clear that the city is itself the site of so many spontaneous Motherwells or Newmans; now, as in Godard's *Two or Three Things I Know About Her*, the city appears as an endless environment of more or less fragmented signification, whose restitution into intelligibility is the artist's task. As *Zorns Lemma*, his most spectacular anatomy of film language, reveals, the modern city is always an Empire of Signs.

In the tradition of the great pedagogical primers, Frampton's *Zorns Lemma* is divided into three parts. The first, which has sound but no images, is concerned with verbal language experienced aurally. Uninflected black leader is accompanied by a male voice reading *The Bay State Primer*, a combination catechism and elementary reading manual from the eighteenth century: "In Adam's fall / We sinned all. / Thy life to mend / God's book attend," and so on. The second part, which is silent, is concerned with the visual experience of words and images; it is organized in cycles of twenty-four shots, each twenty-four frames long. The matrix for these cycles is initially established by shots of words photographed from signs in the streets of a modern city, and arranged alphabetically according to their first letters. By employing the Roman alphabet, in which "I" is not differentiated from "J" and "U" is not differentiated from "V," the film is able to accommodate the words of modern English into cycles of twenty-four units. One-second shots of continuous, live-action imagery, without verbal inscription, are then progressively substituted for the shots of words; a take of a bonfire replaces the

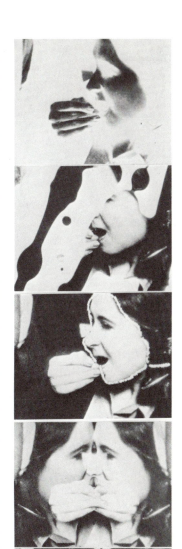

6.17 Variations on a single shot: Hollis Frampton, *Artificial Light*

6.18 Hollis Frampton, *Poetic Justice*

words beginning with "X," for instance, and a stand of cattails replaces those beginning with "Y." Once introduced, these nonverbal images always occupy the same location in the alphabetical sequence. More and more of the letters are replaced until finally the film is entirely nonverbal, with twenty-four different shots, each twenty-four frames long, rotating in regular cycles. The third part, which has both image and sound, combines visual images with spoken language. It appears to be a single long take of a landscape during a snowstorm, though actually it contains three 400′ rolls dissolved one into the next. It depicts two people and a dog walking away from the camera across some fields toward woods. On the sound track, six voices read, at a rate of one word per second, a medieval scientific text, Robert Grosseteste's "On Light or the Ingression of Forms."

Despite this tripartite form, the film is organized around binary oppositions. By playing representation against signification, image against sound, and nonverbal against verbal in quasi-systematic permutations, both within each section and throughout the film as a whole, Frampton generates a panoramic display of the semantic and syntactic possibilities that produce film language and filmic meaning.

In the first section, a verbal language demonstrates some of the principles of its own codification and clarifies the grammatical system that orders it. An aural reproduction of a written text uses a highly formalized selection of English words to manifest the sequence of the alphabet. Regular variations foreground a series of specific nouns ("Adam" in the first stanza, "book" in the second, "cat" in the third, "dog" in the forth, and so on); but while objects are thus proposed as the dominant ordering elements, they do not subtend a realist model of language of the kind that privileges words as the nomenclature for preexistent things. Rather, like structuralist linguistics, the primer demonstrates how words function differentially within linguistic systems. The underlying alphabetical taxonomy that supplies the logic of the primer as a whole also informs the function of the narrative vignettes the stanzas contain and the principle of their interrelationship. The linguistic events in "In Adam's fall / We sinned all" occur not simply to describe the fate of Adam in the extratextual world, but also to produce a syntactically correct linguistic context, commensurate in terms of rhyme, rhythm, and other formal properties with the verbal structures that surround it, that can allow "Adam" to instance a linguistic order. Similarly, in the sequence as a whole, Adam is not related to the cat and the dog by the role each plays in a continuous narrative or coherent diegesis (even though these were to be understood as linguistically constituted); the terms relate to each other by virtue of their role in the demonstration of an axiom of the order of language, the principle of alphabetical position.

In the second and by far the longest section, the film takes this alphabetical system as the point of departure for its own language pedagogy, but now the language to be taught is the visual language of film. By proposing to arrange the material world according to the model supplied by the primer in the first section, the film initially explores a systematization of film order by reference to the verbal language it contains. Made present as words, the world submits to an alphabetical taxonomy. But the nonverbal imagery that ruptures this schematization progressively subverts the hegemony of the verbal system, demanding filmic articulations and generating purely filmic meanings.

The montage is of an elementary kind, Eisenstein's metric montage, and initially it combines verbal and purely filmic orders: the shots are constructed in cycles of twenty-four on the basis of a language function (the alphabetical order of the first letter of the word or that fragment of it that has been photographed), but the length of each shot is determined by filmic priorities (the number of frames that pass through the projector in a single second at standard speed). The units of this montage do, however, have a plastic specificity of their own, a material presence that can never be entirely assimilated to the abstract conceptual system of the alphabet. The different scripts, colors, and substances from which the signs are made, the spatial dramas of their location in the city streets, and also the properties they have acquired in being brought by photography from the three dimensions of the real world to the two dimensions of the film frame—all these demand processes of visual apprehension quite different from those of reading.

The combination of the insistent alphabetical order of the words and the otherwise arbitrary method of their selection generates a weird concrete poetry. Construing abecedarian sequences like "back, cable, dairy, eagle, face, gallery, hair, jack, keen, lace, mad, name" or sorting furiously for meaning through other such colorless green ideas as "Right size toad use wood" or "After bay cedar dark emergency" certainly has its own pleasures, the pleasures of poetry. But as these sequences are experienced in the film's presentation of material words, the progress of those pleasures is impeded (and supplemented) by the processes of filmic apprehension. The reconstitution of sentences is delayed; during the search around the film frame for the word and its initial letter, which will confirm the alphabetical logic and introduce its specific variation, attention alights upon some purely visual property of the word or its environment. Reading through the frame to reconstruct the three-dimensional scene the shot represents involves continuously shifting attention among the optical properties of the visual field and the irrational discourse produced by the meaning of the words—variously locating the sign, perceiving the signifier, comprehending the signified.

Within this lexical shingle factory, nonverbal images appear: a bonfire, cattails, an egg being fried, some men digging a hole, the face of a young woman with a strange split down the middle, a man painting a wall, waves breaking, and so on. Calling into question the system of the alphabet, these images produce a tension between verbal and nonverbal apprehension: having become accustomed to

6.19 Hollis Frampton, *Zorns Lemma*.
Top: Last frame of the final passage of
the raging bonfire—the replacement
image for "X." *Bottom*: Earth: a stand of
cattails—the replacement image for "Y."

reading, even to subvocalizing, the verbal text—indeed having been taught that the key to the images' organization is the language they subtend—the spectator has been conditioned to reduce the sensual extensiveness of these live-action scenes into a single noun and return them to alphabetical order by finding in a shot of waves breaking backwards, for example, that one word which will adequately summarize it: waves, beach, ocean, or whatever. This process is akin to searching through the couplet for the relevant noun in the first section of the film or to reading the word on the signs that have appeared so far in this section. But now such a verbal orientation is discredited as an inadequate or improper method of assimilating the images. And as more and more of the letter slots are replaced by the new images, the film enters into a realm of signification entirely unlike that of verbal language. The new nonverbal system cannot entirely prevent the intrusion of the verbal, and like the clothes in Barthes's investigation of the language of fashion, it perhaps invokes an ongoing verbal gloss. But as the control of the alphabetical sequence falls apart, the terms of an autonomous filmic grammar appear. The properties of a shot—color, movement, direction, articulation of the frame, optical manipulation of imagery, and so on—as well the multiplicity of the effects generated by the juxtaposition of different shots, articulate themselves without reference to a verbal infrastructure. Frampton has opened up to scrutiny and pleasure the way purely filmic meaning is produced at those two stages which, for him, constitute the essential activities of filmmaking: the generation of "the image bearing film strip" and the subsequent structuring of this material (Frampton, 1983: 124).

Though the conclusion to this process is not the simulation of physical reality—it produces not a Bazinian narration but rather an Eisensteinian montage of ecstatic complexity—the last section of the film does move into the realm of Bazin's long take and deep focus. Indeed, the diminution of the couple as they walk into the distance at the center of the screen seems designed to demonstrate precisely these two primary capabilities of the medium. But even here, where the film most completely subordinates its own constitution as language to the unhindered reproduction of extra-filmic space and time, representation and diegetic presence finally seep away, leaving us not with the "redemption" of physical reality, but with a formal film, a pure film (maybe a "Snow" film). Rather than corroborating a visual illusion, the sound track constructs a distance between itself and the visual scene, while the Grosseteste text comments reflexively on light, the means of the visual's reproduction. Broken into one-second fragments, language's ability to mean collapses, and it too dissolves into abstract sound. And so, as the people walk into the distance, the illusion brightens and the white light of the depicted snowstorm evaporates into the white light of the film projection. The oblivion that awaits the travelers is the oblivion of complete light, which, as Frampton himself points out (ibid.: 194), is that total film of which all others are subtractions.

As a meta-filmic demonstration of the points of articulation between verbal and film language and as a systematized meditation on film-as-language, *Zorns Lemma* raises the reflexive project of structural film to its highest abstraction. Though other films will surpass it in inflating verbal reflexivity to the point of hermetic circularity (Michael Snow's *So is This*, for example), here the congruence of structural film with structuralism is most complete; it is at once a film and a theory of film. As such, it presents itself to commentary with a disarmingly aggressive openness, itself establishing the terms of critical engagement.

In subordinating represented content to formal procedures

which, rather than adding cognitive or metaphorical inflection, demonstrate linguistic operations, *Zorns Lemma* redirects its content in the direction of form, eliminating that area where commentary can intervene to decode themes or clarify the relation of style to them. Discouraging reference through the text or out of it and rerouting questions of content to demonstrations of form, the film limits interpretation to the enumeration of filmic activity. Thus hermeneutics, if it is not to be transformed into its opposite, the "erotic" description of "the sensuous surface," according to an influential contemporary formulation (Sontag, 1966: 22), has to find a way of opening this closed linguistic circle. But since passage through the film is forbidden, the only path left is back from the film, to the spectator. Criticism of structural film was therefore initially phenomenological.

*

At their most ambitious, phenomenological readings of structural film proposed quasi-mystical theories of its trans-rational effect on the spectator. Arguments such as Sitney's that "structural film approaches the condition of meditation and evokes states of consciousness without mediation" (Sitney, 1979: 380) were corroborated by, for example, Sharits's "interest in creating temporal analogues of Tibetan mandalas" (Sharits, 1972: 39) or Gehr's desire to "make something out of the film material itself relevant to film for spiritual purposes" (Gehr, 1972: 26), as well as by the optical, "psychedelic" hyper-stimulation common in the films of both. Whatever the final status of such interpretations of the structuralist project—and we shall return to the possibility of their embodying, however distantly mediated, some trace of transcendence—they clearly parallel the great if severe beauty of many structural films and call for a theory of the sublime to mediate between the aesthetic and religious vocabularies. At the other extreme of affective models of structural film, more mundane readings propose the text not as transcendental, but as a puzzle addressed to "the decision-making and logical faculties of the viewer" (Sitney, 1979: 392). Pure forms of Sitney's "participation" films—the later work of George Landow such as *Institutional Quality* (1969), *Remedial Reading Comprehension* (1971), and *What's Wrong with This Picture* (1972), Robert Nelson's *Bleu Shut* (1970); or Hollis Frampton's *nostalgia* (1971), for instance—simply hyperbolize what amounts to a single component of the reflexive processes as a whole, that is, the reconstitution by the spectator of the generating principles of the film in those works that exploit a disjuncture between the filmstrip and the perceptual experience, between the artifact and its performance.[13]

Between these extremes lies a broader area of phenomenological theory which proposes analogies between the experience of the film work and the processes of consciousness itself, according to which exemplary instances of the former provide privileged occasions for the discovery of the contours of the latter. The proposal that "there are cinematic works which present themselves as analogues of con-

13 On this issue see especially Arthur's reading of *Empire* and *Mothlight* (Arthur, 1978), and his further consideration of Sitney's definitional condition—"that shape . . . is the primal impression of the film" (Sitney, 1979: 369)—in Arthur (1979b: 123–24). Le Grice remarks on the difficulty of recovering formal structure from perceptual experience in respect to Paul Sharits's films (Le Grice, 1977: 107).

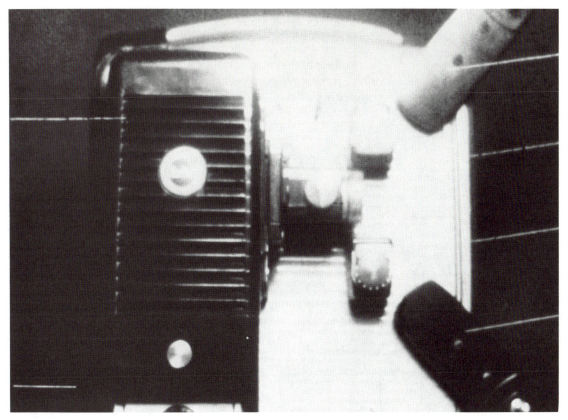

sciousness in its constitutive and reflexive modes" allows the most distinguished exponent of such an approach to read the progress of the zoom in Snow's *Wavelength*, for example, as the turning of the progress of narrative toward self-consciousness of the process of its apprehension: "its 'plot' is the tracing of spatio-temporal *données*, its 'action' the movement of the camera as the movement of consciousness" (Michelson, 1971a: 30, 32). Whatever the strategic value of such readings—and they certainly correspond to such stated intentions of the filmmakers as Frampton's proposals that the task of the cinema is "the founding of an art that is to be fully and radically isomorphic with the kineses and stases . . . of consciousness" (Frampton, 1983: 100), or that the ambition of film and video is "nothing less than the mimesis, incarnation, bodying forth of the movement of consciousness itself" (ibid.: 164)—that value is less important here than the circularity these readings reimpose on the hermeneutic process. For even if structural film does demand a critically self-conscious process of perception that breaks the identification between spectator and film to produce "not a spectator as unified subject . . . but a spectating activity, at the limit of any fixed subjectivity" (Heath, 1981: 167), and even if such revisions in the mode of industrial consumption are understood as having a political effect, commentary must nevertheless return to language as the third term which makes possible the mediation between film text and consciousness. For it is in instancing language functions in general rather than in any specific use of language or message communicated that both structural film and the structuralist way of looking at film (even if phenomenologically relocated) try to negotiate their own unity and their autonomy from society and from history.

Restating the film, formalist and phenomenological commentary can only join with it and extend it. Though the material difference between a film and a critical essay on it sustains between them the disjunction that is erased in post-structuralist commentary on modernist literary texts, still in the structural project, film and criticism come ever closer. As film more self-consciously engages film theory, its appropriate "practical criticism" is theory and it is itself composed more and more of theory. The later works of George Landow, with their references to other filmmakers, other structural films, and even to Sitney's essay on structural film in his book *Visionary Film*, demonstrate this escalation that transforms his earlier concern with the process of filmmaking and his reflexive puns on film's visual and conceptual consumption into a cannibalizing of the critical institutions in which structural film as a whole is embedded. As the critical apparatus was elaborated, the hermeneutic circle was widened but not opened.

The need for a commentary of another order becomes clear, one that can arrest the film's progress into the verbal replication of it and so understand as a historically specific condition the obsession with language that nevertheless strands film and criticism together in the muteness of a false autonomy. Such a "metacommentary"[14] will not primarily address itself to excavating from structural films the traces of social traumas concealed within them, though as the burning in Frampton, the scratching in Sharits, the visual violence in Gehr, and even the shades of concentration camp victims who flicker through *Tom, Tom, the Piper's Son* suggest, such a project is not as fanciful as might be expected. Rather, it will confront the hermeneutic closure itself, taking as its point of departure the fact that commentary of the usual kind is resisted and even precluded. Thus its object must be not this or that structural film but structural film as a whole, together with the social systems in which it is embedded. The historical specificity this commentary can recover is symptomatic in the precise sense of marking the body's attempt simultaneously to announce and accommodate a disorder. This project, that of making "structural analysis . . . pass to the rank of an object-language and be absorbed into a more complex system which will explain it in turn" (Barthes, cited in Jameson, 1972: 208), will again entail a detour through the New York art world of the fifties and sixties, but now this milieu will be argued not as the site of formal and philosophical issues at the terminus of Western representation, but as a specific social formation organized by specific social practices and historical contradictions. Only this formation can explain why, in the hunger of its most rigorous desire, film became structural.

14 The term is Fredric Jameson's (Jameson, 1971) and refers to his elaboration of a critical procedure for reading modernist texts that lack determinate content. Rather than substituting one set of meanings for that manifestly present in the text, what metacommentary seeks to do is explain the "conditions of existence" of the problem that certain texts appear to resist interpretation. In respect to structuralism and Russian Formalism, critical systems which par excellence have refused the issues of interpretation, Jameson suggests that their methodological and ideological impasse may be transcended only by transforming their basic categories into historical ones. This supplies the methodology of my attention to the processes of censorship in both structural film and structuralist criticism as themselves "reflections of a particular and determinate moment of history" (ibid.: 15).

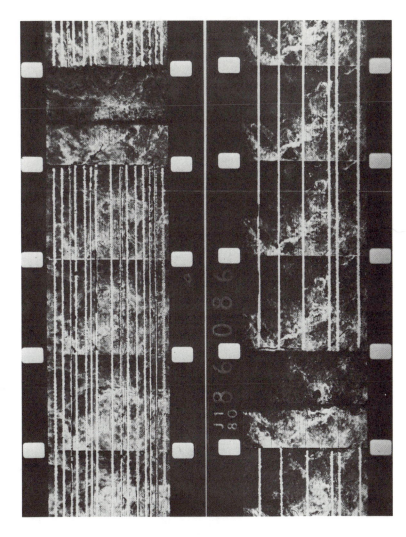

6.21 Paul Sharits,
*S:TREAM:S:S:ECTION:S:ECTION:S:S:EC-
TIONED*

The Contexts

A little formalism turns one away from History, but . . . a lot brings one back to it.
— Roland Barthes

Whether from the point of view of the determinations upon it or
of its own participation in the cultural field, the problem of structural film's political significance is exacerbated by the fact that the
turn toward pure formalism occurred at exactly the height of domestic politicization. The great monuments of structural film were
all made after 1967, and by 1974 the movement was essentially
spent. In its contrast with the underground's use of aesthetic radicalism as the vehicle of social transformation, this paradigmatically
modernist conjunction of aesthetic radicalism and social quietism
demands that the exclusion of content from structural film be
understood specifically as the refusal of *social* content, and that

filmic reflexiveness be read as the repression of cinematic reflexiveness, especially since elsewhere attention to filmic signification was understood as the precondition of political responsibility. In the post-1968 cine-groups in France and almost simultaneously in Cuba, Argentina, and Japan, the critique of representation provided the Brechtian bridge that allowed the filmmakers to claim continuity with the exemplary union of formal and political radicalism in early Soviet art. Within this international avant-garde, which by the turn of the decade included several radically formalist cinemas in Europe, it became common to distinguish between structural film's scrutiny of the materials of film and the critique of Hollywood codes in politically engaged narrative films, preeminently Godard's.

Though each school thought itself politically correct, relations between them were never sympathetic. Godard commonly attacked the co-op movement as merely the occupant of the basement of the house of Hollywood, and while the structural filmmakers and critics were better informed (for example, Paul Sharits's first publication was an appreciative article on *A Woman is a Woman* [Sharits, 1966]), they saw Godard's concern with illusionism as his having "*backed into* the work and the theoretical positions of the American independents" (Michelson, 1972b: 62). While the attempts to provide a theoretical bridge between these "Two Avant-Gardes" (Wollen, 1982) argued them as heirs of the cubist and of the early Soviet cinema respectively, in fact both sides claimed descent from the Russians, despite the fact that, as with structuralism and its uncle, Russian Formalism, structural film's entire lack of political content left it vulnerable to the tradition of Marxist anti-formalism. Thus Trotsky's attack on the Formalist School, Brecht's attack on abstract painting, Lukács's attack on modernism's inability to narrate, and even Plekhanov's argument that aestheticism "arises and takes root whenever people engaged in art are hopelessly out of harmony with their social environment" (Plekhanov, 1957: 38) are all implicit in Godard's attack on the underground's supposed disengagement, or in *Cinéthiques*'s dismissal of the "experimental art" cinema (Harvey, 1980: 162). While none of these positions could adequately account for the social determination of artistic production or for the degree to which even the purest formalist exercise may contain some aesthetic disturbance with the potential for cognitive reorganization, the opposite proposition, that aesthetic renewal or the demystification of the art process effected by formally advanced film necessarily produces an ideological rupture, is entirely idealist.

The crucial figure over whom this issue was contested was Dziga Vertov. Though overshadowed by Eisenstein in the thirties, Vertov was known in the United States and even regarded as a hero by the Workers Film and Photo League, for example. As early as 1962 *Film Culture* republished the selection of his writings that had appeared in 1935 in the Film and Photo League's short-lived journal, *Film Front*. While the *Lef* and *Novy Lef* debates were being taken up again in France, with Vertov championed against Eisenstein as the

6.22 Dziga Vertov, *The Man with the Movie Camera*

model for "making films politically," he was simultaneously being hailed as the progenitor of the phenomenological project of structuralism.

The argument was most lucidly made by Annette Michelson, and her *Artforum* article " 'The Man with the Movie Camera': From Magician to Epistemologist" (Michelson, 1972a) argued that Vertov's hyperbolic extension of the techniques of montage and his use of tropes like reverse motion as the "formal pivot of his epistemological discourse" (ibid.: 66) were the apogee of the mapping of the mind by film language, the place where "epistemological inquiry and the cinematic consciousness converge in dialectical mimesis" (ibid.: 63). Corroborating this specific continuity, Vertov's dismissal of the acted, theatrical film—"the sweet embraces of the romance,/the poison of the psychological novel,/the clutches of the theater of adultery" (Vertov, 1984: 7)—and even his preference for "the poetry of machines" over "man as a subject for film" are variously present in the structural filmmakers' interest in "the higher drama of: celluloid, two-dimensional strips; individual rectangular frames; the nature of sprockets and emulsion; projector operations" (Sharits, 1969: 13).[15] But the supposition that this anti-humanist reflexivity accounts for the totality of Vertov's achievement or even for its significance distorts not only its nature, but also the implications of the real parallels between his work and structural film. By emphasizing the phenomenological and aesthetically "materialist" component in Vertov's work, structural film theorists were able to appropriate it, but they could do so only by suppressing its preconditions. For as well as being the documentarist of the filmstrip, Vertov was the documentarist of Lenin, the poet of a political as well as an aesthetic revolution. However much you wanted Vertov, he could never come without socialism.

15 Though Sharits himself rejected the drawing of morphological analogies between the human body and nonhuman instruments—the "exclamatory presumptions that Vertov's 'Kino Eye' concept typifies" (Sharits, 1972: 36).

16 As Godard himself recognized. See the discussion in Chapter 5 of his contribution to *Far From Vietnam*. The turning of political content into the form of such content is not an aesthetic but a social inevitability, the function not of the manner in which a text is constructed but of the conditions that determine its use. Adorno's remark that the "primacy of lesson over pure form, which Brecht intended to achieve, became a formal device itself" (Adorno, 1977b: 185) is equally applicable to Godard, and in both cases it marks the return of social relations of production and consumption as the determinant of form. The large version of this inevitability is not the historical emergence of structural film and of structuralism, but the tendency of Marxist criticism to become another formalism, which it can only avoid by entering into "non-formalist" relations with working-class movements.

17 A parallel distinction is more thoroughly adumbrated in the difference between Vertov's own *The Man with the Movie Camera* and the film of the same name made by the English structural filmmaker David Crosswaite, in which a small mirror mounted in front of the camera relays into the film the operations of the cameraman. See Le Grice (1977: 132–33). Compare also the various interludes of instructions about the use of the projector in the films of George Landow, Morgan Fisher, and Standish Lawder with the brief sequence in *Ice*, mentioned above, in which a young woman is similarly instructed.

Despite the political turmoil of the twenties and the controversies over the correct line for cinema before the imposition of realism at the All-Union Party Conference in 1928, the specificity of the Soviet artist's situation in respect to the human and technological materials of his art was conditioned by the general nature of social relations in that society. Vertov's ability to be realistic simultaneously in both ontologies, that of the filmic and the profilmic, was a function of the revolutionary transcendence of those distinctions between artist and society, producer and consumer, filmmaker and subject that exist in capitalism. For him reality was a continuum, from the practice of filmmaking to the practice of social construction—from the single film frame to *One Sixth of the Earth*—unsundered by structural contradictions, even if that social wholeness were still under construction. The evidence of this, the precondition of the continuity of the modernist, reflexive documentation of the film practice and the realist representation of social life, is everywhere in his films (even if, as in the *Kino Pravda* series, for example, it includes social chaos); but nowhere is it more visible than in the represented role of the artist and of technology. For in documenting the continuity between the machinery of cinema and the machinery of material production, in documenting the continuity between the worker and the artist, Vertov demonstrated that in socialist societies, art can spring free from its alienation and recognize that cultural production is social.

The difference between Vertov and structural film, which appears as the presence of content in the one and its absence in the other, is a priori determined by the nature of the social relationships involved in their different modes of film production. The ineluctability of capitalist social relations engenders the pure formalism of structural film, as it does the ironies of the films of Godard, who in this sense was no less alienated,[16] inevitably having more in common with Frank Tashlin than with Vertov himself. This social difference is summarized in the difference between the *de ta fabula narratur* trope as it occurs in the intertitle from *One Sixth of the Earth*, which reads "This Film Is About You," and the title "This Is A Film About You," which appears in Landow's *Remedial Reading Comprehension*. In the first case the film addresses the *zoon politikon*, the social being engaged in revolutionary social construction; in the second, the autonomous perceptual faculties of the monadic bourgeois subject.[17] Similarly, in Frampton's clarion call, "From now on we will call our art simply: film" (Frampton, 1983: 114), the orientation toward the materials marks an actual as well as a symbolic repression of the social relations of the medium. As in his entire project of remaking film history as it should have been, for Frampton himself to secure film, he had to exclude cinema. The utopian condition of Vertov's reflexivity was that film and cinema were unified in post-revolutionary labor.

The suppression of the social conditions of structural film's production was the precondition of the sphere of formal integrity it wrested from these conditions. But that alienation from its maker,

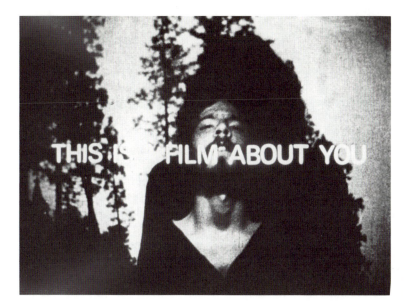

6.23 George Landow, *Remedial Reading Comprehension*

from its social context, and from history—which we must now see allegorized in every structural film—defines it precisely as that form of critical negation that Theodor Adorno attributed to the second Vienna school of composition (and it is surely not uninteresting that one of the first and most rigorous structural films, *Arnulf Rainer*, should have been made by the Viennese, Peter Kubelka). It is in terms of Adorno's model of modernism that the social determination of structural film, both embodied and repressed, begins to yield a theory of it that is at once analytic and evaluative. This is the first level of its metacommentary.

STRUCTURAL FILM AS DETERMINATE NEGATION

Adorno argued that in liberating the intra-subjective elements of expressionism, Schoenberg first made available the "elements of aesthetic objectivity" (Adorno, 1973: 48) and so established the paradigmatic modernist praxis, the pursuit of the formal logic of the medium itself. In Schoenberg's case this entailed the final dissolution of tonality into the systematic variations of the twelve-tone row to produce an art whose relationship to its society was one of *definitive negation*: "Its truth appears guaranteed more by its denial of any meaning in organized society, of which it will have no part—accomplished by its own organized vacuity—than by any capability of positive meaning within itself" (ibid.: 20). Separating itself from the culture as a whole, art of this kind affirms its autonomy as both the reflection of its historical moment and the refusal of it. "Art is the negative knowledge of the actual world" (Adorno, 1977a: 160); and instead of resolving "objective contradictions in a spurious harmony, [it] expresses the idea of harmony negatively by embodying the contradictions, pure and uncompromised, in its innermost structure" (Adorno, 1967: 32).

In forcing a representational tradition into abstraction and thence into the investigation of its own intrinsic procedures, and especially in displacing the spectator's attention from empirical presence to the cognition of the structure of the whole, structural film corresponds much more closely to Schoenbergian modernism than it does to any previous film practice, including Russian constructivism. While it may, then, be valorized according to Adorno's model, in this it becomes vulnerable to the nondialectical idealisms in Adorno that derive from his overestimation of the practical negative potential of modernist art. As later events have made clear, not only does the mass media absorb antagonistic cultural practices, it depends on them. On the other hand, structural film has proven less assimilable and less available as a means of renewing industrial production than virtually any other development in postwar culture; even the academic circulation of structual film remains minimal. In the continued beauty of its resistance, it most justly epitomizes the aspiration of all the marginal cinemas of the period, as well as standing to reproach cultural practices of less integrity.

Structural film's sustained marginality registers a resistance to consumer society that allows us to celebrate it as a cultural second dimension—a "beautiful image of liberation" (Marcuse, 1978: 6) that opens the otherwise total closure of the consciousness industries; such an evaluation, however idealist in this formulation, nevertheless supplies the terms for a properly materialist understanding of the conditions of structural film's production. On this next level metacommentary becomes historical explanation; the various polemical issues used to justify structural film—art as negation, the renewal of perception, resistance to illusion—may be recast as the matrix of its historical intervention, its dialectical situation in respect to the film industry. Here the assumption by film of the formal preoccupations of painting and sculpture appears as a migration between mediums and their different constitutions as social practices; film ceased to be movies in order to become art—in both senses. Structural film's flight from the theater of the popular was a response to the social pressures that also produced the Greenbergian aesthetic imperatives we initially used to understand it. The terms of its very success stand as the sign of social impossibilities.

Though in Adorno's model the prevalence of industrial culture directly influences modernism's own self-formulation, the progress of a parallel influence in the case of American film can best be framed by Clement Greenberg's slightly different formulations, as well as by the history of the mutations in his critical theory. In the 1939 essay "Avant-Garde and Kitsch," he proposed categories essentially parallel to Adorno's (and indeed Adorno cites them in his essay on Schoenberg [Adorno, 1973: 10]), except that rather than identifying the avant-garde as genuine art, he saw it and kitsch together as complementary inevitabilities in a period when real art is impossible. In his conception of Picasso's or Joyce's modernist aestheticism, "the reduction of experience to expression for the sake of expression, the expression mattering more than what is being expressed," is intrinsically reflexive, for "avant-garde culture is the imitating of imitating," a fact that in and of itself "calls for neither approval nor disapproval" (Greenberg, 1961: 8). In place of Adorno's negation, which though proffered as a category of theory is nevertheless subject to empirical verification and dispute, prewar Greenberg proposed an ontological description whose verification displaced evaluation of the art object into evaluation of the society at large; the avant-garde and kitsch are "simultaneous" cultural phenomena, for "if the avant-garde imitates the processes of art, kitsch . . . imitates its effects" (ibid.: 15).

What is valuable about this circuitous Platonism is not simply Greenberg's prescience in focusing on reflexivity in a period when discussion of the avant-garde was dominated by the formal and moral implications of expressionism, but rather his recognition that such a formal redirection corresponded to transformations in the economic nature of the art object and its social situation. When the avant-garde was subsidized by the ruling class, it was able to maintain its aesthetic integrity; but in 1939 Greenberg thought its abandonment by those who supported it, "by those to whom it actually belongs—our ruling class," threatened its survival.

By the sixties, after World War II and the cold war, Greenberg's explicitly Marxist orientation had been lost along with the Marxist culture of the thirties that had made it possible. His attention to the social contexts of modernism's aporias had been subsumed in the essentialism of critical formalism, which demanded the repression of all consideration of the economic and political nature of the art world and of the role of the commodity object within it.[18] This history of American art, of the social conditions under which abstract expressionism and subsequent American painting was produced and the uses, both domestic and international, to which it was put, is the determining context of structural film. The restoration of its complementarity to the mass media, to kitsch, is thus an excavation of Greenberg's original model of the situation of the avant-garde in industrial capitalism, the loss of which analysis may be read not only in structural film but also in its contemporary theorization. Understanding what made structural film both possible and necessary thus demands investigation of the art world as a social practice.

FILM IN THE ART WORLD

In the introduction to the catalogue for the highly influential Rockefeller-sponsored Museum of Modern Art (MOMA) exhibition—*The New American Painting*—that toured eight countries in 1958–59, Alfred Barr presented what had become the official theory of expressionism.

Indeed one often hears Existential echoes in their words, but their "anxiety," their commitment, their "dreadful freedom"

18 On this shift see T. J. Clark (1983).

concern their work primarily. They defiantly reject the conventional values of the society which surrounds them, but they are not politically engagés even though their paintings have been praised and condemned as symbolic demonstrations of freedom in a world in which freedom connotes a political attitude. (Cited in Cockroft, 1974: 41)

Asserting a relationship between American freedom and painting, yet simultaneously defusing any subversive potential in the latter by re-containing it as formal or symbolic only, Barr summarized the terms by which a marginal, parochial art had become culturally central and entangled in all the operations of U.S. capitalism.

The opprobrium of abstraction's supposed affiliation with the communism of the immediate postwar years[19] gave way, certainly in higher social echelons, to recognition of its compatibility with American political ambitions in the cold war years and of its utility in cultural diplomacy. The social anxiety that lay behind the activism of the young Jackson Pollock, for example, or behind the political self-consciousness of Robert Motherwell and the general climate of the thirties had been internalized as formal anxieties about the relationship of the artist to the painting and especially about the relationship of one part of the painting to the others.[20] Thus even the scandalous iconoclasm of Action Painting in fact bespoke a social quietism: "The lone artist did not want the world to be different, he wanted his canvas to be a world" (Rosenberg, 1959: 30). As the School of New York reinvigorated Parisian modernism to reexport it in USIA-sponsored traveling shows, the international prestige and cold-war function of American painting were matched by the transformations in the domestic market; and in the domestic art world of the sixties, contradictions similar to those that surrounded the international use of Abstract Expressionism proliferated.

By the sixties painting had become a profession that could be engaged in "as a career the same as law, medicine, or government" (Larry Rivers, cited in Zukin, 1982: 436), and the painting itself the commodity basis for a self-sustaining, self-validating interlocking system of professions and trades, of aesthetic, critical, commercial, and industrial activities.[21] Unlike Hollywood and the institutional apparatus of other mediums, the New York art establishment was still relatively malleable and accessible to new interests and pressures, though it had stabilized to the point where its institutions and procedures allowed it to be self-sustaining yet integrated into the overall economic and political structures of the country. Within this loose formation three areas may be distinguished: (1) a number of artists, living and working mostly in lower Manhattan, who, through their friends, dealers, and hangers-on, diffused into (2) a critical and marketing establishment based on galleries, museums, journals, and educational institutions that mediated the art object into (3) the larger financial establishment of collectors, investors, corporate donations and patronage, the larger museums, and even-

19 While abstract art of all styles was frequently associated with communism, the majority of attacks on artists during the fifties were focused on left imagery in representational painting and usually succeeded in causing its repression in government-sponsored murals and exhibitions. See Hauptman (1973).

20 Though not unselfconsciously. Motherwell himself remained keenly aware of the artist's alienation but also of the contradictions in the aesthetic, "individualist" freedom achieved by the artist; see his 1944 essay "The Modern Painter's World" (Motherwell, [1944] 1968). On the relations between Abstract Expressionism and the cold war see Kozloff (1973); Cockroft (1974); and the less useful Guilbaut (1983).

21 For the art world "Described as a System," see Alloway (1972). Sociological description of the art world, which began with Rosenberg (1965), has recently become more professionally analytic in studies that link the lower Manhattan social and real estate developments with the uses made of art in contemporary bourgeois society. See especially Simpson (1981) and Zukin (1982). Tomkins (1980), provides an engrossing personal account of life in the art world in the heyday of pop and after.

tually state organizations like USIA with international mandates. Though distinctions within the total system can be made, by contrasting one part against another—artists against dealers, for example, or academic critics against journalists—or by distinguishing between the nature of the art object at different points in its circulation through the total system,[22] privileging any one point in the system at the expense of the others only obscures the contradictions that inhabit all stages of modern art production.

At the center is the double-ness of the art object itself, whose aesthetic, cognitive, or even metaphysical value only ends up as the vehicle of its commodity function, its capacity for speculative investment. As Marx noted, what the artist produces "as a silkworm produces silk, as the actualization of *his own* nature . . . is taken over by capital and only occurs in order to increase it" (Marx, 1977–81, I: 1044); and his idealized organic model only slightly exaggerates a real contradiction. For even as the artist, the process of art making, and the artist's studio were all promoted as reservations of authenticity in an alienated world, they were simultaneously fetishized as such and the whole gestalt then used to authorize the commodity art object. The successful artists' wealth and fame and the glamour of their lives were simultaneously the reward and the indictment of their art.

So while the assumption of any deep conflict between avant-garde painting and its bourgeois milieu is certainly "simplistic" (Kozloff, 1973: 43), the opposite assumption of direct, easy homologies between the form and content of art and its function within American capitalism and imperialism is equally problematical.[23] Even pop art, which frequently narrated its own collusion, typically contained some ironic counter-text that signaled ideological distance; apart from Warhol's savagely complex capitalization, the work of James Rosenquist may best summarize such strategies. And, more clearly in the entire conceptualist, earth-works, body-works phase of early seventies art, alongside the critique of representation there ran a continuous if incomplete attempt to subvert the market function of the artwork. Nor was the art world itself as politically inactive as is often supposed. A continuing political sensitivity that first became openly committed in 1965 with a full-page advertisement in the *New York Times* protesting the war (and including Allan D'Arcangelo, Elaine de Kooning, Richard Diebenkorn, Mark di Suvero, Leon Golub, Red Grooms, Harold Rosenberg, and Tom Wesselman among its five hundred signatories) became especially active between 1968 and 1972. The California Peace Tower, the Angry Arts Week, the protest around the 1968 MOMA dada show, various alternative exhibitions, and the formation of the Art Workers Coalition were some of the signs of a revival of thirties activism.[24] So while aesthetic and political resistance to mass culture and capitalism were undermined by the economic activities that constituted the art world, neither the art nor the artists were totally at the service of the corporate state. The utopian desire and its denial that shim-

22 Though it is available to anyone who can point to someone else more compromised than themselves, the former is often invoked by those artists who have political self-consciousness forced upon them by marketplace failure, or who arrive at it by other means, as happened in New York in the early to mid-seventies. See the first two issues of *The Fox*. For the latter, see Alloway (1972: 29): "Art is a commodity in a part of the system but not in all of it." Alloway notes that the market value of art which before 1960 was a source of prestige subsequently came to be regarded as "the taint of corruption" (ibid.).

23 Kozloff's own blanket assertion that New York School art as a whole has an "allure" that stems from an equivocal yet profound glorifying of American civilization is just such an oversimplification.

24 For further documentation see Therese Schwartz's series of articles "The Politicalization of the Avant-Garde" (Schwartz, 1971–74).

6.24 Paul Sharits, projection installation,
Walker Art Center, 1974

mered together like a mirage in the formal integrity and rigor of the
best sixties art were not absent from the social praxes through
which it came into being.

As film engaged the formal issues of post–Abstract Expressionist
art, it engaged its characteristic mode of production and its institutional support system and so entered into determination by the contradictions of all these. Free to depart from the conditions of theatrical social insertion, structural film moved not toward integration
in communal social processes, as happened with the utopian edge
of the underground, but in the opposite direction, toward achieving
the reified presence of the art object. Art museums, galleries, and
universities became the preferred place of exhibition, with installa-
tions and loop projections common, and often with the projectors
themselves visible—included as part of the process to assert the materiality of the operations of the entire apparatus. In instances like
the work of Anthony McCall, attempts were made to substantiate
the projection of light as essentially a sculpture, while elsewhere the
duration of projection was reduced into the timelessness of painting
by making more or less extensive selections from the film simultaneously visible; Sharits's "Frozen Film Frames" of *Piece Mandala*
and other films and Tony Conrad's "Yellow Movies" are examples

of a practice going back to Warhol's blowups of frames from *Sleep* on plexiglass. Correlated as these activities were with the selling of films that was begun by major sixties galleries like Castelli-Sonnabend, and with the supplementation of the independent distribution apparatuses inherited from the underground by other art world marketing organizations such as Visual Resources, Inc., they should all be understood as attempts to acquire for film the object-hood that created the marketability of the unique painting or the limited-edition print.

At the same time, structural film developed a theoretical support system within the art-critical establishment. Glossy illustrated catalogs with interpretative essays by art critics accompanied domestic exhibitions, such as "Projected Images" at the Walker Art Center in Minneapolis, and international ones, such as "New Forms in Film" at Montreux, both in 1974. Most important, after Sitney's first formulation of the movement's terms in *Film Culture* in 1969, significant criticism appeared not in film journals (though *Film Culture* did continue to represent structural film), but in art magazines, especially *Artforum*. Championing the work of Frampton, Joyce Wieland, Jacobs, Sharits, Snow, Landow, and Joan Jonas and Richard Serra as "an achievement whose importance will eventually be seen as comparable to that of American painting in the 1950s and onwards," Annette Michelson edited a Special Film Issue devoted to these filmmakers (Michelson, 1971b; quotation, p. 9), as well as subsequently writing on several of them herself.

But though structural film was an avant-garde art practice taking place within the parameters of the art world, it was unable to achieve the centrally important function of art in capitalist society: the capacity for capital investment. Massive public indifference to it, its inaccessibility to all but those of the keenest sensibility, and finally its actual rather than merely ostensible inability to be incorporated excluded it from the blue-chip functions, the mix of real estate and glamour, that floated the art world. Since structural film could neither become a commodity nor even support itself, it had to be subsidized by the institutions that supported the art world, while these, rather than delivering the artist to wealthy collectors or corporate investors, now were obliged to become themselves its financiers. Though grants had been awarded to underground filmmakers through the sixties—the Ford Foundation gave several independent filmmakers, including Kenneth Anger, $10,000 in 1964, for instance (Sitney, 1979: 124)—the underground had been supported by the subculture and its sympathizers. But almost from the beginning structural film was supported by museums, by state and federal grants, and marginally by colleges and universities, where jobs for avant-garde filmmakers were becoming available by the early seventies.[25]

In its reflexive attention to filmic signification, structural film reached not only the semiological limits of the medium, but also its economic and social limits. Film's inability to produce a readily marketable object, together with the mechanical reproducibility of

25 Extensive information on this is not generally available, but summaries of two exemplary biographies give a sample. The biography of Paul Sharits in *Film Culture* (Sharits, 1978) records continuous academic employment from 1970 to 1973 with grants in the same period from the American Film Institute, the Ford Foundation (two awards), the National Endowment for the Arts, New York's Creative Artists Public Service Program, and the New York State Council on the Arts. Hollis Frampton began his academic employment as an assistant professor at Hunter College in 1969 and was appointed associate professor at the State University of New York at Buffalo in 1973, where he remained until his death. Although he regularly had major retrospectives—at the Walker Art Center in 1972; at MOMA in 1975; at Knokke-Heist, Belgium, in 1974; at Anthology Film Archives in 1975; at Rijksmuseum, Otterlo, Netherlands, in 1977, for example—grants came tardily until, after a 1975 National Endowment for the Arts award for the completion of *Straits of Magellan*, they virtually became annual. See Jenkins and Krane (1984: 106–19).

its texts, set very narrow limits to the possibility of structural film's being turned into a commodity. Like underground film, it was still subculturally produced, and traces of its social origin are everywhere. Even a thoroughly centripetal work such as Morgan Fisher's *Production Stills* cannot record the means of its production without also recording the group of friends who constitute its amateur company, and in other structural films the delineation of quite rigid social boundaries often accompanies the definition of filmic axioms. The almost unvaried litany of names that runs from Sitney's first list of structural filmmakers through subsequent criticism is invoked in the films themselves so regularly that vestiges of the underground's subcultural definition are clear. Michael Snow's *"Rameau's Nephew,"* "acted" by the luminaries of the New York artists' film world, including its critics and theorists, is exemplary in this respect, but even a film like Hollis Frampton's *nostalgia* can be seen as a displaced beat documentary. The people who come from Frampton's past into the film—Carl André, "a young painter," Frank Stella, James Rosenquist, "a painter friend," Michael Snow, and Larry Poons—are all artists and all friends.

But despite the social milieu that can be recovered, the economic and other determinants of subcultural production could not be for-

6.25 Hollis Frampton, *nostalgia*

mally included among the filmic procedures structural film displayed—except negatively: even as he recognizes his social environment in *nostalgia*, Frampton also destroys it, burning his social bridges behind him, as if he were allegorizing his passage into an aesthetic and institutional system that demanded the cancellation of personal history.

We may see Frampton's denial as an emblem of structural film's need to efface its social function, to burn the evidence of its social context, in order that its formal purity might shine through. The interdependence of formal qualities and the conditions of production thus became completely circular. Relinquishing the populist ambitions of the underground and the revolutionary ones of contemporary political filmmakers, structural film became Art, high culture distinct from and opposed to the mass media in general and the film industry and even other independent film in particular. But in thus repressing its social milieu, it deprived itself of anything to represent. Its anathematization of narrative was as much a social inevitability as a formal choice. Precluded from engaging or even recognizing its own social situation, it had no story to tell. The formal concerns, the absence of content, and the insistent reflexivity all corresponded to an absence of any positive social function, the denial of any audience but the specialist. Its symbolic utopia of uncompromised film was achieved not merely by negating all previous uses and situations of film, but by negating cinema.

POLITICS AND FILM LANGUAGE

The hermeneutic recovery of the social absence upon which structural film is predicated, the return of its repressed milieu, also recovers its social meaning; its acts of repudiation and disengagement oblige the analyst to organize systems of mediation whose complexity correspond precisely to structural film's own need for censorship. As in the paradigmatic instance of the dream-work, an elaborate system of condensations, displacements, and inversions lies between phenomenal appearance and the motivating cause. As in similar cases, like the Revolutionary Ensemble's record, *The People's Republic*, and Jean-Marie Straub's "dedication" of *The Chronicle of Anna Magdalena Bach* (1968) to the North Vietnamese, establishing a connection between absolute formal purity and some kind of political responsibility demands the reconstruction of a tortuous path through the chain of historical determinations: the capitalist mode of material production; the industrial mode of film production; the flight of film from the industry into the art world; the history of the art world; the art world's formal preoccupations and the social relations it depends on. The path is so distended and involves so many complicated maneuvers that to reduce the entire system to a statement of simple causality in the end makes explanation seem like indictment.

But it is possible to summarize the relation between the extremities of this cultural field, between structural film and the social conditions of its period—even the most militant contestation of the Vietnam War—through the single mediating category of film language, specifically, through the crisis in the relation of language to the extra-linguistic world of which structuralism is the ideology. But now we will be able to consider language not as a virtually autonomous, self-regulating, endlessly divisible pattern of formal permutations and combinations—the formalist model of language in general presupposed by structuralism and engaged by structural film— but rather as a historically specific, concrete social practice, integrated with similarly specific social functions. By restoring the structural film's investigation of film language to the historical moment that made it possible and necessary, we may restore the language of stuctural film to its context in cinema.

In the late sixties, the pandemic modernist crisis in language was exacerbated by the crisis in public confidence in the media, a crisis which was given a peculiarly public form as interior psychic tensions were projected as public issues. Following two decades of debate about the advertising industry that accompanied the postwar growth of the consumer society, liberal-pluralist theories of the mass media rapidly lost ground in the face of anxiety about the mendacity of public discourse and especially about the appropriation of public discourse by consumer industries and corporate military interests. Widespread concern about the administration, military, and media accounts of the Vietnam War summarized this anxiety—an anxiety so extreme that official statements about the war coming from Washington could be considered as much a symptom of the national illness as the war itself (Merton, 1969: 100). The war was language. Though the contradictions in public discourse, especially those deriving from actual corporate control of ostensibly public discourse, were probably no more extreme than at any other time, their effect was felt so severely that alternative media sprung up in all areas of cultural activity. The renaissance in independent newspapers is exemplary, fueled as it was by the same pressures that forced underground filmmakers to give over documenting their own marginal life styles and instead to confront the industrial media more aggressively. While the new political cinema was often filmically naive, it was socially—cinematically—very self-conscious. The opposite occurred with structural film; it became invested with all the energies that its position in the art world prevented it from addressing. The social and the cinematic were internalized as questions of film: "we will call our art simply: film" (Frampton, 1983: 114).

It is here, then, at the point where structural film's repression of cinema is juxtaposed to the conditions determining the hegemonic cinema, that the moment of structural film in the history of cinema as a whole becomes clear. Here the instrumentality of its non-instrumentality may be retrieved. The formal exclusion of narrative—the condition of both its transcendence of illusion and its fetishizing of its own materials and of language as such—is the condition of its self-definition against the discourse of the hegemony. As Ernie Gehr demonstrated, in structural film's desire to transcend kitsch and the operations of ideology in mass culture, any history other than that of the seepage of light through the sprocket holes of the optical printer was simply inconceivable. The withdrawal of film from the hopelessly contaminated public sphere of industrial cinema, even from the culturally circumscribed sphere of the underground, into the artificially sustained false autonomy of the art world was thus a social strategy in which nonintervention became the only possible uncompromised or unassimilable intervention. But while history allowed afunctionality the function of figuring integrity, it concealed a final irony.

The apparent lack of use that permitted the sixties art object to enter into the social sphere of the aesthetic was immediately contained by its actual function in the political operations of the art world. However much the restraints on structural film's social insertion and indeed its actual rather than merely ostensible resistance to consumption denied it an equivalent investment and utility, it was not entirely without use, and it did play a limited role in the culture. But the ambiguities involved in proposing aesthetic negation as social resistance increased as attempts to valorize it became more explicit and articulate. In the United States, since the Frank-

6.26 Ernie Gehr, *History*

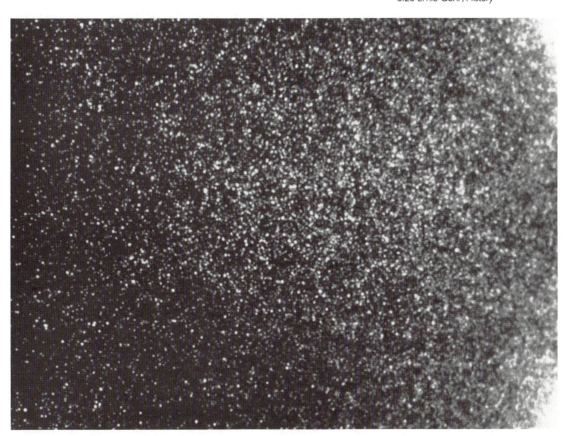

furt school's critical orientation excluded it from the theoretical field, a political function for structural film was not argued except in neoformalist appeals, tenuous at best, to the significance of perceptual renewal. But in Europe, an explicitly political significance was claimed for a mutation, a hyperbolic extension, of at least one aspect of the general gestalt of structural film procedures. And as such claims were made, they brought to light contradictions that forced the rhetoric of transgression to ever more extreme gestures.

The performance in the filmic of negations whose real context was the cinematic set in motion a dialectical reduction that, once initiated, could never retrieve stability this side of absolute negation—the refusal to make films at all. The shift from an ex post facto critical reading of a given work as negatively determined to a critically prescriptive program of social intervention by means of formal gestures of negation opens a hierarchy of degrees of refusal. Like the sublations of the meta-filmic in general, any limitation of this or that aspect of filmic meaning, any rejection of this or that area of filmic pleasure, establishes a position that is immediately vulnerable to the insertion of yet another layer of self-consciousness which will contain it, or to a more severe formal reduction against which it will itself appear collusive or sentimental. While from the outside such successive outflanking maneuvers appear as a filmic version of Freud's "narcissism of minor differences," internally they register the coming into visibility of extreme historical compulsions. In England, in an intellectual milieu nourished by a social moment entirely less opulent than that of Soho, such a vista of imperatives became clear.

In the group around the London Film Co-op and especially in the "Structural/Materialist" filmmaking and theoretical project of Peter Gidal (himself a displaced American), which attempted to infuse the idealist foundations of both French structuralism and American structural film with an explicitly *materialist* component, the repudiation of the illusionist narrative codes of the commercial feature was only the first step in a *via negativa* of unprecedented severity. Claiming an identification between the materiality of the apparatus and the materiality of the Marxian dialectic, this project repudiated even those aspects of the avant-garde, such as the films of Straub and Godard, that had previously been taken as containing exemplary political strategies. Arguing for and making films that could only display but neither represent nor document their own production, Gidal allowed film to operate only "in that space of tension between materialist flatness, grain, light, movement, and the supposed real reality that is represented" (Gidal, 1975: 189). Works like *Room Film* (1973) and *Condition of Illusion* (1975) are, then, filmic events designed to tease the spectator into knowledge of the conditions of their production.

Though Gidal's project originated in the felt need to resist the contamination of the film medium by the film industry, so total and categorical had that contamination become that his reaction against it had the status of a transhistorical absolute that reconstituted a

Greenbergian medium-specific essentialism as a political as well as a logical imperative. It appeared not simply that all images were corrupted, but that dependence on representation per se bespoke an intolerable empiricism; all a film could validly do was produce knowledge—and the only permissible knowledge was the knowledge of its own production. Despite its Puritan urgency, Gidal's position ultimately consumed itself, for even as it discredited all previous film production, it supplied the grounds for its own discrediting. All it could do was point the way to the absolute reduction, making intolerable anything this side of the pure, uninflected light of the projector.

But in taking the project of structural film to its logical conclusion, in discovering structuralism's structuralism and the modernism of filmic modernism, Gidal's project retrospectively illuminated the social determination of structural film in general. It made evident what had been implicit and inevitable all along. The contradictions in capitalist cultural production are irreconcilable and ineluctable, and they force the most extreme responses upon those filmmakers who most love the art. In order to save film, they had to destroy it.

7 The American Art Film: Production as Narration

There is no American "art" film.
— Jonas Mekas

Il copione non ha neanche i pregi di un film di rottura, anche se a volte sembra averne le deficienze.
(The script doesn't even have the values of an avant-garde film, even if at times it seems to have some of the deficiencies.)
— Daumier to Guido, in Fellini's *8 1/2*

Structural film marks an edge of cinema, the apotheosis of modernist aestheticism in which a severe beauty was honed on social despair. So fundamentally recalcitrant that it was completely coherent only when it negated the entire previous constitution of the medium, it summarizes the impossibility of the political intervention of the aesthetic as such. Its innovations also hyperbolically summarize a history of alternative film practices, for as the logical and chronological result of the failure of a genuinely popular narrative cinema to emerge out of the crises of the industry, structural film thus finally justified the ideology of an autonomous avant-garde by generating a totalized antithesis to Hollywood. "American cinema remains in Hollywood and the New York underground. There is no American 'art' film" (Mekas, [1964] 1972: 120).

In Mekas's mid-sixties analysis of the polarization of American film into mutually exclusive modes of production, the missing third term, the absent "art" film, marks the failure of early sixties attempts to reform industrial practice with a cinema responsive to the needs of the general public. That failure notwithstanding, by the early seventies enough individual attempts had been made that something like an American New Wave did exist, and indeed its summary achievement would be Mekas's own magisterial meta-cinematic meditation, *Lost Lost Lost*, in 1976. Before that film, isolated, autonomous productions of the kind cited in the "Statement" of the New American Cinema Group had become sufficiently numerous and their thematic preoccupations sufficiently conventional that they approached the status of a genre, a specifically American equivalent of the European art film, even though the sclerotic hegemony of the studios, together with the more extreme politicization of potentially reformative practices that accompanied the disintegration of the social consensus, prevented any general social function for the "genre" and ensured that it would remain essentially a series of ad hoc entrepreneurial efforts.[1]

1 Coinciding with the late forties crises in Hollywood, the American audience for European films crystallized especially around Italian neorealism. By the mid-fifties, over six hundred cinemas located in large cities and college communities exhibited art films at least part time. See Jowett (1976: 377–79) for the American currency of the European art film, and Turan and Zito (1974) and *The Report of the Commission on Obscenity and Pornography* (1970) for the art film's intersection with exploitation films.

Dissolving at its extremes into the underground on the one hand and into independent industrial productions and eventually even "anti-establishment" studio features like *Bonnie and Clyde* and *Midnight Cowboy* on the other, this tradition of anomalies forms a continuum between them. Its scope, which includes films that date from the early sixties through to the point when the *auteur* productions of the New Hollywood gave way before the mid-seventies revival of studio mega-productions, may be indicated by the following examples: *Pull My Daisy* and *Shadows* (1959); *The Flower Thief* (1960); *The Connection, Guns of the Trees,* and *The Sins of Jesus* (1961); *The Cool World, Hallelujah The Hills,* and *The Queen of Sheba Meets the Atom Man* (1963); *Nothing But A Man, Babo 73,* and *Georg* (1964); *Hold Me While I'm Naked* and *The Chelsea Girls* (1966); *Portrait of Jason, David Holzman's Diary, Beyond the Law, The Edge, Lonesome Cowboys,* and *Nude Restaurant* (1967), as well as Warhol's later features; *Maidstone* and *Night of the Living Dead* (1968); *Brandy in the Wilderness, Duet For Cannibals, Ice,* and *Putney Swope* (1969); *Lives of Performers* (1972); *The Devil's Cleavage* (1973); *Film about a woman who . . .* and *Speaking Directly* (1974), as well as Jost's subsequent films; and *Kristina Talking Pictures* (1976). Additional examples include films independently produced within the industry, such as *Easy Rider, Medium Cool,* and *The Last Movie*; the films of John Cassavetes, Monte Hellman, and Mike Nichols; perhaps those of Woody Allen, and many of Roger Corman's New World Pictures.

Despite their heterogeneity, these films manifested a stronger or more explicit concern with contemporary social, sexual, and philosophical issues than was usual in Hollywood, yet their length and most common gauge reflected the type of theatrical exhibition and the degree of intervention in the general feature market it was hoped they would achieve. Unlike underground film, but like the European avant-garde, they were produced as commodities to be put on the industrial market. Without either regular industrial financing or the assistance of a state support system like those which had initially floated the Italian, Swedish, English, and French New Waves, however, they typically were produced through unique funding efforts and (often unsuccessful) attempts either to sell the finished product for studio distribution or to distribute it independently on the edges of the underground, on the college circuits, or in the art houses themselves. The determining specificity of these films, then, is this occasional and essentially hybrid production—a feature in which they did not differ from the European art film so much as exemplify to a crucial degree the double-ness that defines it.

While the art film did develop formal conventions such as the attenuation of narrative continuity, an unstable synthesis of realism and subjectivity, and a strongly marked authorial signature in visual style (which even when it varied, did so in reaction to changing Hollywood practices), it has been seen less as a genre coexisting with others in a single mode of production than as itself a specific, unique order of production—as a "Mode of Film Practice" (Bordwell,

1979) or as "Institution" (Neale, 1981). Despite their imprecision, both terms draw attention to the intersection in the art film of thematic or formal innovations with the reorganization of the social relations of production that was their precondition. The specificity of the art film as a mode of production lies in its attempt to bridge the industrial operations of the studios with the artisanal practices of the aesthetic and political avant-gardes, to reconcile commercial and personally expressive functions. Given the lethargy of the studios, the American art film demanded that an individual amass the social and technological means of production of the commercial feature in order to make and distribute a film that was nevertheless entirely under his or her personal control. Hence the primacy of directors in the art cinema; since they acted essentially as their own producers, as artist-entrepreneurs who secured control over all stages of production, they acquired the power to inscribe authorship in all aspects of the filmic to the degree otherwise possible only in non-commodity practice.

The American art film thus hyperbolically distended the tension between authorial authenticity and the commercial viability of the studio-produced European art film. Rather than contesting commodity production, the European art film renewed it by competing with the orthodox feature in industrial markets. The assertion of a national cultural identity, commonly appropriating—and negotiating itself through—the codes of high art, mobilized nationalist resistance to American mass culture and competition with it for cultural hegemony in the international capitalist order. The European art film did indeed articulate post-World War II European metaphysical deracination and existential alienation, but the form of that articulation was simultaneously materially determined from the outside by the various national cinemas' attempts to challenge U.S. economic and cultural hegemony—which coincided in the export of the American industrial film. The situation of the European art film vis-à-vis American industrial culture thus became its greatest single preoccupation. Its dominant stylistic traits became allusion to classic American cinema and the foregrounding of its own deliberate misuse or quotation of Hollywood codes; its master narrative allegorized its attempt to secure filmic and political autonomy from the international dominance of the American cinema and of U.S. culture in general.

The formal determination of the American art film was thus double; alongside the address to Hollywood it inherited from the European models, it typically included in its patterns of formal distancing a similar self-consciousness about the art film itself, the *Kulturfilm* proper, compared to which it always remained something of an interloper in the college town art theaters, its pedigree always somewhat sinister. References to the European New Waves were continuous from the early features of the Mekas brothers. Adolfas Mekas's *Hallelujah The Hills*, an American *Jules and Jim* so densely studded with parodic references to Bergman and Resnais that its own narrative emerges mainly as a refraction of its sources, set the pace for what, as *Faces* had it, was hoped would be a series of "*Dolce Vita*s of the commercial world." These references culminated in the ubiquitous Godard quotations of the early seventies that allowed intertextuality to be realigned as reflexiveness proper. Godard's attention to the relationship between the language of industrial film and the conditions of industrial production revealed filmic signification as a function of cinematic practice, and it supplied the vocabulary by which American art film could return its attention to the politics of its own peculiar situation in American film generally. Formal self-consciousness sharpened into a critique of the movie business, with Jon Jost's *Speaking Directly* being the culmination of this specific and explicit articulation of underground film's allegorization of its relation to hegemonic practice. In taking film narrative as its theme, then, the American art film returned to the material conditions of narration, to the social organization of cinema.

Reflexivity is thus a pandemic trope in sixties film, from structural film through the underground to the narrative art film and even to the New Hollywood's rejection of classical, invisible narration in films in which "the director, the process of filmmaking, the conventions of story-telling, and the act of viewing [were] all placed in the foreground" (Schatz, 1983: 21–22). Indeed, by the early seventies, ostensibly Brechtian devices were common in the Hollywood mainstream. Mel Brooks's generic self-consciousness that opens the fictional diegesis to the conditions of its production (the quotation of western motifs in *Blazing Saddles* and the finale in which the cowboys break through the screen into the studio commissary) was not that unusual, though on the edges of the industry a more complex layering of meta-filmic modes was possible. Jon Davidson's pastiche *Hollywood Boulevard*, for example, superimposes the representation of its own production over references to the whole classic era and previous industrial reworkings of it (the film's own point of departure is, of course, *Sunset Boulevard*): outtakes from and additional references to other films in the Roger Corman canon; the sociology of mass cultural consumption which includes a drive-in showing of parts of the present film; and even quasi-structuralist devices in which the film is allowed to burn in the projector gate.

In light of this ubiquitous reflexivity, the Formalist proposal that emphasis on the message itself over the other components of the communication is the condition of art discourses in general may be extended to assert the reflexivity of all films (or virtually all, if a "prosaic" transparency be allowed to certain technical or other representationally neutral films of one kind or another). They all generate meaning by signaling points of contrast and similarity with other films, from the micro-level of the reproduction of three-dimensional space in the two-dimensional photographic image, through the requirements of generic codes, even to the prescriptions of the entity, "film," and of the transaction, "cinema." To expand the concept of reflexiveness to the point where it becomes indistinguishable from film itself—a Shklovskian inversion which would finally ordain structural film not as deviation or anomaly, but as the "most typical" film practice—does indeed inhibit naive conflations of film with its profilmic; but the argument that all films are reflexive short-circuits the concept's usefulness in locating the accommodation to specific historical tensions that different modes of reflexiveness register, the specific strategy of various responses to seismic shifts in the history of cinema.

Though both participate in the general crisis of signification in late capitalism, structural and art film (which we may now understand as cousins) responded differently to the cinematic form of this crisis. The hermetic closure of signification in structural film marks a negation in the face of social contradictions that made extratextual meaning impossible, a semiological accommodation to inhibitions on expressivity imposed by the collusiveness of industrial cinema. The reflexiveness of the art film, on the other hand, was the inscription of those contradictions in the film narrative. Structural film withdrew to the materials of signification, like concrete poetry displaying the absence of narrative or discourse as the objectified form of the impossibility of narrative or discourse. The most significant instances of art film narrated that impossibility—the impossibility of significant individual authorship in the realm of industrial commodity production, the impossibility of the social story being industrially told. Its analogues were thus simultaneously the nonfiction novel and the reflexive novel, both of which genres emerged, hypertrophied, and burst in the same decade, the one the complement of the other in the same dilemma, the fictitiousness of history and the historicity of fiction.[2] As the novel became history and vice versa, so cinéma vérité became narrative fiction and vice versa. The art film documented the sublation of all these dialectical contraries.

The field of narrative reflexivity as a repertoire of formal devices may be classified several ways: by reference to the categories of Jakobson's analysis of speech acts (Fredericksen, 1979); by distinguishing between generic self-consciousness and simply the affirmation of authorial presence (Braudy, 1977: 114); or by distinguishing between films that document their own production and those that document the production of some other film, the *construction en abŷme* of films that are then "divided and doubled, thus reflecting on themselves" (Metz, 1974b: 228). This last distinction between works in which a dominant diegesis (what I will call the a-film) records the production either of itself or of another (the b-film) is especially powerful when transposed into materialist terms, since it allows analysis of differences between various productive methods, between a given mode of production and some other one it may intradiegetically represent. The extremes yielded by such a classification are presented in the table on the next page.

The first category—independent films about making independent films—is very large. The anxieties of alternative production together with the centrality of the aesthetic as the category of alterity make the autobiography of production a common theme in independent cinema, though in cases like *Lost Lost Lost* or the later films of

2 These are the summary terms used by Norman Mailer as the subtitle of his most crucial investigation of the relationship between subject and object in historiography, his account of the 1968 March on the Pentagon (Mailer, 1968).

Category	a-film	b-film
1	independent	independent
2	industrial	industrial
3	industrial	independent
4	independent	industrial

George Landow, that autobiography can also include reference to other modes of avant-garde practice that have been rejected. The second category is relatively small, for despite the recurrent classic Hollywood films about one or another aspect of the movie business, the effacement of production has been the general orthodoxy. When it does occur, reflexive industrial production is itself, however, frequently predicated on a disparity between the a- and the b-film, proposing one as a critique of the other: King Vidor's distinction between *films d'art* and popular entertainment in *Show People* (1928), for example. Often, this film-within-a-film motif is used nostalgically, with the documentation of the b-film and its fragmentary presentation offered in lieu of its actual impossibility, or in lieu of the fact that it is the last of a vanishing kind; the lament for films like *I Want You To Meet Pamela* in Truffaut's *Day for Night* is exemplary. This disparity can be pushed even further so that rather than mirroring itself, the film differentiates itself absolutely from the other film whose production it documents. Thus, the third and fourth categories set the b-film (or several interpolated b-films, or even one b-film inside another—a c-film) against the hegemonic diegesis: the industrial documentation of an alternative practice and vice versa.

Since any recognition, favorable or not, of non-commodity cultural practices contradicts the industry's need to naturalize its own production and the spectator's function in respect to it, Hollywood typically displaces representation of such practices into other mediums—for example, romanticized portraits of doomed genius musicians or painters such as Van Gogh, Gauguin, Gaudier-Brezeska, and Gulley Jimson. The third category is then very small, and in industrial film any alternative film practice must intrinsically be denigrated, marked as deviant (*Peeping Tom*) or dangerously naive (*Sullivan's Travels*). Independent films about Hollywood films, the fourth category, are similarly critical, though ranging from the affectionate and parodic treatments of the disparity between their own scale of production and that of the studios (the Kuchars' films or those of Warhol's middle period) to explicit critiques of the relationship between Hollywood and American capitalism, as in the collages of Bruce Conner or Bruce Baillie.

Between these extremes, however, a number of films explored the tensions between private and industrial production specific to the art film in this period. In recounting the cinematic determinants of film narrative, they revealed how semiological possibilities were determined by the material conditions of production. Their investigation of the social conditions of independent feature production allowed them to represent, in a synecdochic or symbolic form, the operations of power in society at large. The difficulties of mobilizing resources sufficient to compete with the studio product, the hierarchies of power that generate industrial division of artistic labor, the filmmaker's real or vicarious participation in the glamor of the media industries—all were spheres in which the social transactions of film production intersected with the social and economic transactions of the corporate state.

As they provided a vocabulary for the analysis of the relations between the media industries and American politics in general, films about independent feature production demanded formal deviation from Hollywood codes. All were thus reflexive, and all were constructed not across homologies between their mode of production and their formal properties, but across contradictions between them. Torn between a filmmaking practice they embodied and one they depicted, they were all in contradiction with themselves. Here we consider four: *David Holzman's Diary* (Jim McBride, 1967); *Maidstone* (Norman Mailer, 1968); *Medium Cool* (Haskell Wexler, 1969); and *The Last Movie* (Dennis Hopper, 1971). As the financial and productive resources for these films ranged from the shoestring private funding of *David Holzman's Diary* through the more extensive but still personal financial outlay of Wexler and Mailer to the unrestricted studio backing of *The Last Movie*, so they were able to depict increasingly elaborate modes of production that engaged political issues of increasingly wider implications. In *David Holzman's Diary*, the amateur diarist's project expressed the problems of domestic filmmaking, especially its effect on personal relationships. *Maidstone* and *Medium Cool*, the adventures of an independent feature filmmaker and a television news cameraman, respectively, explored the function of film and television in the two-party and presidential political systems. And in depicting a studio production, *The Last Movie* analyzed the role of that mode of production's essential genre, the western, in the history of the Americas.

Jim McBride produced *David Holzman's Diary* on weekends and using equipment borrowed from his job as a television news cameraman. A fictional, acted film masquerading as an underground documentary, a film diary, it so distends the reflexive component of the latter mode that self-consciousness occupies it entirely to call into question the relation between fiction and documentation in it.

Losing his job and receiving his draft notice at the same time, the hero confronts social and ontological dislocation by filming a diary on the explicit Godardian assumption that it will make "truth 24 times a second" available to him and so allow him to bring himself "into focus." The social environment the film engages is restricted to the filmmaker's immediate acquaintances, especially his girlfriend, Penny, a model. David's insistence on photographing Penny, even when she is asleep, so angers her that she leaves him. But his obsession has its own compensations: a voyeuristic relationship with a woman in a nearby apartment, a photographic rape of a woman on the subway, and a prolonged photographic encounter with a woman in a car that substitutes for actual sexual contact. His desire to film his diary thus generates the events that compose his life, establishing his filmmaking equipment as simultaneously the means of documenting personal life and a participant in it.

Though the apparatus is on the one hand the mediating agency of social relationships, it assumes a quasi-human status of its own. Initially alternating between real social contacts and relations only with the apparatus, Holzman eventually becomes entirely preoccupied by the latter. The Eclair camera and the Nagra tape recorder replace his friends and accompany him wherever he goes. Introduced in erotic terms, they become the object of both his desire and his anxiety. He quarrels with them, then apologizes and makes up, and the crisis of the film is not the failure of sexual relationships but the theft of the filmmaking equipment. In the way that the resolution of the woman-question allows narrative closure in orthodox features, here the loss of the camera brings the drama to its termination. Discovering the theft, Holzman uses a public photo machine and audio recording booth to recount the theft and to announce the consequent end of the film.

This coda is of course duplicitous, a represention of its own impossibility. We receive notice of how the theft of its material prereq-

7.1 Jim McBride, *David Holzman's Diary*: L. M. Kit Carson

uisites terminates the film, not from an actual paper photograph or recorded disk but from visual and aural filmic tracks that are materially continuous with all the film that has preceded them; the fact of the absence of the apparatus can only be demonstrated by the deployment of its replacement, the surrogate of its presence. Parallel contradictions inhabit the whole film. As a fictional diary made by a filmmaker using an actor to play a character, it is entirely a duplicitous dissimulation. But once set in motion, as simulation, it generates a veracity of its own—the reality of the illusion, in Godard's phrase—distinct from the illusoriness of the ostensible documentation. Once instigated, this interpenetration of the two ontologies destabilizes all moments in the film; the instances when autobiographical honesty is called into question by implications of fictitiousness are matched by the immediacy with which the artificiality of what the medium presents is redeemed by the actuality of the presentation.

Such a sublating of *cinéma* into *vérité* and vice versa, the narrative extension of structural film dialectics, has social relevance to the extent that the relations around the production of the film engage society at large. Though the Vietnam War in the form of radio reports is a constant background (as indeed it is in the very similar *Brandy in the Wilderness*) and though contemporary urban disintegration is crucially figured in the theft of the camera, the chief social issues *David Holzman's Diary* sets into play are sexual politics, as these revolve around David's desire to photograph women, especially his girlfriend.

As a model, Penny professionally makes her body into a commodity for commercial photographers in the service of commodity marketing in general. From her point of view, domestic life is a reservation outside the self-reification she professionally embraces. David's desire to photograph her, specifically to photograph her naked, is for her not an act of intimacy or truth, but rather the vehicle by which her public inauthenticity would rape the personal self she attempts to retain. Marking a point of tension between public and private spectacle, her decision to limit spectatorship of her body to

7.2–7.3 Jim McBride, *David Holzman's Diary*

her professional function and to deny her image to David and his
amateur film brings her role in his film into contradiction with her
role outside it. Her wish to preserve a private space outside photography demands that she exist outside David's film. It forces the
quarrel with him, for his compulsion is such that only by breaking
the social relation between them can she break the filmic one—even
though that break continues to motivate his subsequent activity and
the rest of the movie.

These intradiegetic tensions between personal domestic use of the
film apparatus and public, commodity spectacle also summarize
and dramatize the film's primary conceit—its simulation of the private diary film designed for public exhibition in the commodity
market. The moments of its intradiegetic authenticity—the use of
film in intimate self-examination or, in the case of Penny's anger,
the refusal to allow it such a function—are fabricated illusions of
such. A commodity produced for the market, the film masquerades
as the trace of the quest for its opposite, a non-commodity film practice. The scenes in which the camera faces itself in the endless re-
treating reflections of parallel mirrors that seem to lay bare the
filmic processes of Holzman's uncompromised interior quest—
where, in Metz's terms, the film is most clearly "divided and doubled . . . , reflecting on [itself]" (Metz, 1974b: 228)—in fact lie
across the contradictions of McBride's cinematic adventure.

The larger the scope of the filmmaking represented in a film, the
more significant such contradictions between the medium as a recording process and the medium as an agency in social production
become. The tensions between practice and representation in the
film itself are especially fertile when they may be made to engage,
symbolically or actually, parallel tensions between the mass media's
participation in the operation of social power and its representation
of such power. *Medium Cool*, which considers news photography
as both a means of representation and a participant in the political
process, is the fullest extension into the public media world of the
tensions that McBride opens on a domestic level while using an amateur mode of production.

The hero of Haskell Wexler's *Medium Cool*, a television news cameraman named John Cassellis, is substantially a persona for Wexler
himself, both in his general career as a photographer in the commercial media and in his specific capacity as writer, director, and
photographer of *Medium Cool*. As Wexler's own understanding of
politics had changed, so during the film Cassellis discovers how the
mass media are integrated into the operations of the state. Initially,
he is politically naive. He enjoys shooting exploitative and even explosive social situations without any regard for their implications,
and like his soundman who claims to be merely the elongation of a
tape recorder, he believes himself to be separate from any responsibility for what he reports. But the events of the film force him to
acknowledge that he and the institutions for which he works col-
lude in the authoritarian operations that control political reality.

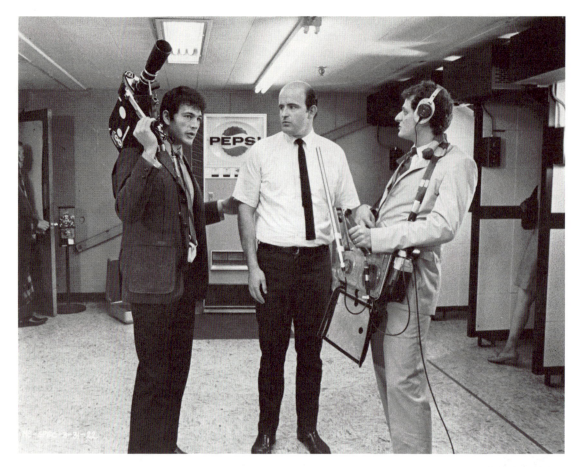

7.4–7.6 Haskell Wexler, *Medium Cool*

While following up a story about police persecution of a Black cabdriver, Cassellis is verbally assaulted by Black militants, who see him as an agent of a communications industry that misrepresents or excludes them; and when he objects to his station's practice of supplying his news footage to the FBI, he is fired from his job. His social and ideological displacement continues in his relationship with a

7.7–7.8 Haskell Wexler, *Medium Cool*

Vietnam War widow; together they descend into the hell of a psychedelic disco, and, searching for her truant son through the parks and streets of Chicago during the disturbances and police riots that accompanied the 1968 Democratic convention, they come face to face with the violence of the state. She is killed and he critically injured when their car crashes, and in a reprise of the first scene of the film, in which Cassellis had photographed a freeway accident, a child takes a snapshot of their burning car.

This narrative of a journey from ideological illusion to reality is recapitulated filmically. As the plot is increasingly penetrated and surrounded by real history, the film is besieged and absorbed by elements of cinéma vérité; and as the actor and actress playing Cassellis and his lover search for the missing boy amid the real political violence, they—and Wexler and his crew—fall out of the intradiegetic security of the story into the exigencies of their historical moment. Thus like the exactly contemporaneous *Memories of Underdevelopment*, which also places a fictional character in a real revolution, the film is a mix of more or less improvised acting with different modes of documentary. Sequences of virtually straight news reporting alternate with the intradiegetic representation of television news programs; and sequences of documentary, initially staged for the camera but which generate their own urgency (interviews with the Black militants, for example), are interspersed with others in which it is impossible to tell whether the profilmic action is real or staged.

As the fiction loses its power to dictate the progress of the filmic, the public world takes charge of the film and forces it into consciousness of its own role in the operations of the media. For example, a voice shouting "Watch Out, Haskell. It's real" as a tear gas cannister falls in front of a group of demonstrators testifies to the filmmaker's physical presence in the events he represents. But more integral political functions of the media are also invoked. In Chicago it became clear that rather than merely reporting the political process, the press actively participated in it. The dissidents depended on the news media not merely to document their protest, but to ensure that their opposition to domestic racism and international imperialism could become part of the national political agenda. Press coverage of the riots deflected that project, displacing it with the local scandal of police brutality.

While this sensationalism assisted the dissidents in uncovering the violence of the corporate state, it also demonstrated the limited possibilities of turning the establishment press to their own purposes. Shots of television cameramen photographing the protesters who cry "Stay with us, NBC" illustrate the possibility that the media could safeguard the demonstrators against the worst of the police violence and so preserve the democratic right to free speech; and *Medium Cool* served something of the same function. But the impotence of any individual within NBC or within any other component of the corporate media to act on any but the government's behalf has already been dramatized by the case of Cassellis himself. He figures the impossibility of an individual's sustaining political responsibility in the network organization, the impossibility of turning the industrial media to progressive purposes. The car accident that ends the film is an arbitrary but inevitable resolution to the narrative contradictions the film encounters, for it cannot imagine a way in which as a photographer Cassellis could implement the political insight he has gained. And so Cassellis completes the allegorized self-representation of Wexler himself; torn between the compromises Paramount demanded as the condition of distributing *Medium Cool* and his engagement in radical politics, Wexler rejected the commercial cinema to work on marginal documentaries like *Underground* that took him back to the Chicago radicals, but in a mode of film production that was consonant with their political program, not in contradiction with it.

Like *Medium Cool*, Norman Mailer's *Maidstone* is set in the context of the civil violence of 1968, though the assassination of Robert Kennedy, not Chicago, is the shadow behind it. The filmic premise to which it harnesses the possibility of a reenactment of that violence is its attempt to achieve the existential fullness that is generated in live theater by the presence of the audience. Mixing actors and non-actors and including in the cast representatives from various militant social groups, Mailer introduced into performance extradiegetic social animosities that set one part of the cast in competition with the other, making the profilmic the space of collective improvisation and charging fictional interaction with real tensions. The conceit goes back through a decade of avant-garde theater to *Shadows*, and, like that film, *Maidstone* is an attempt to use the specifically improvisatory tradition of underground film to revitalize the commercial feature.

The fiction celebrates a highly popular though esoteric director, Norman T. Kingsley, played by Mailer himself, who is casting a remake of Buñuel's *Belle de Jour* in which a male brothel populated by Kingsley's cronies is visited by its female clientele. At the same

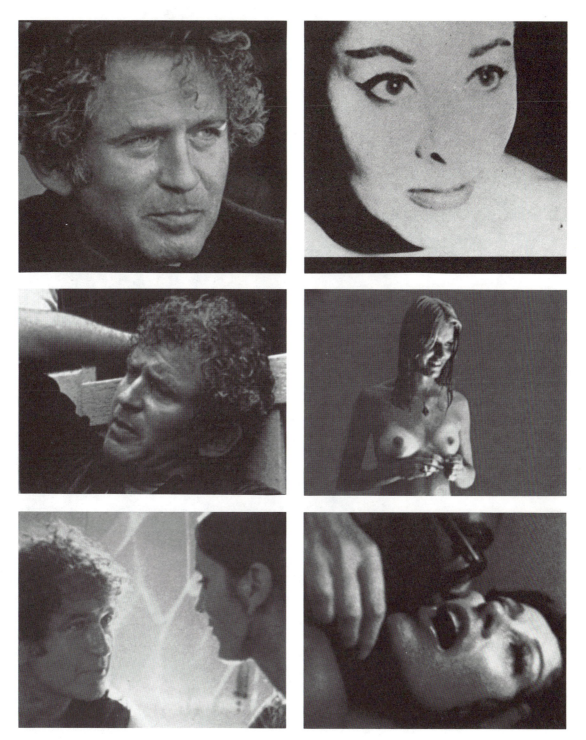

7.9–7.14 Norman Mailer, *Maidstone*

7.15–7.17 Norman Mailer, *Maidstone*

time, Kingsley is considering running for the U.S. presidency and is being scrutinized by both the Eastern establishment and an elite secret police organization, PAX,C, which ostensibly was formed to prevent assassinations but is popularly rumored to carry them out and, in fact, perhaps murders Kingsley in the film. The desired confrontational energy in performance comes as overflow from the sexuality and violence of the roles, and the highly volatile social mix constantly erupts in exchanges that force histrionic artifice into more authentic contact. The body becomes a moment of presence subtending the fictive world, because both sexual intercourse and physical violence do not allow the performer either to remain separate from the act or to be entirely constrained in the mode of simulation.

The interlaced diegetic frames thus break; frequently, scenes are narratively indeterminate and without a matrix, and many shots float without anchor between the disjunctive levels of representation of the several nested films. The encounters between Norman Mailer and Rip Torn (who plays Kingsley's bodyguard, but also perhaps his assassin) and those with the other actors and with photographers Ricky Leacock and D. A. Pennebaker constitute the movie *Maidstone*; but in this story of Kingsley and the bankers, and of the thugs and actresses who surround him, nests a third, the shots from the *Belle de Jour* remake. And inside all these, or certainly indeterminate in respect to them, is the most audacious interlude, a sequence called "The Death of the Director." Consisting of more than two hundred shots in ten minutes, it culls fragments from all the others into an assembly in which the assassination of Kingsley, whether real or imagined, annihilates film syntax. Neither the separate shots in this and other sequences, nor their sequential combination, allows a hierarchical ordering of reality and artifice; instead, they articulate their intermittent interpenetration.

The difficulty of deciding which diegetic order is referred to by a given shot—say, of two people in sexual congress or of an altercation between Blacks and Whites—may be understood formalistically as an aesthetic fragmentation that produces spectator distance or brackets issues of general film ontology. But it is also a response to a social imperative. As the events that take place while the film is being shot generate confrontations between individuals that refract the tension of the body politic, filmmaking becomes a microcosmic arena where issues of general biographical or social import are symbolically enacted. More than a mechanism for generating modernist narrative fragmentation, the central conceit of having filmmaking the subject of the film and its hero a filmmaker who is running for president provides a narrative vocabulary through which the interpenetration of politics and the media—the spectacular nature of modern politics and the political nature of the modern spectacle—could have been thoroughly explored. That this finally happens only in a particularly circumscribed way follows simultaneously from elements in Mailer's own political thinking and from the specific mode of film production historically available to him, as together these produce *Maidstone*.

The personalization of history that informs Mailer's political and aesthetic philosophies, the belief that social and moral truths are known viscerally, felt upon the pulses or not at all, privileges the individual body as the site of social renewal. His is one of the decade's exemplary formulations of the politics of authenticity[3] and, in the interchangeability of the aesthetic and the political within it, the most sophisticated elaboration of beat ideology. Informing the conflation of individual and social experience in *Maidstone*, this somatic politics also informs the film's successes and limitations. For

7.18–7.19 Norman Mailer, *Maidstone*

3 And, in fact, Mailer's own account of *Maidstone* concludes, "We are a Faustian age determined to meet the Lord or the Devil before we are done, and the ineluctable ore of the authentic is our only key to the lock" (Mailer, 1971: 180). Similar sentiments are voiced by Kingsley throughout the film, and indeed inform all Mailer's writing.

the great moment in the film (and it is one of the great moments in American cinema) in which the metaphor of breaking through the artifice of fiction into the reality of history is justified, is not the explosion of the assembled social energies in an assassination attempt on Kingsley. Instead, it comes as an explosion of the anger of one of the actors in what is virtually an assassination attempt on Mailer himself. When the shooting of *Maidstone* is apparently complete, the cast dismissed, and Mailer is walking away with his wife and children, suddenly Rip Torn attacks him, beating him on the head with a hammer while Mailer fights back by punching and biting. Captured as the spontaneous eruption of manic jealousy, the attack gives the film its climax and conclusion, an exergual validation of Mailer's project that is legitimately incorporable into the work by virtue of the expanding frames of the meta-textual documentation that have been its premise.

The social violence to which the collective improvisation provides access, then, is finally that of the domestic and the psychological, a family plot in which Mailer's wife and children are terrorized by an explosion from the projection of Mailer's own alter ego. For as the costar of the film and Mailer's best buddy, as an under-recognized actor and a disturbingly intimate male friend, Torn can live tensions only as large as those spanned by the film's production. And despite its feature length, *Maidstone* remains a domestic production, put into motion by Mailer's private resources, a hyperinflated underground film. Totally financed by Mailer, totally controlled by him, it is his self-projection and so can unleash only the dynamics of his self. Though in *Maidstone* he represents himself as an art filmmaker like Antonioni or Fellini, in the American system this private fantasy could only be privately enacted and so could engage personal violence, a fight between friends, but not the systemic violence of the state. The politics of the film as industry and its reproduction of the social conditions of capitalism could only be fully realized, however anomalously, within the industrial mode of production.

Standing with *Wind from the East* as one of the most comprehensive narrative analyses of capitalist cinema, *The Last Movie*, like that film, articulates its critique through a meta-generic consideration of what has been identified as the essence of that cinema, the western, "cinema par excellence" (Bazin, 1971: 141). Its address to film as a commodity within specific material and psychological economies and to cinema as a practice with a similarly specific system of social institutions politically motivates its Brechtian procedures of distancing and formal disintegration.

It narrates the adventures of a movie stuntman and wrangler, Kansas (played by Hopper himself), on location in Chinchero, a remote village in Peru, where Samuel Fuller is shooting a movie about Billy the Kid. Expecting the location to be used by other companies, Kansas stays behind after the Hollywood crew is finished. He lives with Maria (Stella Garcia), a Peruvian woman from a nearby bordello, and drifts into various escapades with a motley of U.S. expa-

7.20 Dennis Hopper, *The Last Movie*:
Samuel Fuller directing a western

triates that includes Neville Robey, a gold-prospecting Vietnam vet, and Mr. Anderson, a U.S. businessman, and his wife. Eventually he becomes involved with the Chinchero Indians, who have taken over the sets left by the Hollywood crew. With cameras, lights, and booms made out of straw, they are making their own "movie," *La Ultima Pelicula*, by reenacting the shooting of Fuller's movie as exactly as possible, except that they refuse to believe that the Hollywood violence was simulated. Initially recruited by the local priest who is distressed that their obsession with the movie is drawing the villagers away from the church, Kansas unsuccessfully attempts to teach the Indians the artifice of movie violence. In a drunken rage precipitated by Robey's suicide when he realizes that he lacks sufficient funds to develop a mine he has discovered, Kansas attempts to destroy the sets; but he is captured by the Indians and is chosen to play the role of "el muerte," the scapegoat-hero of their ritual and the best part in *La Ultima Pelicula*, whose completion will coincide with the Good Friday and Easter celebrations. Maria, who herself has won a part in the movie, returns to the bordello, while Kansas, realizing that the violence in the village has been introduced by Hol-

7.21–7.25 Dennis Hopper, *The Last Movie*

lywood, accepts his fate in expiation of his culture's guilt. It appears that he is killed in the same location used for the final shootout in Fuller's movie.

Though a skeletal chronological reference to this narrative is maintained throughout the film, and in fact the central phase of Kansas's adventures with Robey and the Andersons is relatively conventional, elsewhere continuity is fragmented by interpolations of shots from both Fuller's and the Indians' movies, and the diegetic frames separating these are entirely lost. This scrambling of various levels of illusion and reality recurs as a major theme of the narrative; the social role of Hollywood is analyzed, literally and specifically but also metaphorically, in implied analogies between the cinematic and other forms of spectatorship.

In these narratives the other characters use Kansas to fulfill otherwise impossible dreams, all of which are associated in some way with Hollywood. For Fuller, Kansas's stunts, such as being shot off a moving horse, are necessary to the illusion of the Billy the Kid movie, a spectacle in which Kansas participates only by selling his labor but in whose glamour and other rewards he can only marginally share. For Robey, whose knowledge of gold mining is only what he learned from *The Treasure of the Sierra Madre*, Kansas is needed to help develop a mine he discovered in the Peruvian wilderness. For Maria, Kansas holds the promise of a refrigerator and other consumer goods touted by the American-oriented media. For the Andersons, he is the guide to a lesbian sex show which resembles a movie in its voyeuristic commercialization of female sexuality, while for Mrs. Anderson he is the embodiment of a movie cowboy, a fantasy lover. For the priest, he represents the possibility of turning the Indians back to religion. And for the Indians, he is first their technical advisor in movie-making and then the victim of their ritual. For this entire microcosm of American society, then, Kansas is the vehicle of illusions of wealth, violence, and sex as these circulate through cinema. But as the embodiment of the American movie industry, the embodiment of capitalism's penetration of the indigenous cultures of the West, he is the means by which that cultural imperialism achieves both an individual psychic registration and a social historical form—but also the means by which the Chinchero Indians may symbolically exorcise that which oppresses them.

Hopper's analysis of the social effects of the western in the biographical narrative of Kansas is recapitulated in the larger form of the contrast between Fuller's exemplification of Hollywood practice and the exemplary transformation of it the Indians make. The former, a classic instance of the ratification of the mass production of ideology in commodity cultural production, is negated in the latter, an anti-imperialist cinema of decolonization in which revolutionizing the means of film production allows contestation of the myths for which Hollywood has been the vehicle.

Although in their enthusiastic emulation of Fuller the Indians appear to abandon their own culture, they are in fact incorporating film into their own, already transformed, version of the Passion in a way that clarifies the similarities between the movies and that other ritual observance they resemble, religion. Like Christ, Billy the Kid was an outlaw whose ritual execution inspired cultic practices that compensate for and so sustain exploitation in daily life. Both cults produce architectural monuments more or less decorated with representations of their saints, and both have produced a legitimizing social apparatus which interprets their parables and encourages the distinction between true and false gods. But in using Kansas as a conjoining third term between the myth of Christianity and that of the silver screen, the Indians exorcise both.

When Kansas tries to destroy the sets, he thinks he is striking a blow against Hollywood, which he blames for Robey's fantasy and suicide. But the Indians have already repossessed what had been literally and metaphorically stolen from them; they have symbolically reclaimed the landscape stolen in the past by white imperialism in North America and in the present by a contemporary form of that imperialism. Their appropriation of the sets is thus a symbolic liberation from imperialism, just as their possession of cinema, of the western, is a rejection of what *The Last Movie* has shown to be both typical of and metaphorical for contemporary exploitation of all kinds. In Chinchero, Kansas, by name a middle American and by trade a cowboy actor, is sacrificed in the exorcism of imperialism, while the art form of his culture finds both its purgation and a model of its transcendence.

La Ultima Pelicula does not create a division of labor in production, and it does not produce the larger distinction between production and consumption. It is, then, an extravagant extrapolation of underground innovation that completely redefines cinema as practice. Without real cameras or real stock, nothing is produced; the social improvisation of the symbolic shooting is all there is, a perfect "Imperfect Cinema," in which the medium is realized as a popular practice "carried out as but another life activity." But, as it achieves this utopian disappearance into everything, it also disappears into nothingness (Espinosa, n.d.: 25–26). The shots we see are not those made by the Indians; they are made by Dennis Hopper.

The fragmented narrative texture of *The Last Movie*—its apparently arbitrary mix of objective and subjective shots, of repeated takes of a single action with shots of the actors out of role, of outtakes with shots that are unedited and on which the clapboard titles remain, even of titles like "Scene Missing"—all these mix Fuller's movie and Hopper's movie with documentation of the production of both. And this collage may include documentation of the Indians' film, but it cannot logically include shots from it. Sometimes it *appears* to do so, most crucially in the scene of the death of Kansas-as-Billy the Kid. In the last of three takes of this shot, Billy (Hopper-as-Kansas-as-Billy) staggers across the village square and falls down with his face very close to the camera. After a few seconds of being "dead," Hopper thumbs his nose at the camera and gets up. This could be an unedited shot from *The Last Movie*, in which Kansas only *acts* the death of Billy for the Indians; when they have their take, still as Kansas he thumbs his nose at them. Or it could be an unedited take from (Hopper's simulation of) the Indians' movie, in which case Kansas-as-Billy is actually killed and the nose-thumbing is done by Hopper, who thus steps out of both his roles. Hopper's transgression of editing codes allows the shot to float between various diegetic moorings, but though it generates both objective demystification of the process of production and subjective interpenetration of several diegetic modes, the indeterminacy of the shot also summarizes the ontological and practical contradictions that Hopper sets into play. For while the Indians' practice of cinema can be represented, their film never exists and so cannot be re-presented. *The Last Movie* cannot display *La Ultima Pelicula*; all it can do is frame its absence, the absence of a revolutionary film, the negation that constitutes a revolutionary cinema.

This exemplary meditation on the film industry remains, however, the trace of a biographical anomaly, a peculiar combination of Hollywood expertise and recalcitrance. An actor since childhood, with impeccable credentials (*Rebel Without A Cause*, *Giant*, *The Sons of Katie Elder*), Hopper adeptly deployed the success of *Easy Rider* to the point where Universal allowed him the resources of a major studio for use as essentially his home movie crew. But through that career ran another career, a history of failure and rejection. Though it may have been Hopper's legendary obstinate independence, which had caused him to be blacklisted for years, that provided him with the insight to elaborate his intervention in the industry through the metaphor of a revolutionary cinema that would deny it, still his power was not sufficient to make *The Last Movie* a commercial success in the popular market, or even in the world of art film.

The revile of its public reception thus completed *The Last Movie* on several levels, its cinematic failure reflecting its filmic integrity. Testifying to the force of its affront, the pre-release publicity coupled with its immediate complete disappearance more importantly allowed Hopper to create a perfectly lucid *conceptual film*, one that unwittingly recapitulated in the industrial arena the interdependent valorization of the ritual of shooting and the devaluation of the commodity object, which together constitute the radical significance of *La Ultima Pelicula*. In the context of an exploitative cinema of pleasure, its own constitution as analysis amounted to its constitution as negation that could be legitimized only by the absoluteness of its rejection by the degraded public.

As a narrative act of framed silence, an industrial *hapax legomenon*, *The Last Movie* thus epitomizes the art film. With absolute personal control over all aspects of the artwork and access to industrial means of production, Hopper secured a golden opportunity; but by forcing the discrepancies between art and industry to their furthest reaches, he forced the social contradiction between them from the level of theme to the realm of practice. He thus excluded himself from all markets, attaining a hermetic purity rarely equaled even by the most ascetic structural film. As in structural film, the final absence he constructed was social, the absence of any audience, even the hippie audience of *Easy Rider*. For the meta-critical undertaking of the art film to discover a real social viability, individual appropriation of industrial narrative had to be undertaken by an individual from a social group that had an interest in narrative and the public cinema, an individual from a social group that still had a story to tell and a desire to tell it. In the early seventies the only such group was women.

8

Cinema and Sexual Difference

I WAS PERMITTED TO BE AN IMAGE / BUT NOT AN IMAGE-MAKER CREAT-
ING HER OWN SELF-IMAGE.
— Carolee Schneemann

Images and symbols *for* the woman cannot be isolated from images and
symbols *of* the woman.
— Jacques Lacan

Women in Theory

The women's movement and its cinemas had a double relation to
the alternative movements of the sixties. On the one hand, the situation of women in both the social formation as a whole and the
dominant cinema in particular was in certain respects parallel to
that of the other, more properly minority groups who produced the
innovations in sixties film. For women, as for Blacks and the working class, social disempowerment was reflected in cinematic disenfranchisement. Though women were anomalous in that this disenfranchisement corresponded not to exclusion from the filmic but to
a hyper-exposure within it, their presence in cinema was confined
to the use of the actresses' bodies in film narratives, a use that was
thought ipso facto to objectify women and to repress their own sexuality (Gledhill, 1978: 475). More or less informed by psychoanalysis, feminist accounts of this presence eventually argued that what
was represented was not really women at all, certainly not real
women, so much as the projection of men's desires and fears or
some initial enabling moment in phallocentric discursive systems—
or they argued that the insistence of these stereotypes stood in for
an actual unrepresentability.[1] Radical intervention could logically
be thought of, then, as a matter of withdrawing rather than securing
representation. Despite this difference from other groups marginalized by the industrial cinema, women's attempts to determine their
own representation by securing power in the industry or by developing cinemas of their own recapitulated the projects of the beats,
of Black people, and of other dissident groups.

On the other hand, such parallels between women and other marginal groups must be restored to history, first to the diachronous
relation of the women's movement to other political contestations
and the different conditions under which their respective cinemas
were constructed, and then to the ideological disputes within and

1 For example: "Within a sexist
ideology and a male-dominated cinema, woman is presented as what
she represents for man. . . . Woman
represents not herself, but by a process of displacement, the male phallus" (Johnston, 1973: 25–26). See
also Mulvey (1975) and Gledhill
(1978: 480). On the unrepresentability of women, see especially
Doane (1981).

around feminism about the structure of the social formation and the relative importance of gender, race, and class within it. Here the fact that, along with the gay rights movement, the women's movement was the *last* of the major mobilizations to be organized speaks plangently of the struggles of its birth. Considered either as a new departure or as a revival of a participatory impulse lost since the twenties, sixties feminism followed in the wake of other programs. Like nineteenth-century feminism, it grew from opposition to racism and may well have been "inspired" (Mitchell, 1973: 50) by the Black movement, and certainly consciousness-raising, its most innovative and effective social mechanism, had much in common with the "Speaking Pains to Recall Pains" of the Maoist cells. Despite its ancestry in these radical movements, American feminism forged itself in the face of violence from men and women of all classes, races, and political persuasions, and only slowly through the decade did it clarify itself as a political program. President Kennedy's committee on the status of women in 1961, Betty Friedan's *The Feminine Mystique* in 1963, the formation of NOW under her presidency in 1966, the beginnings of consciousness-raising, the first mass action by women at the Miss America pageant in 1968, Kate Millett's *Sexual Politics* in 1970, the *Roe v. Wade* abortion decision in 1973—all these were crucial crests in a swell that peaked in the early seventies when women constituted 40 percent of the 1972 Democratic convention. But American feminism only gained public prominence as a mass movement or a vanguard ideology as it discovered its difference from the left in general and separated itself strategically from other social movements.

Whatever its contingency upon previous radical programs, the history of feminism and its cinemas after the turn of the decade differs markedly from that of the other movements. The seventies' recision of the previous decade's advances affected the women's movement less than any of the other social movements, and as varieties of feminism became powerful in a way different from any other program of social change, the condition of certain women did significantly improve. Though sexual equality was not attained, and not even the Equal Rights Amendment could be nationally ratified, nevertheless feminism was the only contestation whose gains were not annulled, the only one whose entry into the political arena still appears irreversible. Virtually unhindered by the state, the women's movement was on all levels "the most public revolutionary movement ever to have existed" (Mitchell, 1973: 13).

As the failures of 1968 and of Eurocommunism, the end of the Vietnam War, and the redirection of Chinese politics after the death of Mao in 1976 eliminated the major focuses of utopian aspirations, feminism remained the only social movement with an international momentum. In contrast to the rout of the left in the United States and the extirpation of the Black movement—not merely of its Marxist vanguard—some forms of feminism became institutionally secure; and while the vocabularies of race and class were banished from the media, the political process, and the academy, women's liberation was the only radicalism to retain its voice. If Betty Friedan had been right in 1963 in her claim that the woman's question was "buried, unspoken," "the problem that has no name" (Friedan, 1963: 15), fifteen years later the argument, in either its social or its psychoanalytic form, that women were innately prohibited from discourse and were constituted as the unsayable was bruited about widely and forcefully. For while the social and ideological implications of some feminisms were fundamentally incompatible with the status quo, the concrete social form these took was in most cases assimilable to it and even functional within it; in marking the culmination of sixties radicalism, feminism coincided with its termination. And while other alternative cinemas were essentially depleted by 1974, their necessity and function dispersed, feminist film and feminist film theory were enjoying their maturity.

However painfully they fell short of their objectives, the achievements of the women's movement make clear the need for a historical understanding of the emergence of the ideologies of feminism, as it was facilitated by shifts in the economic role of women that culminated in the sixties.[2] "Women's liberation did not *create* the working woman; rather the working woman—especially the working housewife [on the public market]—created women's liberation" (Harris, 1981: 89). The long-term anti-natal tendency, interrupted by the postwar baby boom which peaked in 1957 (the period from 1940 to 1960 saw the only increased birthrate since 1800), continued as the shift from agrarian, labor-intensive family subsistence to an urban, market existence accelerated. More effective means of birth control and better infant health care freed women from the regime of serial childbearing and the dangers of multiple or undesired pregnancy, while technological innovations reduced the time needed for domestic labor. These changes in the structure of the economy, which *preceded* the period of consciousness-raising, spurred the entry of women, especially married women, into the job market. And this market, which now consisted predominantly of jobs in low-level information processing and social services—that is, women's work—rather than in heavy manufacturing, eagerly awaited them: by 1979, two out of every three new jobs were filled by women.

The fact that the emergence of the women's movement was contingent upon large-scale economic changes in no way invalidates the knowledge it made available—any more than the labor theory of value's equivalent dependence for its discovery upon nineteenth-century labor-intensive industrialization discredits it. In no way does it exculpate either the history of oppression the movement at last made visible or the inequality that persists. But the historical necessity that provided the singular staying power which other movements could only envy also determined the particular forms the ideologies of feminism would take. In general constituted at the expense of the historically obsolete industrial proletariat and especially at the expense of unassimilable minority males, American feminism was at root severed from class consciousness and racial

2 The following information is drawn from Harris (1981).

awareness, and was capable of only precarious and partial articulation with historical materialism. But in competition with this dominant bourgeois feminism, which envisaged the remedy of the condition of women within extant social structures and was assimilable to prevailing class relations, two other main positions on the relation of gender and class were developed—those of radical and socialist feminism.

Capable of more sophisticated theoretical elaboration, radical feminism understood capitalism as merely one among other modes of production that were part of the continuing oppression of women which characterized patriarchy. More responsive to the specific situation of working-class women as well as to lesbians and others outside the bourgeois hegemony, it extended coruscating polemics into comprehensive theories of gender difference with resonant, internally consistent historical analyses. At their most innovative these theories aimed to subsume historical materialism by arguing that the roots of class division and all other social hierarchies lay in the biological division of the sexes (Millett, 1970: 25; Firestone, 1970: 12), and that the exchange of women formed the basis for both the symbolic and the social orders. "Male supremacy is the oldest, most basic form of domination. All other forms of exploitation and oppression (racism, capitalism, imperialism, etc.) are extensions of male supremacy. . . . *All men* receive economic, sexual, and psychological benefits from male supremacy. *All men* have oppressed women" ("Redstockings Manifesto": 534). Since the general social division of labor merely extends the sexual division of labor produced around childbirth and nurturing, gender and indeed other forms of social equality can come about only with the complete obliteration of primary sex roles. But until biology may be thus transcended in an ultimate wresting of freedom from the necessity of nature, radical feminism is stranded as an ahistorical essentialism. For the fact that "like all other historical civilizations" capitalism is patriarchal (Millett, 1970: 25) implies that the contestation of it or any other historical mode of production as such will inevitably be fruitless. Consequently, however powerfully it influenced other theories of women, radical feminism led only to separatism and life-style politics which, like those of the beats and other idealisms that preceded it, could be only locally and incidentally disruptive to the status quo.

Attempting to articulate the concept of patriarchy that was developed by radical feminists with the Marxian concept of mode of production,[3] socialist feminism differentiated the forms of patriarchy produced in different modes of production. Extending the materialist analysis of the division of labor by means of the concept of the sexual division of labor, rather than simply replacing one with the other, it was able to recognize the special role of women in reproducing the human means of production. Since it could both recognize privileges enjoyed by men across class lines and distinguish the specificity of different classes of women positioned differently in relation to material production, it could diagnose the dual oppres-

3 On the "unhappy marriage" of feminism and Marxism, see especially the essays collected in Sargent (1981). For a Marxist critique of socialist feminism, see Burnham and Louie (1985).

sion of working-class women: their exploitation as women and as workers. But since the relation between the two systems could not conclusively be determined, within socialist feminism sexual inequality was accorded varying degrees of autonomy from the mode of production, and so the women's movement was allowed corresponding degrees of autonomy. But all positions in it to some extent qualified the orthodox Marxist understanding of the determining structure of society and of the agency of social change.

Since each of these feminisms differently understands the constitution of the social formation, logically each is situated differently in respect to the hegemonic media. Bourgeois feminism is generally oriented toward increased and improved representation of women by and in the industrial media, but it cannot contest the media's function within capitalism. Radical feminism implies an alternative cinema, for, by, and of women, outside the industrial media. And socialist feminism, equally concerned to contest the industrial function, does so only in affiliation with the working class generally, especially with racial minorities who are almost totally contained in the working class. In practice, however, these different cinematic priorities and the ideological distinctions they attend were not categorically distinguished. Though the ideological differences among these feminisms recurred in their attempts to make cinema, early seventies feminisms generally repressed class and racial differences to propose women as a noncontradictory, trans-class commonality. Early attempts to develop a feminist cinema in this vein were crucially realigned by an encounter with psychoanalysis, which supplied the dominant vocabulary for the production in film theory of the idea of the commonality of women. The consequent tension between psychoanalysis and historical materialism runs through the recent semiology of women.

After the turn of the decade, a specifically feminist film culture was constructed at the intersection of two cinematic practices: the increased participation of women in Hollywood, in political filmmaking, and in various art cinemas and the increasingly sophisticated attention to the representation of women in the mass media. Analysis of the formal and thematic conventions of the feature film clarified the ideological function of traditional women's roles, while against-the-grain readings of unusual or unstable films proposed progressive sub- or counter-texts in them. These specific investigations stimulated the meta-critical project of developing conceptual frameworks for the understanding of film and cultural production generally. Timing thus ensured a pivotal authority for women in what emerged in the seventies as a distinct regime of cinema: theory. No less than other radical innovations, academic film theory may be understood as a subcultural practice of cinema; and together with its affiliates in independent feature production on the edge of the industry or in academic institutions, feminist theory displays social and intellectual preoccupations parallel to those of previous subcultural cinemas.

The growth of academic film theory and most crucially of femi-

nist theory is historically determinate in respect to the sixties. The
demand for relevance in education; the prestige of the European art
film with the legitimizing, quasi-scientific methodology of the *auteur* theory, especially as hitched to structuralism; and the interests
of those sixties intellectuals who found in cultural studies the hope
of maintaining some echo of social intervention—all these fueled
the expansion of academic cultural studies. As sixties activism and
alternative cultural practices disintegrated, the academy seemed to
provide a sphere outside the marketplace where progressive work
could be continued. While resistance seeped away from almost all
art practices, American criticism was meeting French post-structuralism, itself after 1968 putatively the displacement of a social program. As film studies intersected with feminism—the only radical
discourse tolerated in the academy—theory appeared to itself as the
chief surviving arena of dissent, the main site of negation. With the
decline of both radical and structural film after the early seventies,
theory became the best part of cinema, and the best part of theory
was feminist. Recapitulating the sequence of French intellectual life
from structuralism to post-structuralism, avoiding Marxism in all
but formalist dalliances with Brecht, feminist film theory came to its
maturity in the crucial encounter with Lacanian psychoanalysis.

In the early days of American feminism, psychoanalysis had been
considered an ideological cornerstone of patriarchy, with Freud
himself commonly taken as "beyond question the strongest individual counterrevolutionary force in the ideology of sexual politics"
(Millett, 1970: 178). With the shift away from equal-rights confrontational activism to a theoretical interest in sexual difference
per se, away from a concern with sexual roles to a concern with
sexual identity, materialist analysis of the social condition of
women was succeeded by the investigation of femininity as an unconscious positioning, coincident with the construction of the subject in language. Though the immediately previous debate about the
relevance of verbal language to film had been abandoned without
resolution, feminist theory occupied itself with Jacques Lacan's linguistically based model of the unconscious.

Because Lacan's own writings were either unavailable or unintelligible, Lacanian feminism was disseminated by variously initiated
acolytes in re-presentations of re-presentations that resembled nothing so much as the film practices they succeeded, the distortions produced by successive reprintings in structural films like J. J. Murphy's
Print Generation. Nevertheless a general orthodoxy did emerge
(Mulvey, 1975; Gledhill, 1978; Heath, 1978; Kuhn, 1982; Metz,
1982; Kaplan, 1983). According to this orthodoxy, Lacan had returned to Freud's understanding of the female's lack of male geni-
talia as a constitutive function of sexual difference, but he had reinterpreted that absence semiologically. Instead of Freud's limited
anatomical concept of penis envy, for Lacan possession of the phallus, of which the penis is only the sign, allows the male a position in
the symbolic order, the realm of language and signification. Without
access to the phallus, women can only play a negative role in lan-

guage; they merely embody lack, the primary moment of differentiation that sets the signifying process in motion.

Whatever the metaphysical status of this exclusion from language in general, it seemed to correspond to and so could be validated by the actual historical situation of women in language production, and nowhere more clearly than in the absence they manifested as authors of film. Their only voice in cinema was that spoken for them by men, their only place that constructed for them in men's sight. Since Lacan's concept of the "mirror stage" apparently made looking crucially important in the formation of the subject, feminist film theory turned to the gaze as the cinematic agency of sexual difference. In the three basic looks identified (that of the intradiegetic participant, that of the camera, and that of the spectator in recapitulating the camera's look), women were historically over-determined as the objects but never the subjects of a relay of gazes. They could be looked at in the filmic and by the filmic, but they could not themselves either look at men or look back at the camera, for such a return of the gaze would break the imaginary identification of the spectator. While this analysis supposed a biological and social femininity as the object of the scopophilic drive, it also recognized that historically women have occupied the nominally male position of the spectating subject. Though the gaze of the spectator at the screen was not literally male, appropriation of it inscribed women in a linguistically masculine position. Hence among the ideological effects produced in cinema was the splitting of women between identification with the female object—the visual sex object—and identification with the male subject. The shift in emphasis away from the spectators' sociological identification with the intradiegetically reproduced roles of patriarchy to their psychological identification with the apparatus itself, with the look of the camera as relayed by the projector (Metz, 1982: 49), completed this dislocation, from actual men and women, of sexuality as a filmic function.

In the event, this disjuncture had been anticipated by developments within Lacanian theory that supplied masculine and feminine with a similar metaphoricalness. Initially, the special relation between the penis and the phallus had allowed Lacan to establish the terms male and female as functions in language. Still, in early texts such as "The Signification of the Phallus" in 1958, the ostensibly symbolic function of the phallus retained more than a degree of biological determinism; for example, it was chosen as the privileged signifier because "it is the most tangible element in the real of sexual copulation. . . . [And] by virtue of its turgidity, it is the image of the vital flow as it is transmitted in generation" (Lacan, 1977: 287). When Lacan turned in the early seventies to the question of female sexuality, he de-emphasized this residual biological differentiation in a theorization of the phallus as purely a function of signification, as an attribute not of the natural but of the symbolic order. Men had no privileged access to it, and, in fact, it could be possessed only by the analyst. Now anatomical difference did not subtend sexual difference in either language or society; it only *figured* a difference (Rose, 1985: 44). Having abandoned the historical family as the mediating sphere between the individual and the social formation for a series of positions in the realm of the symbolic, Lacanian psychoanalysis finally proposed not just a trans-historical, trans-cultural, trans-racial, trans-class subject, but a trans-sexual one. It thus completed itself as theology.

Though Lacan's project did not yield a theory of a specifically female language, Derridean and Nietzschean work subsequent to it did, either by reversing the terms of pre-Freudian models of female specificity, even those of the Aristotelian dyads, or by deconstructing the oppositions that organized them. Post-Lacanians such as Hélène Cixous, Julia Kristeva, Monique Wittig, Luce Irigaray, and Michèle Montrelay[4] all propose conceptions of women and of female language in which terms that initially appear as biologically essentialist are elaborated socially and historically to the point where "woman" becomes the summary other of all history, an umbrella category, subsuming the dispossessed in general.

Presently the most useful of these conceptions is Irigaray's critical reading of psychoanalysis, particularly of Lacan's selection of the phallus as virtually a transcendental signifier, the signifier of all subsequent signifiers. Irigaray argues that Lacan reproduces the Western tradition's privileging of a unified, objective, preeminently male subject, figured in the penis and its erection. Against this phallocentrism, which has excluded women even while incorporating them into its systems of representation, Irigaray proposes a female specificity figured in the infolding lips of the vagina: "Woman 'touches herself' all the time . . . for her genitals are formed of two lips in continuous contact. Thus, within herself, she is already two—but not divisible into one(s)—that caress each other" (Irigaray, 1985: 24).

This radical, unsutured plurality, the constantly shifting site of difference and nonidentity, implies woman as the other of phallocentrism; her language is correspondingly the other of phallocentric discourse (of phallogocentrism, to use Derrida's term). It does so not simply by reversing the value system of the binary opposition between male and female, but by subverting the binary itself. Female differs from male, but only as one and two together are different from one—or two. This plurality, the trace of *différance*, inhabits both women and their language.

> "She" is indefinitely other in herself. This is doubtless why she is said to be whimsical, incomprehensible, agitated, capricious . . . not to mention her language, in which "she" sets off in all directions leaving "him" unable to discern the coherence of any meaning. . . . One would have to listen with another ear, as if hearing *an "other meaning" always in the process of weaving itself, of embracing itself with words, but also of getting rid of words in order not to become fixed, congealed in them.* (Irigaray, 1985: 28–29)

Woman must thus tentatively and provisionally seek for her language within male discourse, even while she knows that it cannot be fully realized and that even to raise the issue of a complete female

4 In the United States, Mary Daly proposed a similar model of feminist language as the spinning and weaving of Hags and Crones that would "dis-spell the language of phallocracy" (Daly, 1978: 4), while Jane Gallop relocated plurality from the text to the reading process in her project of working through the French texts with "attention to small details" that refuse "imperialistic, idealizing reductions," especially to errors that make holes in texts (Gallop, 1984: 93, 104).

language, certainly an *authentic* female language, would only articulate a concept still within patriarchy; unable to "leap outside"
phallocentric discourse, she situates herself "at its borders and . . .
move[s] continuously from the inside to the outside" (ibid.: 122).

Irigaray's own writing is programmatically indeterminate in its
definition of woman. What woman's language is cannot yet be written and so, as in the extracts above, the definition of woman can
only appear framed by patriarchy, enclosed in parentheses such as
"this view," "in this sexual imaginary," or "within this logic." Irigaray's indeterminacy is especially important in relation to her informing metaphor, that of the figuration of female plurality in vag-
inal bi-labialism. Her use of this metaphor has permitted her to be
read reductively, as a biological determinist who restates Lacan's
equivocation between the phallus and the penis in the obverse perhaps, but still in a manner determined by him. In fact, the rejection
of a self-referential univocality in her re-presentation of male representations of women sustains her deconstructive intervention, as
well as non-metaphysically mirroring the actual historical construction of women between biology and culture. Even if it begins by
appearing to invoke an essential femininity, Irigaray's vulva-logo-
centrism defers it, shifts it from the trans-historical body to the historical imaginary. Since woman has been (un)known under patriarchy only as its other, what her nature outside patriarchy might be
cannot presently be asserted.

By unfolding a multiple, dispersed female from phallocratic sin-
gularity, Irigaray makes it possible for the radical division of all
post-humanist subjects to be rewritten as female. Consequently, in
this and similar paradigms of woman as the (non)categorical other,
the two main theoretical issues that traverse feminism merge: that
of the nature of sexual difference and that of the relation between
sexual and other forms of discrimination, especially class and race.
When patriarchy is understood as a function of Western discourse,
with capitalism and imperialism its complete forms, its other becomes equally as extensive. As a social category historically constructed rather than a biological essence, woman loses gender specificity in identification with all others marginally or oppositionally
placed in respect to patriarchy—with all other Others. Thus, in a
complete formulation of such a syncretism, the "difference between
the sexes is not whether one does or doesn't have a penis, it is
whether or not one is an integral part of a phallic masculine economy" (Fouque, 1981: 117). Outside this economy are groups who
are not gender-specific—the Chinese, for example, or schizophren-
ics—and also those whose gender would otherwise include them—
male homosexuals or male feminists. And so, as revolutionary and
liberated, Third World and avant-garde men secede, the phylum
shrinks, leaving only the capitalist patriarchs themselves in their
corporate towers, alone with their erections. But since these can be
unified only as social positions, the actual "men" who occupy them
are themselves always divided, psychologically and linguistically
dispersed over the abyss of post-structural difference. They too can
only be *women*.

Feminism finally completes the revision of historical materialism begun in the sixties when the concept of the Third World supplanted that of class as the hegemonic category of difference. Then we were all to be Vietcong; now we are all to be women. Though working-class, Third World women retain a privileged position, finally "feminist" becomes the synoptic term for resistance—at its most utopian, capable of synthesizing as complementary what male discourse reifies separately as the realms of the personal, the cultural, and the political. Situated simultaneously on the terrains of history and (un)consciousness, post-structural feminism retains a special place for writing; first, for feminist writing, but then, since the work of difference that defines feminist writing also defines writing per se, for Writing, for *Écriture*, for the avant-garde: "The avant-garde, the women's struggle and the battle for socialism, are merely symptomatic of the 'impossible,' on different levels" (Kristeva, 1981: 139).

Though the institution of woman as the exemplary post-modern subject occurred after a women's film culture developed in the United States, this body of theory supplies the terms by which the feminist cinema may best be understood. The tensions within feminist theory between the search for the intrinsically female and the recognition that such essences could only be supplementary to androcentric institutions that preceded them recurred in feminist film. That supplementarity, summarized in Kristeva's argument that "a feminist practice can only be negative, at odds with what already exists" (Kristeva, 1981: 137),[5] ensured that women's cinema would be constructed against previous practices—languages of difference intervening in an economy of the same. Feminist film thus discovered a special consanguinity with the avant-garde; for the general terms of femininst film language—it had to be an anti-Aristotelian, non-teleological, anti-systematic language of interiority, plurality, and autoeroticism—were also those in which previous alternative film modes had constructed an unstable specificity for themselves as the other of the teleological, sutured, patriarchal narrative industrial film. The play of the authentic within the inauthentic, and then of the inauthentic within the authentic, that echoed back through the structural film and the art film's reshuffling of the codes of the commercial feature, through Brakhage and the homosexual ironists—Warhol, Smith, the Kuchars, and Anger—and finally through the matrix, Maya Deren herself—all this tradition could logically be recognized as latently feminist.

In practice, neither the mobilization of a women's alternative cinema nor even women's intervention in the avant-garde was this easy. Filmmaking by groups organized as feminist did not flourish until the mid-seventies, and even then a real feminist film practice was often considered impossible (Doane, 1981: 23). But that self-conscious feminist cinema was prefigured in the period of this study by numerous interventions by women in previous oppositional cinemas. Women participated in underground, radical, structural, and art film, and in each case their situation in the subcultural cinema duplicated the conditions of the alternative practice itself. In each instance women were marginalized within already marginalized

5 Cf. "A politically and aesthetically avant-garde cinema is now possible, but it can still only exist as a counterpoint" (Mulvey, 1975: 8).

subcultures. Their determining contexts were thus crucially doubled; as well as having to develop formal practices consonant with a particular conception of women and to define themselves in respect to the industrial media and the general social conditions, these women's films could only come into being as a sub-category among but also *within* pre-feminist marginal cinemas. Each had to distinguish itself against the male discourses that surrounded it, against the sexism that was systemic in the mass media, but also endemic among the independents. Each was doubly at odds with what existed, the other within the other.

Women in Cinema

The special case of actresses aside, women participated more substantially in the independent cinemas than in the industry, and in several instances their interventions have been crucial. Following Mary Ellen Bute's important abstract films of the thirties, Maya Deren virtually invented the avant-garde film for Americans as both genre and mode of production, and *Meshes of the Afternoon* (1943) established major paradigms for the next twenty years of the underground. Shirley Clarke, a prime mover in the New American Cinema Group, made exemplary works within that aesthetic for twenty-five years. Marie Menken, Sara Arledge, Barbara Rubin, Storm de Hirsch, Carolee Schneemann, Anne Severson, Chick Strand, Freude, Yoko Ono, Gunvor Nelson, and Dorothy Wiley all worked with distinction in underground or cognate modes. Apart from Marie Menken's *Notebook* (1962–63), a virtual lexicon for the next decade's formalist explorations, films made by women in the classic underground period were preoccupied with women's experience, especially the politics of domestic life and parturition. In their attention to female sexuality they reproduced the aesthetics and rituals of their subcultural location, taking to its logical extreme a main function of the underground.

The anxieties surrounding the contemporary changes in sex roles and sexual mores, felt but repressed in Hollywood,[6] were a primary motivation for several alternative cinemas. First came the beats' renegotiation of homosexuality, and then the polemical display of the female body and of eroticism in general by the underground and art cinemas. Publicly tagged as a sex cinema,[7] underground film was always identified with proscribed eroticism. No less an authority than *Playboy* noted a continuity of concern with sex from the classic avant-garde, through Hans Richter's re-creation of Duchamp's "Nude" in *Dreams That Money Can Buy*, to the subject matter of Warhol et al., which it found "a compound of exotica, erotica, neurotica and lurid samplings of psychopathia sexualis" (Knight and Alpert, 1967a: 138).

It is scarcely possible to isolate a "sincere" concern with sexuality from the merely sensationalist or exploitative in this tradition, for not only could sexually explicit representations be made to serve

6 Marjorie Rosen charts the emergence of the "diminutive sex goddesses" (Rosen, 1973: 309) of the youth market that revitalized the industry in the late fifties, but she notes that even the tardy attempts to confront social issues after *Easy Rider* in the late sixties did not extend to the presentation of new roles for women: "In most of these movies, female roles were negligible—nonexistent, purely sexual, or purely for laughs" (ibid.: 342).

7 See Chapter 4, note 7.

8.1 Maya Deren in her *Meshes of the Afternoon*

any number of purposes, but also, in an environment of acute censorship, such representation as a deliberate act of social transgression would not finally be separable from the attempt to restore it to some pristine unselfconsciousness outside socially imposed guilt. The (finally impossible) task of safeguarding the erotic from the pornographic at the level of representation forced late-underground (or "high" countercultural) filmmakers to diffuse explicit imagery through various filmic effects; the soft focus in Scott Bartlett's *Love-making* is exemplary. In such works, where explicit representation of sexuality was made to signify social freedom, women's bodies became the site of contestation, even when what was at issue was not female sexuality per se so much as censorship and repression of any kind. But though women were thus objectified as the sign of the sexual in general, initially the most contentious issue, especially in the New York underground, was not female but male sexuality.

In the films of Kenneth Anger, Gregory Markopoulos, Jack Smith, and Andy Warhol, themselves like the beats predominantly homosexual, the profilmic is the scene for the gamut of male sexuality—the genital, the mythic, and the operatively everyday. As the critical epicenter of this sphere of underground film, homoeroticism

8.2 Marie Menken, *Notebook*

was valorized for itself but also as the vehicle for other interventions. Since sex was the sign of social and aesthetic values suppressed in straight society, it could signify deviance and resistance in general, and so social repression of all kinds could be contested via the codes of sexual representation. Jonas Mekas's observation that the films of the Baudelairean cinema "all contain homosexual and lesbian elements. The homosexuality, because of its existence outside the official moral conventions, has been at the bottom of much great poetry since the beginning of humanity" (Mekas, 1972: 86) and his imprisonment for showing Smith's *Flaming Creatures* and Genet's *Un Chant d'Amour* summarize such a reading of male sexuality and its public effect. Similarly committed to the erotic as the self-justifying source of liberation, women's underground film had to disentangle a specifically feminist use of woman's body, a specifically feminist female sexuality, not only from mass media appropriation but also from the misogyny of the male underground.

Given the ideological and commercial use of the female body, the contradictions involved in any attempt to rearrange its codification, to modify "the syntax which constitutes the female body as a term" (Doane, 1981: 34), are most crucial in respect to the genitals. The sensationalizing of the female body, explicit in pornography and implicit in the mass media, makes any representation of it problematic, but the body is most politicized at the site of most categorical sexual difference. The dialectic of exposure and concealment that constitutes the body as erotic is most precisely hinged at that site, and so the vagina is valorized in an over-determination by biological, moral, psychological, economic, and aesthetic shibboleths—an over-determination that loads but also destabilizes the vagina's potential as a signifier. Privileging of the vagina as the figure of female language provides a powerful vocabulary for a feminist intervention in the representation of women, in which the polemic affirmation of the propriety of the vagina as an object of representation may authorize a language of representation organized in reference to its particular morphology.

Irrespective of the significance of any other practices with which it might be correlated, vulva-logocentric representation is thus doubly transgressive: it violates the patriarchal control of images of the vagina that is integral to control of women themselves, and it violates the languages that maintain that control. Thus the paintings of Georgia O'Keefe and Judy Chicago, for example, criticize even as they invoke the use of genital imagery in advertising and pornography. Such practices always exist precariously next to men's use of the same images, and representations of this kind are always in danger of approaching what they seek to differentiate themselves from, of making themselves available for the uses they abhor. Films as early in the underground as Barbara Rubin's *Christmas on Earth* (1964) or as late as Anne Severson's *Near the Big Chakra* (1972) are extreme and extremely ambivalent instances of women's attempts to reclaim anatomy in acts of sexual decolonization.

Christmas on Earth is a twin-projection superimposition of one

8.3 Scott Bartlett, *Lovemaking*

film inside another. Figuring female bi-labialism both in its representation of the vagina and in the intercourse of one screen with the other, it suggests allegorical readings of image production and reproduction. It polemically asserts the double-ness, the plurality moving toward the polymorphous-ness, of the female against the fetishizing of the male that is figured, filmically, in the phallomorphism of single projection and, socially, in the circle of filmmakers associated with the New York Cooperative at that time. Responsive to a different current in women's liberation, *Near the Big Chakra* documents the vaginas of thirty-seven women of all ages, allowing the biological reality of women's anatomy, the diversity of its forms, to desensationalize it and retrieve it from the sanitized cosmetics of the media. Between these two films, and similarly transgressive in its representation of the genitals of both sexes, is the remarkable *Fuses* (1964–67), the film Carolee Schneemann made of her lovemaking with James Tenney.

CAROLEE SCHNEEMANN: *Fuses*

But *woman has sex organs more or less everywhere.*
— Luce Irigaray

In the visual density of its heavily worked style, in its domestic, artisanal practice that identifies home movies as art film, and in its use of film as a participant in erotic activity, *Fuses* is an essay within the mode developed by Stan Brakhage. But it also extends that mode, organizing a critique of it and bringing to a fuller articulation cinematic possibilities Brakhage discovered but did not entirely resolve. In *Fuses*, a new copulation between the filmic and the erotic is traced, one in which female sexuality is enacted in a practice of

8.4–8.7 Carolee Schneemann, *Fuses*

mutuality. Dissatisfied with Brakhage's representation of her sexuality in *Loving* and *Cat's Cradle*, the films he made about her relationship with Tenney, Schneemann made her own vision, one that addresses the phallocentric imbalance of even Brakhage's best attempts to share authorship with a lover in the profilmic space. In doing so she was able to address the repression in culture generally of what she understood as the female principle. Her film is, then, a polemically female representation of heterosexual eroticism, one that demonstrates its difference in almost all the phases of its production.

Schneemann's intimate and graphic representation of sexual intercourse is historically anomalous; its explicitness appeared antifeminist in the context of feminist attempts to differentiate erotica from pornography, and its fascination with the male as much as with the female body was unusual outside homosexual pornography. As in Brakhage's participation films, this egalitarian representation follows from the lovers' photographing each other during lovemaking, though Schneemann also photographed herself and used camera stands to photograph herself and Tenney together. The editing was entirely Schneemann's own work, but otherwise labor was not divided in the production of the profilmic or in its recording. Thus reproduction of gender in power relations in the profilmic or in the control of the apparatus was avoided, as was phallocratic

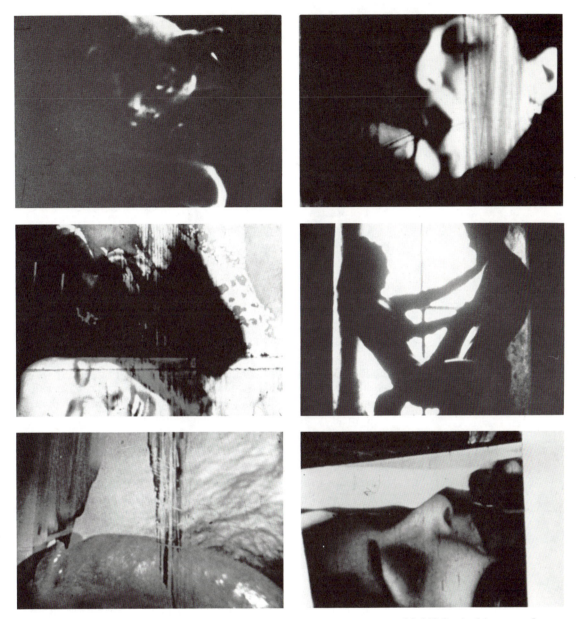

8.8–8.13 Carolee Schneemann, *Fuses*

distribution of roles—the male as the scopophilic subject and the female as its object. The film so thoroughly interweaves shots of Schneemann and shots from her point of view, shots of Tenney and shots from his point of view, and shots of the two of them from no attributable point of view that narrator positioning is entirely dissolved. The only stable persona implied is a black cat; its manifest sensuality is a purring correlative to the action, reminding us that in the textual plurality of the film's infolding, it illustrates the pussy's point of view.

Within this plurality, the organizing telos of the male orgasm—the end that orders the narrative and representational systems of contemporary pornography—is shunned. The montage does not insert the shots into the rhetorical figures of orthodox narrative economy, but rather disperses authorship and subjectivity as generalized functions of an indeterminate erotic field. Emotions are legible on the participants' faces, and their existence outside sexual passion is fragmentarily glimpsed (but then only in contexts that feed back metaphorically into the iconographic field—she running on the beach and he driving a car), but these do not articulate psychological dimensions of character. The lovers are not unified, discrete subjects within the erotic activity, so much as the vehicle of an eroticism that possesses them.

The urgency in which the lovers' individual lineaments are subsumed inheres as thoroughly in Schneemann's physical encounter with the material of film as it does in her encounter with the body of James Tenney. Emerging as the totalizing, polymorphous, introverted energy and self-absorbed hypersensuality of the sexual activity of the profilmic, the erotic power of *Fuses* overflows into the filmic, is reproduced there as a filmic function. For the physical passion traced photographically is returned upon in Schneemann's excitation of the physical body of the film in editing—the touch of her hand on the film's flesh in her painterly and sculptural work on the emulsion. In the film's own eroticism, its autoeroticism, its skin is slipped upon the celluloid, displaced from the closure of mimetic identification and freed from the economy of its syntax, suddenly a tactile material, palpably aroused. This texturing of superimposition, of rhythmic disjunction and return, the scratching, painting, and dyeing, the fusing and refusing of represented flesh, is thus both correlative in its visceral energy to the sexual encounter it reproduces (its dalliance with memory) and itself the site of a textural eroticism in which the work (or play) on the body of film renews the congress, coming back to it (its encounter with desire).

The experience of the projected film, the trace of this epidermic intimacy, reproduces Schneemann's palpation in another sensual register, that of light. An optical promiscuity in which the slippage of the boundaries of the self experienced in lovemaking recurs visually in the seepage of figure into ground and of image into medium; the bodies not fixed, not spatially, not materially, not temporally; they merge and rhythmically emerge into a clarity that cannot be held but is carried away in the flux of unlocalized optical sensation (produced without return to humanist narrative economy), sterile, profligate; as color, texture, form, and other properties of the photographic find themselves free from the self-effacement of transparent representation, they become attributes of concupiscent light, a psychedelic projection which, as it illuminates the lovers' bodies, receives its body from them, indulgence shimmering, echoing and supplementing the pleasure of the engorged penis as the mouth takes it, pandering to the vagina's pleasure as fingers open its lips to light: outside commerce: the film fuses.

In completing Brakhage's domestication of the apparatus for libidinal autobiography, Schneemann opened up the full register of his notion of the artist as *amateur*—one who loves—in an entirely eroticized language and practice; filmmaking became the site of sexual performance, a contract transacted outside the historical and political conditions of women. The possible effect on contemporary film of Schneemann's love in the medium was defused and diffused by the terror her vision evoked. The film could hardly be seen, either by the avant-garde establishment or by the women's movement. For the latter, her exaltation of woman as an erotic body too closely resembled the exclusion of social responsibilities inherent in the male projection of pornography. Those responsibilities became unavoidable as a feminist position emerged in the political subcultures into which beat disengagement was forced.

Feminist Documentary: *The Woman's Film*

But women do not constitute, strictly speaking, a class, and their dispersion among several classes makes their political struggle complex, their demands sometimes contradictory.
— Luce Irigaray

During the activist phase of the women's movement, a number of independent documentaries about politicized women were made in order to assist and encourage others in their steps toward liberation—a function that transformed the representation of women into a feminist practice of cinema. Typically, these films were constructed around first-person direct-address narration, with lip-sync images of the women talking variously interspersed with cutaways. The genre is represented in Geri Ashur and Peter Barton's *Janie's Janie* (1971) (one woman); Kate Millett's *Three Lives* (1971) (three

8.14 Geri Ashur and Peter Barton, *Janie's Janie*

8.15 "Women are using technical equipment": *The Woman's Film*

women); and in San Francisco Newsreel's *The Woman's Film* (1969) (several women).

The Woman's Film is a compilation of interviews, interspersed with rapid collages, in which half a dozen women, including both Black and White women and one Chicana, almost all of whom are working-class, talk about their past expectations, their present lives, and their plans for the future. In direct address to the camera or in discussion with other women, they share accounts of their problems with men, expressing discontent with males ranging from husbands to bosses, and of their attempts to organize cooperatives and labor actions, so as to take control of their lives.

Such films may be understood cinematically; they provide a public voice to people unrepresented in industrial cinema, and they extend documentation into suasive, legitimizing, and other characteristic functions of group organization that together constitute a practice of cinema. Given the history of women's cinematic disenfranchisement, the participation allowed women in these films itself constitutes a political intervention. In *The Woman's Film*, women's filmmaking skills are appropriately emphasized by a shot of the sound recordist, as well as stills of her and the camerawoman that are included in a final collage of women activists, and also by one of the interviewees who declares the pleasure of participating in a film made by women: "Women are using technical equipment. . . . I thought that the ability to use a tape-recorder was something that men were born with." The fact that it is a film made by women about women and for women, in which women tell the story as well as serve as the story, involves an appropriation of the apparatus that is both metonymic for and instrumental in the seizure of more general social power—a transgression correctly understood at the time as so primary that it was ipso facto radically feminist.

The point of reference for the valorization of women's discourse

8.16–8.21 San Francisco Newsreel, *The Woman's Film*

was the consciousness-raising group, a semipublic forum where private histories were mediated into public activities. In these feminist developments of the principles of psychoanalysis and group therapy,[8] the healing of the analysand through the account of her own experience was understood as the reclamation of a realm of women's experience, repressed and unspeakable in patriarchy; it was a "talking cure," but one without the authoritarian control of the male analyst. The autobiographical account of oppression thus produced an ostensibly objective mode, one that appeared to circumvent filmic discursiveness by presenting the profilmic speakers without interference.

8 Thus: "The structure of the consciousness-raising group becomes the deep structure repeated over and over in these films. Within such a narrative structure, either a single woman tells her story to the filmmaker or a group of women are filmed sharing experiences in a politicized way. They are filmed in domestic space, and their words serve to redefine that space in a new, 'woman-identified' way" (Lesage, 1978: 521).

The realism claimed by films of this order is open to political criticisms of two kinds: first, to the extent that the filmmaker does efface herself, the politics of the film are circumscribed by the politics of the profilmic speakers; and second, the documentary objectivity, whether it includes direct address or pretends to a cinéma vérité unselfconsciousness of the camera, is illusory. Since the pragmatic priority of these films—to generate solidarity among women—overrode expression of differences among the speakers—through the ironic juxtaposition of interviewees, for example, or through other forms of authorial critique—the latter criticism is more important. In this feminist version of the thirties modernism/realism debate, accessibility to a mass, filmically unsophisticated audience was pitted against the need for critical attention to filmic illusionism. The pull between these responsibilities was especially tense in films about specific local issues and in films designed for working-class audiences, cases involving a conflict between pragmatic priorities in social organizing and the theoretical investigation of film form—a conflict which reiterated the separation of practice from theory in Western Marxism generally.[9]

Critiques of documentary realism argued that the emotional identification between the audience and the profilmic speaker prevented analysis and allowed elision of profilmic coding and of the effects of the apparatus.[10] Such blanket dismissals of realism preclude recognition of authorial organization and of ideological differences inside formally similar filmic modes (Kaplan, 1983: 125–30), differences that can otherwise be charted in the political analyses presented by different speakers. The extent to which gender distinction is accommodated to class difference, for example, is quite different in *Three Lives* than in *The Woman's Film*. But even as it allows a range of positions to pass through the uncritical juxtaposition of various women's voices, maintaining the specificity of actual women within the wide terms of their collective situation, the polyvocality of the "talking heads" film is always finally held in place by the filmmaker's authority.

Of the filmic codes that articulate this authority, the most important is editing, which in *The Woman's Film* is so sophisticated that the profilmic voices can hardly be distinguished from the activities of those other women, the filmmakers, through whom they speak. In this case, then, the ostensible realism of the illusionist presentation of actual women speaking, including the transparent ploys they create for identification and other forms of self-conscious self-presentation, is contained within a calculated discursiveness—the editorial arrangement of the fragments of the women's voices. Their speeches are broken down and reassembled to create an orderly passage from one concern to another, and they are interspersed with other material that directs apprehension of them. By these means the film rewrites as class struggle conditions it introduces as sexual exploitation.

Black and White alike, the women begin with complaints about the accepted female sphere: the disillusion of marriage, the drudgery

9 Cf. "And if the Feminist filmmakers deliberately used a traditional 'realist' documentary structure, it is because they saw making these films as an urgent public act and wished to enter the 16 mm circuit of educational films especially through libraries, schools, churches, and YWCAs to bring Feminist analysis to many women it might otherwise never reach" (Lesage, 1978: 508).

10 See, for example, the position of *Camera Obscura*: "We had come to question the political effectiveness of films which depended on emotional identification with characters. What we felt we needed was not a person to identify with, but situations in which we could imagine ourselves, within a structure of distanciation which insures room for critical analysis" ("Yvonne Rainer: An Introduction," 1976: 59).

of housework, the viciousness of men. Here they speak specifically as women, as victims of patriarchy. But as they pass on to the discrimination they experience at work—in agriculture and in low-level urban jobs such as typing, cleaning, and switchboard operating—the focus on the public sphere prompts the introduction of the special exploitation of racial minorities (a Black woman talking about her work segues into a collage history of racism since slavery); and from that condition they proceed to working-class collective activism in social protest and strikes. The account given by one of the women will illustrate. She describes a failed first marriage in which for sixteen years she was "a slave" to her husband, obliged to perform his dictates in her work, at home, and in sex. This enslavement, subsequently literalized in the collage history of Black women, ended when she left her first husband for a better man. When he is brutalized by the police while on picket duty, she supports the strike with other women and then organizes around it. Finally, at the end of the film, when the journey to similar social action has been charted for several other women, she expresses the opinion that "the working class, whether Black, Chicano or White, should be leading the fight."

The rhetorical integration of the women's movement into class struggle—the former is necessary, but only "to teach us how to be good fighters"—is possible because virtually all the women in the film are from the working class. By avoiding the specific problems of bourgeois women, racial tensions within the working class, and the situation of Black males, the film can sustain a hortatory (if historically illusory) image of solidarity among women of all classes. Since most of the women, Black and White, recur from section to section, domestic, racial, labor, and class issues appear continuous with each other, each the implication and concomitant of the others. The similarities in the experiences of these women thus present a composite biography, the situation and concerns of a representative woman (none of them are named), a social position which specific women occupy and illustrate. At the same time, the logic of their sequential presentation supplies the viewer with increasingly wide contexts, so that the emergence of class as the comprehensive form of injustice proves that action on behalf of the working class is the proper response to the victimization all the women have lived.

If from a radical feminist position *The Woman's Film* appears as a Marxist excursus, its provenance reveals its politics as a feminist intervention in a previously Marxist cinema. Initially, the influence of the Bay Area counterculture ensured that San Francisco Newsreel was as anti-Marxist as the founding New York branch; but the larger proportion of working-class members in it and the influence of the Black Panther party (with whom it made several films) quickly made it "the most working-class, Marxist oriented Newsreel office" (Nichols, 1972: 175), allowing it to develop a collective mode of film production in which participation in community affairs responded to community input. Its first two major films, *Black Panther* (1968) and *Oil Strike* (1969)—the latter a documentation of a wildcat workers' strike which culminates in a call for joint worker-student resistance—were informed by Marxist analysis, and they exemplify this unusual and unusually early integration of a filmmaking collective with the working class. *The Woman's Film*'s extension of this popular integration in its addressing the problem of working-class women evidences the filmmakers' appropriation for feminism of an apparatus previously organized around other concerns—an appropriation emblematized by the accompaniment of the film's opening collage of still images of women by Aretha Franklin's version—her rewriting—of the aggressively male song "Satisfaction." The film retains the traces of Newsreel's working-class orientation by being itself partially constructed from fragments of specifically working-class films. The woman whose experience was recounted above was the wife of a Santa Clara steel plant worker, whose strike was documented in an earlier Newsreel film, *PDM*, and many of the scenes of the women protesting are from *Los Siete*, a film about the railroading of seven Latino youths by the San Francisco police. The recontextualization and the recoding of such footage represent its adaptation to the situation of women, the discovery of a feminist component in labor and racial contestation. Thus, though the film was made by Newsreel women, researched in collaboration with women's groups, and subjected at rough-cut stage to their criticism (Nichols, 1972: 190), its specifically feminist orientation occurred as a revision of a practice organized in different terms.

In confronting the industrial cinema's reproduction of repressive sex roles and images of women, the feminist documentary did not give filmic codes or the mode of film production the kind of attention that defined the concerns of structural and art film. Despite important exceptions such as Joyce Wieland and Yoko Ono in the first mode and Susan Sontag in the second, both types of film were even more exclusively male-dominated than either underground or radical film. The most important intervention in both, and one that proved especially fertile for feminism, was made by Yvonne Rainer. By playing the compositional procedures of structural film against the narrative extensions of the art film, she produced a macaronic mode—including both types of film but constructed at a critical distance from each—that broke the terminal impasse each had reached in the early seventies.

YVONNE RAINER: *Film about a woman who . . .*

We would have needed, at least, two genres.
— Luce Irigaray

Starting out "trying to make dance like sculpture" (Koch, 1972: 55) in the post-Cunningham Manhattan art world, Yvonne Rainer was among those choreographers who most radically rejected theatricality and kinetic virtuosity. Her interest in the specificity of ordinary body movement, clarified by the repetitive performance of simple tasks that also demonstrated the process of composition, resembled the minimalist sculptors' concern with object-hood. As we have seen, the terms of this similarity—and she invoked them in a 1968 essay outlining "a one-to-one relationship between aspects of so-called minimal sculpture and recent dancing" (Rainer, 1968: 264)—also broadly informed structural film: the substitution of phrasing, development and climax, character and performance by equality of parts, repetition of discrete events, and neutral performance. These priorities ensured that the tropes of structural film would inform Rainer's forays into cinema; they are summarily visible in a section, entitled "An Emotional Accretion in 48 Steps," that represents a crisis in a love affair in her melodrama of sexual passion, *Film about a woman who . . .*

Though it has a narrative continuity that is untypical of both structural film and her own filmmaking in general, "An Emotional Accretion in 48 Steps" demonstrates how Rainer's previous career in minimalist dance initially supplied the formal paradigms for her filmmaking and so placed it within structural film's dominant frame of reference. It may be understood as the performance of a predetermined set of compositional procedures. Numbered so as to eliminate dramatic inflection of the whole, the steps manifest various possibilities in the combination of words and images: the verbal text may be narrated in either the first or third person, on- or off-screen, with or without lip sync, by a male or a female voice; the text may be realized in either sound or written words, in white on black or black on white, accompanying or disjunct from actions it refers to. The image track may be blank, or it may contain either text or figures, the latter either silent or speaking and more or less accurately performing the roles described for them. Reminiscent of Hollis Frampton's cross-referencing of visual and verbal languages, the sequence may be read either as the didactic presentation of the forms of sound and image that constitute film language (in Rainer's own words, "the *acting* of the narrative film, the *inter-titles* of the silent movie, the *sub-titles* and *dubbing* of the foreign language film, the *voice-over* of the documentary and the flash back, and the *face-front-to-camera delivery* of Godard" [Rainer, 1974: 278]), or as the formalist juxtaposition of them, their mutual negation in a self-ironizing paradigm.

But unlike classic structural film, in which such axiological reductions to the materials of the medium demand that represented iconography be either sufficiently neutral to allow the formal procedures to efface it or figuratively apposite so that it may be reclaimed as a metaphoric restatement of those procedures, here content asserts itself as such; through the didactic display of the forms of film language a melodramatic plot of sexual passion unfolds. The filmic processes certainly foreground themselves; but they never efface the diegesis they carry or entirely contain its emotional resonances. The unstable plurality of the forms of the signifier, which nevertheless sustains signification, opens a tension between formal and narrative content, between filmic and extra-filmic meaning, cueing the di-

Who is the victim here?

8.22 Yvonne Rainer (*right*) in her *Film about a woman who . . .*

vided reading process that is the dominant experience of Rainer's films. Recognition of the more or less systematic permutations of filmic codes is held against the possibility of reading through them, a possibility they simultaneously propose and resist.

This tension inhabits all the structural binaries of photographic codes (surface/depth, stills/motion, frontality/diagonality, real time/film time, color/black and white, in-frame/out-of-frame) by which the film produces itself. In one sequence, for instance, a vacationing family assumes a series of artificial, still-camera poses which are all

8.23–8.24 Yvonne Rainer, *Film about a woman who . . .*

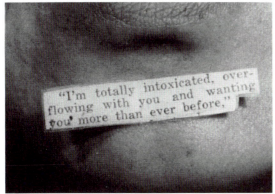

48
She had wanted to
bash his fucking
face in.

"I'm totally intoxicated, over-
flowing with you and wanting
you more than ever before,"

and also by funding from

The American Theater Laboratory
National Endowment on the Arts
Castelli-Sonnabend
Tapes and Films
Change, Inc.

8.25–8.28 Yvonne Rainer, *Film about a woman who . . .*

mis-aligned with the frame; in another the body of a young woman, unusually foregrounded so that it dominates the frame, encloses a man and produces spatial discontinuity that makes him appear impossibly small; and in another the woman frames the same man in a barely visible sheet of glass, a surrogate screen that contradictorily layers profilmic space, internally modeling the optical intervention of the apparatus. But in each of these sequences, which would otherwise be read formalistically as the permutation of filmic codes, some narrative relation between the people, typically an erotic implication, asserts itself against the map of formal procedures. Rather than being synchronized, the formal and narrative codes are articulated virtually autonomously, one across the other, so that neither establishes hegemony or totally occupies the film. Reading—on a local level, as a general procedure, and as a totalizing interpretation—is suspended between them.

In refusing structural film's self-restriction to the material of the signifier and especially in introducing narrative, the order it had anathematized, *Film about a woman who . . .* refers to the art film; the tension between narrated content and structural film's insistence on purely filmic specificity falls into place as the investigation of filmic narration. This rejection of pure minimalism had been prefigured in Rainer's choreography. By the late sixties, she was habitually using film projection and verbal texts in her performances; stimulated by Kathakali narrative dance in India, she assembled a mixed-media performance, *Grand Union Dreams*, in which she interspersed her earlier dance compositions not only with fragments from other texts, but also with functions that she had previously abjured: spectacle, emotion, and character. *Lives of Performers* (1972) was drawn from *Grand Union Dreams*, and after it, performance work and dance were always understood as preparatory to film projects. The text of her next mixed-media dance work, "This is the story of a woman who . . . ," a melodramatic tale of sexual jealousy, is largely the shooting script for *Film about a woman who . . .*

As a film of a performance, *Film about a woman who . . .* inevitably engages the thematics of the art film. Its principal devices oscillate around the art film's ontological figure/ground reversals, the ambiguities produced in the collapse of illusion into reality and vice versa, which is inherent in the documentation of a simulation: a "real" photograph is succeeded by a photograph of it; the characters of the drama are seated watching a screen on which appear elements of their performance; references to other movies, both intradiegetic ("Doesn't this remind you of . . . *2001*?") and by quotation (stills from *Psycho*) occur. As a feature-length citation (rather than representation) of personal obsession, *Film about a woman who . . .* cues the distance from illusionist narrative codes that is the art film's own space of self-consciousness, and, in fact, it fragments diegetic unity more radically than any but the most analytic of Godard's films.

Rainer juxtaposes different levels of abstraction, with characters, performers, and activities alternately represented in a naturalistic verisimilitude, presented in the stylization of dance, or recounted verbally by an omniscient narrator. In this abstraction of drama into dance and back again, each narrative function is distributed among several players; the central drama of the relationship between a man and a woman is variously presented by two couples, with aspects of it also distributed among a number of supporting players. But the film most fundamentally assaults narrative integrity by representing not an action as such, but only discrete episodes from it, unsutured shards chopped obliquely from a possible narrative. The frame of an action is implied by certain crises, including the woman's self-betrayal in asking the man to hold her when really she "wanted to bash his fucking face in," her fight with the other woman, her anger at his preference for the other woman's breasts, and finally the recognition that discovery of the truth about her feelings makes her "free to love him again." But the chronological matrixing is so weak and the texturing of character interaction so meager and indeterminate that instead of asserting a strong diachronic progression, these episodes remain virtually autonomous.

Manifesting the appearance of content rather than content itself, they organize on the surface of the text a *combinatoire* of interactions and confrontations that could, elsewhere, make narrative pos-

n all is the opposi-
, even the sporadic
btended by this
, and all are return-
but only as *functions*
rimposed
signed to enumerate
rosexual re-
del of all pos-
tive then, the
ey are *actants*,
model of nar-

o . . . , that is, as a
it can finally propose
ed about anything ex-
an mobilize the forms of
litics and elusive in its at-
titude t   in a major scene, for example, the lead wo   ically stripped and her body
presented to the came   ntal exposure. However one
might wish to justify this as dem   rating a real or imagined objectification of a woman, the scene itself is uncomfortably, indeed bru-
tally, exploitative. Again, at the end of the scene, as the woman is
dressed, the camera leaves her body for the face of Rainer herself,
now revealed as a spectator to this ritual, the director of the visual
rape. On pieces of paper stuck to her face are typed statements of
erotic infatuation ("Love you, love you with a love even more un-
bounded, even more unconquerable. Your life-long wife"). Because
these protestations are quoted as instances of discourse, their actual
discursiveness is framed and their implications vague; but equally
indeterminate is the further political register opened up by the fact
that they are all quotations from the letters of Angela Davis to
George Jackson. The spurious recruitment of the politics of class
and race into the bourgeois psychodrama of the rest of the film only
unsettles its political pretensions. The refusal of political commitment elsewhere, and especially the refusal to attempt an articulation
of sexual and class politics, reduces the political realities the quotations signify to terms within a formalist exercise.

Rainer's inability to confront politics in any but formal terms corresponds to her position in the bourgeois art world, a position
which itself is figured in the major omission in her display of filmic
devices: her repression of the material processes of her film's own
production. As we have seen, the American art film's examination
of the social conditions of its own production allowed it to examine
the film industry's ideological and economic participation in the
capitalist state. Rainer's gesture toward political statement could
similarly have been opened up had she attended to the economics of
her own production, which combines the art world subsidies of
structural film and the personal investment of the art film—both of

which derived ultimately from government funding. This she can acknowledge only in an introductory title. Her refusal to confront the contradictions entailed in her dependence on state support, her refusal to include that dependence in the conditions which make narrative possible, ensured that her politics would be circumscribed by the irony of her modernist formalism. They would at best be pseudo-politics.[11]

The repression of the social conditions of production is intrinsic to idealist aesthetics. So despite the absence of a feminist stance and despite Rainer's own doubts about the political content of her early films, readings of her work in feminist terms were quickly proposed. Widespread discomfort with the (male) hyper-intellectuality of structural film allowed the *implication* of content to stand in for the actual absence of content in her films. Especially since it privileged the domestic, the melodramatic, and the verbal over physical action, Rainer's work could be understood as a refurbishing of the "woman's film" intrinsic to the revalorization of a specifically female realm of experience (Rich, 1981: 10–12). The invocation of women's real life experience in a mode that simultaneously invoked the codes of the industrial feature yet secured a self-critical distance from them was taken as a feminist resolution of the closure of formalism, one that made Rainer's work pivotal in the inauguration of feminist film theory and feminist cinema. Thus in 1976, the first issue of *Camera Obscura* hailed *Lives of Performers* and *Film about a woman who . . .* as exemplary in that their "modernist self-reflexiveness and formal rigor made a decisive break with illusionistic practice, and, at the same level of priority, explored problems of feminism" ("Yvonne Rainer: An Introduction," 1976: 59).

Coming the year after Laura Mulvey's seminal account of the metapsychology of spectatorship (Mulvey, 1975), and together with the strong feminist orientation of *Jump Cut*, the establishment of *Camera Obscura*, subtitled *A Journal of Feminism and Film Theory*, signaled the strength of U.S. feminism and its occupancy of the critical center of academic film studies. From this point on, rather than simply documenting or interpreting feminist film, theory produced feminism. For example, despite her resistance to *Camera Obscura*'s interpretation of the formal strategies of *Film about a woman who . . .* as Brechtian alienation (when what she claimed interest in was "plain old Aristotelian catharsis" [Rainer, 1976: 80]),[12] and indeed despite her resistance to the editors' general sense of the feminist implications of the film, it was her debates with them and other feminists that caused Rainer "to identify, rather reluctantly, with feminism" (Kaplan, 1983: 113). The interaction between mid-seventies academic feminism and post-structuralist film theory produced an international subculture, organized as virtually a new form of cinema, whose mode of practice was theory. Film is, of course, an especially privileged moment in cinema, but in over-privileging it idealist aesthetics have allowed the social system of which it is the vehicle to be repressed. Apart from marketing the stars'

11 Rainer's formalist citation of political issues is equally problematic in her appropriation of Baader-Meinhof resistance in the later *Journeys From Berlin/1971* (1979). Her remarks about *Journeys* summarize the neutralization of political reference, including that of sexuality, in all her films: "The film has no theoretical position on politics, feminism, or psychoanalysis. Rather than theoretical exposition, *Journeys* offers contrast and contradiction. . . . I didn't make a filmic dissertation" (Carroll, 1980: 45–46). Not until *The Man Who Envied Women* (1985), when Rainer confronted the contradictions of her own privileged location in the art world, would she transcend this impasse.

12 For Rainer's account of the disagreement, see Carroll (1980: 45).

private lives, bourgeois cinema has so entirely concealed the operations that produce it—the procedures of fabrication, for instance, and film's role in general ideological reproduction—that sustained attention to the other parts of cinema inevitably entails revisions in the mode of film consumption. Feminism and theory came together to propose a new model of consumption—one that is multiple, critical, and thoroughly verbalized rather than single, acquiescent, and nonverbal—and so a new practice in cinema.

Like previous avant-garde cinemas, then, feminist theory both contested the cinema of the hegemonic social formation and consolidated alternative communities. Recapitulating the organization of feminist theory as a whole around the critical reconsideration of history, this feminist practice of film theory was also a determinate option within the historical situation of feminism; it made it possible for a dispersed, highly educated, bourgeois community, without ready access to production, to engage in cinema, even as it made cinema the means by which that community could produce and organize itself. The privileging of high-level theory informed feminist cinema in two ways, as itself the central site of the cinematic practice of feminism and as the point of origin for feminist films.

As a semi-autonomous practice, feminist theory helped pry industrial film from its corporate uses, turning it against its industrial function in a rewriting of its texts and a redeployment of its apparatus in the manner of the subversive recontextualizations of collage. It thus resembles the re-presentation of Hollywood codes by the Kuchars or Warhol, and more generally the re-appropriation of mass cultural forms by modernist painting, modern jazz, and intellectual punk. Symptomatically, one of the major controversies within feminist film theory was whether its proper practice consisted of feminist rereadings of the classic cinema, especially of "ruptured" texts within it, or of productions of new, specifically feminist (and by that necessarily "avant-garde") texts.[13] Though this issue was exacerbated, theoretically and institutionally, by academic film studies' preoccupation with the industrial feature, the different positions ultimately rejoin each other at the point where the defining project of feminist avant-garde filmmaking is itself clarified as the critique of the mass media.

The mutual reciprocation of the two main feminist projects made theory and production integrally interdependent in a way not seen since the early days of the Soviet cinema. Critical writing acquired a new importance in disseminating avant-gardist projects to women at large, and it often had to stand in for the films themselves; but theory also commandeered film production. Films have always been made after literary texts—poems, plays, novels, and, of course scripts; but by the mid-seventies the most interesting films were being made in virtual illustration of theoretical issues developed in feminist scholarly articles. The exemplary case is the interdependent critical and filmic production of Laura Mulvey and Peter Wollen. In the United States, though such a rigorous prosecution of principles was hardly possible, still a sizeable tradition of quasi-structuralist

13 For a summary form of this argument, see Bergstrom (1979). Critical reinterpetation can be understood as an essential feminist practice. Thus, "a feminine text has no fixed formal characteristics, precisely because it is a relationship; it becomes a feminine text in the moment of its reading" (Kuhn, 1982: 13).

filmmakers attempted analogous integrations of feminist politics and didactic film forms. The worsening political climate of the late seventies, however, saw the interrogation of patriarchal narrative in these projects dissolve into independent feature production barely different from and, in fact, in competition with the edges of the industry. Yet some work of the late seventies, outside the period of this study, did integrate the theoretical advances of the mid-decade with innovations pioneered in the sixties.

The collectively authored *Sigmund Freud's Dora* (1979), for instance, was a highly articulate recapitulation of the themes of feminist theory: of biography and autobiography and women's claiming the right to speak for themselves; of the theoretical issues involved in the foregrounding of the codes of narrative realism; of the relation of the gaze and its conventions to sexuality; of masculinist representation of women in film (but also in television); and of the mobilization of filmic strategies that locate women not as individual people, but as roles, as positions within social and filmic systems. And while the tension between the main text and the footnotes in Freud's *Dora* is a classic moment in which a normative heterosexuality begins to crumble, the informing tension of at least the opening section of the film is between Marxism and psychoanalysis. Remarkably, the film begins by associating the Marxist position with the voice of the woman, who indicts her male interlocutor's belief in the "bourgeois pseudo-science" of psychoanalysis. But though the film subsequently wreaks havoc upon Freud's attempts to manipulate Dora, the debate that structures most of the film is one within psychoanalysis, rather than one between it and materialism. By the end, historical materialist theory and socialism have been totally forgotten, as if in the succession of its own conceptual sche-

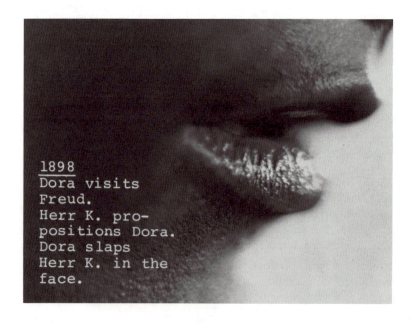

1898
Dora visits
Freud.
Herr K. pro-
positions Dora.
Dora slaps
Herr K. in the
face.

8.29 Sigmund Freud's Dora

mas, the film allegorized the itinerary of seventies feminist theory.

Not the least remarkable aspect of the critical examination of the languages of sexuality in *Sigmund Freud's Dora*, however, is its attention to what historically had been one of the most prominent of them, a subtext that ran through most of the films discussed here, even though until this time it had been anathema to theory and to feminism alike: pornography.

The Erotic Text

Think how pornography would fulfill Hollywood. Remember that it never will.
— Charles Boultenhouse

Since the kiss in the Edison short of 1896, *John Rice–May Irwin Kiss*, the cinema has been moved by sex; as André Bazin noted, of all the arts it is in cinema alone that "eroticism is there on purpose and is a basic ingredient . . . , a major, a specific, and even an essential one" (Bazin, 1971: 170). But at no time did the representation of sexuality and its relation to social movements appear with more vividness and less clarity than in the sixties. In books, in the periodical press, in the theater, and in still and motion picture photography, the succession of challenges to censorship by increasingly explicit depiction registered a revision of popular and judicial notions of obscenity and pornography so fundamental and extensive that a presidential commission was formed to study it. In film the dramatic inflation in explicitness took place in cinemas of widely different social positions, leading to the migration of explicit representation from the social margins to the center, and the creation of essentially new genres with new apparatuses of production and exhibition. As pornography coalesced, not indeed as a stable term, but as a category where competing moral, iconographic, judicial, and semantic projects intersected, it was understood as a vocabulary of *representation* of sexuality. But after Foucault, we cannot separate this function from that of the *production* of a mode of sexuality, one with its own specificity, not merely a displaced, perverse, or substitute form of some other, more authentic, activity. Nevertheless, it is clear that whatever personal freedoms were won either in this exponential increase in sexual material or in the changes in sexual mores of which it was a signal feature, they were coextensive with an unprecedented invasion of the private sphere, in fact, by the industrialization of the entire field of sexuality.

At the beginning of the decade three distinct systems of production manufactured three equally distinct modes of filmic sexuality: 35mm films that suppressed reference to physical sexuality, especially outside marriage, made for general release by major studios; 35mm "exploitation" or "art" films that were beginning to include female nudity, made by independent producers for public distribution in special theaters; and 16mm "stag" films that depicted sexual intercourse, made for private distribution and exhibition in brothels and men's clubs.[14] By 1970 distinctions among the generic conventions and the systems of production of these three modes had almost entirely broken down. In the first area, the loosening of the proscriptions against sexual content that had been growing since the war, especially since Otto Preminger's decision in 1953 to release *The Moon Is Blue* without code approval, accelerated through the sixties so that a previously unimaginable sexual self-consciousness became integral to the New Hollywood. After the Production Code was replaced by a ratings system in 1968, Hollywood responded with a new freedom and a surge in sexual content, beginning with *Myra Breckinridge* and *Carnal Knowledge* in 1970, that allowed the presidential commission of the same year to report that the major themes of even general release features included "perversion, abortion, orgies, wife-swapping, prostitution, promiscuity, homosexuality, nymphomania, lesbianism etc." (*Report*, 1970: 77). Developments in the second category of filmic sexuality were even more remarkable.

Since the Motion Pictures Producers and Distributors Association founded the Hays Office in 1922, and especially after the adoption of the Production Code of 1934, small independent companies, totally outside the studio system, had maintained public exhibition of mildly risqué films. The conventions and stability these marginal industrial operations had established through the thirties and forties were upset in the mid-fifties by a vogue for the partial nudity exhibited in pseudo-documentaries about nudist colonies. Though these were entirely without sexual implication, one of them, *Garden of Eden*, was prosecuted. In its ruling on the case in July 1957, the New York Court of Appeals found that nudity was not in itself obscene. Exploiting the distinction established by this ruling, Russ Meyer made a comedy in 1959 about the affliction of a middle-aged man to whom all women appear naked. Returning over $1 million on a $24 thousand investment, *The Immoral Mr. Teas* quickly spawned 150 imitations, establishing a pattern for the developments of the next decade: a standard of representation is breached; it encounters first judicial harassment, then vindication; this vindication clears the way to new challenges and new judicial rulings. After 1963–64, the purely voyeuristic attractions of the nudie genre could no longer sustain the *frisson* of transgression. Beginning with melodramas of violence and sexuality like Herschell Gordon Lewis's *Blood Feast* (1963), Russ Meyer's *Lorna*, (1964), and the subsequent productions of David F. Friedman, various generic mutations supplemented the nudity: actual sexual contact; lesbianism; sadism and violence, including violence by women against men (Knight and Alpert, 1967b: 187); and eventually the use of name stars, such as Jayne Mansfield in *Promises, Promises* (1963).

These developments coincided with the increasing explicitness of the European imports shown in the art houses in the late fifties. Not bound by the Production Code, films like *Hiroshima Mon Amour*, *Les Liaisons Dangereuses*, and especially *And God Created Woman* had exceeded domestic standards, generally without hindrance. But

14 *The Report of the Commission on Obscenity and Pornography* distinguished three main categories: general release, art, and exploitation films (*Report*, 1970). Though the films in the second group were almost entirely European-made and the third group domestic, I include them together because they were ideologically similar, and their modes of production were virtually identical. *The Report* also noted a recent appearance of "quite a number of highly sexually oriented hybrid films," combining elements of all three categories, as well as more explicit 16mm films (ibid.: 75–76). *The Report* argued that these constituted a new genre, even while recognizing their similarity to stag films (ibid.: 85–86). For further information on erotic films of the period, see especially Knight and Alpert (1967a, 1967b, 1967c); Di Lauro and Rabkin (1976); and Turan and Zito (1974).

Louis Malle's *The Lovers* was prosecuted. The Supreme Court verdict in the case (*Jacobellis v. Ohio*) in 1964 ruled that "customary standards of candor" should be those of the nation as a whole rather than of any local community, and so it opened the way for a second wave of imports of even greater explicitness. With domestic filmmakers stimulated to present more nudity and more sexual activity, the remaining barriers quickly fell. The graphic depiction of intercourse in *I Am Curious (Yellow)*, released in the United States in 1968, was followed by domestic quasi-documentaries about stag films (*History of the Blue Movie* and *Pornography in Denmark*) and then sexually explicit features. *Mona, the Virgin Nymph* (1970) was the first 16mm hard-core feature to be distributed nationally, the first of an essentially new genre that culminated in the *succès de scandale* of *Deep Throat* (1972), *Behind the Green Door* (1972), and *The Devil in Miss Jones* (1973), along with parallel homosexual features after Wakefield Poole's *Boys in the Sand* (1971). These publicly exhibited features, playing in the Main Streets of cities across the country, were widely reviewed, widely discussed, and enormously successful. Estimates on *Deep Throat* suggest a return of $25 million on a $25 thousand investment, while *Devil in Miss Jones* was sixth in 1973 box office grosses. They were also as graphic as the stags had ever been.

Deep Throat was the most celebrated case of the migration of explicit sexual representation from the illegal underground, if not to the studios themselves at least to a social prominence and legitimacy adjacent to them. This migration recapitulated in several ways the emergence of the industry itself from the disrepute of its origins. Like the stags, early cinema had consisted of short loops, with anonymous actors and directors, and it was valued for the fact of representation or the sensationalism of what was represented rather than for any formal artistry. During its second decade Hollywood isolated stars and directors and developed longer narratives with individually realized characters. Similarly, as the stags "grew up" in the seventies, what would henceforth be known as "Adult" films developed an increased concern with production values. With a production system that included directors, writers, actors, a star system, an awards system, and the rest of the studios' legitimizing apparatus, they too claimed the status of art. Extended narratives with individually differentiated characters meant longer films and theatrical projection rather than the kinetoscope-like private booths. All these developments blurred the differences between hard-core films and the industry generally, whereas previously stags had constituted an autonomous tradition, an entirely illegal independent cinema.

A true underground, shown only in brothels and men's clubs, stags had no theatrical or other public exhibition and no influence on the public cinema. Although the earliest extant stag film, *A Grass Sandwich* (also known as *A Free Ride*), dates from 1915, a sizeable market for films depicting sexual intercourse existed in the United States as early as 1904 (Knight and Alpert, 1967c: 156). Though such films had in various phases been imported from Latin America and Europe, their production in the United States was essentially regional, on the coasts and around Chicago, with no national distribution. Postwar technical developments did cause some mutations in this otherwise static genre; as 16mm projectors became cheaper, domestic exhibition and increased female spectatorship became possible, and then in the fifties production rapidly increased as 8mm film allowed the industrial form to pass back and forth into home entertainment. By 1967 the standard format was a single, 200' roll of black and white 8mm film. With no pretense of having any function other than erotic arousal, the narrative existed only to frame sexual display, and the late sixties "beaver" films of female genitals carried the mode to its logical reduction. With no mediating institutions, stags are supposed to reflect directly the desires and prejudices of their audience—middle-class American males. A 1967 survey of 1,000 stags produced since 1920 found that only 4.9 percent of them included any kind of male homosexual contact, while 19.2 percent included lesbianism, 68.8 percent included fellatio and 46.1 percent included cunnilingus (Knight and Alpert, 1967c: 170).

Stags continued to be produced for consumption in the home or in clubs, and for private viewing in booths in specialty stores (an innovation beginning in Chicago in the early fifties), but after the end of the sixties they were no longer entirely separate from other forms of filmic sexuality. On the one hand, the quasi-legal depiction of sexual activity in theatrical films and the increased legitimation of pornography after *Deep Throat* and, on the other hand, the partial integration of both film codes and individual filmmakers into the studio system (instanced by Russ Meyer's making *Beyond the Valley of the Dolls* for Twentieth Century-Fox in 1970) confounded the terms by which the different modes had been distinguished. And in place of the clear formal division of studio, art, and stag film and the distinct social position each occupied, filmic sexuality was constituted in a constantly transforming reticulation of multiple industrial modes, an open field of sexual discourses.

As well as involving very interesting formal anomalies, these transformations are crucial in respect to questions of alternative cinema in general—to questions of the conditions of transgressive representations and the social relations constructed around them, of the relation between performance and representation in pornographic histrionics (is it possible to "act" sexual intercourse?), and of the interdetermination of industrial and subcultural practices. Both Brakhage and Warhol, for instance, are critically situated by the aesthetics of pornography, though in very different ways. But consideration of sexually explicit cinema has been almost entirely limited to the supposed effects of the iconography, especially as these have intersected with the concerns of the women's movement. The liberal celebration of increased candor, understood through the sixties as freedom from censorship, ground to a halt with the surge in pornography between 1969 and 1972 that coincided with the emergence of feminism and of a position within it that saw sexually explicit representation as a pivotal practice within patriarchy.

Beyond this coincidence, the relation between feminism and the growth of pornography and the critique of pornography is not clear. Some positions within feminism understood pornography as "part of a male backlash" to the women's movement (Lederer, 1980: 27), while others retained a place for sexually explicit representation—if only in theory or in the future. But most argued a causal relation between it and violence toward women, summarized in the slogan "Pornography is the theory, rape is the practice." Three main positions were developed. The first, stimulated by Kate Millett's accounts of misogynous literature (Millett, 1970: 45–46) and advanced in the seventies by organizations such as Women Against Violence in Pornography and the Media,[15] either argued that pornography was typically accompanied by images of violence or defined it as such.[16] The second, predicated on the symbolic vulnerability of nakedness or on the degradation intrinsic to a woman selling her body (in which case pornography returned to its etymological roots in prostitution), argued that even if other violence was not present, sexual representation was itself violent; thus *"pornography is in itself a sadistic act"* (Griffin, 1981: 111). The third argued that whether or not it contained violence or was itself violent, pornography was an integral moment in an ideological system that implicitly sanctioned violence, and hence rape was a consequence of pornography's objectification of women (Lederer, 1980: 24).

Like the similarly misleading association of pornography with pedophilia, these positions lack supporting evidence and typically are predetermined by other political agendas. Sadistic pornography exists, but as a distinct genre, and sadism is not present in pornography in general. In fact, in most popular media (broadcast television, for instance) more often than violence accompanies eroticism, it substitutes for it. Similarly, the virtually exclusive consumption of filmic pornography by males is derived from the conditions of its availability, rather than from qualities innate in males (a fact underscored by the growing female market for home video pornography), and it is learned amidst other forms of socialization. Since neither conclusive statistical information[17] nor an adequate psychology of pornography is available, any causal relation between pornography and violence remains speculative. Nor can either a causal relation between pornography and other individual or social pathologies or a continuity between it and Western representation of women in general be posited with any certainty. For although in some respects pornography appears as an extreme instance of the use of women in the mass media, in other respects it catastrophically interrupts the traditional functions. The presentation of the unconcealed vagina, for example, contradicts the theories of fetishism and of the phallic woman proposed in psychoanalytic accounts of spectatorship (Ellis, 1980: 99; Pollock, 1977: 30) and also ends the anathematization of woman's genitals in Western art. But while the erroneous insistence on a connection between pornography and violence has unfortunately inhibited consideration of sexual representation per se, the putative misogyny of pornography has ensured that consideration

15 Women Against Violence in Pornography and the Media was founded in 1978, coinciding with the beginnings of the Take Back the Night marches and feminist attempts to disrupt the urban places where pornography intersects with other sexual industries.

16 Cf. "What feminists usually object to in pornography are non-sexual elements such as violence and domination [but which have] as a specific purpose direct, sexual arousal of the spectator" (Lesage, n.d.: 46).

17 In its summary of the effects of sexual materials, the presidential commission "found no evidence to date that exposure to explicit sexual materials plays a significant role in the causation of delinquent behavior among youth or adults" (*Report*, 1970: 27). For statistical analysis of the decrease in sex crimes in Denmark after pornography became freely available, see Kutchinsky (1973).

of it has taken for its point of departure the actual historical relations between men and women, rather than some essentialist model of sexuality.

All critical moments in the various interlocking controversies about pornography are situated, then, on two axes—between competing theories of the nature of sexual representation per se and between theories of its differential relation to men and women; proposals for a general liberating potential commonly turn on gains for men purchased at the specific expense of women. Analogous to Marxist objections to the depiction of harmonious relations between owners and hands in the nineteenth-century industrial novel, the feminist denial of the possibility of the representation of sexual activity free from immediate or indirect coercion reflects structural social contradictions. For even if it were possible to instance non-exploitative sexual representation, its heuristic or utopian function would be preempted by present inequality, the reproach of things as they are upon the representation of things as they might be. Homosexual pornography on the other hand, even though it constructs hierarchies of discrimination and subjection according to criteria other than gender, can figure the possibility of a nondiscriminatory mutuality and a plurality of spectator positions unavailable to heterosexual pornography. But as long as men control women, the representation of women's pleasure can never be more than a masquerade, the representation of a male fantasy of woman's pleasure, and one that speaks male fears and male desires. Like the question of a feminine language in general, the possibility of nonsexist sexual representation must be deferred.

The necessity of this deferral does not close the issue of pornography, however, so much as open it up to the conditions of its historical form, to its place among the other discourses of sexuality—sex manuals, psychotherapy, women's magazines, advertising, and prostitution—and to its place with these in the overall relations of power. In the present this larger context produces a pornography with a specific combination of progressive and collusive functions. It is essentially organized by the operations of the mass media, in which the sexual is privileged as the sign of pleasure and possession. A totalized account of the discourses of sexuality would include the social changes produced in the shift from manufacturing to information industries that constitutes late capitalism, the different kinds of labor demanded, and the different kind of socialization appropriate to the new priority assumed by consumption. Here, as sexuality is liberated from reproduction and constituted as potentially a sphere of pure pleasure without social responsibilities or repercussions (the utopian component in pornography), it is immediately recolonized by the very economy that made its autonomy initially possible.

Since the traditional family has all but disintegrated, the previously mandated return of nonutilitarian sexuality to that arena is no longer necessary. Sexual pleasure in general and women in particular have become free signifiers, capable of attachment to almost anything in consumer society. This industrialization of sexuality turns it into a commodity fit for integration into other social exchanges, but it does so only by reifying the individual subject as a machine in which all pleasures are experienced as sexuality. As the micro-social form of the spectacular society, impelled not by the production of goods but by the production of consumption, sexuality appears as pure display. The apogee of sexual achievement is not the satisfaction of one's own desire, but the production of desire in others; scopophilia is only possible when it is introjected into narcissistic identification. Exhibitionism, not voyeurism, is the modern mode of mastery; we possess not those we look at, but those whom we oblige to look at us.

Such functions for sexuality have been on the agenda at least since the early fifties, when it began to be recognized as a consumer good (Riesman, [1950] 1971: 146). But its industrialization took a qualitatively different leap forward with the explosion of leisure industries in the sixties. As sex became the privileged nexus in the symbolic exchange between private life and the media environment, the body, especially the female's but increasingly also that of the male, signified pleasure in itself and also the pleasure of all other commodities. The sexual text, consumption of which magically promised possession of all the goods that constituted consumer society, was itself organized according to the principles of marketing. Both advertising texts and other forms of mass media are ordered by concealment and frustration that impose restraints on bodily display and desire. The amount of body revealed by the advertising model is the measure of how much she and the product she entails is available; the amount she withholds is the measure of what remains to be obtained. A similar tension between possession and privation provides the basis for narrative, which in film is organized around the "woman question." The enigmatic unavailability of the woman produces the extension of the plot for both the protagonist and the spectator, in which possession must be delayed because it is synonymous with narrative closure. "Precisely because it must never take place, everything centers upon copulation" (Horkheimer and Adorno, 1972: 141).

This ideological and indeed material production of aesthetic conventions provides the context in which older ideas of the subversiveness of pornography might be reconstituted. In the satiric literary mode of "moral" pornography (Carter, 1980: 19), absolute sexual license functions as a critique of social constraints upon sexuality, including those which in integrating sexuality with nonsexual economies exploit women specifically. This mode does have its analogues in film, notably in a largely surrealist tradition that has seen film as intrinsically erotic. From Robert Desnos's claim that in "cinematic eroticism . . . consolation for everything that is disappointing in everyday life must be sought" (Desnos [1923] 1978: 122), through Bazin, to Parker Tyler's picture of Hollywood as "a sort of mundane Olympia where men and women led the 'ideal' lives of gods and goddesses" (Tyler, 1969: 10), the cinema has been associated with illicit eroticism, not simply representing it, but in its darkness itself providing the refuge for the most delicious consolations. But it was especially in the stags that sex figured revolt, with the display of sexual pleasure ratifying the challenge to social mores in the rudimentary narratives (the anticlericalism of European stags is prototypical). When this model of the pornographic as both the logical expression of a repressive society and "its subversive, demotic antidote"[18] is relocated from the moral system of bourgeois ethics to the industrial system of image manipulation, a new level of contradiction appears: graphic representation of sexuality extends the use of sex in advertising, but it also undermines the sexual repression advertising depends on.

A "pure pornography," a "moral pornography" of revolt, cannot, then, exist in the present; its utopian alterity is constantly pricked by actual social relations, and by the industrialization of the erotic. The realignment of the social function of sexuality in the sixties as it became ubiquitous throughout the cultural landscape, and the relocation of pornography from social marginality into dominant industrial production, robbed both sexuality and pornography of their other dimension. Where previously proscription had registered the threat of pornography, total acceptance signaled its impotence. A false liberation preempted an authentic negation.

To all the previous tensions within the pornographic image, then, must be added those that follow from the full industrialization of sexuality, specifically as these derive from the conditions of its manufacture. The production stage of industrial pornography is not primarily organized according to distinctions in gender, and it exploits the women who perform in it no more (or less) than the men. Any understanding of it, including that derived from prostitution, must contain gender distinctions within the structural relations of capitalism in general. If, as Walter Benjamin remarked, prostitution is anomalous in that the seller is also the commodity (Benjamin, 1973: 171), this is true only at a rudimentary stage. Organized prostitution reintroduces the distinction between seller and commodity; the prostitute's labor is sold by the pimp. Similarly, in industrial pornography the distinctions between seller and commodity and between capitalist and workers are categorical. Like actors and actresses in Hollywood, actors and actresses in pornographic film all work to valorize invested capital. Male and female alike, they are the vehicles of the exchange between producers and consumers.

As the pornography industry became integrated with capitalist industry generally in the late sixties, its reproduction of the industrial function of the sexual revolution itself compromised whatever subversive potential it had inherited from older pornography. This modulation of infraction into collusion is especially clear in *Deep Throat*, the film whose success as scandal summarized the contradictions in the new social functions of explicit sexuality. In fact, since the formal transformations entailed in the development from the stag loops to the 35mm feature, as well as the changes in social function these represent, are all still visible in *Deep Throat*, it con-

18 Cf. "Ours is a flourishing example of a [pornographic society], a society so hypocritically and repressively constructed that it must inevitably produce an effusion of pornography as both its logical expression and its subversive, demotic antidote" (Sontag, 1969: 38).

tains both a condensed history of the modes of sexually explicit film and an allegory of the process by which it was itself produced out of them. Like *Easy Rider* (whose title it could well share), it is a generic amalgam in which underground people and an underground mode are refurbished for mainstream consumption. The tension between the recalcitrant underground and the integrated industrial function is sedimented in the formal tension between the virtual narrative stasis of the episodes of sexual contact (the heritage of the stags, and in several instances involving the incorporation of previously extant shorts) and the larger narrative economy (the vehicle of industrial entertainment) which more or less spuriously motivates and justifies them.

Formally invoking the legitimate feature film, *Deep Throat* offers narrative itself as the exculpation of promiscuous sexuality and the restoration of a moral order. But this economy in no way contains or motivates the sexual activities; it exists merely to bring them about. Like the early pseudo-documentary histories of stag films (or like Warhol's *Couch*), the film is essentially a string of separate sexual encounters which have little narrative or thematic connection. Unlike the image of the woman in orthodox features, these encounters cannot be said to retard the plot, since the plot is entirely subordinate to them. But they do allow the attributes of the humanist subject to be shed in a reduction to purely genital transactions—a dehumanization that is the terror of pornography but also its liberation. In the sequences of sexual intercourse, the shots are not fixed in a frame of narrative or any other order, not clearly linked to specific people. Often, one scene of copulation is intercut with brief shots from others in rapid rhythmic montages that even further fragment individual subjectivity. Here sterility as a principle of subversive anti-narrative comes into dominance, spilling "the libidinal forces outside the whole, at the expense of the whole (at the price of the ruin and disintegration of this whole)" (Lyotard, 1978: 54).

But while the episodes of sexual play retain the subversiveness of earlier pornography, what narrative logic there is attempts to return them to the moral order, as a summary of the rudimentary plot will make clear. A young woman, played by Linda Lovelace, complains to her roommate that she cannot get married because sex is not satisfying; it provides only tingles of sensation, not overwhelming experiences equivalent to rockets exploding or dams being burst. When she has sex with fourteen men in a single afternoon of excess but still gains no relief, she visits a doctor, who discovers that her clitoris is in her throat. By fellating him she is able to experience orgasm for the first time, and to be able to repeat the experience, she becomes a sex therapist. This allows her a series of sexual encounters. The conclusion revolves around one of her patients, Wilbur, who wishes to marry her; she refuses because his penis is four inches away from the nine inches she needs. The way to their marriage is finally cleared when the doctor promises to solve this problem—by making the necessary abbreviation!

Rather than celebrating unrestrained sexuality, the logic of the

8.30–8.32 Gerard Damiano, *Deep Throat*

narrative closure nostalgically invokes social norms of a bygone era. As the doctor removes the impediments to marriage, first for Linda and then, in the inverted recapitulation of the main plot, for her prospective spouse, marriage is endorsed as the preferred arena of sexual pleasure, and Linda's promiscuity is denigrated as a dissatisfactory deviation. This entirely orthodox proposal that modern medicine can cure sexual irregularity and other barriers to marriage is also endorsed, both in the two main narrative reversals and in the interludes when, as an agent of medicine, Linda heals several wounded or aberrant men: one who drinks soda from her vagina, one who has not been sexually active since his wife died, one whose penis is bandaged, and finally Wilbur, who despite his surreal endowment is incapable of sex unless Linda plays a role in a rape fantasy.

Similar contradictions pervade the narrative of gender difference. Ostensibly, the film's quest is for woman's pleasure, and cunnilingus is prominently featured (indeed, arguments that the film was progressive were made on these grounds). But while the dominant narrative logic appears to celebrate the female orgasm, Linda's biological abnormality is such that even as it does so, it simultaneously invokes the male pleasure of fellatio. Within this latter activity, however, lurks the male fear of castration, figured in Linda's ability totally to consume the penis in what amounts to a relocated *vagina dentata*. The parade of wounded men that culminates in the mix of impotence and superpotence in Wilbur, together with the re-invocation of the castration motif in his being cut down to size, summarize what is at best a highly ambivalent celebration of phallic power.

Given the primacy of the phallus in psychoanalytic theories of signification, it is not surprising that this ambivalence returns in the processes by which sexual pleasure is represented. Pornography is, whatever else, one of the most critical of realisms. As much as other iconic texts, it depends on transparency, on encouraging the illusion of passage through the filmic to the profilmic scene. The sight of the male ejaculation is the fullest sign of presence, where if somatic rhythms have coincided with their optical pattern, the (male) spectator may complete narcissistic identification and find himself and his pleasure represented in the text. The climax is both a physical and a semiological one, the instance that proves the system of filmic codes by which it is represented. But this moment when reality is overwhelmingly affirmed is physiologically gendered; it reaches its apogee in the male orgasm but can find no equivalent validation around female pleasure. Since a woman's orgasm is not manifest materially or on the outside of the body, it cannot be directly represented.

Unimportant in films which serve male pleasure or in phallocentric cinemas generally, this unrepresentability is crucial for feminist film theory. It is especially crucial in *Deep Throat* which, whether or not it is a feminist film, is narratively organized around a woman's capacity for orgasm. Linda's inability to experience orgasm is thus the site of a double lack, a physiological and a textual one. The pleasure she can know only as absence cannot be illustrated, but only figured in the nonsexual metaphors by which she describes her desire to her roommate at the beginning of her odyssey. Alongside her quest for orgasm runs the film's own quest for a means of expressing it; both succeed by infraction. The rewards of her biological ungrammaticalness are matched in the film's parallel revision of the grammar of pornography; when she does finally come, the film shifts from representation to signification by making visually present the metaphors through which she had originally spoken her desire and lack. Intercut with the shots of the pleasure of her face, we see fireworks exploding, rockets taking off, and bells being rung. We are precipitated into the ontology of the poetic avant-garde film, the vertical montage elaborated some thirty years before, at the beginning of the American feminist film, by Maya Deren.

Afterword

The Democrats were going to nominate a man who, no matter how serious his political dedication might be, was indisputably and willy-nilly going to be seen as a great box-office actor, and the consequences of that were staggering and not at all easy to calculate.
— Norman Mailer, 1960

It is both logically and chronologically appropriate that this study should have ended with pornography. The recent history of this mode, the epitome of contemporary industrial cultural production, summarizes the transition between the social possibilities of the period with which this essay has been concerned and those of the period in which it has been written. Figuring an obdurate contraction of social aspiration and substituting the spectacle of mutual prostitution for the renovation of the body politic (or even of the total sensual body), contemporary pornography entails a retreat from the political that mirrors in reverse the utopian explosion of popular participation in the political that characterized the sixties. Despite the overwhelming literality of its images, it is experienced as sheer affect, as a socially unlocalized indulgence that can be fixed upon by virtually any propaganda project. As its representations of the most intimate of human experiences—the most precious and yet the most common—are parlayed through the circuits of economic exchange and integrated into industrial culture generally, what once was understood as a storming of the walls of repression has become an alienated and entirely administered diversion.

Similar appropriations are regularly exercised upon all aspects of sixties utopianism. The period is far enough away that its cultural remains, retaining only the vaguest traces of their original function, may be excavated and put to new uses. That commodity culture depends for its renewal upon misplaced images of resistance or confrontation is now well understood; we know that however they challenge industrial culture, marginal or disruptive social movements also sustain it on many levels. The sixties thus have a special utility for the culture industries, for while the social projects of the period are ignored or condemned, their vocabularies and stylistic innovations may be made to serve projects antithetical to those from which they derived. As a consequence of this enforced deracination, sixties culture must appear ambiguous, while really the shifts within its semiosis only reflect the uncertainty of the present; we do not finally know how to insert the period either into a chronology of modernity or into the various narratives of modernity's end.

This essay is itself inevitably an appropriation of the period, a rewriting in competition with other rewritings to make the past useful to the present. But even as we try to retrieve the lost dimensions of resistance, we must not pretend that their practices in film can be imitated or simply renewed. Such a supposition, which has allowed fragments of these practices to be commercially recycled as style only, is the functional form of the erasure of history it ostensibly laments. The present return to that social history has, on the contrary, demanded that we historicize this or that practice in order to see sixties films not as texts, but as traces of social activities. The same project also obliges us to historicize *film*, to recover that determinate connection between the sixties and the fact that then film was uniquely privileged, available and ripe for symbolic investment and social mobilization. Only by recovering the historical meaning of the medium as a whole can we understand how people could so energetically have believed that revolutions in film could supply revolutions in society, and how, like Taylor Mead, people could have believed that "the movies are a revolution" (Mead, 1963: 9).

The role of film as the dominant medium in this century, inflecting and directing the others, reached a curious apogee in the sixties. Its potential hegemony over other mediums had been apparent since this century's first decade, and when Jean Epstein remarked in 1921 that "the cinema saturates modern literature" (cited in Lawder, 1975: 76), he could easily have included painting, music, and theater as well. According to Arnold Hauser's notion of the twentieth century as "the Film Age," the medium's technical capabilities allowed it to summarize other modernist projects and supplied it with formal strategies appropriate to all that the Bergsonian flow called into being: "The agreement between the technical methods of the film and the characteristics of the new concept of time is so complete that one has the feeling that the time categories of modern art altogether must have arisen from the spirit of cinematic form" (Hauser, n.d.: 239). Although Hauser admitted film's stylistic representativeness, he would not allow it qualitative supremacy. But by the sixties any residual doubts had evaporated, and the example of the French rereading of Hollywood on the one hand and the already nostalgic celebration of film's populism on the other qualified it as the referential medium for what was recognized as a generation formed by it.

Addressing "a film generation," Stanley Kauffman in 1966 acknowledged "a culture in which the film has been of accepted serious relevance, however that seriousness is defined" (Kauffman, 1966: 415). To his mind, what allowed film this preeminence and made it the envy of poets and painters were its use of advanced technologies; its ability to represent both superficial, physical details and interior states of tension; the universality of its appeal; and finally its youth. Though these formulations, as much generalizations from the fact of film's significance as explanations of it, would seem to validate film in general, Kauffman extended his approval essentially to the European art film and did not find in either Hollywood or "certain experimental films" (which he was careful to disparage) the seriousness that legitimized the medium. Nevertheless, his assessment had wide credibility, and in this period populist and intellectual interest in the arts coincided at film. The ubiquitous prestige of the medium and its hegemony on many cultural levels made intervention in it desirable, while Hollywood's weakness and its well-recognized inadequacies made intervention possible and necessary.

The present argument has been that it was precisely the coincidence of the popularity of film and its crisis that made it available for popular intervention. The sixties alternative cinemas were built amid the ruins of an industry, but the unprecedented social maturity they brought to film was its autumnal ripeness. When we look back, it is not only to specific practices of film that have been lost, but to an equally vanquished social presence for the medium as a whole. The end of cinema, at least for the West, came much more quickly than expected, even by those who desired it most.

This termination of film's social urgency bequeaths to the historian the task of preparing an account of film's position among other mediums. Like the reasons why it was a preferred arena for dissident social activity, the particular social possibilities film symbolized or promised cannot be understood apart from its engagement and competition with other cultural practices, or apart from the changes in the relations among cultural practices and other practices, other forms of production. Such a consideration of alternative film practices in their relation to the dominant cinema, but also in their relation to the dominant and marginal forms of other mediums, would constitute a social history of the superstructure, an understanding of the place of cultural production in general in the social developments that call it (and that it calls) into being. In this essay I have given some indication of interdependencies among different mediums—for example, the connections between the social relations produced by underground film and those produced by poetry and jazz; the importance for structural film of the social institutions of painting; and the way the social activities of political film were framed by the mass media. Though I will not undertake here the larger task of organizing into a total cultural history such occasional acknowledgments of the social bases of formal resemblances across mediums, it is necessary to sketch the historical position of film in culture generally, in order to understand what was at stake in this period of its flowering, and also in its subsequent decline. Two other mediums are of particular importance: popular music and television.

Since the heyday of the beats, the baton of the preferred medium for subcultural mobilization has passed rapidly from writing to film and then to rock music (though this last does not designate a single musical form or a consistent social function). We have seen the sequence enacted biographically in Ken Kesey's rejection of writing for film, which he understood as a formal progression dictated by the changing historical relevance of the material qualities of the different mediums. Writing was given up because it was "an old-fashioned and artificial form" (Wolfe, 1968: 91), inherently inadequate to the experience of psychedelics and incapable of communicating their importance to the public. Obsolescence also awaited film; Kesey abandoned his movie and never completed it, turning his attention instead to rock-and-roll bands. This progression, which we should understand in material terms rather than in reference to the intrinsic formal or sensual properties of the various mediums, is also enacted within the history of film.

Despite the audacity of *Scorpio Rising*, rock-and-roll only fragmentarily displaced jazz as accompaniment for underground film. It figured briefly in transitional protest documentaries of the late sixties counterculture, in which urban blues formed the bridge between Black music and an eventually autonomous White adaptation of it. Films like Jerry Abrams's *Be-In* (1967), with music by Blue Cheer, and Leonard Henny's *The Resistance* (1968), which featured the Charlatans, record this coincidence of film, rock, and political dissidence. But at the same time as political developments were undermining the premises of underground film, the youth cultures were finding music more potent than film in producing, organizing, and representing alternative social energies. These cultural forces fueled the rapid innovation of more elaborate musical forms for rock, its own increasing social centrality, and its temporary politicization. While previously music had been supplementary to film, both in the culture generally and within any given film, since the late sixties the reverse has been true. Industrial and non-industrial film alike lost hegemony in their respective cultural spheres, and their place and form have subsequently been dictated by music.

Hollywood had used rock music since mid-fifties teenage terrors like *The Blackboard Jungle*, *The Girl Can't Help It*, and *Love Me Tender*, but after the feature documentaries of the late sixties (*Monterey Pop*, *Woodstock*, and *Gimme Shelter*), which savagely reinvented the musical as genre, rock increasingly entered narrative film. On the sound track, in the story, and as a general frame of reference, it was inescapable, and by the early eighties it seemed that "every third film that comes along falls back on rock for some sense of support" (Ehrenstein and Reed, 1982: n.p.). By 1974 popular music had outstripped film as the most profitable branch of the entertainment industry, earning $2 billion as opposed to the movies' $1.6 billion (Chapple and Garofalo, 1977: xi). Given the greater flexibility of its modes and institutions, music became the privileged form of the culture industries and also the chief vehicle of individual or subcultural attempts to challenge them. As industrial, commodity music came to be organized in patterns similar to those of cinema in the previous decades, with subcultural production and industrial appropriation feeding off each other in cycles of innovation and decay, it displaced film from any but the most archaic and academic role in alternative social organization. At the same time, surviving remnants of art film began either to resemble television (Arthur, 1987: 69) or to surrender their function in the art world to video.

Broadcast television had been substantially responsible for the fifties crisis in the film industry that opened the way for alternative cinemas, and by the late sixties electronic technology was on all levels more useful than the mechanical technology of film. As broadcast television became even more thoroughly integrated into corporate production than film ever had been, the boundary of the television industry dissolved into the general operations of the corporate state. Similarly, the boundaries of the television text dissolved into electronic visual information processing generally, one form of programming among many. On the other hand, noncommercial video, which became available at the time of the greatest prestige of structural film, initially assumed an aesthetic project parallel to that of structural film, even figuring in the work of structural filmmakers (in Hollis Frampton's, for example, after *Travelling Matte* in 1971). But video art's "negative" definition in the early seventies, its organization of languages and procedures exactly counter to those of broadcast television, could last only as long as the social possibilities of the sixties generally. Along with structural film, it died with the dispersal of those possibilities, though the expectation that artists' video might restage independent film's project in a modernist, "writerly" critique of a putatively "realist" broadcast television text was preempted by broadcast television's own appropriation of the formal devices of high modernism. Similarly, the possibility of its sustaining social opposition was choked in advance by the medium's increasingly internalized dependence on corporate technology.

Each bypassing the vestiges of the filmic avant-garde, popular music and television eventually met in the early eighties in music videos. In the convulsive recyclings of post-punk, which themselves reflected the absence of any social basis for formal invention, the tropes of underground film were eventually called on, though the form in which they reappeared shredded in ridicule the social aspirations that first brought them into being. The backside of the pornography industries, music videos exploited all underground film's stylistic innovations—surrealist motifs; the representation of marginal and criminal subcultures; the fracturing of diegetic time and space; rapid cutting and nonlinear, nonlogical editing; and especially the denaturing of representations within the materiality of the photographic image. But rather than mobilizing either aesthetic or political alternatives, or articulating any decentralized practice or other difference from the industry, all these stylistic elements were rewritten in the codes of television commercials, finally to find a place in the industrialized consensus, which now celebrated an entirely administered false liberation, a global farce in which the simulacra of social otherness or resistance stood in as advertisements for their actual impossibility.

The dystopian integration of contemporary film in a totalized in-

dustrial system, existing at a higher logical level than any one medium within it, is the context in which we inherit the traces of sixties
cinemas. If any function remains for these films, it will not be separable from that of breaking open this closure with invocations of
other forms of social life.

Works Cited

FILMS

Across 110th Street. Barry Shear. 1972
The Act of Seeing with One's Own Eyes. Stan Brakhage. 1971
Alabama March. Alan Jacobs. 1965
Allures. Jordan Belson. 1961
Alphaville. Jean-Luc Godard. 1965
Analytic Studies. Paul Sharits. 1972–76
And God Created Woman. Roger Vadim. 1956
Andalusian Dog. Luis Buñuel and Salvador Dali. 1928
The Anderson Platoon. Pierre Schoendorffer. 1966–67
Andy Warhol Films Jack Smith Filming "Normal Love." Andy
    Warhol. 1963
Andy Warhol's Exploding Plastic Inevitable. Ronald Nameth. 1966
Anticipation of the Night. Stan Brakhage. 1958
Applications. Vito Acconci. 1970
Army. Newsreel. 1969
Arnulf Rainer. Peter Kubelka. 1960
Art Makeup: Green, Black, White, Pink. Bruce Nauman. 1971
The Art of Vision. Stan Brakhage. 1961–64
Artificial Light. Hollis Frampton. 1969
As Long as Rivers Run. Carol Burns and the Survival of the Amer-
    ican Indian Association. 1971
Babo 73. Robert Downey. 1964
Back-Forth. Michael Snow. 1969
Barn Rushes. Larry Gottheim. 1971
Batman Dracula. Andy Warhol. 1964
Beat Girl. Edmund T. Grenville. 1959
Behind the Green Door. Jim Mitchell. 1972
Be-In. Jerry Abrams. 1967
Belle de Jour. Luis Buñuel. 1967
Beyond the Law. Norman Mailer. 1967
Beyond the Valley of the Dolls. Russ Meyer. 1970
Bike Boy. Andy Warhol. 1967
Black Panther. San Francisco Newsreel with the Black Panther
    Party. 1968
The Black Panthers: A Report. Agnes Varda. 1968
Black Power, We're Goin' Survive America. Leonard Henny. 1968
The Blackboard Jungle. Richard Brooks. 1955
Blazing Saddles. Mel Brooks. 1974
Bleu Shut. Robert Nelson. 1970

Blonde Cobra. Ken Jacobs. 1959–63

Blood Feast. Herschell Gordon Lewis. 1963

Blood of a Poet. Jean Cocteau. 1930

Blow Job. Andy Warhol. 1963–64

Blue Moses. Stan Brakhage. 1962

Blue Movie. Andy Warhol. 1968

Bonnie and Clyde. Arthur Penn. 1967

Boston Draft-Resistance Group. Newsreel. 1968

Boys in the Sand. Wakefield Poole. 1971

Brandy in the Wilderness. Stanton Kaye. 1969

Break and Enter (*Rompiendo Puertas*). New York Newsreel. 1970

Breakfast for Children. Los Angeles Newsreel

Breathless. Jean-Luc Godard. 1960

The Brig. Jonas Mekas. 1964

Buck and the Preacher. Sidney Poitier. 1972

Bucket of Blood. Roger Corman. 1959

Bush Mama. Haille Gerima. 1975

Canyon. Jon Jost. 1970

Carnal Knowledge. Mike Nichols. 1970

Cat's Cradle. Stan Brakhage. 1959

Chakra. Jordan Belson. 1972

The Chelsea Girls. Andy Warhol. 1966

Cheyenne Autumn. John Ford. 1964

Christmas in Vietnam. CBS. 1965

Christmas on Earth. Barbara Rubin. 1964

The Chronicle of Anna Magdalena Bach. Jean-Marie Straub. 1968

Chumlum. Ron Rice. 1964

Citizen Kane. Orson Welles. 1941

City. Jon Jost. 1964

Cleopatra Jones. Jack Starrett. 1973

Cobra Woman. Robert Siodmak. 1944

Coffy. Jack Hill. 1973

Columbia Revolt. Newsreel. 1968

Come Back, Africa. Lionel Rogosin. 1959

Condition of Illusion. Peter Gidal. 1975

The Connection. Shirley Clarke. 1961

Contempt. Jean-Luc Godard. 1963

Controlling Interest. Newsreel. 1978

The Cool World. Shirley Clarke. 1963

Cosmic Ray. Bruce Conner. 1961

Cosmos. Jordan Belson. 1969

Cotton Comes to Harlem. Ossie Davis. 1970

Couch. Andy Warhol. 1964

Critical Mass. Hollis Frampton. 1973

Cybernetik 5.3. John Stehura. 1969

David Holzman's Diary. Jim McBride. 1967

Day for Night. François Truffaut. 1973

The Dead. Stan Brakhage. 1960

Deep Throat. Gerard Damiano. 1972

Desistfilm. Stan Brakhage. 1954

The Devil in Miss Jones. Gerard Damiano. 1973

The Devil's Cleavage. George Kuchar. 1973

Diaries, Notes and Sketches (Walden). Jonas Mekas. 1968

Dionysus '69. Brian De Palma, Robert Fiore, and Bruce Rubin. 1969

Dog Star Man. Stan Brakhage. 1961–64

Dreams That Money Can Buy. Hans Richter. 1944–46

Duet for Cannibals. Susan Sontag. 1969

Duplicity. Stan Brakhage. 1978

Dutchman. Amiri Baraka (Leroi Jones). 1967

Easy Rider. Dennis Hopper. 1969

Eat. Andy Warhol. 1963

The Edge. Robert Kramer. 1967

8 1/2. Federico Fellini. 1963

Empire. Andy Warhol. 1963–64

Entry-Exit. George Brecht. 1965

eyes. Stan Brakhage. 1971

A Face of War. Eugene S. Jones. 1967

Faces. John Cassavetes. 1968

FALN. Peter Gessner with Robert Kramer. 1965

Far From Vietnam. Chris Marker. 1967

Festival Mix. Jud Yalkut. 1968

Fifty Fantastics and Fifty Personalities. Andy Warhol. 1965

Film about a woman who . . . . Yvonne Rainer. 1974

Film in which there appear sprocket holes, edge lettering, dirt particles etc. George Landow. 1966

Films By Stan Brakhage: An Avant-Garde Home Movie. Stan Brakhage. 1961

Finally Got the News. Stewart Bird and Peter Gessner with the League of Black Revolutionary Workers. 1970

Fireworks. Kenneth Anger. 1947

Flaming Creatures. Jack Smith. 1963

Flesh. Andy Warhol. 1969

The Flicker. Tony Conrad. 1966

The Flower Thief. Ron Rice. 1960

* * * * (Four Stars). Andy Warhol. 1966

Four Women. Julie Dash. 1978

Foxy Brown. Jack Hill. 1974

Fragment of Seeking. Curtis Harrington. 1946

Frankenstein. Andy Warhol. 1974

The French Connection. William Friedkin. 1971

Fuses. Carolee Schneemann. 1964–67

Ganja and Hess. Bill Gunn. 1970

Garden of Eden. Max Nosseck. 1954

Georg. Stanton Kaye. 1964

G.I. José. Norberto Lopez. 1974

Giant. George Stevens. 1956

Gimme Shelter. David and Albert Maysles. 1971

The Girl Can't Help It. Frank Tashlin. 1956

A Grass Sandwich (A Free Ride). 1915

The Great Train Robbery. Edwin S. Porter. 1903

The Green Berets. John Wayne. 1968

Guess Who's Coming to Dinner. Stanley Kramer. 1967

Guns of the Trees. Jonas Mekas. 1961

Haircut. Andy Warhol. 1972

Hallelujah the Hills. Adolfas Mekas. 1963

Hand Catching Lead. Richard Serra. 1968

Hanoi, Martes Trece. Santiago Alvarez. 1967

Hapax Legomena. Hollis Frampton. 1972

Hard Core. Walter de Maria. 1972

Heat. Andy Warhol. 1972

Hedy. Andy Warhol. 1965

Henry Geldzahler. Andy Warhol. 1963–64

Hiroshima Mon Amour. Alain Resnais. 1959

History. Ernie Gehr. 1970

History of the Blue Movie. Alex de Renzy. 1970

Hold Me While I'm Naked. George Kuchar. 1966

Hollywood Boulevard. Jon Davidson. 1976

The Horseman, The Woman and The Moth. Stan Brakhage. 1968

Hospital. Frederick Wiseman. 1971

Hud. Martin Ritt. 1963

The Hustler. Robert Rosen. 1961

I Am Curious (Yellow). Vilgot Sjöman. 1967

I, an Actress. George Kuchar. 1977

I and I: An African Allegory. Ben Caldwell. 1977

Ice. Robert Kramer. 1969

The Immoral Mr. Teas. Russ Meyer. 1959

In the Event Anyone Disappears. Third World Newsreel. 1974

In the Year of the Pig. Émile de Antonio. 1969

Inauguration of the Pleasure Dome. Kenneth Anger. 1966

Incident at Owl Creek. Robert Enrico. 1961

Information. Hollis Frampton. 1966

Inside North Vietnam. Felix Greene. 1968

Inside Women Inside. Third World Newsreel. 1978

Institutional Quality. George Landow. 1969

Interim. Stan Brakhage. 1952

Interview with Bobby Seale. San Francisco Newsreel. 1969

Interviews with My Lai Veterans. Joseph Strick. 1971

Intolerance. D. W. Griffith. 1916

Intrepid Shadows. Al Clah. 1966

Invocation of My Demon Brother. Kenneth Anger. 1969

Janie's Janie. Geri Ashur, Peter Barton, et al. 1971

Joe. John G. Avildsen. 1970

John Rice-May Irwin Kiss. The Edison Company. 1896

Journeys From Berlin/1971. Yvonne Rainer. 1979

Jules and Jim. François Truffaut. 1961

July '71 in San Francisco, Living at Beach Street, Working at Canyon Cinema, Swimming in the Valley of the Moon. Peter Hutton. 1971

Killer of Sheep. Charles Burnett. 1977

Kino Pravda. Dziga Vertov. 1922–25

Kirsa Nicholina. Gunvor Nelson. 1970

Kiss. Andy Warhol. 1963

Know Your Enemy—The Viet Cong (AFIF 172). U.S. Army. 1968

Kristina Talking Pictures. Yvonne Rainer. 1976

Kustom Kar Kommandos. Kenneth Anger. 1965

La Chinoise. Jean-Luc Godard. 1967

La Région Centrale. Michael Snow. 1971

Lady Sings the Blues. Sidney Furie. 1972

L'Amour. Paul Morrissey. 1973

Lapis. James Whitney. 1966

The Last Movie. Dennis Hopper. 1971

Last Year at Marienbad. Alain Resnais. 1961

Law and Order. Frederick Wiseman. 1969

The Learning Tree. Gordon Parks. 1969

Les Liaisons Dangereuses. Roger Vadim. 1959

The Liberal War. Nick Macdonald. 1972

Life and Death of 9413—A Hollywood Extra. Robert Florey and
    Slavko Vorkapich. 1928

The Life of Juanita Castro. Andy Warhol. 1965

Lincoln Hospital. Third World Newsreel. 1970

Line. Yvonne Rainer. 1969

Line Describing a Cone. Anthony McCall. 1973

Little Big Man. Arthur Penn. 1971

Little Stabs at Happiness. Ken Jacobs. 1959–63

Lives of Performers. Yvonne Rainer. 1972

Lonesome Cowboys. Andy Warhol. 1967

Loose Ends. Chick Strand. 1979

Lorna. Russ Meyer. 1964

Los Siete. San Francisco Newsreel. 1969

Lost Lost Lost. Jonas Mekas. 1976

Lot in Sodom. James Watson and Melville Webber. 1933

Love Me Tender. Robert Webb. 1956

Lovemaking. Scott Bartlett. 1970

The Lovers. Louis Malle. 1958

Loving. Stan Brakhage. 1957

Lucifer Rising. Kenneth Anger. 1966–80

Lupe. Andy Warhol. 1965

Lurk. Rudy Burckhardt. 1965

The Mack. Michael Campus. 1973

Made in U.S.A. Jean-Luc Godard. 1966

The Magical Mystery Tour. The Beatles. 1967

Maidstone. Norman Mailer. 1968

A Man Called Horse. Elliot Silverstein. 1970

The Man Who Envied Women. Yvonne Rainer. 1985

The Man with the Movie Camera. Dziga Vertov. 1928

March on the Pentagon. David Ringo. 1968

Mass for the Dakota Sioux. Bruce Baillie. 1963–64

Mayday. San Francisco Newsreel with the Black Panther Party. 1968

Meditation. Jordan Belson. 1971

Medium Cool. Haskell Wexler. 1969

Melodic Inversion. Richard Hugo. 1958

Memories of Underdevelopment. Tomás Gutiérrez Alea. 1968

Meshes of the Afternoon. Maya Deren. 1943

Midnight Cowboy. John Schlesinger. 1968

A Midsummer Night's Dream. Max Reinhardt. 1963

Moment. Bill Brand. 1972

Momentum. Jordan Belson. 1969

Mona, The Virgin Nymph. Bill Osco. 1970

Monterey Pop. D. A. Pennebaker. 1968

The Moon Is Blue. Otto Preminger. 1953

Moon 69. Scott Bartlett. 1969

More Milk, Yvette. Andy Warhol. 1965

Mothlight. Stan Brakhage. 1963

A Movie. Bruce Conner. 1957

The Murder of Fred Hampton. Mike Gray Associates. 1971

My Hustler. Andy Warhol. 1965

My Mountain Song. Stan Brakhage. 1969

Myra Breckinridge. Mike Sarne. 1970

A Navajo Weaver. Susie Benally. 1966

Near the Big Chakra. Anne Severson. 1972

New Left Note. Saul Levine. 1969–75, released 1983

New York Ear and Eye Control. Michael Snow. 1964

Night of the Living Dead. George Romero. 1968

Nine Minutes. James Riddle. 1966

No Game. Newsreel. 1967

Normal Love. Jack Smith. 1963

nostalgia. Hollis Frampton. 1971

Notebook. Marie Menken. 1962–63

Nothing But A Man. Michael Roemer and Robert Young. 1964

Nowsreal. Kelly Hart. 1968

Nude Restaurant. Andy Warhol. 1967

Oil Strike. San Francisco Newsreel. 1969

On the Bowery. Lionel Rogosin. 1956

One Plus One. Jean-Luc Godard. 1968

One Sixth of the Earth. Dziga Vertov. 1926

Paradise Now. Sheldon Rochlin. 1970

Passing Through. Larry Clark. 1977

Paul Revere. Richard Serra and Joan Jonas. 1971

PDM. San Francisco Newsreel. 1970

Peace March. Anthony Reveaux. 1967

Peeping Tom. Michael Powell. 1960

The People Are Rising (El Pueblo Se Levanta). Newsreel. 1971

People's War. Newsreel. 1969

Performance. Nicholas Roeg. 1972

Phenomena. Jordan Belson. 1965

Piece Mandala/End War. Paul Sharits. 1966

Pink Flamingoes. John Waters. 1973

Pittsburgh Trilogy. Stan Brakhage. 1971

Playing a Note on the Violin While I Am Walking Around the Studio. Bruce Nauman. 1968

The Plow that Broke the Plains. Pare Lorentz. 1936

Poetic Justice. Hollis Frampton. 1972

Pornography in Denmark. Alex de Renzy. 1970

Portrait of Jason. Shirley Clarke. 1967

Prelude. Stan Brakhage. 1961

Print Generation. J. J. Murphy. 1973–74

Production Stills. Morgan Fisher. 1970

Projection Instructions. Morgan Fisher. 1976

Promises, Promises. King Donovan. 1963

Psyche. Gregory Markopoulos. 1947

Psycho. Alfred Hitchcock. 1960

Puce Moment. Kenneth Anger. 1949

Pull My Daisy. Robert Frank and Alfred Leslie. 1959

Putney Swope. Robert Downey. 1969

The Queen of Sheba Meets the Atom Man. Ron Rice. 1963

The Quiet One. Sidney Meyers and Janice Loeb. 1948

Quixote. Bruce Baillie. 1964–68

A Raisin in the Sun. Daniel Petrie. 1961

"Rameau's Nephew" by Diderot (Thanx to Dennis Young) by Wilma Shoen. Michael Snow. 1974

Rate of Change. Bill Brand. 1972

Rebel Without A Cause. Nicholas Ray. 1953

Red Squad. The Pacific Street Film Collective. 1972

Re-Entry. Jordan Belson. 1964

Reflections on Black. Stan Brakhage. 1955

Remedial Reading Comprehension. George Landow. 1971

Reminiscences of a Journey to Lithuania. Jonas Mekas. 1971

Report. Bruce Conner. 1967

The Resistance. Leonard Henny. 1968

The Riddle of Lumen. Stan Brakhage. 1972

Room Film. Peter Gidal. 1973

Saigon. Leslie Fenton. 1947

Samadhi. Jordan Belson. 1967

San Francisco State: On Strike. San Francisco Newsreel. 1969

The Savage Eye. Ben Maddow. 1959

Scarface and Aphrodite. Vernon Zimmerman. 1963

Scenes From Under Childhood. Stan Brakhage. 1967–70

Science Friction. Stan Vanderbeek. 1959

Scorpio Rising. Kenneth Anger. 1963

Screen Test #2. Andy Warhol. 1965

Script. John Baldessari. 1973

See Through. Vito Acconci. 1970

Senseless. Ron Rice. 1962

Serene Velocity. Ernie Gehr. 1970

79 Springtimes (79 Primaveras). Santiago Alvarez. 1969

S.F. Trips Festival, An Opening. Ben Van Meter. 1966

Shadows. John Cassavetes. 1959

Shaft. Gordon Parks. 1971

Shaft In Africa. John Guillermin. 1973

Shaft's Big Score. Gordon Parks. 1972

Show People. King Vidor. 1928

Sigmund Freud's Dora. Anthony McCall, Claire Pajaczkowska, Andrew Tyndall, and Jane Weinstock. 1979

Sincerity. Stan Brakhage. 1973

The Sins of Jesus. Robert Frank. 1961

Sins of the Fleshapoids. Mike Kuchar. 1965

Sirius Remembered. Stan Brakhage. 1959

Slaughter. Jack Starrett. 1972

Slaughter's Big Rip-Off. Gordon Douglas. 1973

Sleep. Andy Warhol. 1963

So is This. Michael Snow. 1982

Soft Fiction. Chick Strand. 1979

Soldier Blue. Ralph Nelson. 1970

Songs. Stan Brakhage. 1964–69

The Sons of Katie Elder. Henry Hathaway. 1965

Spartacus. Stanley Kubrick. 1960

Speaking Directly: Some American Notes. Jon Jost. 1974

Special Effects. Hollis Frampton. 1972

Spiral Jetty. Robert Smithson. 1970

Stagecoach. John Ford. 1939

Straits of Magellan. Hollis Frampton. 1975

The Strawberry Statement. Stuart Hagmann. 1970

S:TREAM:S:S:ECTION:S:ECTION:S:S:ECTIONED. Paul Sharits. 1970

The Subterraneans. Ranald MacDougall. 1960

Sullivan's Travels. Preston Sturges. 1941

Summer of 68. Newsreel. 1969

Sunset Boulevard. Billy Wilder. 1950

Superfly. Gordon Parks. 1972

Superfly T.N.T. Ron Neale. 1973

Sweet Sweetback's Baadasss Song. Melvin Van Peebles. 1971

Tarzan and Jane Regained . . . Sort of. Andy Warhol. 1963

Teach Our Children. Third World Newsreel. 1973

Tell Them Willie Boy Is Here. Abraham Polonsky. 1970

10 Feet. George Maciunas. 1966

The Text of Light. Stan Brakhage. 1974

Thigh Line Lyre Triangular. Stan Brakhage. 1961

The Thirteen Most Beautiful Boys. Andy Warhol. 1965

The Thirteen Most Beautiful Women. Andy Warhol. 1964

Three Lives. Kate Millett. 1971

Time of the Locust. Peter Gessner. 1966

To Kill a Mockingbird. Robert Mulligan. 1963

Tom, Tom, The Piper's Son. Billy Bitzer. 1905

Tom, Tom, The Piper's Son. Ken Jacobs. 1969

Trash. Andy Warhol. 1970

Travelling Matte. Hollis Frampton. 1971

The Treasure of the Sierra Madre. John Huston. 1948

Trick Baby. Larry Yust. 1973

The Trip. Roger Corman. 1967

Triptych in Four Parts. Larry Jordan. 1958

Troublemakers. Norman Fruchter and Robert Machover. 1966

Truck Turner. Jonathan Kaplan. 1974

23rd Psalm Branch. Stan Brakhage. 1966

Two or Three Things I Know About Her. Jean-Luc Godard. 1966

2001: A Space Odyssey. Stanley Kubrick. 1968

Un Chant d'Amour. Jean Genet. 1950

Uncle Josh at the Moving Picture Show. Edwin S. Porter. 1902

Underground. Émile de Antonio, Mary Lampson, and Haskell Wexler. 1975

Vietnam. Roman Karmen. 1955

Vinyl. Andy Warhol. 1965

Visual Variations on Noguchi. Marie Menken. 1945

Watermelon Man. Melvin Van Peebles. 1970

Wavelength. Michael Snow. 1967

The Way to Shadow Garden. Stan Brakhage. 1954

We Demand Freedom. Third World Newsreel. 1974

We Shall March Again. Lenny Lipton. 1965

Wedlock House: An Intercourse. Stan Brakhage. 1959

The Weir-Falcon Saga. Stan Brakhage. 1970

Western History. Stan Brakhage. 1971

What's Wrong with This Picture. George Landow. 1972

Why Vietnam? United States Government, Department of Defense. 1965

The Wild Angels. Roger Corman. 1966

The Wild Bunch. Sam Peckinpah. 1969

Wild in the Streets. Barry Shear. 1968

The Wild One. Laslo Benedek. 1953

Wind from the East. Jean-Luc Godard. 1970

Window Water Baby Moving. Stan Brakhage. 1959

Winter Soldier. Winterfilm Collective. 1971

The Woman's Film. San Francisco Newsreel. 1969

Women in Revolt (Sex). Andy Warhol. 1971

Woodstock. Michael Wadleigh. 1970

World. Jordan Belson. 1970

The Wreck of the New York Subway. New York Newsreel. 1970

Yantra. James Whitney. 1955

Young Puppeteers of Vietnam. National Liberation Front of Vietnam

"*Z.*" Constantine Costa-Gavras. 1969

Zabriskie Point. Michelangelo Antonioni. 1969

Zen for Film. Nam June Paik. 1962–64

Zorns Lemma. Hollis Frampton. 1970

Adair, Gilbert. (1981) *Vietnam on Film: From the Green Berets to Apocalypse Now*. New York: Proteus.

Adorno, Theodor. (1967) *Prisms*. London: Spearman.

———. (1973) *Philosophy of Modern Music*. New York: Continuum.

———. (1977a) "Reconciliation Under Duress." In *Aesthetics and Politics*, ed. Ronald Taylor. London: New Left Books.

———. (1977b) "Commitment." In *Aesthetics and Politics*, ed. Ronald Taylor. London: New Left Books.

Affron, Charles. (1977) *Star Acting: Gish, Garbo, Davis*. New York: E. P. Dutton.

Alexander, Thomas Kent. (1967) "San Francisco's Hipster Cinema." *Film Culture* 44 (Spring): 70–74.

Alexander, William. (1981) *Film on the Left: American Documentary Film from 1931 to 1942*. Princeton, N.J.: Princeton University Press.

Allen, Donald, ed. (1960) *The New American Poetry*. New York: Grove Press.

Alloway, Lawrence. (1972) "Network: The Art World Described as a System." *Artforum* 11, 1 (September): 28–32.

Alpert, Jane. (1981) *Growing Up Underground*. New York: William Morrow.

Althusser, Louis. (1971) "Ideology and Ideological State Apparatuses." In *Lenin and Philosophy*, trans. Ben Brewster. New York: Monthly Review Press.

Altieri, Charles. (1979) *Enlarging the Temple: New Directions in American Poetry During the 1960's*. Lewisburg, Pa.: Bucknell University Press.

Anger, Kenneth. (1965) *Hollywood Babylon*. Phoenix, Ariz.: Associated Professional Services.

Arlen, Michael. (1969) *Living Room War*. New York: Viking.

Arthur, Paul. (1978) "Structural Film: Revisions, New Versions, and the Artifact." *Millennium Film Journal* 1, 2 (Spring): 5–13.

———. (1979a) " 'Quixote' and its Contexts." *Film Culture* 67/68/69: 32–56.

———. (1979b) "Structural Film: Revisions, New Versions and the Artifact. Part Two." *Millennium Film Journal* 4–5 (Summer/Fall): 122–34.

———. (1987) "Last of the Machine: Avant-garde Film since 1965." *Millennium Film Journal* 16/17/18 (Fall/Winter 1986–87): 69–93.

Balio, Tino. (1976) *The American Film Industry*. Madison: University of Wisconsin Press.

Baraka, Amiri. (1963) *Blues People: Negro Music in White America*. New York: William Morrow.

———. (1966) *Home: Social Essays*. New York: William Morrow.

———. (1967) *Black Music*. New York: William Morrow,

———. (1971) "Black (Art) Drama Is the Same as Black Life." *Ebony* 26, 4 (February): 74–82.

———. (1972) *Spirit Reach*. Newark, N.J.: Jihad Productions.

———. (1976) *Black Music*. New York: William Morrow.

Barnouw, Erik. (1974) *Documentary: A History of the Non-Fiction Film*. New York: Oxford University Press.

Barthes, Roland. (1972a) "The Structuralist Activity." In *Critical Essays*. Evanston, Ill.: Northwestern University Press.

———. (1972b) *Mythologies*. New York: Hill and Wang.

———. (1974) *S/Z*. New York: Hill and Wang.

———. (1977) *Image—Music—Text*, trans. Stephen Heath. New York: Hill and Wang.

Battcock, Gregory. (1967) "Four Films by Andy Warhol." In *The New American Cinema: A Critical Anthology*, ed. Gregory Battcock, 233–52. New York: E. P. Dutton.

———. (1968) *Minimal Art: A Critical Anthology*, ed. Gregory Battcock. New York: E. P. Dutton.

Baudry, Jean-Louis. (1974) "Ideological Effects of the Basic Cinematographic Apparatus." *Film Quarterly* 28, 2 (Winter 1974–75): 39–47.

Baxter, John. (1972) *Hollywood in the Sixties*. London: The Tantivy Press.

Bazin, André. (1967) *What is Cinema?* trans. Hugh Gray. Berkeley: University of California Press.

———. (1971) *What is Cinema? Volume II*. trans. Hugh Gray. Berkeley: University of California Press.

Benjamin, Walter. (1969) *Illuminations*, ed. Hannah Arendt. New York: Schocken Books.

———. (1973) *Charles Baudelaire: A Lyric Poet in the Era of High Capitalism*. London: New Left Books.

———. (1979) "The Author as Producer." In *Reflections: Essays, Aphorisms, Autobiographical Writings*, ed. Peter Demetz. New York: Harcourt Brace Jovanovich.

Berger, John. (1974) "The Changing View of Man in the Portrait." In *The Look of Things*. New York: Viking.

Bergstrom, Janet. (1979) "Rereading the work of Claire Johnston." *Camera Obscura* 3–4: 21–32.

Boe, Eugene. (1966) "Lights, Camera, But Where's the Action." *Status* (March): 71–74.

Boorstin, Daniel J. (1961) *The Image: Or What Happened to the American Dream*. New York: Atheneum.

Bordwell, David. (1979) "The Art Cinema as a Mode of Film Practice." *Film Criticism* 4, 1: 56–64.

Boultenhouse, Charles. (1963) "The Camera as God." *Film Culture* 29 (Summer): 20–22.

Bourdon, David. (1971) "Andy Warhol as Filmmaker." *Art in America* 59, 3 (May): 48–53.

Brakhage, Stan. (1963) *Metaphors on Vision*. New York: Film Culture.

Brakhage, Stan. (1968) "Closed-Eye Vision." *Caterpillar* 2 (January): 26–34.

———. (1971) *A Moving Picture Giving and Taking Book.* West Newbury, Mass.: Frontier Press.

———. (1975) *The Seen.* San Francisco: Zephyrus Image.

———. (1977) *Film Biographies.* Berkeley, Calif.: Turtle Island.

———. (1978) "Brakhage Uncensored." *Cinemanews* 6: 14–15, 24–27.

———. (1979) "Stan Brakhage Speaks on '23rd Psalm Branch' at Filmmaker's Cinematheque, April 22, 1967." *Film Culture* 67/68/69: 109–35.

———. (1982) *Brakhage Scrapbook: Collected Writings 1964–80.* New Paltz, N.Y.: Documentext.

———. (n.d.) "Stan Brakhage: The Text of Light." *Cantrill Filmnotes* 21/22: 33–35.

Braudy, Leo. (1977) *The World in a Frame: What We See in Films.* New York: Doubleday.

Brooks, Cleanth. (1971) "Irony as a Principle of Structure." In *Critical Theory Since Plato*, ed. Hazard Adams, 1041–48. New York: Harcourt Brace Jovanovich.

Brustein, Robert. (1971) *Revolution as Theatre.* New York: Liveright.

Burch, Noël. (1979) *To the Distant Observer: Form and Meaning in the Japanese Cinema.* Berkeley: University of California Press.

Burnham, Linda, and Miriam Louie. (1985) *The Impossible Marriage: A Marxist Critique of Socialist Feminism.* Oakland, Calif.: Line of March.

Cage, John. (1961) *Silence.* Middletown, Conn.: Wesleyan University Press.

———. (1970) "On Film." In *John Cage*, ed. Richard Kostelanetz, 115–16. New York: Praeger.

Carmichael, Stokely, and Charles V. Hamilton. (1967) *Black Power: The Politics of Liberation in America.* New York: Vintage.

Carroll, Noël. (1980) "Interview With A Woman Who." *Millennium Film Journal* 7/8/9 (Fall): 37–68.

Carter, Angela. (1980) *The Sadeian Woman.* New York: Harper and Row.

Chalfen, Richard. (1975) "Cinema Naivete: A Study of Home Moviemaking as Visual Communication." *Studies in the Anthropology of Visual Communication* 2: 87–103.

Chapple, Steve, and Reebee Garofalo. (1977) *Rock'n'Roll is Here to Pay: The History and Politics of the Music Industry.* Chicago: Nelson-Hall.

Charters, Ann. (1973) *Kerouac: A Biography.* San Francisco: Straight Arrow.

Choy, Christine. (n.d.) "Interview with Christine Choy: Third World Newsreel: Ten Years of Left Film." *Jump Cut* 27: 21–22, 39.

"Cinema Underground." (1963) *The New Yorker* 13 (July): 16–17.

Clark, T. J. (1983) "Clement Greenberg's Theory of Art." In *The Politics of Interpretation*, ed. W.J.T. Mitchell, 203–20. Chicago: University of Chicago Press.

Clarke, John et al. (1976) "Subcultures, Cultures and Class." In *Resistance Through Rituals*, ed. Stuart Hall, John Clarke, Tony Jefferson, and Brian Roberts. London: Hutchinson.

Cleaver, Eldridge. (1968) *Soul On Ice*. New York: Delta Books.

Cockroft, Eva. (1974) "Abstract Expressionism: Weapon of the Cold War." *Artforum* 12, 10 (June): 39–41.

Collier, James Lincoln. (1979) *The Making of Jazz: A Comprehensive History*. New York: Delta.

Comolli, Jean-Luc, and Paul Narboni. (1971) "Cinema/Ideology/Criticism." *Screen* 12, 1 (Spring): 27–36.

Cook, David A. (1981) *A History of Narrative Film*. New York: Norton.

Coplans, John. (n.d.) *Andy Warhol*. New York: Graphic Society.

Cornwell, Regina. (1980) *Snow Seen: The Films and Photographs of Michael Snow*. Toronto: PMA Books.

Corr, Eugene, and Peter Gessner. (1974) "Cine Manifest: A Self-History." *Jump Cut* 3 (September): 19–20.

Cripps, Thomas. (1978) *Black Film as Genre*. Bloomington: Indiana University Press.

Crowdus, Gary. (n.d.) "The Murder of Fred Hampton." *Cinéaste* 5, 1: 50–51.

Curtis, David. (1971) *Experimental Cinema: A Fifty Year Evolution*. New York: Delta.

Daly, Mary. (1978) *Gyn/Ecology: The Metaethics of Radical Feminism*. Boston: Beacon Press.

Davis, Angela. (1981) *Women, Race and Class*. Random House: New York.

De Antonio, Émile. (n.d.) "*Year of the Pig*: Marxist Film." *Jump Cut* 19: 37.

Debord, Guy. (1977) *Society of the Spectacle*. Detroit: Black and Red.

Deleuze, Gilles, and Félix Guattari. (1983) *Anti-Oedipus: Capitalism and Schizophrenia*. Minneapolis: University of Minnesota Press.

Delillo, Don. (1971) *Americana*. New York: Houghton Mifflin.

Deren, Maya. (1960) "Cinematography: The Creative Use of Reality." *Daedalus* (Winter): 150–67.

Desnos, Robert. (1923) "Eroticism." In Paul Hammond (1978: 122–23).

Diagnostic and Statistical Manual of Mental Disorders. (1980) 3d ed. Washington: American Psychiatric Association.

Dienstfrey, Harris. (1962) "The New American Cinema." *Commentary* 6, 33 (June): 495–504.

Di Lauro, Al, and Gerald Rabkin. (1976) *Dirty Movies: An Illustrated History of the Stag Film, 1915–1970*. New York: Chelsea House.

Doane, Mary Ann. (1981) "Woman's Stake: Filming the Female Body." *October* 17: 23–36.

Dorn, Edward. (1977) "Afterword." Anselm Hollo. *Sojourner Microcosms*. Berkeley, Calif.: Blue Wind Press.

Dulac, Germaine. (1978) "The Avant-Garde Cinema." Reprinted in Sitney (1978).

Dwoskin, Stephen. (1975) *Film Is: The International Free Cinema*. Woodstock, N.Y.: The Overlook Press.

Eagleton, Terry. (1976) *Criticism and Ideology: A Study in Marxist Literary Theory*. London: New Left Books.

Eco, Umberto. (1976) "Articulations of the Cinematic Code." In *Movies and Methods*, ed. Bill Nichols, 591–607. Berkeley: University of California Press.

Ehrenstein, David, and Bill Reed. (1982) *Rock on Film*. New York: Delilah Books.

Ellis, John. (1980) "On Pornography." *Screen* 21, 1 (Spring): 81–108.

Enzensberger, Hans Magnus. (1974) *The Consciousness Industry: On Literature, Politics and the Media*. New York: The Seabury Press.

Espinosa, Julio Garcia. (n.d.) "For an Imperfect Cinema." *Jump Cut* 20: 24–26.

Farber, Manny. (1957) "Underground Films: A Bit of Male Truth." *Commentary* 24, 5 (November): 432–39.

Farrell, James T. (1944) "The Language of Hollywood." *Saturday Review of Literature* 5 (August): 29–32.

"Filming for the City: An Interview with the Kartemquin Collective." (1975) *Cinéaste* 7, 1 (Fall): 26–30.

Film-Makers' Cooperative Catalogue No. 6. (1975) New York: Film-Makers' Cooperative.

"Films in Vietnam." (1969) *Film Comment* 2 (Spring): 46–88.

Finkelstein, Sidney. (1948) *Jazz: A People's Music*. New York: Citadel.

Firestone, Shulamith. (1970) *The Dialectics of Sex: The Case for Feminist Revolution*. New York: William Morrow.

"The First Statement of the New American Cinema Group." In Sitney (1970: 79–83).

Fitzgerald, Frances. (1972) *Fire in the Lake: The Vietnamese and the Americans in Vietnam*. New York: Vintage.

Foucault, Michel. (1972) *The Archaeology of Knowledge*, trans. A. M. Sheridan Smith. New York: Harper and Row.

———. (1978) *The History of Sexuality*. New York: Pantheon.

Fouque, Antoinette. (1981) "The MLF is you, is me." In *New French Feminisms: An Anthology*, ed. Elaine Marks and Isabelle de Courtivron. New York: Schocken Books.

Frampton, Hollis. (1972) "Interview by Simon Field." *Afterimage* 4 (Autumn): 45–77.

———. (1983) *Circles of Confusion*. Rochester, N.Y.: Visual Studies Workshop Press.

Franchi, Rudy M. (1962) "The Coming of Age of the X-Film." *Cavalier* (July): 25–27, 83–85.

Frank, Robert. (1969) *The Americans*. Rev. ed. New York: Grossman.

Franklin, H. Bruce. (1971) *From the Movement Toward Revolution*. New York: Van Nostrand Reinhold.

Fredericksen, Don. (1979) "Modes of Reflexive Film." *Quarterly Review of Film Studies* 4, 3 (Summer): 299–320.

Fried, Michael. (1968) "Art and Objecthood." In Battcock (1968: 116–47).

Friedan, Betty. (1963) *The Feminine Mystique*. New York: Norton.

Gallop, Jane. (1984) *The Daughter's Seduction: Feminism and Psychoanalysis*. Ithaca, N.Y.: Cornell University Press.

Gans, Herbert J. (1962) *The Urban Villagers: Group and Class in the Life of Italian Americans*. New York: The Free Press.

Gayle, Addison, Jr., ed. (1972) *The Black Aesthetic*. New York: Doubleday.

Gehr, Ernie. (1972) "Ernie Gehr Interviewed by Jonas Mekas, March 24, 1971." *Film Culture* 53/54/55 (Spring): 25–36.

Georgakas, Dan. (1972) "They Have Not Spoken: American Indians in Film." *Film Quarterly* 25, 3 (Spring): 26–32.

———. (1973) "*Finally Got the News*: The Making of a Radical Film." *Cinéaste* 5, 4: 2–6.

Gessner, Peter. (1966) "Films from the Vietcong." *The Nation* 202, 4 (24 January): 110–11.

Gidal, Peter. (1975) "Theory and Definition of Structural/Materialist Film." *Studio International* 190, 978 (December): 189–96.

Gifford, Barry, and Lawrence Lee. (1978) *Jack's Book: An Oral Biography of Jack Kerouac*. New York: St. Martin's Press.

Gill, Brendan. (1966) "Easeful Death." *The New Yorker*, 23 April, 130–32.

Ginsberg, Allen. (1968) *Planet News, 1961–67*. San Francisco: City Lights.

Gitlin, Todd. (1980) *The Whole World Is Watching: Mass Media in the Making and Unmaking of the New Left*. Berkeley: University of California Press.

Gledhill, Christine. (1978) "Recent Developments in Feminist Criticism." *Quarterly Review of Film Studies* 3, 4 (Fall): 457–93.

Godard, Jean-Luc. (1972) *Weekend/Wind from the East*. New York: Simon and Schuster.

Green, Samuel Adams. (1966) "Andy Warhol." In *The New Art*, ed. Gregory Battcock, 229–34. New York: Dutton.

Greenberg, Clement. (1961) *Art and Culture*. Boston: Beacon Press.

———. (1965) "Modernist Painting." *Art and Literature* 4 (Spring): 193–201.

Griffin, Susan. (1981) *Pornography and Silence: Culture's Revenge Against Women*. New York: Harper and Row.

Guilbaut, Serge. (1983) *How New York Stole the Idea of Modern*

Art: Abstract Expressionism, Freedom, and the Cold War. Chicago: University of Chicago Press.

Gurevitch, Michael et al. (1982) *Culture, Society and the Media*, ed. Michael Gurevitch, Tony Bennett, James Curran, and Janet Woollacott. New York: Methuen.

Haller, Robert. (1980) *Kenneth Anger*. Minneapolis: Walker Art Center.

Hamill, Pete. (1963) "Explosion in the Movie Underground." *Saturday Evening Post*, 28 September.

Hammond, Charles Montgomery, Jr. (1981) *The Image Decade: Television Documentary, 1965–75*. New York: Hastings House.

Hammond, Paul, ed. (1978) *The Shadow and Its Shadow: Surrealist Writings on Cinema*. London: British Film Institute.

Harris, Marvin. (1981) *America Now: The Anthropology of a Changing Culture*. New York: Simon and Schuster.

Harvey, Sylvia. (1980) *May '68 and Film Culture*. London: British Film Institute.

Hauptman, William. (1973) "The Suppression of Art in the McCarthy Decade." *Artforum* 12, 2 (October): 48–52.

Hauser, Arnold. (n.d.) *The Social History of Art*. Vol. 4. New York: Vintage.

Heath, Stephen. (1978) "Difference." *Screen* 19, 3 (Autumn): 51–112.

———. (1981) *Questions of Cinema*. Bloomington: Indiana University Press.

Hebdige, Dick. (1979) *Subculture: the Meaning of Style*. London: Methuen.

Herr, Michael. (1978) *Dispatches*. New York: Avon.

Hess, John. (1981) "Notes on U.S. Radical Film, 1967–80." *Jump Cut* 21: 31–35.

Higgins, Dick. (1969) *foew&ombwhnw*. New York: Something Else Press.

Hoffman, Abbie. (1969) "Media Freaking." *The Drama Review* 13, 4 (Summer): 46–51.

Holmes, John Clellon. (1965) "15c Before 6:00 P.M.: The Wonderful Movies of 'The Thirties.' " *Harper's*, December 1965, 51–56.

Horkheimer, Max, and Theodor W. Adorno. (1972) *Dialectic of Enlightenment*. New York: Herder and Herder.

"The Independent Film Award." In Sitney (1970: 423–29).

Irigaray, Luce. (1985) *This Sex Which Is Not One*. Ithaca, N.Y.: Cornell University Press.

Jacobs, Lewis. (1968) *The Rise of the American Film*. New York: Teachers College Press.

James, David. (1978) "Semiology and Independent Film: A Review of Research and Criticism." *Quarterly Review of Film Studies* 3, 3 (Summer): 389–404.

Jameson, Fredric. (1971) "Metacommentary." *PMLA* 86, 1 (January): 9–18.

———. (1972) *The Prison-House of Language: A Critical Account of Structuralism and Russian Formalism*. Princeton, N.J.: Princeton University Press.

———. (1979) "Reification and Utopia in Mass Culture." *Social Text* 1: 130–49.

———. (1984) "Periodizing the 60s." In *The 60s Without Apology*, ed. Sohnya Sayres, Anders Stephanson, Stanley Aronowitz, and Fredric Jameson. Minneapolis: University of Minnesota Press.

Jenkins, Bruce, and Susan Krane. (1984) *Hollis Frampton: Recollections/Recreations*. Cambridge, Mass.: MIT Press.

Johnston, Claire. (1973) "Women's Cinema as Counter Cinema." In *Notes on Women's Cinema*, ed. Claire Johnston. London: Society for Education in Film and Television.

Jowett, Garth. (1976) *Film: The Democratic Art*. Boston: Little, Brown.

Kaplan, E. Ann. (1983) *Women and Film: Both Sides of the Camera*. New York: Methuen.

Karenga, Ron. (1972) "Black Cultural Nationalism." In *The Black Aesthetic*, ed. Addison Gayle, Jr. New York: Anchor.

Katz, Ephraim. (1979) *The Film Encyclopedia*. New York: Thomas Crowell.

Kauffman, Stanley. (1966) *A World on Film*. New York: Harper and Row.

Kelman, Ken. (1964) "Anticipations of the Light." *The Nation*, 11 May 1964, 490–94.

Kerouac, Jack. (1958) "Essentials of Spontaneous Prose." *Evergreen Review* 2, 5 (Summer): 72–73.

———. (1959) "The Origins of the Beat Generation." *Playboy* 6, 6 (June): 31–32, 42.

———. (1972) *Visions of Cody*. Introduction by Allen Ginsberg. New York: McGraw-Hill.

Kirby, Michael. (1969) "The Uses of Film in the New Theater." In *The Art of the Times*. New York: E. P. Dutton.

Klotman, Phyllis Rauch. (1979) *Frame by Frame: A Black Filmography*. Bloomington: Indiana University Press.

Knight, Arthur, and Hollis Alpert. (1967a) "A History of Sex in the Cinema. Part XV: Experimental Films." *Playboy* 14, 4 (April): 136ff.

———. (1967b) "A History of Sex in the Cinema. Part XVI: The Nudies." *Playboy* 14, 6 (June): 124ff.

———. (1967c) "A History of Sex in the Cinema. Part XVII: The Stag Film." *Playboy* 14, 11 (November): 154ff.

Koch, Stephen. (1972) "Performance, A Conversation." *Artforum* 11, 4 (December): 53–58.

———. (1973) *Stargazer: Andy Warhol's World and His Films*. New York: Praeger.

Kofsky, Frank. (1970) *Black Nationalism and the Revolution in Music*. New York: Pathfinder Press.

Kostelanetz, Richard, ed. (1978) *Esthetics Contemporary*. Buffalo, New York: Prometheus Books.

Kozloff, Max. (1973) "American Painting During the Cold War." *Artforum* 11, 9 (May): 43–54.

Kramer, Robert. (1969) "Towards a New Definition of Propaganda." *Leviathan* 1, 6 (November): 27–31.

Krauss, Rosalind. (1972) "A View of Modernism." *Artforum* 11, 1 (September): 48–51.

———. (1976) "Video: The Aesthetics of Narcissism." *October* 1 (Spring): 51–64.

Kristeva, Julia. (1981) "Woman Can Never Be Defined." In *New French Feminisms: An Anthology*, ed. Elaine Marks and Isabelle de Courtivron, 137–41. New York: Schocken Books.

Kuhn, Annette. (1982) *Women's Pictures: Feminism and Cinema*. London: Routledge and Kegan Paul.

Kutchinsky, Berl. (1973) "The Effects of Easy Availability of Pornography on the Incidence of Sex Crimes: The Danish Experience." *Journal of Sociological Issues* 29, 3: 163–81.

Lacan, Jacques. (1977) *Écrits: A Selection*. New York: Norton.

———. (1985) *Female Sexuality: Jacques Lacan and the école freudienne*, ed. Juliet Mitchell and Jacqueline Rose. New York: Norton.

Lawder, Standish. (1975) *The Cubist Cinema*. New York: New York University Press.

Le Grice, Malcolm. (1972) "Thoughts on Recent 'Underground' Film." *Afterimage*. (London) 4 (Autumn): 78–95.

———. (1977) *Abstract Film and Beyond*. Cambridge, Mass.: MIT Press.

Lederer, Laura, ed. (1980) *Take Back the Night: Women on Pornography*. New York: William Morrow.

Lesage, Julia. (1978) "The Political Aesthetics of the Feminist Documentary Film." *Quarterly Review of Film Studies* 3, 4 (Fall): 507–23.

———. (n.d.) "Women and Pornography." *Jump Cut* 26: 46–47.

Levertov, Denise. (1970) *Relearning the Alphabet*. New York: New Directions.

Levine, Mark et al. (1970) *The Tales of Hoffman*, ed. Mark L. Levine, George C. McNamee, and Daniel Greenberg. New York: Bantam Books.

Lippard, Lucy. (1978) "10 Structurists in 20 Paragraphs." In *Esthetics Contemporary*, ed. Richard Kostelanetz. Buffalo, N.Y.: Prometheus Books.

Lippard, Lucy, and John Chandler. (1968) "The Dematerialization of Art." *Art International* 12, 2 (February): 31–36.

Lipton, Lawrence. (1959) *The Holy Barbarians*. New York: Julian Messner.

Lukács, Georg. (1973) "Idea and Form in Literature." In *Marxism and Human Liberation*. New York: Delta.

Lynd, Staughton. (1969) "Towards a History of the New Left." In *The New Left: A Collection of Critical Essays*, ed. Priscilla Long, 1–13. Boston: Porter Sargent.

Lyotard, Jean-François. (1978) "Acinema." *Wide Angle* 2, 3: 52–59.

MacBean, James Roy. (1975) *Film and Revolution.* Bloomington: Indiana University Press.

Maccabe, Colin. (1980) *Godard: Images, Sounds, Politics.* Bloomington: Indiana University Press.

Macherey, Pierre. (1978) *A Theory of Literary Production.* London: Routledge and Kegan Paul.

Maciunas, George. (1970) "Some Comments on 'Structural Film' by P. Adams Sitney." In Sitney (1970: 349).

Mailer, Norman. (1958) *The White Negro.* San Francisco: City Lights.

———. (1960) "Superman Comes to the Supermarket." *Esquire,* 54, 5 (November): 119–30.

———. (1968) *The Armies of the Night: History as a Novel, The Novel as History.* New York: Signet.

———. (1971) *Maidstone.* New York: Signet.

Mandel, Ernest. (1975) *Late Capitalism.* London: New Left Books.

Mapp, Edward. (1972) *Blacks in American Films: Today and Yesterday.* Metuchen, N.J.: The Scarecrow Press.

Marcuse, Herbert. (1964) *One-Dimensional Man.* Boston: Beacon Press.

———. (1978) *The Aesthetic Dimension: Toward a Critique of Marxist Aesthetics.* Boston: Beacon Press.

Marx, Karl. (1973) *Grundrisse: Foundations of the Critique of Political Economy.* New York: Vintage.

———. (1974) *The Eighteenth Brumaire of Louis Bonaparte,* in *Surveys From Exile.* New York: Vintage.

———. (1977–81) *Capital: A Critique of Political Economy,* trans. Ben Fowkes et al. Vols. I–III. New York: Vintage.

Mason, B. J. (1972) "The New Films: Culture or Con Game." *Ebony* 28, 2 (December): 60–68.

Mead, Taylor. (1963) "The Movies Are a Revolution." *Film Culture* 29 (Summer): 9.

Mekas, Jonas. (n.d.) "Notes After Reseeing the Movies of Andy Warhol." In *Andy Warhol,* ed. John Coplans. New York: New York Graphic Society.

———. (1955) "The Experimental Film in America." *Film Culture* 3 (May-June): 15–20.

———. (1960) "Cinema of the New Generation." *Film Culture* 21 (Summer): 1–20.

———. (1962) "Notes on the New American Cinema." *Film Culture* 24 (Spring): 6–16.

———. (1968) "Movie Journal." *The Village Voice,* 29 February 1968, 40.

———. (1972) *Movie Journal: The Rise of a New American Cinema, 1959–1971.* New York: Collier.

Merton, Thomas. (1969) "War and the Crisis of Language." In *The Critique of War: Contemporary Philosophical Explorations,* ed. Robert Ginsberg, 99–119. Chicago: Henry Regenery.

Metz, Christian. (1974a) *Language and Cinema*. The Hague: Mouton.

———. (1974b) *Film Language*. New York: Oxford University Press.

———. (1982) *The Imaginary Signifier*. Bloomington: Indiana University Press.

Michelson, Annette. (1971a) "Toward Snow." *Artforum* 9, 10 (June): 30–37.

———. (1971b) "Foreword in Three Letters." *Artforum* 10, 1 (September): 8–10.

———. (1972a) "The Man With the Movie Camera: From Magician to Epistemologist." *Artforum* 10, 7 (March): 59–72.

———. (1972b) "Screen/Surface: The Politics of Illusionism." *Artforum* 11, 1 (September): 59–62.

———. (1973) "Camera Lucida/Camera Obscura." *Artforum* 11, 5 (January): 30–37.

———. (1974) "Paul Sharits and the Critique of Illusionism: An Introduction." In *Projected Images*. Minneapolis: Walker Art Center.

Millett, Kate. (1970) *Sexual Politics*. New York: Doubleday.

Mills, C. Wright. (1969) "Letter to the New Left." In *The New Left: A Collection of Critical Essays*, ed. Priscilla Long, 14–25. Boston: Porter Sargent.

Mitchell, Juliet. (1973) *Women's Estate*. New York: Vintage.

Motherwell, Robert. ([1944] 1968) "The Modern Painter's World." *Dyn.* 6 (1944). Reprinted in *Readings in American Art Since 1900*, ed. Barbara Rose. New York: Praeger.

Mulvey, Laura. (1975) "Visual Pleasure and Narrative Cinema." *Screen* 16, 3 (Autumn): 6–18.

Murray, James P. (1973) *To Find an Image: Black Films From Uncle Tom to Superfly*. New York: Bobbs Merrill.

Neale, Steve. (1981) "Art Cinema as Institution." *Screen* 22, 1: 11–39.

Newfield, Jack. (1966) *A Prophetic Minority*. New York: New American Library.

Newsreel. (1968) "Newsreel." *Film Quarterly* 22, 2 (Winter): 43–48.

Newsreel Catalogue No. 4 (March 1969).

Newton, Huey P. (1972) *To Die for the People*. New York: Random House.

Nichols, William J. (1972) "Newsreel: Film and Revolution." Master's thesis, University of California, Los Angeles.

———. (1973) "Newsreel: Film and Revolutions." *Cinéaste* 5, 4: 7–13.

———. (1976) *Movies and Methods: An Anthology*. Berkeley: University of California Press.

———. (1980) *Newsreel: Documentary Filmmaking on the American Left*. New York: Arno Press.

———. (1981) *Ideology and the Image: Social Representation in the Cinema and Other Media*. Bloomington: Indiana University Press.

Oglesby, Carl. (1965) "Let Us Shape the Future: An Address to the November, 1965 March on Washington to End the War in Vietnam." Reprinted in Franklin (1971: 41–44).

Olson, Charles. (1966) *Selected Writings*. New York: New Directions.

Parkinson, Thomas, ed. (1961) *A Casebook on the Beat*. New York: Crowell.

Partridge, William H. (1973) *The Hippie Ghetto: The Natural History of a Subculture*. New York: Holt, Rinehart and Winston.

Peterson, Sidney. (1963) "A Note on Comedy in Experimental Film." *Film Culture* 29 (Summer): 27–29.

Plekhanov, G. V. (1957) *Art and Social Life*. Moscow: Progress Publishers.

"Poetry and the Film: A Symposium." In Sitney (1970).

Poirier, Richard. (1971) *The Performing Self: Compositions and Decompositions in the Languages of Contemporary Life*. New York: Oxford University Press.

Pollock, Griselda. (1977) "What's Wrong With Images of Women?" *Screen Education* 24 (Autumn): 25–33.

Polsky, Ned. (1969) "The Village Beat Scene: Summer 1960." *Dissent* 8, 3 (Summer 1961): 339–59. Reprinted 1969 in *Hustlers, Beats and Others*. New York: Anchor.

Powers, Thomas. (1971) *Diana: The Making of a Terrorist*. Boston: Houghton Mifflin.

"Propaganda Films About the War in Vietnam." (1966) *Film Comment* 4, 1 (Fall): 4–22.

Rainer, Yvonne. (1968) "A Quasi Survey of Some 'Minimalist' Tendencies in the Quantitatively Minimal Dance Activity Midst the Plethora, or an Analysis of Trio A." In Battcock (1968: 263–73).

———. (1974) *Work 1961–73*. New York: New York University Press.

———. (1976) "Yvonne Rainer: Interview." *Camera Obscura* 1 (Fall): 76–96.

Rayns, Tony. (1969) "Lucifer: A Kenneth Anger Compendium." *Cinema* (London) 4 (October): 24–31.

"Redstockings Manifesto." (1970) In *Sisterhood Is Powerful: An Anthology of Writings from the Women's Liberation Movement*, ed. Robin Morgan. New York: Random House.

Renan, Sheldon. (1967) *An Introduction to the American Underground Film*. New York: E.P. Dutton.

Report. (1970) *The Report of the Commission on Obscenity and Pornography*. U.S. Government Printing Office.

Rexroth, Kenneth. (1957) "Disengagement: The Art of the Beat Generation." In *New World Writing No. 11*, 28–41. New York: The American Library.

Rice, Ron. (1962) "A Statement." *Film Culture* 25 (Summer): 71.

Rich, B. Ruby. (1981) *Yvonne Rainer*. Minneapolis: Walker Art Gallery.

Richter, Hans. (1947) "A History of the Avantgarde." In *Art in Cinema*, ed. Frank Stauffacher. San Francisco: Art in Cinema Society.

———. (1957) "Hans Richter on the Nature of Film Poetry." *Film Culture* 11: 5–8.

Riesman, David. ([1950] 1971) *The Lonely Crowd*. New Haven: Yale University Press.

Rigney, Francis J., and L. Douglas Smith. (1961) *The Real Bohemia: A Sociological and Psychological Study of the Beats*. New York: Basic Books.

Rose, Jacqueline. (1985) "Introduction II." In Lacan (1985).

Rosen, Marjorie. (1973) *Popcorn Venus: Women, Movies and the American Dream*. New York: Avon.

Rosenberg, Harold. (1959) "The American Action Painters." *Art News* 51, 5 (September 1952). Reprinted 1959 in *The Tradition of the New*. New York: McGraw-Hill.

———. (1965) "The Art Establishment." *Esquire* 63 (January): 43–46.

———. (1972) *The De-Definition of Art*. New York: Horizon Press.

Rosenblum, Robert. (1979) "Andy Warhol: Court Painter to the 70's." In Warhol (1979).

Roszak, Theodore. (1969) *The Making of a Counterculture*. Garden City, N.Y.: Doubleday.

Rubin, William. (1963) "Arshille Gorky, Surrealism, and the New American Painting." *Art International* 7, 3 (February): 27–37.

Sale, Kirkpatrick. (1973) *SDS*. New York: Random House.

Sargent, Lydia. (1981) *Women and Revolution: A Discussion of the Unhappy Marriage of Marxism and Feminism*. Boston: South End Press.

Schatz, Thomas. (1983) *Old Hollywood/New Hollywood: Ritual, Art, and Industry*. Ann Arbor: UMI Research Press.

Schlesinger, Arthur. (1960) "The New Mood in Politics." *Esquire* 53, 1 (January): 58–60.

Schneemann, Carolee. (1979) *More Than Meat Joy*. New Paltz, N.Y.: Documentext.

Schwartz, Therese. (1971–74) "The Politicalization of the Avant-Garde," Parts 1–4. *Art in America* (November 1971): 97–105; (March 1972): 70–79; (March 1973): 67–71; (January 1974): 80–84.

Seale, Bobby. (1970) *Seize the Time: The Story of the Black Panther Party and Huey P. Newton*. New York: Random House.

Sharits, Paul. (1966) "Red, Blue, Godard." *Film Quarterly* 19, 4 (Summer): 24–29.

———. (1969) "Notes on Films/1966–1968." *Film Culture* 47 (Summer): 13–16.

————. (1972) "Words Per Page." *Afterimage* 4 (Autumn): 27–42.

————. (1978) "A Cinematics Model for Film Studies in Higher Education." *Film Culture* 65/66: 43–68.

Shklovsky, Victor. (1965) "Sterne's *Tristram Shandy*: Stylistic Commentary." In *Russian Formalist Criticism: Four Essays*, ed. Lee T. Lemon and Marion J. Reis, 25–60. Lincoln: University of Nebraska Press.

Silber, Irwin. (1970) *The Cultural Revolution: A Marxist Analysis*. New York: Times Change Press.

Simpson, Charles R. (1981) *SoHo: The Artist in the City*. Chicago: University of Chicago Press.

Sitney, P. Adams. (1969) "Structural Film." *Film Culture* 47 (Summer): 1–10.

————, ed. (1970) *Film Culture Reader*. New York: Praeger.

————. (1975) *The Essential Cinema: Essays on Films in the Collection of Anthology Film Archives*. New York: New York University Press.

————. (1977) "Autobiography in Avant-Garde Film." *Millennium Film Journal* 1, 1 (Winter): 60–106.

————, ed. (1978) *The Avant-Garde Film: A Reader of Theory and Criticism*. New York: New York University Press.

————. (1979) *Visionary Film: The American Avant-Garde*. 2d ed. New York: Oxford University Press.

Sklar, Robert. (1975) *Movie-Made America: A Cultural History of American Movies*. New York: Vintage.

Smith, Julian. (1975) *Looking Away: Hollywood and Vietnam*. New York: Scribners.

Solanas, Fernando, and Octavio Gettino. (1976) "Towards a Third Cinema." In *Movies and Methods*, ed. Bill Nichols. Berkeley: University of California Press.

Sontag, Susan. (1966) *Against Interpretation*. New York: Laurel.

————. (1969) *Styles of Radical Will*. New York: Farrar Straus and Giroux.

Spellman, A. B. (1970) *Black Music: Four Lives*. New York: Schocken Books.

" 'A Statement on Civil Disobedience' by the Leaders of the Vietnam Day Committee." Reprinted in Franklin (1971: 44–47).

Stern, Susan. (1975) *With the Weathermen: The Personal Journey of a Revolutionary Woman*. New York: Doubleday.

Taylor, Clyde. (n.d.) "New U.S. Black Cinema." *Jump Cut* 28: 46–48.

Taylor, John Russell. (1975) *Directors and Directions: Cinema for the Seventies*. New York: Hill and Wang.

Thurston, Wallace. (1961) "Creative Film Award Winners: 1959 and 1960." *Film Quarterly* 14, 3 (Spring): 30–34.

Tomkins, Calvin. (1976) *The Scene: Reports on Post-Modern Art*. New York: Viking.

————. (1980) *Off the Wall: Robert Rauschenberg and the Art World of Our Time*. New York: Doubleday.

Trilling, Lionel. (1965) *Beyond Culture*. New York: Viking Press.

Trotsky, Leon. (1960) *Literature and Revolution*. Ann Arbor: The University of Michigan Press.

Truffaut, François. (1967) *Hitchcock*. New York: Simon and Schuster.

Turan, Kenneth, and Stephen Zito. (1974) *Sinema: American Pornographic Films and the People Who Make Them*. New York: Praeger.

Tyler, Parker. (1962) "For *Shadows*, Against *Pull My Daisy*." *Film Culture* 24 (Spring): 24–33.

———. (1969) *Underground Film: A Critical History*. New York: Grove Press.

Unger, Irwin. (1974) *The Movement: A History of the American New Left, 1959–1972*. New York: Dodd, Mead.

Vanderbeek, Stan. (1961) "The Cinema Delimina—Films from the Underground." *Film Quarterly* 14, 4 (Summer): 5–15.

Vertov, Dziga. (1984) *Kino-Eye: The Writings of Dziga Vertov*. Berkeley: University of California Press.

Warhol, Andy. (1975) *The Philosophy of Andy Warhol*. New York: Harcourt Brace Jovanovich.

———. (1979) *Andy Warhol: Portraits of the Seventies*. New York: Random House.

———. (1980) *Popism: The Warhol 60's*. New York: Harcourt Brace Jovanovich.

Washington, Michael, and Maruin J. Berlowitz. (1975) "Blaxploitation Films and High School Youth: SWAT/*SUPERFLY*." *Jump Cut* 9 (October): 23–24.

Weinbren, Grahame. (1979) "Six Filmmakers and an Ideal of Composition." *Millennium Film Journal* 3 (Winter): 39–54.

Whitney, John. (1980) *Digital Harmony: On the Complementarity of Music and Visual Art*. Peterborough, N.H.: Byte Books.

Whitney, John, and James Whitney. (1947) "Audio-Visual Music." In *Art In Cinema*, ed. Frank Stauffacher. San Francisco: Art in Cinema Society.

Wittgenstein, Ludwig. (1968) *Philosophical Investigations*. Oxford: Basil Blackwell.

Wolfe, Tom. (1968) *The Electric Kool-Aid Acid Test*. New York: Farrar, Straus and Giroux.

Wollen, Peter. (1982) *Readings and Writings: Semiotic Counter-Strategies*. London: Verso Editions.

"Workers' Films in New York." (1931) *Experimental Cinema* 1, 3: 37.

Worth, Sol, and John Adair. (1972) *Through Navajo Eyes: An Exploration in Film Communication and Anthropology*. Bloomington: Indiana University Press.

Young, Nigel. (1977) *An Infantile Disorder? The Crisis and Decline of the New Left*. Boulder, Colo.: Westview Press.

Youngblood, Gene. (1970) *Expanded Cinema*. New York: E. P. Dutton.

"Yvonne Rainer: An Introduction." (1976) *Camera Obscura* 1: 53–70.

Zukin, Sharon. (1982) "Art in the Arms of Power: Market Relations and Collective Patronage in the Capitalist State." *Theory and Society* 11, 4 (July): 432–50.

Index